D0225706

Culture and Redemption

2 BR
526
F48
2007

Culture and Redemption

RELIGION, THE SECULAR, AND
AMERICAN LITERATURE

Tracy Fessenden

PRINCETON UNIVERSITY PRESS

PRINCETON AND OXFORD

Nyack College Librar.

Copyright © 2007 by Princeton University Press
Published by Princeton University Press, 41 William Street, Princeton, New Jersey 08540
In the United Kingdom: Princeton University Press, 3 Market Place, Woodstock,
Oxfordshire OX20 1SY
All Rights Reserved

Portions of chapters 3, 4, 5, and 8 appeared in the following journals, respectively:
Church History: Studies in Christianity and Culture 74.3 (December 2005);
Journal of Women's History 14.1 (Spring 2002); *Prospects: An Annual of American
Cultural Studie*s 25 (2000); and *U.S. Catholic Historian* 23.3 (Summer 2005).
Those materials are used here with permission of the publishers.

Library of Congress Cataloging-in-Publication Data

Fessenden, Tracy
Culture and redemption : religion, the secular, and
American literature / Tracy Fessenden.
p.   cm.
Includes bibliographical references and index.
ISBN-13: 978-0-691-04963-2 (cloth : alk. paper)
ISBN-10: 0-691-04963-7 (cloth : alk. paper)
1. United States—Church history. 2. Secularism—United States.
3. Christianity and culture—United States. 4. American literature—
History and criticism. 5. Religion and literature—United States. I. Title.
BR526. F48 2006
201′.681—dc22   2006007752

British Library Cataloging-in-Publication Data is available

This book has been composed in Sabon

Printed on acid-free paper. ∞

pup.princeton.edu

Printed in the United States of America

1   3   5   7   9   10   8   6   4   2

64624885

To my family

CONTENTS

ACKNOWLEDGMENTS

MANY PEOPLE and institutions have helped me to finish this book, and it is a pleasure to thank them here.

The Pew Program in Religion and American History at Yale University and the National Endowment for the Humanities provided welcome affirmation in the form of research fellowships; I owe thanks not only to their officers, readers, and referees but to the College of Liberal Arts and Sciences at Arizona State University for supporting in each case an extended period of leave. I made grateful use as well of a Littleton-Griswold Research Grant in Legal History from the American Historical Association and a Summer Research Award from the Program in Women's and Gender Studies at ASU.

I was fortunate to be able to bring parts of this book or early rehearsals of its arguments to many academic conferences and to more intimate scholarly gatherings at Berkeley, Colorado, Harvard, Indiana, Santa Cruz, Tulane, Vassar, and Yale. Among the friends and colleagues who made such occasions so pleasurable I wish especially to thank those who made them possible, or whose insights set me thinking in new ways: Carrie Tirado Bramen, Jon Butler, Carlos Eire, Rosemarie Garland-Thomson, Rosemary Graham, Paul Harvey, Joan Hedrick, Susan Juster, Colleen McDannell, Marian Ronan, Peter Silver, Steve Stein, Harry Stout, Cornel West, and Magdalena Zaborowska.

Conversations with Gauri Viswanathan during a partial summer's residence at the Quaker House in London over a decade ago did more to shape this book than I could ever have anticipated, not least by introducing me to the bracing challenges and satisfactions of her own work. I don't know whether Jenny Franchot would have liked this book, but I know I would not have written it without the lasting motivation of her passion and example. Janet Jakobsen responded to an earlier version of chapter 7 with unsparing insight and care; her intellectual generosity and her own indispensable thinking about secularism have made this a better book. Without Lucy Maddox's unfailingly gracious encouragement at the beginning, I might long ago have laid the work aside. Of all the forms of affirmation that came my way, Tom Ferraro's comes closest to channeling the dazzling, ever-discerning reassurance of Jay Gatsby's famous smile; this book is in many ways the product of his lavish faith in it and in me.

John Corrigan has been a friend to me and to this project for many years; no one has done more to make me feel at home among scholars of American religion or to smooth my passage into their ranks. In this I am indebted also to the Young Scholars Program in American Religion at Indiana University–Purdue University Indianapolis, and to the irreplaceable network of scholarly friends formed there who continue to nurture, inspire, and enliven: Ava Chamberlain, Kate Joyce, Laura Levitt, Liza McAlister, Deborah Dash Moore, Leonard Primiano, and Jennifer Rycenga. For their genuinely enabling encouragement at earlier stages of my career I owe a special debt of gratitude to Larry Bouchard, Walter Sokel, Elaine Scarry, and the late Robert M. Cover. To Sheila Curran, Aline Kalbian, and Charles Marsh for their gifts of friendship over many years, my abiding thanks.

Deborah Malmud was my editor and champion at the proposal stage; to her and to Fred Appel and the production staff at Princeton University Press, my thanks for *really* getting the book into print. Special thanks go to Kathleen Cioffi for copyediting the manuscript with such elegance and care. I am also exceedingly grateful to the Press's anonymous readers, whose sparkling insights have brought clarity to these pages.

Among those at Arizona State whose warm collegiality has furthered this project, I owe special thanks to three who have chaired the Department of Religious Studies: Linell Cady, James Foard, and Joel Gereboff. Their professionalism, gifts for fostering intellectual connection, and extraordinary kindness have made my years on their faculty more pleasurable and rewarding than academics generally have any right to expect. I am particularly grateful to Linell Cady for welcoming my participation in the activities of ASU's Center for the Study of Religion and Conflict, which she directs, and for our rich conversations over many years. The fruits of both kinds of collaboration have found their way into this book. Two exceptional research assistants, Roxane Barwick and Loretta Bludworth, gave generously of their time and energy to help me prepare the manuscript for publication. I know how lucky I am in the students past and present whose friendship, imagination, and intelligence have comforted and inspired me during the period of writing; they include Crista Cloutier, Doe Daughtrey, Jeni Drinen, Lee Seale, Laurin Stennis, Toni Trapani, Josh Vidich, and especially Brandon Cleworth, who read every word.

Brief acknowledgment feels particularly inadequate for my family and extended family, including Dennis and Sharron Dalton, for whose loving and supportive presence in my life "in-laws" seems as poor a term as could be devised. My parents, Frank and Maureen Fessenden, gave me what must have been every possible resource for my flourishing and every freedom to pursue it as I would; for their love and unwavering faith in me I owe a debt I can never measure or repay.

My thanks above all to Kevin Dalton, who sustains me in all things, and to our beloved children, Hadley and Blaise, whose radiance puts every bright idea in the shade.

Culture and Redemption

INTRODUCTION

I DISCOVERED early in my work on this book that the short answer I usually gave to the polite question of what I was writing about—"American literature and secularization"—invariably failed to conjure, in the listener's imagination, a vivid panorama of persons, events, and literary works that might unfold under that rubric. (I typically drew a puzzled silence, followed quickly by a compassionate redirection of the conversation along different lines.) But neither did the alternate answer I sometimes gave to the same question—"American literature and *religion*"—succeed any more in conveying a world of vibrant and many-layered possibility, beyond eliciting, now and then, a follow-up question about the Puritan divines.

Nor did such responses come quite as a surprise. The assumption that the "secular" consists simply in the unremarkable absence of once-dominant "religion" has shaped both American literary history and American religious history, the two fields this book moves freely between, as well as the smaller subfield that bills itself "religion and literature," where it had its beginnings in a vague dissatisfaction with the way that relationship was configured within the discipline of religious studies. According to the institutional genealogy given by Giles Gunn, for example, critical interest in the "coalescence of the literary and the religious" took shape in the nineteenth century as the attempt to "reconstitute something admittedly in a state of collapse"—that is, religion—"on a different basis."[1] Such figures as Matthew Arnold, says Gunn, took it upon themselves to "keep alive a sense of the normative and its bearing upon beliefs and practices no longer felt to derive their legitimacy from traditional religious sources."[2] Arnold famously relocated religion's powers of legitimation to "culture," intimating the supersession of religion by great works of imaginative literature and other, erstwhile secular forms—a shift given theological endorsement in the last century by Paul Tillich, among others.[3] Far from attending to the presence of religion in literary contexts, then, students of religion-and-literature learned instead to seek after its absence, its displacement by or reconstitution as the newly empowered secular, freed from the trappings of ritual, the limitations of historical communities, or the embarrassments of outmoded belief.

Religion-and-literature in this way played its role in upholding what Robert Orsi calls the "embedded moral schema" that has long governed the academic study of religion, a discipline organized, says Orsi, "around the (usually hidden and unacknowledged) poles of good religion/bad religion." "Good" religion is good in the measure that it tends toward invisibility, or at least unobtrusiveness: "rational, word-centered, nonritualistic, middle class, unemotional, compatible with democracy and the liberal state . . . [good religion] was what was taught and endorsed in academic environments; for everything else the discipline developed a nomenclature of marginalization (cults, sects, primitives, and so on)."[4] For its part, the study of American religious history promoted a developmental narrative in which "good" religion emerges hand in hand with the new nation as a uniquely American achievement, the Puritans' sense of chosenness democratized and domesticated by Enlightenment tolerance, with the blessings of free exercise extended most liberally to matters of privately held belief and not to those allegedly irrational, regressive, or inscrutable forms of religious life—cults, sects, primitives, and so on—deemed foreign to democracy.

The salutary transparency of good religion and the attribution of antidemocratic leanings to any other kind made it inevitable that, beyond the discipline of religious studies (and frequently enough within it), *all* visible forms of religion might easily be regarded as irrational, regressive, and threatening to the democratic project. Particularly in American literary studies, a field historically given shape by its own narrative of democratization, religion receives little attention except when it figures as crucial to a progressive, emancipatory politics (Christian antislavery being the readiest example), and often not even then. Secularism enters into American literary studies as both a historical assumption (religion figures only minimally in the development of American literature, and less so over time) and a critical practice (religion therefore fails to warrant the kinds of attention we give to other social formations in American literary history, including gender, race, sexuality, and class).

However distorting a lens for reading this history, secularism flourishes as an operative rubric in American literary studies because it appears to be the best answer to the limitations ascribed to religion.[5] Thus when a hero of American literary studies' own formative narrative of democracy—a Ralph Waldo Emerson, for example—is discovered to align himself with a social-evolutionary paradigm of race (as when Emerson confesses his conviction that African and Indian races are destined not to "progress" but to disappear),[6] alarms are sounded and the work of exposure or exculpation begins, but when the same figure is seen to align himself with a social-evolutionary paradigm of religion (as when Emerson notes easily that Roman Catholicism, too, is destined to disappear),[7] no such expiatory labors are called into play. And this is so because the assumption that some religions or aspects of religion have simply played themselves out, or ought to, or eventually will, is crucial to the developmental schema of good and bad religion—the first associated with freedom and enlightenment, the second with coercion and constraint—implicit in the progress narrative of democracy.

Of course one may well share Emerson's discomfort with the kind of religious authority he identified with the Catholic Church, which seems a very different thing from wishing to see some races evolve out of existence. To question the secularization narrative, moreover, is to risk appearing to advocate an expanded role for religion at a moment when a newly emboldened Christian right seems bent on remaking the erstwhile secular domains of science and law in its image. (With blessings from a president who urges that "both sides" of the alleged controversy over evolution be taught in schools, for example, the Kansas Board of Education voted in November 2005 to amend its official definition of science to accommodate supernatural explanations; eleven months earlier the Bush administration had filed a legal brief on behalf of the Kentucky counties prohibited by the U.S. Court of Appeals for the Sixth Circuit from posting framed copies of the Ten Commandments in courthouses, alongside a proclamation from President Ronald Reagan marking 1983 as the Year of the Bible. "Official acknowledgement and recognition of the Ten Commandments' influence on American legal history," the White House assures any doubters in the brief, "comport with the Establishment Clause [of the First Amendment].")[8]

But consider how a simplified narrative of secularization may in fact work to strengthen the hold of a particular strain of conservative Christianity in American public life. When secularism in the United States is understood merely as the absence of religious faith, or neutrality in relation to religious faith, rather than as a variety of possible relationships to different religious traditions—for example, an avowedly secular United States is broadly accommodating of mainstream and evangelical Protestantism, minimally less so of Catholicism, unevenly so of Judaism, much less so of Islam, perhaps still less so of Native American religious practices that fall outside the bounds of the acceptably decorative or "spiritual"—then religion comes to be defined as "Christian" by default, and an implicit association between "American" and "Christian" is upheld even by those who have, one imagines, very little invested in its maintenance.[9] So pervasive is the identification of religion in America with this unmarked Christianity, even among ardent secularists, that the debate about whether and how to teach about religions in public schools, for example, routinely reverts to a version of the debate between "evolution" and "creationism," between an Enlightenment faith that subordinates all religions to an allegedly disinterested rationality and a conservative Protestant rereading of a Jewish text that eclipses at once the Jewishness of Genesis, different religious perspectives on Genesis, and the multiplicity of religious narratives of origin.[10]

How have specific forms of Protestant belief and practice come enduringly to be subsumed under the heading of "Christian"—to the exclusion of non-Protestant and differently Protestant ways of being Christian—and how, in many cases, does the "Christian" come to stand in for the "religious" to the exclusion of non-Christian ways of being religious? Part of the answer surely lies in the ability of a Protestantized conception of religion to control the meanings of both the religious *and* the secular. "What has often been forgotten," Max Weber reminds us, is "that the Reformation meant not the elimination of the Church's control over everyday life, but rather the substitution of a new form of control for the previous one. It meant the repudiation of a control that was very lax, at that time scarcely perceptible in practice and hardly more than formal in favor of a regulation of the whole conduct which, penetrating all departments of private and public life, was infinitely burdensome and earnestly enforced."[11] Evacuating religious authority from its institutional locations, the Reformation generated its presence "everywhere," not least in secular guise—an outcome, it further bears reminding, given as "truth" or "freedom" in the measure that the Reformation frames its program as liberation from the errors and superstitions of Rome. In this sense Protestantism's emancipation from Catholicism both provides the blueprint for, and sets the limits of, secularism's emancipation from "religion" itself.

Far from being a neutral matrix, then, the secular sphere as constituted in American politics, culture, and jurisprudence has long been more permeable to some religious interventions than to others. The co-implication of secularism and Reformed Christianity has meant, for example, that Christian religious polemic could remain compatible with America's vaunted history of religious liberty and toleration by being cast in strictly secular terms. Thus at various points in American history, Muslims, Catholics, or Mormons could be construed as enemies of republican institutions, Jews as a racial or economic threat, and Native American ritual practice as an affront to environmental or drug policy, all without apparent violence to cherished notions of religious freedom.[12] At the same time, an implicitly Christian culture puts pressure on all who make claims on American institutions to constitute themselves as religious on a recognizably Protestant model.[13] (Recall the all-but-mandatory confessions of faith in the last several presidential elections, or the more recent calls of party leaders for Democrats to "get religion" in the wake of their 2004 defeat by a Republican campaign emphasizing conservative Christian values.)[14] Protests against such public displays of Christianity from secularists, meanwhile, are unlikely to create favorable conditions for the expression of *other* forms of religious knowledge, leaving the forum—

discussions of the meaning of "faith-based," for example—entirely to those who lay claim to it.

To consider the career of secularization in American culture is therefore also necessarily to consider the consolidation of a Protestant ideology that has grown more entrenched and controlling even as its manifestations have often become less visibly religious. Charting the American religious landscape in terms of "manyness" and "oneness," religious historian Catherine Albanese unflinchingly identifies "public Protestantism" as the "*one* religion" of the United States, a dominant if tacit "religious system" that gives "cultural cohesion [to] American society" over time by eliciting and shaping "the religious adaptations of even the most 'other' of new Americans." "Although many times they were unaware of it," says Albanese, "Catholics and Jews, Buddhists and Eastern Orthodox Christians" were induced or compelled to assimilate themselves to Protestant norms in order to be recognized as legitimately American. "So [were] countless others from among the many."[15]

Other American religious historians have clamored over the last decade or two to tell any story *but* this one. To judge from recent textbooks and anthologies, the classic narrative of American religious history as one of ever-expanding "tolerance" and "accommodation" radiating from a Protestant center is rapidly losing ground to what historian David Hackett calls "a multicultural tale of Native Americans, African Americans, Catholics, Jews, and other[s]" told by scholars whose work "cut[s] across boundaries of gender, class, and region."[16] But if, as Hackett suggests, the "older, Protestant consensus narrative has, at best, come to be seen as a convenient fiction for the sake of narrative movement,"[17] that discovery by itself does little to explain how the "convenient fiction" became so powerful and enduring, nor why it remains so ingeniously difficult to counter. Even as the story of persecution-fleeing Puritans and their more broadly Protestant legacy of religious freedom gives way to a more varied and inclusive story of America's religious development (as scholars now work "conscientiously, often feverishly," William Hutchison attests, "to chronicle diversities that our predecessors ignored or slighted"),[18] the metanarrative of ever-increasing "tolerance" remains intact.

To put this in a different idiom: the patriarchal deity of Hebrew and Christian scripture may well be regarded as a narrative fiction, but one that a global move to inclusive-language biblical scholarship would by itself do nothing even to *read*, much less to unwrite. I agree therefore with Hutchison that to tell the story of America's religious development without locating the "enormously dominant and influential Protestant establishment" at its center is in fact to tell a different story, one that could scarcely be called a history of American religion.[19] I do so, however, in order to ask how North Atlantic Protestants came to place themselves at this center, how the "convenient fiction" of a Protestant consensus at the heart of American culture came to take on the status of truth.[20]

This book seeks to demonstrate, then, how particular forms of Protestantism emerged as an "unmarked category" in American religious and literary history, in order also to show how a particular strain of post-Protestant secularism, often blind to its own exclusions, became normative for understanding that history. Part 1 of this book, "Protestantism and the Social Space of Reading," reflects on those literary works and reading practices by which Protestant culture in America became entrenched, serving, in Andrew Ross's phrase, as "bearers and shapers of a language that makes some forms of discursive experience available while it ignores, excludes, or suppresses others."[21] Setting the institutionalization of literacy and the emergence of a distinctive national literature in eighteenth- and nineteenth-century America alongside more visible projects of Anglo-Protestant consolidation and expansion, these chapters argue that what religious historian Nathan Hatch calls the "democratization of American Christianity" and literary historian Cathy Davidson the "democratization of the written word" proceeded together,[22] less toward the end of generalized equality than toward particular distributions of knowledge, mobility, and cultural authority.

Chapter 1 examines New England Puritan contributions to the making of what Edward Said calls "a privileged, genealogical useful past," an account of American origins from which "unwanted elements, vestiges, narratives" are erased.[23] It argues that the Puritans' violent dealings with New England's native inhabitants were intricately tied to their own literary achievements, including their ardent promotion of literacy as a tool for the conquest of spiritual enemies as well as their development of genres designed to expand the Protestant presence in the New World. By figuring their rights to habitation as bound up in their possession of scripture and literacy, for example, Puritans constituted Indians as bereft of legitimate means of conferring or withholding their authorization to Puritans' use of their lands. Puritan reflections on the Pequot War and King Philip's War, moreover, show Puritan violence against Indians to have extended the dynamic by which Puritans constituted Indian lands as void of human occupants, open to and even requiring Puritan habitation, a corollary to the view that Indians were themselves "ruines of Mankind" whose destruction was foreordained in the Reformation impulse toward iconoclastic violence against images.[24] The narrative form of Puritan spiritual biography, meanwhile, further rendered Indians invisible by rewriting contact with them as part of an ongoing dialogue between God and the Puritan soul, a rewriting that both veiled and underwrote the violence required of Puritans to empty Indian lands of the resistant spiritual and physical difference of Indians themselves.

"Indians" who do appear in Puritan writings figure principally as the unregenerate Other to the Puritans' salvific Word, a representational practice that resonates even and perhaps especially in those accounts where Indians do not appear at all. Chapter 2 examines the *New England Primer*, in which Indians do not appear, as a tool for the creation of a literate, Christian self in whom what Cotton Mather called the "Indian vices" that afflicted wayward Puritans had been vanquished. Continuously in print in various editions from at least the early eighteenth to the mid-nineteenth century, the *New England Primer* facilitated the construction of a redeemed self in part by constructing a "redeemed" political order, an account of the nation's beginnings from which not only Indians but histories of violence against Indians have disappeared. If the *New England Primer* rewrites Puritan origins as innocently untroubled by Indian conflict, however, it nevertheless makes subtle use of the Puritan connection between Indians and childhood, in order both to figure "Indianness" as the vanishing state the maturing nation is bound to leave behind, and to signal the danger that the recalcitrant child or national subject, willfully unredeemed from symbolic captivity to Indians, poses to the national project. In this way the *New England Primer* banishes Indians to the invisible reaches of New England experience, only to retrieve them in the reconstituted form of incorrigible or unassimilable Americans whose otherness threatens the project of white Protestant expansion signaled by the Indian's anticipatory "removal" from its own pages.

The aim of the *New England Primer*, which typically begins with a picture alphabet and culminates in the Shorter Westminster Catechism, was to induce Bible literacy in children as a means to spiritual maturity. In this way the *New England Primer*'s centrality to children's education also made the King James Bible central to children's education long after the *Primer* itself disappeared from classrooms in the early nineteenth century. Chapter 3 examines Protestant arguments for the creation of a public, tax-supported, Bible-based school system, together with the Catholic-Protestant "Bible wars" that erupted in Philadelphia and Cincinnati between the 1830s and the 1870s. To Catholic objections that the compulsory reading of the King James Bible in schools made them into instruments of a de facto Protestant establishment, Protestants insisted that schools were nonsectarian, and that it was Catholics instead who dangerously sought to impose their religious views on public institutions in violation of the separation of church and state. The anti-Catholic vocabularies invoked on the Protestant side of these battles were long entrenched and had "separation" built into them as a feature of the nation's independence both from popish religious tyranny and foreign political tyranny—a staple of textbook representations of American's founding from the late eighteenth century. Implicit in this notion of separation was not only a Protestant understanding of religion—defined largely in terms of the sanctity of individual belief, which presumably lay beyond the coercive reach of government or other powers—but also a Protestant understanding of America. While the Bible riots have usefully been cast as class and ethnic conflicts, little attention has been paid to the Catholic objections to compulsory Bible reading as a specifically political critique, namely, an indictment of the exclusionary nature of civil protections for religion within an implicitly Protestant state. As a Philadelphia newspaper put it, a man "may be a Turk, a Jew, or a Christian, a Catholic, a Methodist or Presbyterian, and we say nothing against it," but "when we remember that our Pilgrim fathers landed on Plymouth rock to establish the Protestant religion, free from persecution, we must contend that this was and always will be a Protestant country."[25] Such views left nativist Protestants in the Bible conflicts free to lift "Christianity" away from both denominational affiliation and privately held belief and to identify it all the more closely with national symbols, most prominently the American flag, which were then invoked as the mantle of "freedom of religion" whose fabric Catholic claims to free exercise of religion could only be figured as rending in pieces.

Chapter 4 sets the public school movement alongside the literature of the American Renaissance, including its classic manifestations in the canon of Whitman, Emerson, Melville, and others as well as the larger body of sentimental and domestic fiction more recently championed as belonging also to this period of literary flourishing. As Protestant arguments for a Bible-based public school curriculum came to represent such schools, quite erroneously, as havens of religious, racial, and ethnic diversity, so the sentimental novel of the nineteenth century was marked by its concerted extension of Christian sympathy to what figure in its pages as the distressed slaves, Indians, wage workers, and others marginalized by the expansion of middle-class Protestant culture. But so also have the "classic," male-authored works of nineteenth-century American literature characteristically been valued for just those capacities—the extension of fellow feeling across races and classes, the incorporation of vernacular and subaltern voices—that, in their association with the literature of evangelical Christianity, are derided (or recuperatively defended) as feminine or sentimental. To distinguish such writings as belonging to separate, gendered spheres, or to competing American Renaissances, I suggest, both polarizes the cultural production of the white Protestant middle class and exaggerates the scope of that production, making it stand in for the whole. But it is precisely the "whole," of course, that such works aspire to in the breadth of their democratic address. Harriet Beecher Stowe's evangelical melting pot, in which the discernment of Christ within makes "one blood [of] all the nations of men," was called by other writers simply "America," "a teeming Nation of nations," in Whitman's words, where, as Emerson famously predicted, "the energy of the Irish, Germans, Swedes, Poles, and Cossacks, and all of the European tribes—and of the Africans, and of the Polynesians,—will construct a new race, a new religion, a new state, a new literature."[26] This literature's conversion of religious, racial, and ethnic diversity into the materials for a new, inclusively American sensibility whose hallmarks are progress and tolerance uncannily mirrors what Protestant voices in the Bible wars convey as the strategies of an avowedly secular culture for dealing with overlapping forms of racial and religious "excess."

The second part of the book, "Secular Fictions," takes up the desires, investments, and anxieties seen to govern the narrative practices discussed thus far as these come to inform the work of four celebrated literary figures who wrote at—and of—crucial periods in American history: Harriet Beecher Stowe, Mark Twain, Charlotte Perkins Gilman, and F. Scott Fitzgerald. Ranging widely over the fiction and nonfiction of each author, these chapters look to the ways each projects a vision of American democratic space that, in varying measure, underscores or upends the Protestant-secular continuum examined in the earlier part of the book, and to the ways that religious, racial, and other differences are variously accommodated (or not) within that space.

A recurring theme of the book's earlier chapters is the discourse of anti-Catholicism that served from the seventeenth century onward to underpin the social, political, cultural, and economic dominance of North Atlantic Protestants in the United States. Chapter 5 examines the modulation of this vocabulary in the writings of Harriet Beecher Stowe, including *Uncle Tom's Cabin* and other fiction, devotional narratives, and domestic writing. In *Uncle Tom's Cabin*, I suggest, Stowe drew on traditional anti-Catholic rhetoric, familiar from the sermons and polemics of her father, Lyman Beecher, to associate slavery and Southern culture with Romanism. In this way Stowe joined the long-standing fight against Catholic influence in the United States to antislavery activism, even as race and not religion was on its way to becoming the primary language through which white Protestants in the United States struggled to articulate a cohesive identity against a backdrop of growing immigration, westward expansion, and sectional unrest. As Stowe's vision of a Christian America becomes less overtly religious—Stowe and Catharine Beecher's domestic handbook *The American Woman's Home* would equate "the principles of Christianity" with "the great principles of democracy"[27]—Stowe carefully nurtured her readership and her reputation in Great Britain, connecting the new, racialized basis of American Protestant legitimacy to a wider Atlantic political culture of Anglo-Saxon supremacy. In this way Stowe subtly hastened the conversion of a Protestant discourse of religious otherness into a secular discourse of racial otherness.

A different set of connections between religion and race and a different relation to the secularized Protestant culture of the United States shaped the career of Mark Twain. Twain's own religious skepticism, I suggest in chapter 6, tends to bolster the civic piety that makes a national icon of Twain's most famous novel: perhaps no moment in American literature is more canonical, or celebrated as "quintessentially" American, than Huckleberry Finn's decision to "*go* to hell" to free a slave,[28] to defy in one turn a religious convention and the social injustice it allegedly supports. In a single, brilliant flash of resolve Huck appears to reject a coercive Christianity for a do-it-yourself apostasy, the law and custom of slavery for the riskiness of outlawed freedoms, the privileges of whiteness for solidarity with blackness. Of the oppositions that undergird these either-or choices, however—belief/unbelief, slavery/freedom, black/white— none is entirely stable and belief/unbelief perhaps least of all, since dissent from Christian belief (itself a diversity, and one that accommodated a robust abolitionism on which *Huckleberry Finn* remained silent) could take the form not only of resolute or wavering unbelief but also of varying degrees of allegiance within a vast range of alternative faiths. Twain's writings in fact show an abiding fascination with religions that resist being plotted along a spectrum extending from Protestant conviction to its absence, including the new American religions of Mormonism, spiritualism, and Christian Science; the Old World faiths of Catholicism, Judaism, and Islam; the Asian religions encountered in *Following the Equator*; and the "heathen" belief systems of Hawai'ian natives, American Indians, and black slaves. Unevenly accommodated within conventional renderings of either religion *or* race in Mark Twain's America, these positions beyond the Protestant-secular continuum put questions to readings of Huck's apostasy as a clear strike in favor of racial equality. Most pressing among them, for Twain, was the question of what happens when secular values—patriotism, for example, or scientific "proof"—reveal themselves to be as hostile to racial justice as any constraint of dogma, religious custom, or sect. Grappling with the shortcomings of secular forms of authority produced some of the most searching, if also the murkiest, moments in Twain's writing, for while institutional religion could easily be made the target of his zeal for exposing frauds and superstitions, neither humor nor outrage could as readily undermine these secular values' increasing presumption to legitimacy, or reveal their complicity in the forms of injustice he sought to redress.

No such ambiguity clouds the progress narrative of secularization to which Charlotte Perkins Gilman laid claim in the name of feminism. Chapter 7 reads Gilman's utopian novel *Herland* with her other fiction and nonfiction alongside the first stirrings of the American women's movement, the nineteenth-century anthropological discourse of world religions, and the expansion of America's geopolitical boundaries to include newly enfranchised African American men; new waves of Irish, European, and Asian immigrants; and the inhabitants of the recently annexed territories of the continental United States. Unlike her great-aunts Catharine Beecher and Harriet Beecher Stowe, who imagined the white, Christian home as a blueprint for the civilized world, Gilman argued that the home was a primitive survival whose demands keep white women from achieving the cultural and economic potential of their race. Gilman brought her claims for women's equality to bear on hierarchical models of religious development: in her view, Christianity was a central factor in the relative freedoms of white Western women in comparison to women of other races, but real gender equality, again for white women, depended on Christianity's giving way to what Gilman identified as "the final merging of religion and life which shall leave them indistinguishable."[29] For Gilman, the bridging of the separate spheres of "religion and life" diminishes the gender difference between white women and men by heightening the difference between Anglo-American men and women, on the one side, and racial and religious minorities, on the other. Gilman's stark mapping of a supersessionary model of racial development (culminating in white/ Western dominance) onto a supersessionary model of religious progress (culminating in a wholly secularized Christianity) under the banner of feminism challenges the widely held view that secularism is a necessary precondition for democratic, pluralistic societies. In Gilman's universe, the violence of colonialism and the continued subordination of non-Western women are instead the necessary preconditions for the spread of secular (read American) "freedoms" across the globe.

Gilman understood the disappearance of religion (into "life") as the inevitable and welcome consequence of Protestant Christianity's continuing triumph over its more primitive rivals and antecedents, even as her reliance on colonial models of development undermines her celebratory narrative of secularization as emancipation. F. Scott Fitzgerald tells a different story of secularization than the one that renders religion invisible because wholly transparent to everyday life, or wholly interiorized in the hearts and minds of adherents. Chapter 8 reads Fitzgerald's novels, essays, and stories together with his reflections on his Catholic upbringing and more general debates surrounding the assimilation of non-Protestant immigrants in the early twentieth century. Unlike critics who find a thinly veiled nostalgia for the vividness of childhood faith at the heart of Fitzgerald's melancholy grandeur, I read Fitzgerald as concerned far less about the impossibility of remaining a believing Catholic than about the challenge of remaining a *secular* Catholic, of recovering Catholic difference as something richer, thornier, and more variegated than a difference of belief. Over the course of his career, I suggest, this Catholic secularism moved Fitzgerald toward engagement with new ways of being American, with varieties of otherness—sexual, racial, national—that call to account a culture of "pluralism" that most readily embraces diversity in the form of a marketplace of private religious faiths.

My reading of Fitzgerald's Catholic secularism might seem to mark a break from the preceding chapters in its effort no longer to probe the contradictions of a secularized Protestant culture, but to identify a rival fracturing within the register of the secular itself. To pluralize and complicate the meaning of religion in American cultural history, as I seek to do throughout this book, however, is to raise all along the question of differently descended, differently constituted secularisms. Put another way, to unmask the exacting religious, national, racial, and other specifications that have passed themselves off as a blandly accommodating Christianity is also to begin to expose the similarly exacting specifications concealed within an allegedly universal secular. My hope is that others might follow these alternative trajectories forward and backward from the middle decades of the twentieth century, where I leave off, in the service of a newly energized awareness of the role of religion in American culture, including its literary canon. The last thing I would wish, however, is for religion to be seen as a legitimate category of analysis in American literary and cultural history *only* insofar as it can be reconstituted in terms of the pressures it exerts on race, nationality, gender, sexuality, and other varieties of difference, for such a move would replicate the process by which religion disappears from critical inquiry by being dismissed as epiphenomenal. My interest in exploring the interplay of different religions and different secularisms in American literary history, rather, is to return *these* differences to a discussion from which a simplified narrative of secularization-as-progress has erased them, obscuring a great deal else besides.

PART ONE

Protestantism and the
Social Space of Reading

Chapter One

LEGIBLE DOMINION:

PURITANISM'S NEW WORLD NARRATIVE

> Radical Protestants demanded that the sacred be
> brought into everyday life, into history itself; and to do
> so they abolished the separation of holy from secular
> days, insisting that the divine leave its old haunts—
> churches and pilgrimage sites—to become a part of the
> workplace, the household, to be identified with the his-
> tory of peoples (at first reforming sects, later with
> whole nations) chosen by God to carry out his divine
> purpose in secular time and space. At its most extreme
> the goal was nothing short of the deinstitutionalization
> of religion and its internalization in the hearts and
> minds of all believers. . . . In the end, the Reformation
> contributed not to the sacralization of the world, but
> to its secularization.
> —John Gillis, *Commemorations:*
> *The Politics of National Identity*

WHEN CRISTÓBAL COLÓN arrived on the shores of the Bahamas in 1492, he staked his claim to their possession in a flourish of Catholic theatricality, calling members of his expedition duly to witness his consecration of the land "in the name of our most illustrious Monarch, with public proclamation and with unfurled banners."[1] Some fourteen decades later, the English Puritans who arrived in the New World territories they seized as their refuge from popish and prelatical worldliness described their taking of the land as initiated simply, as John Winthrop put it in his *History of New England from 1630 to 1640*, "by building an house there."[2] John Cotton elaborated the Puritan theory of ownership: "in a vacant Soyle, hee that taketh possession of it, and bestoweth culture and husbandry upon it, his Right it is."[3]

The resonantly anticeremonial quality of what Patricia Seed names the Puritans' "ceremonies of possession" suggests how deeply their material and spiritual claims to their New Jerusalem were grounded in the practice of everyday life. When John Eliot enumerated the means by which the

Puritan attained the "ancient and excellent character of a true Christian"—by keeping not only the Sabbath but the "so many Sabbaths more" devoted to Bible reading, to lectures, to "family-duties" and "daily devotions in our closets," indeed to all "civill callings" and "employment[s]" ("we buy and sell, and toil; yea we eat and drink, with some eye both to the command and honour of God in all")—he concluded that those so occupied were left not "an inch of time to be carnal; it is all engrossed for heaven": "If thou art a believer, thou art no stranger to heaven while thou livest, and when thou diest, heaven will be no strange place to thee; no, thou hast been there a thousand times before."[4]

The creation of a world where eternal life is found in earthly "employment" and the Sabbath undifferentiated from the days of the week that make "so many Sabbaths more" required not only that the difference of the religious per se be dissolved in the conduct of day-to-day life, but also that religious difference itself be constituted as a threat to that life, since manifestly different forms of religious practice and observance point to fissures between the spiritual and worldly realms the Puritans sought to fuse and make one. William Bradford answered the objection of returning colonists that there "was diversitie about Religion": "We know no such matter, for here was never any controversie or opposition, either publicke or private, (to our knowledg,) since we came."[5] "Diversitie about Religion" remained invisible as long as its representatives, as Edward Johnson put it in his *Wonder-Working Providence*, "fled into holes and corners": "*Familists, Seekers, Antinomians* and *Anabaptists* . . . cry out like cowards, If you will let me alone, and I will let you alone, but assuredly the Lord Christ hath said, *He that is not with us, is against us*; there is no room in his Army for toleratorists."[6] While the "gathered church" of the first generations of Puritans limited its membership to the few who could give an acceptable verbal relation of grace, their civil persecutions of spiritual renegades and outsiders—the hanging of Quakers or the maiming of blasphemers, the exile of dissidents or the proscribing of Catholics, all acts that took place against a backdrop of genocidal violence against Indians—maintained the insularity of the New England Way while also making it coextensive with the civil community.[7] As Philip Fisher suggests, "where there are two [or more] systems of belief there are 'religions,' but where there is only one there is only how things are and must be. Social life, when uniform, creates a transparency that we call familiarity, and it is this feeling of familiarity that lets us move from place to place without much effort."[8]

While no one would mistake the relentlessly enforced precariousness of Puritan spiritual life for "effortlessness," the very vigor of the Puritan effort to render heaven and earth commensurable gave rise by the nineteenth century to what many accounts of America's religious development depict as a form of national life in which the religious and the civil are barely distinguishable. Only in America, as Richard Rapson puts it, has "religion ever been so exclusively addressed to this world, so accessible, so awe-uninspiring, so common-sensical, so unmysterious, so simple, so sympathetic to everyday human needs."[9] According to what would take shape as a "consensus narrative" of U.S. religious history, the emergence of this unremarkable, distinctively American religion proceeded through successive acts of democratic inclusion, whereby the failed experiment of the Puritan gathered church eventually yielded a tolerant form of secularized Protestantism that nevertheless remained synonymous with the national community.[10] In its mid-nineteenth-century versions—Robert Baird's *Religion in America*, for example—the consensus narrative portrays an American population united by a common Protestant faith into a single, freedom-loving people, even as nine in ten African Americans were then in bonds, Native Americans were being forcibly driven from their lands, white congregations in the South had begun to secede from their national communions in defense of slavery, and native-born Protestants in northeastern cities rioted in the streets against the Catholic immigrants who would soon outnumber them. The acts of aggression, intolerance, and triumphalism that worked to secure the effect of Protestant consensus for American religious historiography, meanwhile, continued to disappear into the benign vision of the religiously accommodating culture they produced: in its post–World War II versions, the story of America's religious development—beginning, again, with the Puritans—typically credits American's vaunted Protestant heritage with fostering a culture of democracy and religious tolerance unequalled by any nation on earth.[11]

How has New England Puritanism come to stand at the origin point of this quintessentially American narrative of religious tolerance and accommodation? Not, I suggest, for shielding its own violent exclusions—no shortage of bloodshed in Puritan writings—but rather for subsuming these acts of violence under the transcendent, redemptive authority of the Christian Word.[12] Associating both literacy and their removal from an ensoiling Europe with freedom from prelatical spiritual tyranny and monarchical political tyranny, American Puritans sought to project themselves decisively beyond the dividing line they drew between Catholic "matter" and Protestant "spirit," between a moribund, wandering past and a dynamic, providential history, between the dangerous attractions of sensuous ritual and the disembodying powers of the Word.[13] The redemptive power they accorded to literacy and to what the Puritan Richard Baxter called "Self-Examination," or "the serious and diligent trying of a man's heart . . . by the rule of scripture" resulted, according to Andrew Delbanco, in habits of "obsessive self-chronicling" that "guaranteed for [the Puritans] a unique afterlife in American culture."[14] American history "begins" with Puritans insofar as this history is rendered as progress away from hierarchy, ritual, and corruption, and as the gradual triumph of democracy, literacy, and plainspoken truth. Puritans are foundational to this history because this is the history their "obsessive self-chronicling" defines.[15]

It is not simply that New England's native peoples (to take the paradigmatic case) were excluded from a progressive narrative of history they could not easily be brought into. Rather, the providential narrative of history itself both authorizes and obscures the acts of violence by which cultures in competition with the Puritans' own were marginalized or destroyed. "The Lord takes care to make us spiritual in our Imployments," wrote Joshua Moody in *Souldiery Spiritualized, or the Christian Souldier Orderly, and Strenuously Engaged in the Spiritual Warre*, "by spiritualizing all our Imployments. Yea, all our Relations and Conditions, as well as our Imployments, are . . . improved to our Hands by the Spirit of God in his Word [so] that they may . . . further us in those matters that are of most solemn and momentous, because of Eternal concernment."[16] "Spiritualizing" conflictingly suggests both intensification and erasure: to spiritualize material "Imployments" is both to elevate and to demote their importance, to make them matters of "Eternal concernment" and at the same time immaterial, neither here nor there. This is the peculiarly Protestant ethos Weber would call this-worldly asceticism, a "combination of vertues," John Cotton wrote, "strangely mixed in every lively holy Christian, And that is, Diligence in worldly businesses, and yet deadnesse to the world." The Puritan could "bestir himself for profit" and yet "bee a man dead-hearted to the world"; he could seize Indian lands and defend them by violence, "yet his heart is not set on these things, he can tell what to doe with his estate when he hath got it."[17]

Here I seek to follow this "strangely mixed" quality of Puritan reflection by refusing the easy separation implied in the calls of literary and religious historians alike to attend anew to the complexity of Puritan narrative rather than to the brute facts of Puritan violence,[18] or, conversely, to shift focus (at least occasionally) from the Puritans' "sincere desire to establish Christian colonies" to their "stealing of Indian land, and their habit of displacing and murdering these Indians whenever it was convenient."[19] The Puritans' violence against religious and racial outsiders, I argue, was intricately and inseparably linked with their own dealings with the Word, including their ardent promotion of literacy as a tool for the conquest of spiritual enemies as well as their development of genres designed to further projects of Protestant consolidation and expansion.[20] My own aim in starting with Puritans is *not* to privilege as definitively American the New England culture that, beginning with the Puritans, sought to make American identity continuous with Anglo-Protestant identity, but rather to shed light on the ways New England Protestantism elicited assent to its own claims to historical and national primacy by framing the progress of both history and the nation in Protestant terms.[21]

LANGUAGE AND POSSESSION

Where other legal systems—French, Spanish, Portuguese, Dutch— brought from Europe to the New World required authorized written documents to establish title to new lands, only English law made the construction of fixed dwellings and the cultivation of soil the legal mark of ownership.[22] But this right of ownership as constituted in English law was itself a function of literacy and of the spread of print culture more broadly, since it emerged from the linkage between the absolute value of private property and the absolute possession of one's own conscience, a linkage that developed from the Protestant Reformers' insistence that the relationship between God and the individual soul was not to be mediated by ecclesiastical authorities but secured *sola scriptura*, via the agency of the Word. This construction of Protestant inwardness, cultivated in Bible reading and private devotion, fitted Protestant men for the exercise of personal responsibility and contractual obligations that a society based on property ownership required.[23]

Thus Cotton Mather linked the absence of private property among Indians to what he saw as their failures of language: "our shiftless *Indians* were never so much as Owners of a *Knife*, till we came upon them; their Name for an *English-man* was a *Knife-man*."[24] Proper language use constituted what Samuel Purchas aptly called the "litteral advantage" that set English Protestants over those to whose worlds they laid claim by building houses and planting crops: "God hath added herein a further grace, that as Men . . . exceed beasts, so hereby one man may excell another; and amongst Men, some are accounted Civill, and more both Sociable and Religious, by the Use of letters and Writing, which others wanting are esteemed Brutish, Savage, Barbarous."[25]

To establish plantations, to signal possession by building and planting, was also for English colonists to sow the Word in the wilds of the Indian world. The goal of the Plymouth plantation, according to Robert Cushman, had been "to plant a rude wildernesse . . . chiefly to displaie the efficacie & power of the Gospell both in zealous preaching, professing, and wise walking under it, before the faces of these poore blinde Infidels."[26] In his arguments for the establishment of institutions of higher learning in Massachusetts Bay, Charles Chauncey urged Puritans to "consider *what benefit and comfort all sorts have by us*, when our *sonns & young men* are not only indued with *the seed of knowledge & grace*, but such as are sent forth as seedsmen *to sow the Lord's good seed in the hearts of oth-ers.*"[27] For Cotton Mather, to plant the seeds of Puritan culture in the wilds of the New World was to "irradiate . . . an Indian wilderness . . . with a Sweet Light reflected from . . . the Word, which is our Light."[28]

Justifications of Puritan possession that figure the Indian world as prov-identially "irradiated" by the scriptural Word not only spiritualize the Puritans' everyday, proprietary practices of "habitation and culture" but also enforce a hierarchy of literate, English-speaking culture over brute "nature." In the terms of that hierarchy, what John Winthrop called the Puritans' "civill right" to the land overpowers the "naturall right" they share with the New World's native inhabitants. "God hath given to the sonnes of man a double right to the earth," Winthrop wrote; "there is a naturall right, and a Civill Right. The first was naturall when men held the earth in common every man sowing and feeding where he pleased: then as men and theire cattel encreased they appropriated certaine parcells of grownde by inclosinge and peculiar manuerance, and this in time gatte them a Civill right." Indians lack any civil right to the lands they occupy: "As for the Natives in New England, they inclose noe Land, neither have any setled habytation, nor any tame cattle to improve their Land by and soe have noe other but a Naturall Right to those Countries. [S]oe as if we leave them sufficient for their use, we may lawfully take the rest . . . [and] come in with the good leave of the natives who finde benefight allreaddy from our neighbourhood."[29]

The Puritans' "civill right" thus trumped the Indians' "naturall right" whenever and wherever the Puritans "inclosed" the land they claimed for their own. In choosing where they would live, Puritans discussed all of what Winthrop alludes to in his elaboration of Puritans' "civill right": where the soil was best for cultivating, where cattle that provided "im-proving" manure could be grazed, the availability of the kinds of timber that made for the best enclosures. What they did not discuss was the necessity of entering into any kind of agreement with the land's current occupants as to where they might be allowed to live.[30] Indeed, Puritan writings continually refer to the "emptiness" of Indian lands that are man-ifestly populated by Indians. According to Robert Cushman, "their [the Indians'] land is spatious and void & there are few and doe but run over the grasse, as doe also the Foxes and wilde beasts. . . . As the ancient Patriarkes therefore removed from straiter places into more roomthy, where the Land lay idle and waste, and none used it, though there dwelt inhabitants by them, as Gen. 13.6.11.12. and 34.21. and 41.20. so is it lawfull now to take a land which none useth, and make use of it."[31] Indian lands are "spatious and void," in Cushman's account, not because they do not contain human inhabitants but because the only human inhabi-tants they do contain are Indians.[32] Likening Indians to beasts and English colonists to biblical personae, such accounts rhetorically empty Indian lands by making Indians continuous with a wilderness that is ripe for the planting of the Word.

Puritan justifications of land tenure incorporated the biblical linkage between seed and Word (e.g., in the parable of the sower, Matt. 13:18–23; Mark 4:13–20) in their frequent recurrence to scriptural precedents for taking Indian lands by planting them. John Cotton's defense of the Puritans' right to claim title to "vacant soyle" paraphrases Genesis: "*Fulfill the earth and multiply*: So it is free from that common Grant for any to take possession of vacant Countries."[33] John White, in *The Planter's Plea*, defends Puritan appropriation of Indian lands by reference to Psalm 115 ("The lord shall increase you more and more, you and your children," Ps. 115:114): "The gift of the earth to the sonnes of men . . . necessarily inforceth their duty to people it. . . . [N]ow how men should make benefit of the earth, but by habitation and culture cannot be imagined."[34] New England's native inhabitants were also adept at cultivation; Francis Higginson's *New-Englands Plantation* notes that "there is much ground cleared by the *Indians*, and especially about the Plantation. . . . [A]bout three miles from us a Man may stand on a little hilly place and see divers thousands of acres of ground as good as need to be, and not a Tree in the same."[35] Indeed, as Francis Jennings notes, early generations of Puritans frequently evaded the difficult labor of clearing the land, preferring to take over lands cleared prior to their arrival.[36] Biblical typology, however, made the English and not the Indians planters and settlers. According to John Cotton, "a man that is enlightened with the knowledge of God's Will, and the mystery of Salvation; may lawfully . . . make use of diverse Creatures or Things, that are apt and fit to represent Spirituall things unto him."[37] Indians might "make use" of the land and its creatures, but because such uses did not "represent Spirituall things" to Puritans, even those Indian lands that had already been cleared and planted could be conscripted by them to uses authorized by the Word.

THE LITERAL-SPIRITUAL ENTERPRISE

Appeals to scripture to justify Puritan occupation, like Puritan rhetorical practice more generally, made no strict separation between literal and metaphorical usage, or between what Augustine called the carnal and spiritual significations of words. Classical conceptions of metaphor like Cicero's—"words that are transferred and placed, as it were, in an alien place"—made metaphor an oddly "literal" rendering of the experience of exile more generally.[38] The Puritans' self-understanding as a people of exile conflated literal and spiritual significations, most prominently, as

Sacvan Bercovitch argues, by "conferr[ing] upon the continent they had left and the ocean they crossed the literal-spiritual contours of Egypt and Babylon."[39] According to William Hubbard, the ability of Puritans to survive in the New World, far from signaling a debt to Indian assistance, instead reminded them "of God's promise to the people of Israel in their passage towards the possession of the land of Canaan, where he engaged to them concerning the Canaanite and the Hittite, that he would by little and little drive them out from before their people, till they were increased, and did inherit the land."[40]

The Puritans' "discover[y] [of] America in scripture," according to Bercovitch, brought the sacred immediately into the everyday and "changed the focus of traditional hermeneutics, from biblical to secular history."[41] At the same time, the Puritans' "literal-spiritual" enterprise, which set their religion of the word ("faith cometh by hearing," Rom. 10:17) against the embodied excesses of Anglican and Roman Catholic religious practice—"oft starting up, and squatting downe, nodding of heads, and whirling about"[42]—needed at all costs to be distinguished from popery's idolatrous minglings of spirit and flesh. The Boston Synod's 1679 *Confession of Faith* framed the relationship between spirit and flesh as one of "continual and irreconcilable war," war that ultimately issues not in the stalemate of polar opposition but in a tenuous hierarchy, fortified by grace: "in which war, although the remaining corruption, for a time, may much prevail, yet through a continual supply of strength from the sanctifying spirit of Christ, the regenerate part doth overcome."[43] The fragility of the spiritual realm's autonomy, however, also meant that spiritual and material realms frequently blur together in Puritan writings, as in those accounts where the metaphorical absence of Indians stipulated by the scriptural ideology of Puritan land tenure shades into the literal, brutal "disappearing" of Indians in Puritan acts of genocide. So also in John Winthrop's famous account of the dissident Anne Hutchinson's delivery of a malformed birth: "she had vented misshapen opinions [on spiritual matters], so she must bring forth deformed monsters."[44] If this precariously though necessarily close association between spirit and flesh, between the Word and the world, enabled the Puritan project of spiritualizing everyday life, that project further required that the fleshly residue of unregenerate life be continually exorcised by violence.

From the Lenten sermon of the London minister John Hooper in 1550, urging listeners to transform "altars into tables," to the violent dismantling of the cross, statuary, and stained glass windows in John Cotton's Boston, England church in 1621, to John Endicott's defacing of the British flag in Salem, Massachusetts in 1634, acts of material harm directed against tangible representations of the religious worlds from which Puritans sought to exempt themselves punctuate a century of practice culminating in Puritan settlements in the New World.[45] For Puritans, to engage in destruction of what Calvin called the "visible forms" associated with those who "depart from" God was to draw closer to Him:[46] on "hearing . . . the news of the destroying of the cross at Cheapside and those on steeples in England," wrote Cambridge, Massachusetts pastor Thomas Shepard, "I saw how good a thing it was, because in opposing such small evils we resemble God in his holiness the more."[47]

Such acts of iconoclasm take part in the larger Reformation project of asserting the primacy of the "living" word over the "dead" image. The English Book of Common Prayer that retained the "popish" forms of the mass and set prayer, according to Shepard, "has stunk above the ground twice 40 yeeres, in the nostrills of many godly, who breathed in the pure ayre of the Holy Scriptures."[48] The Puritan found the living God in his own words and in the words of scripture; "popish" followers of deadening ritual could be seen by extension as themselves unworthy of life. Though actual Catholics were forbidden by law to reside in Massachusetts Bay, the figure of "popery" proved capacious enough for John Cotton to indict the "Popish ignorance" of the "Indians, and Jews, and Pagans" whose "counterfeit religions" were so many "refuges of lies."[49] Like Catholics and Jews, Indians could be plotted on an unfortunate detour from providential history: "The wandring Generations of *Adams* lost posteritie," according to Roger Williams, "having lost the true and living God their Maker, have created out of the nothing of their own inventions many false and fained Gods and Creators,"[50] habits of worship that in turn confirmed the depravity Cotton Mather signaled in describing Indians as "ruines of mankind."[51]

INDIAN MATERIALITY AND THE TRANSCENDENT WORD

To apprehend native peoples as "ruines" was to ground their destruction in the calls of Reformers to destroy the material forms of idolatrous worship. It was proof of "the wickedness of mans nature," according to William Perkins, that "a man may and can easily transform himselfe into the counterfeit and resemblance of any grace of God."[52] Thus not only did a cross, a flag, or a stained glass window fall under the prohibition against images, but so too could "a man" (or woman) who counterfeited God's grace or participated in allegedly idolatrous devotion. As literal embodiments, to Puritans, of the Second Commandment's violation, Indians were ripe to be targeted in a rhetoric and practice that fused living persons with dead images and spiritual with literal warfare.[53]

Ann Kibbey has documented these processes in suggestive detail in her reading of the Pequot War of 1637–38, the war instigated by the same

John Endicott who destroyed the British flag as an idolatrous image.[54] Although he took issue in that instance with Endicott's "zeal," Governor Winthrop defended Endicott's iconoclastic vandalism on the grounds that since the cross on the British flag was a Catholic image, it was a "superstitious thing, a relique of the anti-Christ."[55] The Pequot War, in which Puritans surrounded the Pequots' Mystic, Connecticut settlement and burned it to the ground, extended the scope of Endicott's and others' acts of iconoclasm by directing them against Pequot men, women, and children, who were, as Kibbey puts it, "not only murdered but destroyed totally in their material being."[56] (The mass conflagration of Pequot bodies not only freed their territories for legitimate Christian uses but also neatly continued the logic of signaling ownership by what Winthrop called "peculiar manuerance": according to Mason's *Brief History of the Pequot War*, the Puritans were "burning them [the Pequots] up in the Fire of [God's] wrath, and dunging the ground with their Flesh.")[57]

The extension of iconoclastic violence toward Indians continued in King Philip's War of 1675–76, where Philip, the Wampanoag Indians' sachem, was in Increase Mather's account "like as Agag . . . hewed in pieces before the Lord."[58] Puritan victors displayed Philip's head at Plymouth for twenty years, and sent his hands to Boston to be ritually mounted as trophies. Noting that "this hand which now writes, upon a certain occasion took off the jaw from the exposed skull of that Blasphemous Leviathan [Philip]," Cotton Mather rejoiced that "the renowned *Samuel Lee* hath since been a pastor to an English congregation, sounding and showing the praises of Heaven, upon that very spot of ground where *Philip* and his Indians were lately worshipping of the Devil."[59]

Mather's "hand which now writes" for posterity; the prayers of Samuel Lee's English congregation, ascending heavenward; Philip's dismembered jaw silenced in its "worshipping of the Devil": Mather's accounting subtly grounds the efficacy of Puritan words in a violent retraction of Indian personhood, as though it were precisely the erasure of Indian speech and spiritual agency that granted Puritan words their disembodying power.[60] Like the attention to Philip's mute jaw, terms like "heathen" and "savage" denote deficient spirituality by contracting Indian humanity to the scope of the body, bereft of interiority. As a space of contracted materiality, the Indian world becomes both a physical obstacle to Protestant expansion and, at the same time, a testament to the limitless reach of the Word. "'Twas . . . unto a Shiloh, that the planters of New England have been making their progress, and King Philip is not the only Python that has been giving them obstruction in their passage and progress thereto," wrote Cotton Mather. "But . . . all the *Serpents*, yea, or *Giants*, that formerly molested that Religious Plantation, found themselves engagd in a fatal Enterprize. We have by a Plain and True History secured the Story of our Successes."[61] Interpreting their contact with Indians by the light of scripture, the Puritans found literal meanings to authorize their acts of war and possession and spiritual meanings to insulate themselves from the corrupting brutality of such acts. Observing that "there are two or 3000 *Indians* who have been killed or taken [captive] . . . [and] not above an hundred men left of them," Increase Mather read the body count to mean that "Salvation is begun."[62]

The rhetorical imposition of surplus physicality on Indians—"some of . . . whose bodyes," according to Edward Johnson's *Wonder-Working Providence*, "were not to be pierced by . . . sharp rapiers or swords [for] a long time, which made some of the Souldiers think the Devil was in them, for there were some Powwowes among them"[63]—gave urgency to the Puritan project of claiming the world for the Gospel to a degree that left, as John Eliot put it, "not an inch . . . to be carnal." As Increase and Cotton Mather wrote of King Philip's War,

> it is observable that several of those nations which refused the gospel, quickly afterwards were so *Devil driven* as to begin an unjust and bloody war against the English, which issued in their speedy and utter extirpation from the face of Gods earth. It was particularly re-marked in *Philip* the ringleader of the most calamitous war they ever made upon us; our *Eliot* made a tender of everlasting Salvation to that king, but the monster entertained it with contempt and anger, and after the Indian mode of joining signs with words, he took a button upon the coat of the reverend man, adding, *That he cared for his gospel just as much as he cared for that button.* The world has heard what a terrible ruine soon came upon that monarch, and upon all his people.[64]

In the Mathers' account, Philip's "monstrousness" is most visible in his vexatious relation to the Word: his deafness to the gospel and, what is here inseparable from it, his peculiar, "Indian mode" of joining bodily signs and physical objects to speech.[65] This reduction of Indian spiritual difference to the scale of the body and its damning gestures inverts the geography of Puritan settlement, casting the Indian world as a space of containment and Puritan habitation as the sign of the Gospel's limitless, invisible reach. Although the Puritans' charter had given as their mission "to incite the natives . . . to the knowledg and obedience of the onlie true God and Savior of mankind,"[66] their self-identification with the Word, what David D. Hall calls the Puritans' "fusion of identity, print, and reli-gion,"[67] functioned as a mandate less to extend the blessings of Christian literacy to Indians—Indian conversion efforts numbered among the Puri-tans' more spectacular failures—than to maintain their own distinc-tiveness.[68] A self-appointed "onely people," Puritans as a group were adept at finding reasons *not* to include Indians in their spiritual, cultural, or linguistic worlds, in which their sense of election was conveyed in their possession of what rendered them not-Indian. Roger Williams observed that when the Narragansett Indians of Rhode Island "talke amongst themselves of *English* ships, and great buildings, and the plowing of their Fields, and Especially of Bookes and Letters, they will end thus: *Manitto-wack* They are Gods."[69]

Because Indian deficiencies were assumed and built into the language of Puritan Christianity, Puritan Christianity entailed as a corollary assumption that Indian languages were themselves deficient. Cotton Mather, here quite unmindful of his own prolixity, urged readers to "count the Letters!" in the transliterated Massachuset words "Nummatchkodtantamooonga-nunnonash," "Noowomantammoonkanunonnash," and "Kummogkoda-nattoottummooetiteaonggannunnonash": "One would think, they had been growing ever since Babel."[70] Rather than subject themselves to the extensive and compromising contact with Indians required for the learning of Indian languages, languages that were, in the Mathers' and other accounts, resistantly opaque to the news of the Gospel,[71] Puritans by and large elected to preserve the blessings of the Word for themselves. "*Children* should learn to READ the *Holy Scriptures*," Cotton Mather enjoined his congregation, "and this, as *Early* as may be."[72] Insofar as history was contained for Puritans between the books of Genesis and Revelation, then withholding biblical literacy from Indians could function to deny both past and future to the New World's native inhabitants except insofar as they figured within the Puritans' own providential designs.[73]

Indians nevertheless remained a living presence even in those territories from which their communities had been forcibly removed, whatever the tendency of the Puritans' chroniclers, as James Merrill notes, to push them off the historical stage even faster than the script demands. Figuring Indians as "utter[ly] extirpat[ed] from the face of God's earth," as Cotton and Increase Mather do, belies the Indians' continued presence as trade partners, interpreters, servants, and slaves.[74] In the majority of Puritan accounts, however, contact with Indians, whether present or absent, living or dead, was conceived as part of an ongoing dialogue between God and the Puritan settlement. "The real interaction," as Richard Slotkin puts it, "was that which took place between the Puritan and the 'invisible world' behind the Indian world. What happened to the mediating Indian world was of secondary importance."[75]

Although Puritans who departed from England sought salvation not in the world but in the interior precincts of the soul in the throes of grace, the confounding Indian world and its inhabitants often proved the more immediately accessible counterpart to that darkened interior landscape.[76]

(Of the forty-nine Puritan saints whose completed conversions were recorded by Thomas Shepard in his church notebooks, only nine first felt the stirrings of their election *before* they arrived in the New World.)[77] In the narrative form of the Puritan spiritual relation, contact with Indians becomes an inward rather than an outward encounter: "You are not now the Slaves of Indians, as you were a few Dayes ago," Mather addressed a congregation that included some recently redeemed from Indian captivity, "but if you continue unhumbled, in your Sins, you will be the Slaves of Devils. . . . Become the sincere Servants of the Lord, who by his *Blood* has brought you out of that *Dungeon*, wherein you were lately Languishing. *Oh! Deny not the Lord*, who has thus *Bought* you, out of your *Captivity*."[78] Here, the Puritan focus on inward spiritual states results in a one-to-one comparison of external and internal otherness, as the "dungeon" of the unregenerate soul takes the form of the Indian camp.

Puritans' conversion narratives show their subjects experiencing the Indian world as a source of continual affliction, and then interpret that affliction as the needlings of grace. As Bercovitch shows, their spiritual inventories in this way take metaphorical form as geographic sojourns: *Jacob Found in a Desert Land, Asking the Way to Zion, A Long Travel to Bethel.*[79] Literal trials in the wilderness became for Puritans occasions for rigorous inward examinations of their un- or only precariously regenerate souls. As Thomas Hooker explained, "The Heart must be broken and humbled, before the Lord will own it as His, take up his abode with it, and rule in it. . . . This was typified in the passage of the Children of Israel towards the promised Land; they must come into, and go through a vast and a roaring Wilderness, where they must be bruised with many pressures, humbled under many overbearing difficulties . . . before they could possess that good Land. . . . The Truth of this Type, the Prophet Hosea explains, and expresseth at large in the Lords dealing with his People in regard of their Spiritual Condition, Hos. 2. 14, 15. *I will lead [her] into the wilderness, and break her heart.*"[80] For Puritan converts, the bruising "pressures" of inward affliction needed, like Indians, to be overcome by spiritual warfare, abandoned in gestures of verbal self-abasement to "dung-hills" and "bogs of Filth," or burned away before God could take possession of and cultivate the wilderness within,[81] in what Hooker called "the soules implantation."[82]

INDIAN CAPTIVITY AND PROTESTANT EXPANSION

Had Puritan conversion efforts remained focused only on the inner life, an entirely different vocabulary might have been expected to authorize external violence and territorial expansion. Instead, verbal attempts at control of the wilderness within also licensed the ordering of the wilderness without; as Cotton put it, the convert has "not only lawfull right" to the fruits of the land "but some right and title to them by the blood of Christ."[83]

The geography of conversion, whereby the uncharted landscape of the new Indian world and its internal correlative, the unredeemed soul, yield each to the proprietary claims of the sanctifying Word, was available most immediately to the first generation of Puritans, for whom separation from a familiar landscape initiated the trial of faith that tested the conviction of the devout. For later generations of Puritans, however, Indian captivity, experienced literally by some and vicariously by the many more who read the accounts of their redemption, could displace the purificatory wandering in the wilderness represented by the first generation's exodus to the New World. Thus Mary Rowlandson structured her narrative of Indian captivity in a form that repeated the first settlers' trauma of emigration and the sequence of the transplanted soul's regeneration: first by conveying her sense of separation, then her perception of her own sinfulness and the strength of her temptations to "Indianization," her recognition of absolute dependence on God's grace, and finally her chastened return to the community of the saints.[84]

As the sanctification of earlier converts by the blood of Christ licensed their appropriation of Indian lands (as in Cotton), so also did accounts of redeemed captives inspire new settlements, even as they effected a gradual loosening of the ties that bound the original covenantal communities. William Hubbard wrote in 1677 of *The Present State of New England*: "It hath been observed of many of these *scattering Plantations* in our Borders, that many were contented to live without, yea, desirous to shake off, all *yoake of Government,* both *sacred* and *Civil,* and so *Transforming* themselves as much as well they could into the manners of the Indians they lived amongst, and some of them are therefore *most deservedly* (as to *Divine Justice)* left to be put under the *yoke and power* of the Indians themselves."[85] Although not all captives welcomed their redemption from captivity, those who did return, particularly in their vivid narratives of arduous sojourns in the wilderness, conveyed by their survival what Jay Fliegelman calls a "secret" teaching: "how to live self-sufficiently alone, how to make a virtue of the theological vice of self-dependence."[86]

The weakening bonds of the Puritans' original covenantal community were given doctrinal expression in the form of the Half-way Covenant, a response to the growing gap between church members and the English population as a whole. Although church attendance was legally required of all Christians, few who attended church were actually full-fledged converts. Among the first generations of Puritans, full church membership was restricted to those who had given an acceptable relation of the workings of grace in their souls. Since that experience eluded the majority of second-generation Puritans, and since baptism was reserved for children of whom at least one parent had made a full conversion, many in the third generation could not be baptized. The Half-way Covenant allowed baptism for children whose parents had themselves been baptized, whether or not they had experienced the grace of conversion. The Cambridge Synod first formulated this compromise in 1646, but waited to implement it until a ministerial assembly of 1657; even then, New England churches waited until after 1675 to apply the broader criteria universally. The Half-way Covenant was the first in a series of doctrinal concessions by which the white Christian community of New England gradually came to comprise not only Puritan congregations but also breakaway sects, among them Baptists, who opposed the Half-way Covenant; Presbyterians, who made its criteria the sole requirement not only for baptism but for full church membership; and later the New Light/Old Light factions within Congregationalism, all of whom claimed to be the legitimate spiritual heirs of the founding Puritan settlements.[87]

That the full implementation of the Half-way Covenant awaited the decimations of King Philip's War points to an intricate shift in the way that Indians demarcated the horizon of the New England Christian community. As long as resistant Indian communities remained a viable threat to Puritan occupation in the areas where Puritans had planted their colonies, the potentially divisive spiritual differences among Puritan Christians could be analogized to the religious difference of the Indians in their midst. This was so even as Puritans portrayed Indians as having, indeed, no religion: John Cotton's counsel to "[o]ffend not the poore Natives, but as you partake in their land, so make them partakers of your precious faith: as you reape their temporalls, so feed them with your spiritualls,"[88] assumes that Indians have "temporalls" but no "spirituals" for Puritan dispossession. Thomas Mayhew, who knew the Wampanoag Indians' language and was acquainted with their spiritual beliefs, described those beliefs thus:

[T]hese poor Indians . . . were mighty zealous and earnest in their Worship of False gods and Devils; their False gods were many, both of things in Heaven, Earth, and Sea. . . . This Diabolical way they were in, giving heed to a multitude of Heathen Traditions of their gods, and many other things, under the observation whereof, they with much slavery were held, and abounding with sins, having only an obscure Notion of a god greater than all, which they called *Mannit*, but they knew not what he was, and therefore had no way to worship him.[89]

Even as Indian religious beliefs were portrayed as the absence of the Puritans' true religion, the very depiction of Indians as deficient Puritans made

Indian spiritual lives in some sense commensurate with the Puritans' own. Thus Puritans viewed as spiritually deficient within their communities were likened to Indians. As Increase Mather exhorted in a sermon, "How many that although they are *Christians* in name, are no better than *Heathens* in heart, and in Conversation? How many Families that live like *profane Indians* without any *Family prayer?*"[90] So also were Puritanism's spiritual renegades "Indianized" in their dissent; Edward Johnson compared the Antinomian controversy and the Pequot War of the same year as simultaneous trials with godlessness, and recorded that Anne Hutchinson had "become all one" with the Indians in her exile.[91] Roger Williams, the dissenter who was associated with Indians in his removal to the more religiously tolerant Providence, nevertheless remarked dismissively of Rhode Island Quakers that "the Indians and Quakers [are] of one spirit."[92]

But if the view of Indians as deficient Christians—and of wayward Protestant Christians as Indians—made Indians the inverse of the Puritan ideal, it also permitted the Puritans' gradual recasting of Indians not as the image of the unregenerate Puritan interior but instead as the external periphery of an increasingly incommensurable otherness, against which different varieties of Protestant Christianity could then be subtly consolidated. After 1679, the civil and spiritual reforms of the Puritans were directed less toward individual regeneration than toward securing ministerial leadership and civil order among the new outlying towns and "unwalled villages" of the expanding white frontier.[93] Because Puritans failed to credit Indians with a distinctive interiority, the Indian became a blank slate for Puritan projections of spiritual deficiency, first by being made into emblems of unregenerate Puritans, and then subtly and increasingly as tools of enemy Catholics. The "conversion" of Indians from weak Puritans to vigorous papists was facilitated by the literal removing or subduing of autonomous tribes from southern New England, which meant that the resistant Indians with whom Puritans came into contact after King Philip's War were those who had been "Romanized" in their association with French colonists to the north. "There is a Danger lest your Neighbors be made *Captives*," warned Cotton Mather in 1707; "If they become *Captives*, they fall into the hands of *Papists*. The Papists will use more than ordinary Pains to Debauch them."[94] Indian captivity had earlier provided Mather the occasion to exhort his congregants to examine their spiritual fragility, their own incipient Indianness in the absence of full conversion. As Tara Fitzpatrick argues, however, the threat of captivity to "papists" now enabled Mather to emphasize less the vulnerability of the Puritan community than its theological strengths, its elevation of faith over works and the gracious workings of the Word over the meretricious agency of the sacraments. In Mather's *Humiliations*, for example, the captive Hannah Swarton related that her captivity secured her conversion, not through a confrontation with her own need for grace as imaged in the depravities of her Indian captors, but through the meddling of the "Nuns, the Priests, Friars, and the rest" to whom they delivered her, who unwittingly convinced her of the superiority of Protestantism and of the sufficiency of the English Bible's lessons in faith.[95]

To earlier generations of Puritans, the presence of Indians, in mirroring the Puritans' need for full conversion, pointed up the degrees of sanctity that divided Protestant Christians among themselves, differences that needed at all costs to be kept from burgeoning into a threatening diversity. As Nathaniel Ward warned in 1645, "Civill commotions make room for uncivill practices: religious mutations, for irreligious opinions. . . . The State is wise, that will improve all paines and patience rather to compose, than tolerate differences in religion."[96] By the final decades of the seventeenth century, however, the Puritans' recasting of the otherness of Indians as a spiritual difference of kind rather than degree enabled the proliferating sects of white New England Protestants to remain united as solid and worthy heirs of the Reformation against the miscegenate corruption represented to Mather as the "half Indianized French . . . half Frenchified Indians."[97] Although the divergent spiritual experiences of Puritans had led them to "gather churches out of churches,"[98] as Increase Mather put it, New England remained, he insisted, a "Protestant Country . . . and of the Church of England too (whatever is blattered to the Contrary)"; "In the same Church there have been *Presbyterians, Independents, Episcopalians*, and *Antipaedobaptists*, all welcome to the same table of the Lord."[99]

Even the witchcraft trials of 1692 may have reflected a certain ironic complacency about the future of Protestant (if no longer of Puritan) stability in Massachusetts. The events at Salem coincided with the passage of a Massachusetts "Bill for the General Rights and Liberties," which recast colonial civil rights from covenantal rights grounded in a specific religious identity to the rights of Englishmen grounded in property ownership.[100] Covenantal rights had until then been restricted to full church members, that is, to those who had given a relation of the workings of faith in their souls. The test of faith was anxiety about the absence of faith; as William Perkins put it, "To see and feele in our selves the want of any grace pertaining to salvation, and to be grieved therefore, is the grace it selfe."[101] In 1692, those convicted of witchcraft experienced anxiety that might have pointed to their sanctity a generation or more before. The accused reported nightmare visitations from Indians, failures at private prayer, feelings of spiritual deadness after baptism or at religious meetings, carnal temptations, and soul-churning doubts, all of which might earlier have signaled the throes of conversion. Cotton Mather appeared to recognize the similarity between demonic possession and the afflictions of the incipient convert when he advocated "lesser punishments" than the "halter or fagot" for "every wretched creature that shall be hooked into some degree of witchcraft." Mather recommended "solemn, open, public, and explicit renunciation of the devil" as an alternative, a verbal purging of inward depravity on the model of the spiritual relation.[102] Even for Mather, however, the afflictions of the possessed were now no longer felt to be internal to Puritanism, from whence they could be purged, but instead to signal an alliance of spiritual enemies without. "One who was Executed at Salem for Witch-craft had confessed That at their Cheef Witch-meetings," Mather wrote, "there had been present some French canadians, and some Indian Sagamores, to concert the methods of ruining New England."[103] By that time, the identity of New England's white inhabitants was explicitly bound up as much in rights of liberty and property as in any claim to doctrinal purity, with Indians and Catholics now marking an expanding Anglo-Protestantism's receding American frontiers.

• • •

"If God were not pleased with our inheriting these parts," John Winthrop wrote to John Endicott, "why did he drive out the natives before us? . . . Why dothe he still make roome for us, by deminishinge them as we increace?"[104] The "increace" of the Puritan presence in the New World has been most visible and accessible to historians less in the decimations they inflicted than in the sheer volume of writing the Puritans produced. "Whether *New England* must live anywhere else or no," wrote Cotton Mather, "it must *Live* in our *History*."[105] Producing their written "History," the Puritans bequeathed to subsequent generations a desire to record America's origins not as religiously and racially plural but instead as white and Protestant, and to read the nation's subsequent history through the lens of the Puritans' providential designs.[106] As Bercovitch summarizes the legacy of this literary deposit, "It gave the nation a past and a future in sacred history, rendered its political and legal outlook a fulfillment of prophecy, elected its 'true inhabitants,' the enterprising European Protestants . . . to the status of God's chosen, and declared the vast territories around them to be their chosen country."[107]

A contested inheritance, to be sure. But if the otherness of the Puritans is felt most powerfully today in the peculiar quality of their religiousness, that may only tell us how far they succeeded in putting their designs on the nation beyond question. For giving their chosenness and their destiny the stamp of inevitability required them to figure other forms of spiritual knowledge, which read the Puritans' redemptive mission otherwise, as illegitimate, threatening, strategically unknowable, or finally inconsequential. "As for their religion," William Hubbard wrote of Indians in 1681, "they were never observed by any of the first comers or others, to have any other but was diabolical. . . . [I]t is not worth the while either to write or read what it was."[108]

If religion, as Jenny Franchot suggests, has come in our avowedly secular intellectual culture to constitute the lost or inscrutable Other, "the loss by which, ironically, we come to know ourselves,"[109] this may be among American Puritanism's most subtle and resilient legacies. In removing the otherness of *other* religions beyond their receding frontiers, New England Puritans consigned to irrelevance or oblivion all religious formations not neatly aligned with everyday life and legitimate self-knowledge as constituted within those frontiers. And if we no longer readily recognize even the Puritans' own fraught and idiosyncratic religious desires as crucial to what Delbanco calls their project of "becoming American,"[110] this is perhaps because those religious sensibilities that do not now shade invisibly into "American" sensibilities fail to command our attention as foundational to our national culture, while those that *do* shade imperceptibly into American sensibilities fail to command our attention as religious.[111] To participate in the Puritan project of equating American Protestantism with American culture, however—as historians have done in framing America's religious development as one of expanding and ever more inclusive Protestant consensus, or as scholars of American literature have done in all but ignoring religion and religious difference altogether—is to credit the inevitability of that equation, American with Protestant, against what Puritan writings in fact record as the enormous psychic and physical violence waged against the possibility that it could have ever been otherwise.

Chapter Two

PROTESTANT EXPANSION, INDIAN VIOLENCE,

AND CHILDHOOD DEATH:

THE NEW ENGLAND PRIMER

"TIS NOT ONLY . . . a *Civil Education* that you must give unto your children," Cotton Mather wrote in his 1702 sermon, "Cares About the Nurseries," but also "that which is peculiar to a *Christian*":

> Here is the *Best knowledge* that our children can have. . . . He knows the best *Rhetoric* that knows how to *Persuade* his own Heart unto the service of the Lord Jesus Christ. He knows the best *Logic* that knows how to conquer the *Devil* in disputing against his *Temptations*. He knows the best *Arithmetic* that knows how to *Number his dayes with wisdom*. He knows the best *Geography* that knows how to Trample the *Earth* under his Foot.[1]

As New England Indian worlds gave way to the ground the Puritan "Trample[d] . . . under his Foot" and the Puritans' civilizing, educating, and Christianizing mission focused increasingly on themselves, the image of the Indian as the figure most in need of redemption continued to function for them as a symbol of the depravity in store for those who lived far from the Word. Mather, whose 1702 *Magnalia* puts Indian conflicts in the past tense—all autonomous Indian groups in southern New England having been vanquished by 1676—was nevertheless moved there to remark that "our Indian Wars are not over yet: We have too far degenerated into *Indian Vices*": "The vices of the Indians are these; They are very lying Wretches, and they are very lazy Wretches; and they are out of Measure indulgent unto their Children; there is no Family-Government among them. We have shamefully Indianized in all these Abominable Things. Now, the Judgements of God have imploy'd *Indian* Hatchets to wound us, no doubt, for these our Indian vices."[2]

With a shortage of Indians available to confirm them, "Indian vices" required extensive rehearsal in Puritan texts. Mather's *Magnalia* represented Indian captors as dashing out the brains of white infants who annoyed them with their crying, drowning them, or sadistically inciting them to tears and then giving them to their distraught mothers to be quieted. In his earlier sermon, "A Family Well-Ordered" (1699), however, Mather had compared the uncatechized child of (presumably more godly) white parents to the captive of Indians: "your *Children*, are the *Children of Death*, and the *Children of Hell*, and the *Children of Wrath, by Nature*: And . . . from *you*, this *Nature* is derived and conveyed unto them. . . . Would it not Break thy Heart if thy *Children*, were in slavery to *Turks*, or *Moors*, or *Indians*? *Devils* are worse than *Indians*, and *Infidels*: Til thy *Children* are brought home to God, they are the slaves of *Divels*."[3]

Mather's urgings on behalf of Puritan infants ground themselves in Calvinist notions of original sin and "native" (that is, innate) depravity; as he put it in "A Family Well-Ordered," "Your *Children* are born with deadly *wounds* of Sin upon their Souls."[4] But further reflected in the precariousness of childhood, as Mather renders it—proximate "by nature" to death, divisiveness, and hell—was the fragility of the Puritans' newly asserted spiritual and civic identity. Childhood, like the Indian world, was the state that Puritans vigorously defined their own religious and civil maturity against—hence the violent nature of much reflection on either— but also all the Puritans had from which to shape their future in the New World. In "Cares About the Nurseries," Mather addressed "Them that are Past Their Infancy": "You are in the *Waxy*, the *Ductile* Age, that Age that is most easily *Moulded* into any form. . . . The Time of peoples' transition from their *Infant-state* unto their *Adult-state* is a Time of very Critical Importance."[5]

For Mather, the point of education was to redeem children from their symbolic captivity to Indians, their "natural" condition of Indianness. Early experiments in Puritan education were occasionally undertaken on behalf of Puritan and Indian children alike; a British bookseller wrote to the younger John Winthrop to advertise "an English written Accedence and grammer of such rare method" for "the speedy bringinge of English and Indians to the perfect understandinge of our tonge and writinge truly."[6] Teaching Indian and English children together, as in the first schools at Boston and Roxbury, spared white schoolmasters the perceived ignominy of ministering exclusively to Indians; learning alongside white children would in turn, according to Daniel Gookin, "much promote the Indians learning to speak the English tongue," "to converse with the English familiarly, and thereby learn civility and religion from them."[7]

Even as Indians disappeared from Puritan classrooms, however, the "Indian" was preserved in early New England writing as the negative example of what the Puritan child who ignored his lessons might become. In his arguments with the Quaker George Fox, for example, Roger Williams likened Quaker modes of spiritual knowing not only to the "*Weapons*" of the "*Devil* and the *Papists* . . . *Mahomet* or the *Pope*," but also to the undisciplined ploys of Indians or badly educated white children.

Fox's "loose and wild spirit" in interpreting the scriptures, Williams charged, had goaded him into "Leaps and Skips like a wild *Satyre* or *Indian*, catching and snapping at here and there a Sentence, like Children skipping ore hard places and Chapters, picking and culling out what is common and easie with them to be paid of and answered."[8]

To discourage Puritan children from "skipping ore hard places and chapters," as well as to guard against their seduction by illegitimate religion, colonial primers, which typically served children from the time they could recognize letters until they had mastered all 105 questions of the (mercifully) Shorter Westminster Catechism, moved in sequence from the alphabet to words of one, two, and more syllables, and from there to scriptural and theological lessons of increasing difficulty. In October 1683, London publisher John Gaine went on record as having issued the *New England Primer, or Milk for Babes*. This work was probably compiled by the Englishman Benjamin Harris, who had published a children's reader, the *Protestant Tutor*, in 1679.[9] The *Protestant Tutor*'s object, according to the full title Harris inserted into the *Stationers' Registers*, was to teach young readers to "spell and read English" and to recognize "the true protestant religion" against the "errors and deceitts of the papists."[10] In addition to its alphabet, Lord's Prayer, and words for children in small syllables, the *Protestant Tutor* included a woodcut of the burning of the pope, an illustrated account of the martyrdom of John Rogers at Smithfield in 1544, a "Prospect of POPERY" and attendant calamities should England fall again under the sway of Rome, narratives of the Spanish invasion by the papists and of the massacre of the British in Ireland, a "Dialogue between an Apostate to the Church of Rome and a Young Protestant," and, lest the point be lost, "A Catechism Against Popery."[11]

Harris moved from London to Massachusetts Bay in 1686, and in 1690 placed an advertisement for a second edition of the *New England Primer* in a Boston newspaper. No seventeenth-century edition of the *New England Primer* has been found, and it remains unknown whether the earliest surviving edition of 1727, printed at Boston, was a later version of Harris's text or whether it was patched together from existing alphabets, catechisms, and picture books. In any event, it is likely that at least portions of the 1727 *New England Primer* were in wide use among the children of British colonists in New England before the end of the seventeenth century. A count beginning with the surviving 1727 copy shows that about three hundred subsequent editions of the *New England Primer* were printed in America, and at least three million and as many as eight million copies placed into circulation before the middle of the nineteenth century.[12]

The *New England Primer* eliminated most of the *Protestant Tutor*'s references to papal violence, save a woodcut of the pope as the hairy, beastlike "Man of Sin" in some editions and the verses ascribed to the martyred John Rogers in nearly all. If Puritan divines were eager to adopt British anti-Catholic vocabularies to defend and define themselves against the native presence in the New World, however, the *New England Primer* records no corollary transfer of the *Protestant Tutor*'s reflections on popery to Indians. Indeed, what is remarkable is that, with narratives of Indian captivity a persistent favorite of colonial and early national booksellers, and the "Indianization" of un- or reluctantly redeemed white captives along the American Atlantic so common as to induce Hector Crèvecoeur to remark in 1782 that "thousands of Europeans are Indians,"[13] native peoples figure only as a massive absence in eighteenth-century editions of the *New England Primer*. Instead, the *Primer*, which was printed not only in New England but in Pennsylvania, New York, and Maryland, rehearses the origins of a nation in which kings, queens, biblical personae, Protestant martyrs, and even Catholics are present, but Indians are not.

The absence of Indians from the *New England Primer* has no doubt helped to make it the darling of historians of early American textbooks, whose works typically proceed without reference to Indians.[14] Nor have literary historians considered Indian-white interactions in the New World a factor in shaping the *New England Primer*.[15] Lucy Maddox's point that the construction at once of a new nation and a "new-nation ideology" required the "removal or supplanting of inappropriate forms of discourse" as well as the "physical removal and supplanting" of Indians,[16] however, suggests that the invisibility of Indians in the *New England Primer* was in fact crucial to its strategies for inculcating in its readers the forms of discourse required to constitute the new nation, discourse in which the absence of Indians was simultaneously assumed and enforced.

The design of the *New England Primer*, which typically begins with a picture alphabet and culminates in the Shorter Westminster Catechism, was to induce literacy as a means to spiritual maturity. The absence of Indians from the *Primer*, then, signals as its goal the creation of a literate, Christian subject in whom Mather's "Indian vices"—of lying, of laziness, of resisting the promptings of the Word for the corrupting entanglements of the flesh—had been vanquished. To the degree that arguments (like Mather's) for literacy as a necessary instrument of redemption assume a condition of "natural" depravity, however, they produce a rather more unstable view of the self: on one hand, the self is salvageable, by the agency of the Word, from the depredations of its natural condition; on the other, the self (because innately depraved) remains resistantly natural and so permanently menaced by the fleshly willfulness and brutality that are the markers of its unregenerate state. In Mather's view, this innate disposition toward evil could be seen not only in the susceptibility of Puritans to "Indianization," but in their failures of government in relation to

Indians themselves. Of King Philip's War, for example, Mather wrote that "during the late unhappy War between the *English* and the *Indians* . . . an evil spirit possess'd too many of our English, whereby they suffer'd *Themselves* to be unreasonably Exasperated against all *Indians*."[17]

Insofar as English Americans figured literacy as the key to redemption from their natural state, then, their favored modes of inducing literacy could serve the further function of suppressing the material and historical realities associated with that state, including the reality of their "unreasonable exasperation" against Indians and its effects. In providing tools for the construction of a redeemed self, the *New England Primer* also images a "redeemed" political order, that is, one in which not only the Indian but violence against Indians has been rendered invisible. By including only white subjects in its pages, the *New England Primer* affirms a conception of early American identity as decisively not-Indian, spiritually or politically. But insofar as that ethnically cleansed identity remains unstably divided along the shifting fault line between redeemed and unregenerate selves, the American subject who engages in (or owes his existence and livelihood to) a sordid history of aggression against Indians blurs into the subject whose access to the redemptive power of the Word lifts him out of that history, and into an ideal spiritual order from which the violent realities of Indian conquest have been effaced.[18]

If the *New England Primer* rewrites New England origins as innocently untroubled by Indian conflict, moreover, it nevertheless retains in displaced ways the connection between Indians and childhood, in order both to figure "Indianness" as the vanishing state that the maturing nation is bound to leave behind, and to signal the danger that the resistant subject, unredeemed from symbolic captivity, poses to the national project. In the *Primer*'s pages, the vanquished "Indian" returns as the inappropriately socialized adult, the Catholic "Man of Sin," or the devil who seduces children away from family, community, and Christ. In these ways, the *New England Primer* banishes Indians to the hinterlands of New England experience, only to retrieve them in the reconstituted form of incorrigible or unassimilable Americans who threaten the project of white Protestant dominance signaled by the Indian's anticipatory "removal" from its own pages.

PROTESTANTISM, LITERACY, AND NATIONAL FORMATION

The *New England Primer* tied religious instruction to the alphabet ("In Adam's fall, we sinned all")[19] and from there to spelling and reading, so that children would absorb the anxious lessons of Puritan theology along with the basic information they needed to participate in the social world.

The *Primer*'s audiences learned to read by learning to discern the presence and designs of God, represented to them, in part, as the constant threat of death and the concomitant requirement of spiritual vigilance. (The child's prayer "Now I Lay Me Down to Sleep," for example, comes from the *New England Primer*.)

Elisa New has eloquently argued that the *New England Primer*'s preparation of children for the deprivations and diminishments of Puritan adulthood finds its corollary in the tendency of Puritan preaching to keep adults suspended in a childlike state of dependence.[20] For Puritan children, instruction in biblical and theological literacy prepared them for entry not only into the company of saints, but also into the company of adults.[21] But because conversion was never a once-and-for-all event, Puritan adults remained like children in their perpetually "unfinished" state. John Cotton counseled Puritans to "rest . . . not untill you finde Christ manifested to your spirit as yours; grow up in a Lambe-like frame of spirit and way, untill the mystery of God be finished in you."[22] Insofar as the malleability of the childhood state mirrored the instability of the Puritan soul, the *New England Primer* could over the two centuries of its development nurture not only white children but the white American population as a whole into a spiritual and civic adulthood. Echoing Mather on the "waxy" and "ductile" nature of childhood, Noah Webster, who produced an "amended and improved" version of the *New England Primer* in 1789, wrote that the "the impressions received in early life, usually form the characters of individuals, a union of which forms the general character of a nation."[23]

The *New England Primer* was written for children but composed, printed, bought, and sold by adults; adults, moreover, were instructed to read the *Primer* to children who were not yet readers themselves. Some editions of the *New England Primer* register the book's adult readership by including childrearing advice directed explicitly to parents. Under the heading "Parents' Duty to their Children," the adult reader of the *Primer* was reminded to "[c]hastise thy son, and hold him to labour, lest his lewd behavior be an offense to thee. Withhold not correction from the child, for if thou beatest him with the rod, he shall not die." More in the spirit of Martin Luther's dictum that he would rather a dead child than a disobedient one, however, the *New England Primer*'s lessons in correction were typically severe, often prescribing death or disfigurement for unmannerly children. Alongside its admonishing Bible verses—for example, "The eye that mocketh his father, and despiteth the instruction of his mother, let the young eagles eat it"—the *Primer*'s "Verses for Little Children" set scriptural instances of juvenile capital punishment to rhyme:

When wicked children mocking said,
To a good man, Go up bald head
God was displeased with them and sent
Two bears which them in pieces rent.
I must not like these children vile
Displease my God, myself defile.

If the *Primer*'s representations of God as the agent of fatal or maiming punishments reassured Puritan parents of the divine justice of their own harsh discipline, such images also potentially recalled them to the necessity of violent transformation in their own lives. John Cotton, whose writings for children were staples of the *New England Primer* into the nineteenth century, counseled parental violence against children as the surest means of bringing them to the violence of conversion:

It is a vain apprehension that men have of themselves as good, to say, I thank God I have a good heart, and you shall finde me tractable, and reasonable, (thou they be but naturall) and so their children are very tractable, you may lead them with a twinde theerd, and need not use violence. . . . [W]hat then are you but eggshells? What need then a iron hammer to crush all the power of the enemy? do not you and your children stand in need of the power of the blood of the lamb as much as others have since the world began? . . . [L]et all Parents tell it to their children, and Masters to their servants, and all that have to do with the world; be not deluded with a good affection to your own nature you are in, this is the state of all since the world began; they are all sprawling in wickednesse, and there is such a league between the Devil and them, that unless the Lamb be slaughtered, we cannot be saved.[24]

In light of the less punitive future gradually signaled in different ways by the emergence of the independent nation, the expansion of the market, and the softening of Calvinist Christianity in the heat of revivalism, the images of child death that persist even into nineteenth-century editions of the *New England Primer* would seem to project a certain perilousness onto the Puritan past, suggesting that a transformative break from Puritan conceptions of the self was required to launch the nation securely into its civil adulthood. Even as developments in the *Primer* over the twelve decades of its recoverable history subtly took note of the changes attendant on the transition from colony to nation, however, the text of the *Primer* remained remarkably constant from edition to edition, keeping New England's past from ever receding completely from New England's—and the nation's—advancing present. While the earliest surviving edition of the *Primer* narrowly postdates the Puritan era, and the nation whose emer-

gence the *Primer* records as the symbolic object of its later eighteenth-
and nineteenth-century readers' allegiance had not yet come into being
for Puritans, the *New England Primer* also records the extension and
modes of transmitting Puritan habits of thought into subsequent generations. The woodcuts that appear in eighteenth- and nineteenth-century
editions are identical to those dating back to 1630, and the hallmarks of
nearly all editions—picture alphabets, John Rogers's verses, the Westminster Shorter Catechism, and the "Dialogue Between Christ, a Youth, and
the Devil"—were widely circulated in the seventeenth century. If changes
in the *Primer* over the eighteenth and nineteenth centuries reflect broader
changes made possible by the expansion of a white Protestant America,
we can infer that what does not change from one edition to the next was
preserved for offering tacit support to that expansion. What remains of
colonial materials in later editions of the *New England Primer* indexes
the susceptibility of later eighteenth- and nineteenth-century white Protestants to Puritan accounts of what it meant to be white and Protestant,
and thus to the parts of the Puritan narrative that could stand unrevised
in subsequent projects of nation building.

Religious historians typically mark as the end of Puritanism the beginning of the Great Awakening, the series of religious revivals that took
hold in the 1720s, peaked in the 1740s, and continued into the 1770s.
The Great Awakening represented both the resurgence of Puritan faith
and its transformation, organizing dissent from Calvinism in ways that
permitted many of its tenets to find homes in other contexts. The revival-
ists' revolt against the ceremonial forms of Presbyterian and Congregationalist worship, for example, and their insistence on the need of the
converted to accept Christ in the ecstatic revelation of his grace, continued
the Puritan distrust of ritual and set prayer. The frenetic spiritual style of
the Great Awakening, moreover, was admirably suited to the growth of
white America, whose rapidly receding frontiers made evangelical conversions the more expedient alternative to belabored and ever unfinished
Puritan ones, and whose emerging market system managed social differences more effectively than the failed experiment of the Puritan "gathered" churches ever could. Though originally in some measure a religious
movement of those dispossessed by the insularity of Calvinist elites, the
evangelical revivals eventually bolstered the dominance of white middle-
class Protestantism by enabling its adherents to emphasize what they
shared rather than what divided them into rival sects.[25]

The *New England Primer* registers these changes by gradually coming
to endorse a white, Protestant "ethnoreligion" alongside (and emanating
from) the resolutely Puritan theology of its seventeenth- and early eighteenth-century sources.[26] The ethnoreligion of the *New England Primer*
proved both expansive enough to accommodate new categories of Chris-

tians—some later eighteenth-century editions of the *Primer* were issued under the auspices of the Episcopal Church, for example—and restrictive enough to demarcate the ethnic, racial, and class boundaries of the Christianity it defined as normative. In the *New England Primer*'s early editions and in its Puritan antecedents, children learned a language of limitation, subjection, and containment from lessons that conveyed what David Watters aptly calls "the Puritan distrust of uncontrolled speech."[27] Although the alphabet lessons "*Time* cuts down all / Both great and small" and "*Youth* forward slips / Death soonest nips" appear in nearly all eighteenth-century editions of the *Primer*, from mid-century on children began to learn that the import of such lessons was less privative than privileging: "He that learns these letters fair / Shall have a coach to take the air." While Puritans might well have objected to this framing of the rewards of literacy, their notions of literacy's moral function were not wholly at odds with later celebrations of its utility for conferring economic status, since the accumulation of wealth, increasingly commended as a mark of virtue in later editions of the *Primer*, was compatible with the Puritan theology of visible saints that made prosperity an indication of election.

At the same time that the *New England Primer*'s biblical lessons were being displaced by attention to worldly goods (the alphabet rhyme that forthrightly details David's adultery with *U*riah's wife would eventually become "*U*rns hold, we see / both coffee and tea"), some verses on earthly themes were evangelized, so that "The *C*at doth play / and after slay" becomes "*C*hrist crucify'd / for sinners died"; "the *D*og will bite / a thief at night" becomes "the *D*eluge drowned / the earth around." In general, however, the *Primer*'s portrayal of a gentler Christianity went hand in hand with its depiction of the results of an expanding market. The softening of the *Primer*'s theological lessons further records the influence of developments in educational theory that warned against the Calvinist emphasis on childhood damnation as demoralizing to those on whom the economic future of America depended.

To the degree that the *New England Primer* of the later eighteenth century came (albeit unevenly) to dissent from the harshness of the Puritan childrearing practices residually preserved in its own pages, it anticipated what would take shape by the mid-nineteenth century as a broader network of middle-class opposition to corporal punishment. That opposition was embodied in a range of genres, including antislavery narratives, domestic advice literature, and arguments on behalf of tax-supported common schools. As Richard Brodhead has shown, whatever the divergent aims of these discourses, they shared the goal of converting their audiences from allegiance to the harsh external authority associated with older and ostensibly outmoded religious and political regimes to a form of "disciplinary intimacy" that would "make . . . authority constitutive of identity, and so make . . . the *self* the governor of the self." Brodhead points to the ways in which this new disciplinary model depended on and further enabled the democratization of print culture, since the same discourses that argued for the internalization of middle-class parental authority by "propagat[ing] the figure of the home as an enclosed zone of domestic leisure, consecrated to the creation of character through loving nurture" also "specif[ied] *reading* as the home's other principal activity."[28]

If the *New England Primer* facilitates this transition to increasingly internalized modes of discipline by priming its audiences to take their places in a middle-class culture of reading, it nevertheless illustrates as well the limits of that culture's putatively democratic reach. What the *New England Primer* offers is not only training *in* literacy, but also a rather selectively extended training *for* literacy, for citizenship in the social world that literacy opens up for "good" boys and girls. Those who learned to read from the *Primer* read the language of Protestant religious experience and Protestant religious classification; they learned rules of inclusion and exclusion that governed the reading subject, the home and schoolroom where reading took place, and the forms and levels of citizenship (and noncitizenship) in the public sphere for which readers (and nonreaders) were trained. As the baby talk of the *Primer*'s "easy syllables" (ba, ca, da, fa) precedes words, so the words themselves, as they increase in length, move from nouns associated with nature and the material world ("colt," "leaf") to words that require some acquaintance with white Protestant positionality ("heathen," "nunnery"), then on to those that image both the virtues ("holiness," "godliness," "fidelity") and the proscriptions ("drunkenness, "impudence," "fornication") of its enforcing regimes. The reading child's progress from sounds to syllables to words of increasing length and complexity ideally brings her from a state of nature to the condition of Protestant self-knowledge and inner direction. In this way, the *New England Primer* schooled its readers in what Elizabeth Barnes aptly calls the "union of private and public privilege" implicit in the model of a self-governing nation.[29]

Changes that made for a kinder, gentler *Primer* from the mid-eighteenth century onward were largely the work of Isaac Watts, an educator and evangelical critic of Calvinism whose innocent "Cradle Hymn" ("Sleep my babe, thy food and raiment, / House and home thy friends provide; / And without thy care or payment / All thy wants are well supply'd") and other verses came rather jarringly to accompany the *Primer*'s more frightening admonitions to children from Puritan sources (e.g., "At night lie down prepar'd to have / Thy sleep, thy death; Thy bed, thy grave"). Watts was a Lockean liberal who believed not that children were vipers but that their minds at birth were each "an empty cabinet" that the proper education would supply both with knowledge and with worldly goods.[30]

Editions of the *Primer* that include Watts's hymns also typically feature lessons on the material prosperity that awaited those to whom "God the all powerful being is [the] friend, who is invariably disposed by nature to reward their virtue." Such lessons explicitly connect virtue and its rewards with literacy; thus, for example, a "good boy" "loves his book" and becomes a "great man" who "dies with credit and reputation," while a "bad boy" "hates his book" and "generally dies a beggar." Some of the Watts-influenced editions of the *Primer* also include a gendered allegory of "Prudence":

> Pretty Miss Prudence
> You've come to the fair
> And a very good girl
> They tell me you are
> Here take this fine orange
> This watch, and this knot
> You're welcome my dear
> To all we have got
> For a girl that's so good
> And so pretty as you
> May have what she pleases
> Your servant Miss Prue.

"Miss Prue" is entitled to a form of citizenship that assumes economic mobility, even as her spending power is elided by her representation in the text as one who is plied with all the goods the market has to offer simply for being so good and so pretty. Her powers of acquisition, her ability to win goods through her goodness, mark Miss Prue from the "naughty" girls who are entitled neither to fill their "empty cabinets" nor to enter public space:

> So pert Misses Prate-apace, how came you here?
> There's nobody wants to see you at the fair
> Not oranges, apples, cakes or nuts
> Will anyone give to such saucy sluts
> For such naughty girls we here have no room
> You're proud and ill-mannered—Go hussies, go home.

If what is hidden in literate Miss Prue's story is her purse, the banishing of the Misses Prate-apace signals the corollary need to keep *illiteracy* hidden as a mechanism for linking economic alienation to religious, racial, and other forms of alienation.[31] John Adams famously remarked that "a native [i.e., a colonist of English descent] who cannot read and write is as rare an appearance as a Jacobite or a Roman Catholic, that is, as rare as a comet or an earthquake."[32] Estimates of the extent of illiteracy in Adams's day, however, run as high as 50 percent for white men and 75 percent for white women; illiteracy rates for nonwhite persons were clearly higher still.[33] There is something both normative and insubstantial in Adams's boast, for his characterization of illiteracy as "rare" conflictingly suggests not that illiteracy is precisely unknown, but rather that it is both spectacular—something that, like an earthquake or a Roman Catholic, literate white Protestants did well to be wary of—and at the same time as dim to perception, and as politically weightless, as a shooting star.

In a similar way, the *Primer* teaches its readers both to take cautionary notice of nonreaders and, in the same measure, to give them no notice at all. The lesson is given, implicitly, in the disidentification of the *Primer*'s audience from nonreaders (which the former's very act of reading the *Primer* secures), but more explicitly in its accounts of the perils of keeping nonreading company. In the second alphabet of verses contained in some editions of the *Primer*, eight are about reading ("B was a *Boy* that was fond of his book"; "C was a *Cheese* cake for such as could read") and six in addition depict the consequences of illiteracy ("N was a *Noddy*, as dull as an ass"; "Z a poor *Zany* was left in the lurch.") By absorbing such lessons, children learned not only to read but to position themselves, as readers, against such dunces as Miss Betsy Low, who not only had "no taste for the genteel pleasures of her book" but "would play with those beneath her . . . and learned their airs, their words and manners," and thus was called "hussy, slut, puss, and a great many other naughty vulgar names." When "she grew a great girl . . . she was so rude and ill mannered that her mamma was ashamed of her," so "she then returned to her ignorant company, and . . . was laughed at, despised, and at last routed." Such examples not only warned children of the spiritual, social, and economic consequences of illiteracy, itself never presented as other than voluntary, but taught literate children their place, as readers, in a nation where nonreaders continued to outnumber them.

The Puritan distinction between the company of saints and the much larger company of the unregenerate is thus preserved, in later editions of the *Primer*, as the distinction between readers and nonreaders. In his sermons, Cotton Mather reminded children that their "*Dawning* Time" may well be their "*Dying Time*": "*Children*, go unto the *Burying-place*; There you will see many a *Grave* shorter than your selves. . . . And what needs any more be said, for your Awakening, to learn the *Holy Scriptures*!"[34] Many eighteenth-century editions of the *New England Primer* include a verse based on Mather's sermon: "I in the burial place may see / graves shorter far than I / . . . my God may such an awful sight / awakening be to me / O that by early grace I might / for death prepared be." By mid-century, however, the *Primer*'s audiences learned to read even these

lessons less to avoid an unhallowed death than to elude the embarrassments of penury, the imputation of sluttishness, and the company of
bad men and women: "Good children should keep such company as will
make them wiser and better; for if you play with naughty boys and girls,
and men and women that say naughty words, you will grow naughty
too." In the *Primer*'s Puritan antecedents, all children may die, and death
should be their motivation for study. Editions of the *Primer* from the mid-
eighteenth century on retain these earlier descriptions of grisly child
death, but gloss them with the lesson that it is bad (nonreading) children
and the bad adults they become who die, die penniless, or fear death. In
contrast, the *Primer*'s readers, by reading, "have God for their friend!
They have nothing to fear: they may smile at death, and leave this world
with pleasure."

The entrance of Isaac Watts's gentle hymns into an ordering scheme
that retains the older Puritan images of child death and dismemberment
signals this new distribution of authority in their suggestion that the reading child has Christ for his protector while nonreading children may have
their lives or their liberties cut short at any moment ("He that ne'er learns
his ABC / For ever will a blockhead be"). The gradual if selective softening
of Calvinist theology in Watts's hymns and the lessons that accompany
them also helped to fix the identification between the nascent republic
and the *Primer*'s readership of literate Protestants. As Watters argues,
the *New England Primer* routinely sets the child in relation to parental,
religious, and civil authorities at the same time that it participates (for
example, by replacing the British sovereign's picture in early frontispieces
with George Washington's picture in later ones) in the national project of
disowning the authority of the parent country. In this way, Watters suggests, Watts's soothing lessons in divine love and forgiveness primed children to see divinity not only in the vengeful father but also in the forgiving
son, and so to map onto the relationship of God and Christ both their
own, progressive interiorization of parental authority and the emergent
nation's independence from the parent king.[35]

The gradual diminution of the British crown in the lives of the *New
England Primer*'s readership is registered across several decades of verses
for the letter K. An early rhyme that appeared in primers published by
Benjamin Harris—"King Charles the good, / no man of blood"—was
changed, in England, as reigns changed, requiring some ingenuity at the
accession of a female monarch—"King William's dead / and left the
throne / to Ann our queen / of great renown." The earliest surviving edition of the *Primer* subtly anticipates the casting off of monarchy altogether by skirting the issue of changing sovereigns; the verse for K reads:
"Our *k*ing the good / no man of blood." Later, the *Primer* asserts the
goodness of kings as normative rather than an objective statement: "Kings

should be good, / not men of blood." Some postrevolutionary editions of the *Primer* use the K verse to memorialize the new nation's independence—"The British *k*ing / lost states thirteen"—and bring the message home in the verse for W: "By Washington / Great deeds were done." Other editions cast monarchs in the role of trinkets—"Queens and kings / are gaudy things"—or else forego the pedagogical inducements of rhyme in favor of the stricter lesson that the passage to self-government entails death to the childlike dependence on absolute authority: "Kings and queens / lie in the dust." Still others insist that the sovereignty claimed by the monarch belongs only to God: "God is our *K*ing / His honors sing."[36]

The block illustrations for *K*ing, *Q*ueen, and other letters were British imports that changes in their accompanying verses put to new purposes: as Puritans declared their own forms of independence by studying the Book, and so circumventing the priest or magistrate who would intervene between the reading subject and God, so the *Primer* primed its readers for spiritual and national adulthood by gradually associating human monarchs with systems of unjust rule from which reading emancipates them, or with childish forms ("gaudy things") to be put behind them. A British import that most editions of the *Primer* leave unchanged, however, are the verses ascribed to John Rogers on the occasion of his martyrdom at Smithfield, illustrated by a woodcut of Rogers at the stake, guarded by a sceptered figure representing Rome, with Rogers's wife and ten children looking on from one side. Rogers's verses were first published in England in 1559 and frequently reprinted, notably in the *Protestant Tutor*. There and in the *New England Primer* the narrative that accompanies Rogers's verses reads: "Mr John Rogers, minister of the gospel in London, was the first martyr in Queen Mary's reign, and was burned at Smithfield, February the 14th, 1554. His wife, with nine small children, and one at her breast, following him to the stake, with which sorrowful sight he was not in the least daunted, but with a wonderful patience, died courageously for the Gospel of Jesus Christ."

Rogers's children were unlikely to have followed him to the stake in fact; Foxe's *Martyrs* records that they "met him by the way as he went toward Smithfield."[37] But neither the *Protestant Tutor* nor the *New England Primer* missed the opportunity to turn Rogers's execution into a child's lesson. Identifying with the attentive children (readers were invited to count them) who watched their father burn, the *Primer*'s audience joined Rogers' family in the act of reading, a transformation literalized in an 1828 *Primer*'s observation that "[h]undreds and perhaps thousands" of American children have "read the account of the martyrdom of Rev. John Rogers and wept at the recital of his sufferings and painful death, without knowing that in their veins flowed the blood of him, who was

MR. *John Rogers*, Minifter of the Gofpel in *London*, was the firftMartyr inQ. *Mary's*Reign, and was burnt at*Smithfield*, *Febru* *any* the fourteenth, 1554. HisWife, with nine fmallChildren, and one at

Figure 1. The *Burning of John Rogers* in the *New England Primer* (Boston: S. Kneeland and T. Green, 1727). From Paul Leicester Ford, *The New England Primer: A History of Its Origin and Development with . . . Many Facsimile Illustrations and Reproductions* (1897). Image courtesy of the "19th Century Schoolbooks" website (http://digital.library.pitt.edu/nietz) hosted by the Digital Research Library, University of Pittsburgh.

the first victim of that 'noble army of martyrs' who suffered during the reign of that cruel and bigoted Queen Mary."[38]

In keeping Smithfield a part of *America*'s cultural memory in the eighteenth and early nineteenth centuries, and, more pointedly, in overlaying Rogers's racial and religious identity onto its readers' own, the *New England Primer* borrowed England's strategies for the manipulation of national memory to celebrate England's delivery from papal bondage as the sign of an Anglophilic deity's favor on the new, implicitly Protestant nation.[39] Relocated to the *New England Primer*, however, the Rogers verses could in the 1770s and thenceforward also celebrate America's gradual delivery from bondage to England. As British toleration of a Roman Catholic Bishop in the province of Quebec fomented desires for separation, colonial newspapers condemned the King's "Romish business" with Quebec,[40] and at the same time appealed to the national, *Brit-*

ish pride of the colonists to unite against "*Popish* Superstition and *French* Tyranny," and to "vindicate . . . our Protestant Religion and our *British* Liberties," that there may "never be wanting a Race of Protestants to sway the *British* Scepter, so long as the Sun and Moon endureth."[41]

Following the Revolution that vindicated Americans' British and Protestant liberties, the Rogers verses that could temporarily be cast as a warning against the enslaving designs of a "popish king" now called to mind for the *Primer*'s readers their special status as a Protestant elect, their political independence from England as well as the renewal of their filial claims on New England, and the unchanging need for vigilance against Catholics. If the Royal Oak of the prerevolutionary *Primer*'s O ("It was the tree / that sav'd his / Royal Majestie") schooled children to celebrate Royal Oak Day as commemorating Britain's triumph over papacy, while the "Sturdy Oak" of later editions less felicitously enlisted them in the new nation's defense ("it is the tree / that forms the navy / of America"), both generations were nevertheless primed for the lesson in Rogers's verses to "Abhor that arrant whore of Rome / . . . Obey not her decrees."

IMAGES OF CHILDHOOD

Warnings against Rome were considered especially needful for children by eighteenth-century American Protestants who saw the Catholic Church as deploying, in John Adams's words, "everything which can charm and bewitch the simple and ignorant." Wondering how "Luther ever broke the spell," Adams wrote to his wife in 1774 of the "awfull and affecting" spectacle of Philadelphia Catholics in thrall to "their Beads," to "their Pater Nosters and Ave Maria's" ("not a word of which they understood") and, most vexingly for Adams ("how shall I describe [it]?"), their grisly "Picture[s]" and "little images."[42] The "little images" that adorned the *New England Primer* caused alarm among some parents who scratched out the woodcuts in their children's copies for fear that they would become idolatrously beholden to icons.[43] But Rogers's readers, and the *Primer*'s, implicitly learn a hermeneutics for finding their Father's face, not in images, but solely in the printed word: "I leave you here a little book / for you to look upon / That you may see your father's face / when he is dead and gone." The martyred Rogers receives historical permanence by being transformed in his "Verses" from tortured flesh into incorruptible text: "to you my heirs of earthly things / [this book] I . . . leave behind / that you may read and understand / and keep it in your mind / that as you have been heirs of that / which once shall wear away / you also may possess that part / which never shall decay."[44]

Michael Warner has suggested that the books that counted as wealth in early America were those that materially survived the death of their readers.[45] The value placed on the inheritability of books in middle-class families points to the ways in which a Protestant culture of literacy was predicated on even as it veiled the economic and other forms of privilege signaled by book ownership.[46] Although copies of the *New England Primer* typically did not survive long enough to be passed from generation to generation, the *Primer* and the Rogers verses within likewise advanced the means by which Protestant culture subsumed its material forms of privilege under the invisible, benign, and unimpeachable authority of the Word. Even as they bequeath Rogers's "book" to his children, the Rogers verses identify not this book but its interiorized lessons on mature spirituality and the perils of false religion as that "which never shall decay." Readers of the *Primer* and of the Rogers verses it synecdochically encloses learned to consign to the impermanent realm of "earthly things" not only the material form of the *Primer* itself, copies of which were routinely read to rags, but more specifically the picture blocks (with their concomitant associations of unjust or primitive forms of spiritual authority) that induced their power to read. The Shorter Catechism bound in most editions of the *New England Primer* glosses the Second Commandment as forbidding "the worshipping of God by images, or any other way not appointed in his word." Reading represented a movement away from potentially enslaving dependence on images for children, who confronted the *Primer*'s woodcuts and then moved beyond them to master the letters they prompted. By successively incorporating letters into syllables, syllables into words, and words into sentences, the form of the *Primer* severs images from this chain of development and fixes them as the unassimilable, "earthly" residue of the language-acquisition process.

In keeping with this trajectory away from images as propaedeutic but ultimately illegitimate sites of knowledge, the woodcut illustrations that accompany the *Primer*'s alphabet depict aspects of culture being excised or abjured by both the reading child in the process of development and the colony on its way to becoming a nation. Toy *Tops* are soon discarded, Zanies "left in the lurch," archaic forms of rule (King, Queen) abandoned. Nature in the *Primer*'s woodcuts (Cat, Vine, Young Lamb) is no longer chaotic, mythic, and prodigious (as in Increase Mather's *Remarkable Providences*, for example) but domesticated, contained, made childsized, even as the imagistic child world of the *Primer* is depicted in the process of being cut away ("Youth forward slips, / Death soonest nips"). If letters, syllables, short words, and sentences are subsumed and taken up in their subsequent linguistic formations, the immobile woodcuts and the forms they represent remain lodged in an infantilized, preverbal past, a static reminder of innocent origins from which a disruptive break is required to set the reading child on her way to linguistic, spiritual, and political maturity.

The *Primer* makes the child's acquisition of speech the sign of her readiness for reading instruction: "If I may speak, and go alone / . . . Then I must learn to know the Lord, / and learn to read his Holy Word." Where earlier editions of the *Primer* had assumed that more difficult words could readily be parsed by children who had mastered the sounds of letters, Noah Webster's "amended and improved" *Primer* of 1789 was the first to indicate silent letters in words by italicizing them, and to offer special lessons on pronunciation. Webster's improvements aimed not only to wean children more speedily from the meaningless syllables (ba, ca, da) of infant speech, but to connect primitive sounds more explicitly with a past to be discarded by the maturing child. Webster's *Primer* included, for example, two companion narratives of the same child as first an infant, then an older boy; in the second, the older child hears inchoate sounds but no words and concludes that a "naughty boy" must be nearby: "Good boys do not cry. / Little babies cry. / Little babies that cannot talk, nor run about, / they can do nothing but cry."[47] As the maturing reader of the *Primer* must renounce the illegitimate speech of his younger self, so the maturing nation, Webster believed, needed to abandon the linguistic archaisms and regional speech patterns of its prefederated past. Since "our political harmony is . . . concerned in a uniformity of language," Webster wrote, Americans did well to consider "the necessity, advantages, and practicability of reforming the mode of spelling, and of rendering the orthography of words correspondent to their pronunciation." Such a project required them to amend or abolish those constricting "faults which produce innumerable inconveniences in the acquisition of and use of the language, and introduce order and regularity into the orthography of the american tongue." With regionalisms and archaisms discarded, Webster believed, "people of one quarter of the world will be able to associate and converse together like children of the same family."[48] For Webster, the triumph over dissonant tongues was to be secured by eliminating the "savage" remnants from American speech: "[A]s savages proceed in forming languages, they lose the guttural sounds, in some measure, and adopt the use of labials, and the more open vowels."[49] Webster's amended *Primer* lays the groundwork for removing the "savage" residue that vexed the project of American political unity by italicizing those figures that the progress and expansion of English speech had rendered silent, thus converting them from text to image. Rewriting the unvocalized letters in *k*nowledge or dau*gh*ter as visible silences, graphic nonspeech, Webster's *Primer* consigns silenced, "savage" characters to the imagistic and infantilized national past they occupy together with kings, queens, and zanies.

In his 1828 dictionary, Webster defined "civilization" as "[t]he act of civilizing, or the state of being civilized; the state of being refined in manners, from the grossness of savage life, and improved in the arts of learning."[50] Webster's image of educated Americans as a "family" of children from whose cultured speech all savage remnants have disappeared in this way continued the educational project framed by Cotton Mather as the weaning of candidates for literacy and Christian conversion from their "natural," depraved state. In the same dictionary Webster defined the adjective "savage" as at once "[p]ertaining to the forest; wild; remote from human residence and improvements" and as "cruel," "ferocious," and "brutal"; a definition he illustrated with the question, "What nation, since the commencement of the christian era, ever rose from *savage* to civilized without christianity?"[51] The Christian culture of literacy that both Mather's and Webster's contributions to the *Primer* helped to shape thus elides a history of violence against outsiders to that culture by associating *both* its outside *and* its depredations against that outside with the ruthless state of nature it allegedly dissolves and replaces. At the same time, however, by defining "civilization" as the Christian conquest of "savagery," both Webster's dictionary and Mather's reflections on education as the antidote to "barbarism" effect a subtle incorporation of brutal aggressions against "natural" Others into the modes of learning that fit literate Protestants to govern them.[52]

The *New England Primer* registers this shading of the violence that Mather associated with the "natural" state into its own civilizing project by conscripting nature to do the work of culture. Carrying forward the Puritan emphasis on the perilous "naturalness" of children, the *Primer* figures youth as malleable and in need of cultivation just as nature is malleable and in need of cultivation: "Children like tender trees do take the bow / And as they first are fashioned always grow." But the *Primer* also makes the unbowed state of nature its own punishment for those who refuse to relinquish it. Children were natural and needed to be brought safely to adulthood or else left to languish in a state of nature; those who resisted the promptings of nurture were punished in the context of the nature they refused to leave behind. Thus, among the *Primer*'s examples, the rebellious Absalom is hanged in the bough of an oak, scoffing children are torn to pieces by bears in the woods, and the eye of a disobedient child is plucked out and eaten by eagles. Even Webster's thoroughly rationalized *Primer* charges nature with disciplining willful resistance to its lessons: in Webster's version, a "bold venturesome boy" nearly drowns, a "churlish boy" who sleeps in the garden when he should be working is awakened by the painful bite of a mouse, and a boy who plays truant is forever lost in the woods.

The "Dialogue Between Christ, a Youth, and the Devil" that appears in nearly all editions of the *Primer* tells a similar tale of nature's claims on the child who resists his induction into the adult world of readerly Christian and civic piety. In the "Dialogue," a child playing in the woods determines to "embrace each sweet delight / the earth affords [him] day and night." Enter the Devil who, made "merry" by the child's resistance to parental and civil authority, invites him to add to his repertoire of willfulness: to "fight and scratch and also bite," to "play the truant" and "think not on God." Christ then intervenes on this scene of illegitimate pedagogy to warn the child that though the Devil's ways "seem sweet," they will quickly "into sour turn": "If in those ways thou wilt run / he will thee into pieces tare / like lions, which most hungry are." The fate of the child seduced by the profoundly magnetic Devil, the "Dialogue" implies, is the fate of children who, elsewhere in the *Primer*, neglect the duties incumbent on their maturing and are vanquished by nature.

At this point in the "Dialogue," the child refuses Christ's remonstrance and commits himself anew to the more appealing ways of flesh and youthful stubbornness: "Don't trouble me, I must fulfill / My fleshly mind, and have my will." "Then in wrath I'll cut thee down," Christ replies, "like as the grass and flowers are mown. . . . [C]onsider this, think on thy end / lest God do thee in pieces rend." The Savior's trump, to reveal that the punishments of the "natural" Devil are in fact the punishments of the deity, comes too late to save the incorrigible child from being carried "to shades of death" by the Devil charged to do God's bidding, much as Cotton Mather believed that God had sent the Indians to punish those Puritans who learned their ways too well.

Without once mentioning Indians, the "Dialogue" makes the Devil the spokesman for what Puritan and early national writers alike remarked on as Indian pleasures, which were the pleasures of unregenerate children loosed in a world from which books, good manners, parental discipline, and piety were absent. Ben Franklin observed in 1753 that when "an Indian Child has been brought up among us, taught our language and habituated to our Customs, yet if he goes to see his relations and make one Indian Ramble with them, there is no perswading him ever to return. . . . [But] when white persons of either sex have been taken prisoner young by the Indians, and lived a while among them, tho' ransomed by their Friends, and treated with all imaginable tenderness to prevail with them to stay among the English, yet in a Short time they become disgusted with our manner of life, and the care and pains that are necessary to support it, and take the first good Opportunity of escaping again into the Woods, from whence there is no reclaiming them."[53]

The Indian captivity narrative remained a popular genre in every American century, with four of the more than one thousand captivity titles printed from sixteenth to the early twentieth centuries among all-time bestsellers. The period culminating in the French and Indian War (1754–63) marks a shift in emphasis in these narratives, which increasingly served the dictates of the emerging Protestant ethnoreligion by stressing less God's interventions on behalf of his elect (as had Puritan captivity narratives) than the religious and ethnic otherness of the captor. The subtitle of the bestselling *Narrative of the Sufferings and Surprizing Deliverances of William and Elizabeth Fleming* (1756), for example, was "a NARRATIVE necessary to be read by all who are going in the Expedition [against the French] as well as by every BRITISH subject. Wherein it fully appears, that the Barbarities of the *Indians* is [*sic*] owing to the *French*, and chiefly their Priests." As Puritans had adapted British vocabularies of Catholic depravities to describe their encounter with Indians, so later colonists shifted the aegis of Indian violence back onto Catholics; Jonathan Mayhew, for example, argued in 1754 that it was French missionaries who converted Indians to the duty "of butchering, and scalping Protestants," their "native ferocity" "whetted and improved by a religion, that naturally delights in blood and murder."[54]

The *New England Primer* continues this emphasis by instilling a hatred for murderous Rome (in the Rogers verses) and by cementing the association between Rogers's "arrant whore" of Babylon and all "savage" obstacles to national unity. The *Primer*'s reader learns to identify Nebuchadnezzar as "the proud king of Babylon, who ran mad and was driven among the beasts, lived with them, and ate grass, and grew hairy all over his body." Nebuchadnezzar's conversion to savagery is embodied by the anatomical drawing of the indecorously naked and conspicuously hairy "Pope, or the Man of Sin" carried over into some editions of the *Primer* from the *Protestant Tutor*, whose accompanying "Advise [*sic*] to Children" lodged the conspiratorial designs of the "Man of Sin" in his unwieldy physicality:

Child behold that man of Sin, the *Pope*, worthy of thy utmost hatred.
Thou shalt find in his Head, (A) Heresy.
In his Shoulders, (B) *The Supporters of Disorder.*
In his Heart, (C) *Malice, Murder, and Treachery.*
In his Arms, (D) Cruelty.
In his Knees, (E) False Worship and Idolatry.
In his Feet, (F) Swiftness to shed Blood.
In his Stomach, (G) Insatiable Covetousness.
In his Lyons [*sic*], (H) The worst of Lusts.

If the conquest of brute "nature" without and within provided white Americans a recourse from internal political and religious strife, a way to consolidate their loose confederation of states and sects into a civilizing,

Protestant nation, the *Primer* shows the conquest of nature to be inseparably a conquest of human obstacles to national expansion. Michael Rogin observes, for example, that the conflicts over land title that dominated early America from Puritan New England to the southwestern frontier two centuries later "threatened to reverse the process by which [white Americans] had appropriated land to themselves, and return them to a contentious, unconsoling state of nature."[55] While the *New England Primer* was unhelpful in negotiating the vagaries of land dispute among white Americans, it did enable them to resist the prospect of such conflicts returning them to a state of nature by rehearsing the justifications by which they appropriated native lands. The *Primer*'s Shorter Catechism justifies white Christian land tenure by rote-learned theology: "Q: How does Christ executeth the office of king? A: Christ executeth the office of king, in subduing us to himself, in ruling and defending us, and in restraining and conquering all his and our enemies." As the *Primer*'s lessons in faith authorize the dispossession of enemy territories, moreover, the more generalized savagery of the "Dialogue's" Devil, the grass-eating Semite, or the Catholic "Man of Sin" could mute the specificity of righteous violence against Indians, broadening its scope to address myriad forms of resistance to the consolidation and expansion of the white Protestant republic.

ARRESTED DEVELOPMENTS

As the material of a child's civil and theological ABC, the *Primer* figures violence not only as necessary to national development, but as *innocently* necessary. Locating the power to triumph over savagery in the Word, the *Primer* makes the vanquishing of all opposition to Christian governance a function of literacy and a part of the providential design that literacy fits the child to discern. If this point is registered in the absence of Indians from nearly all editions of the *New England Primer*, it is made equally in the stray edition—I have found only one—in which the vanishing Indian fleetingly appears. In an 1800 *Primer* printed at Newport, Rhode Island, the woodcut alphabet accompanying the familiar verse "He that ne'er learns his ABC / For ever will a blockhead be" includes, in addition to the images for *A*ss, *B*ull, *C*at, *D*og, and so on that had been recycled since their appearance in seventeenth-century British primers, something entirely new: a tomahawk-wielding *I*ndian to illustrate the letter I.[56] All but four of the letters depict animals, plant life, or toys—for example, *L*ion, *M*onkey, *T*op, *V*ine, *W*hale. The other human figures shown are the customary *K*ing and *Q*ueen, the alphabetically handy King *X*erxes (he who "did die, and so must you and I"), and *Z*any. Because alphabet cuts were reused from edition to edition of the *Primer*, it is unsurprising that the Indian looks a little like the Zany, as though the same woodblock had been used for both and the crested cap of the latter doctored to become the feathered headdress of the former. The Indian's tomahawk, moreover, looks like the scythe raised over a child's body in the illustration accompanying the alphabet rhyme for T ("Time cuts down all / Both great and small"), and like the scepter of the Catholic prelate who oversees the immolation of John Rogers as Rogers's ten children look on.

The Indian frozen in his posture of threat might well have served a function similar to that of the Indian skull that the white doctor who attended the death of the Seminole warrior Osceola would hang on his children's bedpost to frighten them.[57] But if the woodblock Indian could image the charismatic authority of parental discipline, taking his place alongside Rogers's verses and the "Dialogue Between Christ, a Youth, and the Devil" to warn the child against captivity to forms of life that would thwart the program of development to which her reading of the *Primer* commits her, its appearance in this alphabetical zoo also inverts the narrative of captivity to make the miniaturized Indian its new subject, anticipating the Jacksonian policy of removal that made the capture and control of Indians necessary to the expansion of the white Protestant nation. The "savage state" to which Indians "appear to have been inseparably connected," wrote Samuel Williams in his *Natural and Civil History of Vermont*, "operated with a certain and fatal tendency, to continue man in a state of infancy, weakness, and the greatest imperfection. The freedom to which it led, was its greatest blessing; but the independence of which the savage was so fond, was never designed for man: And it is only in the improvement of civil society, that the human race can find the greatest increase of their numbers, knowledge, safety, and happiness."[58]

Installing the Indian in a child's menagerie of Cats, Lions, and Monkeys, the alphabet blocks of this 1800 *Primer* continue the Puritan dynamic by which Indian lands were emptied of Indians by first being discursively rendered as continuous with nature. The woodblocks further set the Indian into a preemptive past tense, the harmless, even "zany" register of arrested childhood. If these images narrowly fail to enclose Indians entirely in the category of the nonhuman, still their human zanies, prelates, and kings all belong to a defeated or domesticated past to be succeeded by the triumphal present for which the *Primer*'s reader is on her way to being fitted by learning to discard images for speech. Freezing the Indian permanently at the innocent point of origin from which a violent break is required for both the child and the nation to attain maturity renders the Indian incapable of being brought to adult form. There can be no question, in this lesson, of nurturing the Indian to American adulthood, any more than American adulthood can legitimately include

monarchs, monkeys, and zanies. The woodblock Indian inhabits a territory where the child on his way to membership in "civil society" no
longer exists.

The *New England Primer* further depicts infancy, and the Indian, as
what the maturing nation must permanently if reluctantly leave behind
by figuring childhood itself as possessed of a certain "fatal tendency" that
dissolves its connection to adult life. Whether slain by beasts or devils for
their disobedience or "cut down" without provocation, numbers of the
Primer's "small" subjects are routinely, violently dispatched, even after
the *Primer*'s harsh Calvinist lessons had been partly mitigated by the inclusion of Isaac Watts's hymns. The reader comforted by Watts's "Hush
my dear, be still and slumber, / Holy angels guard thy bed, / heavenly
blessings without number, / gently falling on thy head" also learned to
pray to God "his soul to take" should the angels fail him and he not, in
fact, wake up.

The tension between Watts's child's sound and confident sleep and the
Calvinist intimations of violent death even for godly sons is enclosed in
Watts's own verses.

> Soft, my child, I did not chide thee,
> Though my song might sound too hard,
> Tis thy mother sits beside thee,
> And her arms shall be thy guard.
> Yet to read the shameful story,
> How the Jews abused their king,
> How they served the Lord of glory,
> Makes me angry while I sing.

Watts's verses point the way to a sentimentalized theology that nevertheless continues to attribute violence to *other* religions and to an archaic
sacred universe that its own liberalizing Protestantism is poised to overcome. The images of death and torture the *Primer* continues to set alongside the gentle prayers of those who claim God for their friend and do
not fear death lodge violence in the past as the necessary prolegomena to
the safety the national subject now enjoys: "Twas to save thee, child from
dying, / Save my dear from burning flame, / Bitter groans and endless
crying, / That thy Blessed Redeemer came."

For American readers whose views of children the evangelization of
Calvinism appropriately softened, the past of childhood could nevertheless take on a sense of fatality imaged in the *Primer*'s unstable depictions
of child death. "Barbarism is to civilization what childhood is to maturity," wrote Francis Parkman;[59] the project of educating white subjects
away from barbarism required that the category of barbarism persist as
a kind of permanent childhood that is always about to be cut down and

replaced by adult life, as the children in the *New England Primer* who do
not reach adulthood (or resist its inducements) are summarily done away
with. Adults whom the *Primer* had nurtured away from the "savage state"
of uneducated childhood were thus prepared to see Indians vanquished
in the defeat of the "nature" they would not abandon. As Horace Greeley
wrote in 1859,

> the Indians are children . . . belong[ing] to the very lowest and rudest
> ages of human existence. . . . Any band of schoolboys . . . are quite
> as capable of ruling their appetites, devising and upholding a public
> policy, constituting and conducting a state or community, as an aver-
> age Indian tribe. . . . [T]he average Indian of the woods and prairies
> is . . . a slave of appetite and sloth, never emancipated from the tyr-
> anny of one animal passion save by the ravenous demands of another.
> . . . These people must die out—there is no help for them. God has
> given this earth to those who will subdue and cultivate it, and it is
> vain to struggle against His righteous decree.[60]

The domestication or defeat of Indians, read retroactively as the rehabili-
tation of barbarous childhood tendencies, made violence in the service of
nation building inseparable from the education of subjects for citizenship.

By containing the Indian in time and space and lodging him in America's national infancy, the 1800 *Primer* followed Mather's *Magnalia* in
putting Indians in a permanent past tense. Figuring the miniaturized Indian as a child's toy, a wooden block, memorializes the past away from
which the nation grew as testimony to the superior expansiveness of adult
faith, civil and theological, even as it hides the violence that is that precondition of that expansiveness. Changes in the *Primer* leading up to the
1800 edition register developments which Indians could not easily be
brought into and that were achieved largely at their expense: the transformation from a household to a market economy was fueled by westward
expansion and the acquisition of Indian lands; evangelization became a
favored mode of securing Indian accommodation to white Protestant settlements because the speed of expansion left little time for "civilizing." If
the absence of Indians from most editions of the *Primer* signals the victory
of these expansionist forces, so too does the woodblock Indian of the
1800 *Primer*, whose containment in the act of waging violence testifies to
the blessings of white Protestant deliverance.

•   •   •

In the *New England Primer*, the acquisition of linguistic, civic, and spiritual maturity takes place in acts of removal and replacement, as the past
of childhood is replaced by an adult present, images by words, fleshly

pleasures by disciplined work, nature by the market. As Puritan iconoclasm had proceeded as an ultimately secularizing mission—altars into
tables—so the domestication of nature in the *New England Primer* records the secularization of monstrosities and wonders associated with a
defeated Indian, a violent Catholic, and a receding Puritan past. The progressive ordering of the Puritan mind continued to turn its prodigies and
magical events outward, where they could be controlled, if not dismissed,
in part by being associated with *other* religions. (The *Primer*'s woodcut
of the pope as the "Man of Sin," with all its overtones of Indianization, in
fact recycled an image that had appeared in seventeenth-century Puritan
almanacs as an astrological key.)[61]

Anticipating the nineteenth- and twentieth-century historiography
that would frame America's religious development as one of emerging
Protestant consensus, the *New England Primer* set the parameters of what
constitutes legitimate, "American" religious and social behavior. Gradually expanding from a book of Bible lessons and aids to faith to include
advice literature, patriotic verse, pointers on etiquette, and short fiction,
the *New England Primer* gestures toward the more expansive and secular
reading fare of nineteenth-century audiences even as it preserves the
broadly Protestant content of that fare. The *New England Primer* thus
primed Protestant Christianity to remain a dominant cultural force in the
lives of nineteenth-century Americans even as those lives became increasingly secular. Put another way, the *New England Primer* helped to make
the secularization of American Protestantism inseparable from its expansion. In that process, Rome is abhorred, nature domesticated, Puritan
strictures reconstituted as enlightened Protestant freedoms, and Indians
rendered continuous with a childhood that is permanently arrested in the
act of passing away.

FROM DISESTABLISHMENT TO "CONSENSUS": THE NINETEENTH-CENTURY BIBLE WARS AND THE LIMITS OF DISSENT

THE CIVIL AND spiritual maturity to which the *New England Primer* nurtured its generations of readers came by the end of the eighteenth century to entail independence not only from British rule but increasingly also from established American churches.[1] Just prior to the Revolution, religious establishment was the rule in nine of the thirteen colonies. Soon after, New York's state constitution of 1777 abolished establishment, South Carolina's in 1778 for the first time required it, and other states proceeded unevenly to codify their relationship to established churches.[2] The decisive blow to religious establishment came in 1786, when a coalition of Baptists, Presbyterians, and Deists in Virginia managed to pass Thomas Jefferson's model "Bill for Establishing Religious Freedom," and subsequently pressed for the passage of the First Amendment's guarantee of religious liberty.

The sanctity of individual conscience affirmed by denominationalist Christians and Deist statesmen alike constituted religion as inherently free, a matter of private conviction rather than civil allegiance, and as such beyond the reach of government or other powers. In her now-classic *The Feminization of American Culture*, Ann Douglas argues that disestablishment, and the attendant eclipse of the moral authority of a Calvinist elite, marked a disastrous loss of "intellectual rigor and imaginative precision," with the result that religion came to be dangerously sentimentalized, relegated to a mawkish, "feminized" sphere where faith was demoted to "feeling" and accorded cultural representation precisely in exchange for its refusal to interfere in political life.[3] In a similar vein, if less in a spirit of critique, David Reynolds's *Faith in Fiction* points to secularizing currents in late eighteenth- and nineteenth-century American literature and culture whose effect was to subordinate doctrine to "affectionalism," "Calvinist constraint to evangelical persuasion," and theological strictness to sentimental piety.[4] Both in their different ways suggest that the removal of religion to the interior precincts of feeling and belief tended over time to reduce the specificity of religious conviction and religious difference to politically weightless matters of affect. But neither they nor subsequent critics who argue for seeing the sphere of the "sentimental" as more powerfully formative of national interests have remarked on a corollary development to the relegation of religion to the private or domestic margins of public life,[5] which is, as Gauri Viswanathan suggests in her far-ranging discussion of secularism in nineteenth-century Britain, its annexation to the "administrative will" of the state.[6]

In the United States, whose founding documents aimed to unite a presumptively (if diversely) Christian population under the mantle of religious tolerance, the rule of noninterference between religion and government, far from consigning all religions equally to the silent margins of the political, instead created the conditions for the dominance of an increasingly nonspecific Protestantism over nearly all aspects of American life, a dominance as pervasive as it is invisible for exceeding the domains we conventionally figure as religious. The religion clauses of the First Amendment—"Congress shall make no law respecting an establishment of religion, or prohibiting the free exercise thereof"—were understood to preclude *dises*tablishment as well, and Protestant establishment in fact survived in Vermont, Connecticut, and Massachusetts until the early nineteenth century. Many of the eighteenth-century state constitutions that eliminated religious establishment also specified that no Catholic, Jew, or nonbeliever was eligible to hold legislative office; some stipulated further that only Protestant teachers could count on the support of the state.[7] Prior to the passage of the Fourteenth Amendment in 1868, the federal government's neutrality in matters of religious belief extended also to neutrality on issues of statutory protection for religious observance. In *Permoli v. First Municipality of New Orleans* (44 U.S. 589 [1845]), for example, the Supreme Court held that the Constitution "makes no provision for protecting the citizens of the respective states in their religious liberties; this is left to the state constitutions and laws; nor is there any inhibition imposed by the Constitution of the Unites States in this respect on the states."[8] (In its opinion, the Court cited the case of *Commonwealth v. Abram Wolf* [3 Serg. & R. (Pa.), 48], which upheld the right of states to fine Jewish workers for working on Sunday in order to observe the Saturday Sabbath while fulfilling the requirements of a six-day work week.)

Legal disestablishment, meanwhile, left different Protestant churches, in John Wesley's words, with "nothing to do but save souls,"[9] setting them on the collective path of eliciting conformity through evangelical persuasion. "It was as dark a day as I ever saw," Lyman Beecher wrote of the 1817 legislative defeat of Congregational establishment in Connecticut; the "odium thrown upon the ministry was inconceivable. The injury done to the cause of Christ, as we then supposed, was irreparable. For several days I suffered what no tongue can tell, for *the best thing that has ever happened to the State of Connecticut.*"[10] As Beecher discovered, disestablishment made for a salutary change in sectarian alignments: where Baptists, Methodists, and Episcopalians had resented Connecticut's Congregationalist establishment and so ranged themselves alongside "infidelity" against the hegemony of the Calvinist old line, disestablishment removed "the occasion of animosity between us and the minor sects," Beecher wrote, so that "infidels could no more make capital with them against us."[11] In Connecticut and elsewhere, the removal of government support for any single church promoted interdenominational efforts among Baptists, Methodists, Episcopalians, Presbyterians, and Congregationalists, who founded the American Education Society, the American Home Missionary Society, the American Bible Society, the American Tract Society, and the American Sunday School Union, among many other voluntary associations, to bring the nation to the cause of Christ. As Beecher saw it, disestablishment made it the business of citizens, "instead of Select-Men, to see that every family has a Bible, every church a pastor, and every child a catechism."[12] Denominational pluralism simply brought more hands to the task. "The distinctions which till lately destroyed the happiness of different sects of Christians," William Staughton preached to the Baptist Association of Philadelphia in 1796, "lose their importance" before the "common enem[ies]" of infidelity and Rome; the time had come for different Protestant denominations, like the twelve tribes of Israel, to unite in "one great bond," and together "march . . . to contest and victory."[13]

By the middle decades of the nineteenth century, with an end to denominationalism nowhere to be seen, and with official Protestant church membership comprising under a third of the population,[14] Protestant historians came nevertheless to figure America as a de facto Protestant nation. An exemplary instance of such depictions, Robert Baird's *Religion in America* divided religions into evangelical and nonevangelical, the latter including Catholics, Jews, atheists, Shakers, Deists, Unitarians, Swedenborgians, and Mormons.[15] Welcoming the diversity of Protestant sects that fell under the mantle of evangelical religion, particularly those that had left off the charged emotional outpourings of the Great Awakening, the Presbyterian Baird pointedly dismissed nonevangelical religions as the "deluded" fashionings of "fanatical sects" whose "perverted" readings of Christian Scripture conspired to "unsettle the mind."[16] In the glowing assessment of a religious historian writing a full century later, Baird's "grand vision" of a pan-Protestant America, in which different evangelical denominations formed the "branches of one great body, even the entire visible Church of Christ in this land,"[17] would come to "permeate all facets of life . . . and touch all races, social strata, and ethnic backgrounds with a Protestant ecumenicity."[18]

Certainly no race, social stratum, or ethnic group remained beyond the designs of this vision's champions. Baird's stunningly resilient portrait of evangelical Protestant consensus asserted a unified Protestant America in the face of conflicts that would rend denominations, families, and nations; his insistence on American Protestants' "remarkable coincidence of views on all important points" of faith[19] minimized these conflicts by implicitly affirming the unity of white, Northern, middle-class Protestant men against the competing claims of other Protestants—variously poor, non-white, enslaved or slaveholding, female.[20] *Religion in America* further displaced the threat of diversity internal to Protestantism at mid-century by resituating religious diversity as a threat to national unity from outside the ecumenical fold. Commending the spirit of tolerance that enabled Protestants of varying denominations to agree on salient points of doctrine, Baird went on to probe its limits:

> Rights of conscience are religious rights, that is, rights to entertain and utter religious opinions, and to enjoy public religious worship. Now this expression, even in its widest acceptation, can not include irreligion—opinions contrary to the nature of religion, subversive of the reverence, love, and service due to God, of virtue, morality, and good manners. What rights of conscience can atheism, irreligion, or licentiousness pretend to? It may not be prudent to disturb them in their private haunts and secret retirements. There let them remain and hold their peace. But they have no right, by any law in the United States . . . to come forward and propagate opinions and proselytize.[21]

Baird's depiction of those he called nonevangelicals and non-Christians—Catholics, Jews, atheists, Mormons, and so on—as "deluded" and "perver[se]" accorded to "irreligion" a rather wide scope. His implicit figuring of nonevangelical subjects as those whose "subversive" beliefs lodge them beyond the scope of civil protections for religious expression subtly aligns religious identity with political identity, underscoring the way in which the constitutional separation of church and state that allegedly secures such protections means different things for different religions. In the case of Protestant evangelical religions (to remain for a moment with Baird's terminology), the separation of church and state means that the religious subject may pursue his or her religious convictions unmolested by the tolerant state. In the case of nonevangelical religions, however, the effect of church-state separation, in Baird's reading, is just the opposite, namely, that the "perver[sely]" religious (or resistantly nonreligious) subject is an affront to evangelical accommodations of diversity in matters of faith, to "virtue, morality, and good manners," and as such forfeits the protection of a state dedicated to their preservation.[22]

The state-church division that American Protestants gradually came in different degrees to accept or to champion, moreover, was figured throughout the later eighteenth and nineteenth centuries as the division between the implicitly Protestant state and the *Catholic* Church, the most visible of the nonevangelical religions consigned to the margins of Baird's *Religion in America*.[23] Indeed, the distrust of Rome that looms so large in Baird's text suggests that his lengthy list of nonevangelical religions functions on some level to fragment and displace the more monolithic presence of the Catholic Church, on its way at mid-century to becoming the single largest religious body in America. At the same time, *Religion in America* implicitly subsumes *all* religious difference external to Protestantism under the banner of Rome. In Baird's view, what united different Protestant churches was not only their internal agreement on the broadest outlines of the Christian faith but their external, collective opposition to "the errors of Rome" and "other aberrations from the true gospel."[24]

The representation of religious freedom as freedom *from* rather than for Catholics had been a staple of American republicanism's founding documents; Paine's *Common Sense*, for example, which held it to be "the indispensable duty of every government to protect all conscientious professors [of religion]," also declared that "monarchy in every instance is Popery of government."[25] In his 1783 sermon "The United States Elevated to Honor and Glory," Ezra Stiles triumphantly observed that "[i]n this country (out of sight of mitres and the purple, and removed from systems of corruption confirmed for ages and supported by the spiritual janizaries aided and armed by the secular power), religion may be examined with the noble Berean freedom, the freedom of American-born minds."[26] The Baptist Elhanan Winchester, in his 1792 "Oration on the Discovery of America," remarked that "it has pleased God to distinguish [the United States] from other countries in causing it to be the first place upon the globe where equal civil and religious liberty has been established," a distinction Winchester attributed to the temporal enclosure of the European "discovery" of America "between two great events. . . . I mean the art of printing, which was discovered about the year 1440 . . . and the reformation from popery, which began about the year 1517."[27]

Textbook accounts of America's founding made the victory of Protestant liberties over Catholic intolerance a key to the formation of national unity. Noting that he was most "attentive to the political interests of Americans"[28] in framing the nation's history, Noah Webster's *An American Selection of Lessons in Reading* discusses the exemplary objections of the colonists to the British toleration of Roman Catholicism in Quebec, which would have "established absolute government and the Roman Catholic religion, throughout those vast regions that border on the westerly and northerly boundaries of the free, Protestant, English settlements."[29] That lesson precedes a "Scene between Lord Peter, Martin, and Jack," with a note by Webster that "by Lord Peter is meant the pope, by Martin, the Lutheran church, and by Jack, the Calvinists. The design of this Dialogue, is to ridicule the Doctrine of Transubstantiation, the arrogance of the Pope, and the evils of persecution":

> PETER [to Jack and Martin]: What now are you at your doubts again? Here boy. Call neighbor Dominick* [footnote: Saint Dominick, the inventor of the Inquisition] the blacksmith here. Bid him bring his tongs with him. Red hot, d'ye hear? I'll teach you to doubt.
>
> MARTIN: Come Jack. This house is like to be too hot for you and me. He is quite raving mad. Let's get away* [footnote: Separation of the Protestant from the Romish Church] as fast as we can.[30]

Elsewhere, Webster avowed that the tolerant state would make national subjects of Catholics as easily as Protestants: "All the dangers to which any government can be exposed by sectaries, must arise wholly from intolerance; and the Roman Catholics, when indulged in the free exercise of their religion, make as good subjects, as peaceable citizens as any sect of protestants."[31] While Webster vested in the principle of tolerance the power to make citizens who were at once American and Catholic, other commentators saw the same principle as driving a fatal wedge between the Catholic as Catholic and the Catholic as American. As late as 1888, for example, Daniel Dorchester's *Christianity in the United States from the First Settlement Down to the Present Time* confidently pointed to the rise in Protestant church membership to assert that, the increasing strength of the Catholic Church notwithstanding, the United States was in fact "the biggest grave for popery ever dug on earth."[32]

In the middle decades of the nineteenth century, however, Catholic immigrants to America were becoming not more Protestant but more Catholic.[33] In this period, debates over children's education became occasions for Catholics to reject or to challenge the spirit of state-controlled institutions, even when and often because this spirit was given as one of tolerance and accommodation. (As the Andover Seminary professor Bela Bates Edwards put it in 1848, "[p]erfect religious liberty . . . does not imply that the government of the country is not a Christian government," thanks to the "real, though indirect association between the State and Christianity.")[34] In dissenting from a vision of national identity as tolerant, "Christian" identity, these Catholic protests against the Protestant character of public education also register dissatisfaction with a civil society that requires the effacement of the religious difference of its non-Protestant citizens as the price for the nominal protection of the religious liberties of all.[35] To Catholic objections that state-run schools were instruments of a de facto Protestant establishment, Protestants would insist that schools were nonsectarian, and that it was Catholics instead who dangerously sought to impose their religious views on public institutions in violation of the separation of church and state.[36]

Public Schools, Public Protestantism

The assumption that education in America proceeded in a steadfastly secular direction ill equips us for seeing not only how Protestant the character of American public schooling remained throughout the nineteenth century, but also how the vaunted secularization of public education was made an instrument for maintaining its Protestant character.[37] The First Amendment and indeed the entire Constitution were silent on the issue of education, so that the Northwest Ordinance of 1787 left unquestioned the link between religion and schools: "Religion, morality, and knowledge being necessary to good government and the happiness of mankind," Article 3 of the Ordinance ran, not churches but "*schools* and the means of learning shall be forever encouraged."[38] In Massachusetts, whose 1780 Constitution had stipulated that "public protestant teachers" would be supported to foster the "piety, education, and morality" on which civil government must "essentially depend,"[39] an 1827 law gave school committees power over textbooks "provided also that said committee shall never direct any school books to be purchased or used in any of the schools under their superintendence, which are calculated to favor any particular religious sect or tenet."[40] Sectarian objections that the public schools made no provision for specifically religious teachings were answered by interdenominational Protestant assurances that the content of instruction would be broadly Christian.[41] At the center of the curriculum was the King James Bible. As the educational reformer Horace Mann insisted, the public school "welcomes the Bible, and therefore welcomes all the doctrines which the Bible really contains. . . . [I]t listens to these doctrines so reverently, that . . . it will not suffer any rash mortal to thrust in his interpolations of their meanings, or overlay the text with any of the 'many inventions' which the heart of man has sought out"—a policy that rendered the annotated Douay Bible used by Catholics unacceptable, even as it enshrined the edition (the King James Bible) whose dedication referred to the pope as the "man of Sinne" and whose preface refuted the legitimacy of the Catholic Church.[42] As head of the Massachusetts School Committee, Mann vetoed as inappropriately sectarian a book then in wide use, *The Child at Home*, which was staunchly Calvinist in matters of sin and final judgment, but he made the Bible into the principle of tolerance itself: "In every course of studies, all the practical and preceptive parts of the Gospel should . . . [be] sacredly included. . . . In no school should the Bible . . . [be] opened to reveal the sword of . . . polemic, but to unloose the dove of peace."[43]

By the middle decades of the nineteenth century, the public schools' interventionist mission[44]—Mann described it as bringing children "cursed by vicious parentage" "under humanizing and redeeming influences"[45]—was directed increasingly at the growing population of Catholic immigrants, whose arrival magnified existing tensions between races, classes, and regions. Skilled craft workers viewed the immigrants as fodder for industrialists, while factory owners saw them as shiftless and unprofitable. Immigrants threatened industrial and domestic laborers by accepting even the lowest-paying jobs that until then only free black men and women had been called on to fill. To slave owners, Catholic immigrants were instinctive abolitionists who were unwilling to compete with slave labor; Protestant abolitionists who saw Catholicism as inherently despotic, meanwhile, made them natural allies of the slave power. The apparently monolithic structure of Catholicism cast the splintering of Protestant congregations and the presence of new religious bodies into relief, while Catholicism's alternative conception of vocation appeared to threaten both the family and the workplace as bulwarks of Protestant power.[46]

Public school advocates frequently made education the antidote to the religious and cultural foreignness of this new population. In Lyman Beecher's *Plea for the West* (1835), which urged Protestant support for common schools extending to the Pacific, Catholic immigrants—"unacquainted with our institutions, unaccustomed to self-government," and easily manipulated by popish "intrigue" and "sinister design"—served as a "train of powder between the enemy's camp and our own magazine" which, once ignited, would destroy the Protestant republic.[47] If the new arrivals were "inaccessible to education," as Beecher warned,[48] their children might yet be saved: according to the Presbyterian writer and polemicist "Kirwan" (Nicholas Murray), the "son of an Irishman, a Frenchman, or Italian is an American, and he will not be a Romanist. We have a mill, of which the common school is the nether, and the Bible and its institutions the upper stone; into this mill let us cast the people of all countries and all forms of religion that come here, and they will come out in the grist Americans and Protestants. And the highest wisdom of our country is to keep this mill in vigorous operation."[49]

Even prior to the arrival of the first waves of Catholic immigrants in the 1830s, the teaching of general knowledge was frequently a veiled (and sometimes hardly veiled) means of teaching against Catholicism. As a British educator put it, subtly echoing Horace Mann, teaching Catholic students something less than the "genuine principles of the Protestant faith" still allowed the acquisition of knowledge to "humanize" them, and in doing so to thwart "the evil designs of popery."[50] In a study of

nineteenth-century American textbooks, Ruth Miller Elson shows that
anti-Catholic propaganda long remained a staple of allegedly disinterested lessons on nonreligious topics: children learned from nineteenth-
century histories that "the Roman Catholic religion completed" the
Roman Empire's "degeneracy and ruin"; from geographies that "those
nations are most distinguished for justice and kindness in which the Bible
is best known, and Christianity the most pure"; and from lessons in patriotism that the founding fathers would have suffered any fate rather than
to "have bowed to papal infallibility, or paid the tribute to St. Peter."[51]
Even textbooks that commended tolerance in matters of religion as indispensable to American republicanism, Elson notes, were "full of the horrible deeds of the Catholics."[52]

Rather than limit their efforts to the identification of objectionably partisan passages in each of the schoolbooks then in use, Catholics who
chafed at the Protestant character of public schooling increasingly argued
that the schools' central, common textbook—the King James Bible—was
a sectarian one, and therefore that the entire curriculum required revision.
In doing so, however, Catholic parents played into the hands of Protestant
detractors who sought for ways to show that Catholicism was the enemy
of the gospel and that the destruction of popery was therefore a sacred
duty of all, implicitly Protestant, Americans.

CONTENDING FREEDOMS

In Philadelphia, Protestant-Catholic conflicts over Bible reading in public
schools, which had begun in the 1830s, escalated by the summer of 1844
into a series of violent confrontations in which churches and homes were
destroyed by arson and at least seventeen persons were killed. While the
Philadelphia Bible riots have usefully been cast as class and ethnic conflicts,[53] little attention has been paid to the Catholic objections to compulsory Bible reading as a specifically political critique, namely, an indictment
of the exclusionary nature of civil protections for religion within a de
facto Protestant state. "We rejoice in the progress of civil liberty," declared the Philadelphia Baptist Association in 1796, "because so intimately related to the liberty with which Christ has made us free."[54] Such
views left nativist Protestants in the Philadelphia conflict free to lift
"Christianity" away from both denominational affiliation and privately
held belief and to tether it all the more securely to national symbols, most
prominently the American flag and the Declaration of Independence,
which were then invoked as the mantle of "freedom of religion" whose
fabric Catholic claims to free exercise of religion could only be figured as
rending in pieces.

In 1834 a resolution passed by the Board of Controllers of Philadel-phia's public schools, then in the process of being converted from charity schools, enacted a version of the nondenominational compromise being pursued elsewhere in the nation. The ruling relegated sectarian education to Sabbath schools and forbade the use of religious books and exercises in public instruction. In 1838, however, the Board passed a ruling that required the reading of the King James Bible in all schools. Over the next several years, Philadelphia Catholics came to insist with increasing force that a public education that gave pride of place to the King James Bible need not be precisely sectarian (as Protestants understood the term) in order to be exclusionary. In the words of an 1841 editorial under the pen name of "Sentinel" in the Philadelphia *Catholic-Herald*:

> The union of Church and State is virtually effected as soon as public education has become sectarian, or received a sectarian bias: which is the case the moment the Protestant principle of the Bible as the sole rule of faith is adopted by its introduction into the public schools, as the source of religious instruction to the pupils. Protestants cannot conceive that such education should be styled sectarian, as long as it is not professedly in the hands of a sect: but if it assume not the hue of any particular sect of Protestants, it will necessarily be Protestant in its character.[55]

A Jewish newspaper in Philadelphia objected that the city's public schools "took special pains to warp the mind and to implant the peculiar tenets of Christianity clandestinely" by conducting prayers "in which the name of a mediator is invoked," and commending the study of the New Testa-ment "as an authority equal if not superior to the received word of God."[56]

Roundly ignoring Jewish objections to the Christian character of in-struction in Philadelphia's public schools, the Philadelphia *Protestant Banner* responded to Catholic protests with a call to political action and a cornering of the identity of "Christian":

> Protestants must be on the alert and guard against the assaults of papists on our free institutions. Much, of course, will depend on the choice of school commissioners and directors. It is important that men should be selected who love the Bible, and who are therefore not prepared to see it hurled out of our schools. If the priests succeed in erecting the cross of the antichrist over our common school houses, they will have gained a triumph which every Christian and philan-thropist will deplore.[57]

Three years earlier, "Sentinel" had warned that the Board's having made it "a sacred caution not to let a Catholic into the chair of instruction, wherever it can be avoided, afford no doubtful evidences of the genius of sectarianism which presides over our public education. . . . A legal provision is necessary, that the commissioners or directors shall permit no books to be used in the schools, save of a literary or scientific character, and shall allow no religious exercise or instruction whatever."[58]

Bishop Francis Kenrick of Philadelphia, meanwhile, urged the Philadelphia Board of Controllers to enforce and extend their 1834 ruling against sectarianism by allowing Catholic pupils to be excused from communal prayer, the singing of Protestant hymns, and Bible-reading exercises: "We offer up prayers and supplications to God for all men," Kenrick wrote; "we embrace all in the sincerity of Christian affection, but we confine the marks of religious brotherhood to those who are of the household of the faith. Under the influence of this conscientious scruple, we ask that the Catholic children be not required to join in singing hymns or other religious exercises."[59] This the Board grudgingly granted over complaints lodged by the American Protestant Association that Kenrick's objections to the sectarian nature of Protestant hymns constituted a "grotesque phantom of the brain" and that his objections to compulsory prayer "disparages and dishonors its source."[60] (To Kenrick's charges of anti-Catholic bias in textbook portrayals of Christianity, the Association replied that "the complaint is that these books contain misrepresentations of the church to which [Kenrick] belongs; when the fact is, they contain no representations whatever on the subject.")[61] The Philadelphia *Christian Observer* approvingly reported on citizens' efforts to "arrest . . . [the Catholics'] infidel project for controlling the Public Schools,"[62] a mission that some Protestant parents evidently imparted to their children, for the *Catholic-Herald* noted that "since the recent action of the Board of Controllers, exempting the Catholic pupils of the Public Schools from reading or hearing the King James Version of the Bible, there has got up in some of the Schools, a petty persecution of Catholic pupils."[63]

In ensuing exchanges in the Philadelphia press, Protestants and Catholics alike figured themselves as victims of sectarian persecution. The *Episcopal Recorder* urged that "Protestant Christians, —American Christians, awake to the crisis and consider the duty which is before them": "Are we to yield our personal liberty, our inherited rights, our very Bibles, the special, blessed gift of God to our country, to the will, the ignorance, or the wickedness of these hordes of foreigners . . . thrown upon our shores, and sheltered here with a kindness the most tolerant and confiding?"[64] The *Catholic-Herald* warned its readers, meanwhile, that the "Protestant Association will take charge of our youth, and provide them with a Bible, hymns, and prayers, according to their judgment, and we must sit down contented, and be silent, if not grateful. They may afterwards provide us with a national religion, when we shall have been prepared for the blessing, by means of a National Protestant Education."[65]

Those who were unwilling to distinguish Protestantism from religious neutrality were also unwilling to distribute the meaning of "American" and "Christian" across a broader spectrum of religious difference, even as they claimed for Americans and Christians the privilege of extending religious tolerance. According to Peter Sken Smith, the editor of the *Native Eagle and American Advocate*, a man "may be a Turk, a Jew, or a Christian, a Catholic, a Methodist or Presbyterian, and we say nothing against it," but "when we remember that our Pilgrim fathers landed on Plymouth rock to establish the Protestant religion, free from persecution, we must contend that this was and always will be a Protestant country."[66] Another nativist writer, Lewis Levin, vested the principle of religious liberty in the very text that Philadelphia schools forced Catholic pupils to read against their families' religious scruples: "The Declaration of Independence is but a transcript of the Bible, which is the original fountain of human liberty and the rights of man."[67] A third Philadelphia nativist, John Hancock Lee, went further in making the Bible the proof text for republican principles, finding in its pages "the Divine authority for the rights of man, as well as for the separation of church and state, on which depends so essentially the pursuit of happiness and freedom of conscience."[68]

On May 6, 1844, a Protestant crowd in the working-class Kensington section of Philadelphia confronted Catholic protesters as they gathered to hear an anti-Catholic address by Samuel Kramer, editor of the Protestant *Native American*. When the Catholic protesters upended wheelbarrows full of dirt in the midst of the flag-waving crowd, scuffling broke out, followed by gunfire in which a young Protestant man, George Schiffler, was killed. Schiffler, the first casualty in the skirmishes that followed over the next several days, was widely hailed in the Protestant press as a martyr for "defending the American flag."[69] In the protests that followed, several Catholic homes and two Catholic churches were burned. Protestants marched through the streets of Philadelphia carrying flags and open Bibles; a placard carried by one Protestant flag waver proclaimed that this was "the FLAG that was trampled UNDERFOOT by the IRISH PAPISTS."[70]

Two months after the May riots, a tense ceasefire ended when rioting again broke out in the wake of agitated Fourth of July demonstrations by Protestant nativists in the working-class Philadelphia neighborhood of Southwark. In the days that followed, Catholics armed themselves against nativist threats, called out the militia to protect Catholic churches, and fired shots when Protestant rioters refused to disperse. The Protestant press framed the conflict as one between tolerant Protestant forbearance and violent Catholic conspiracy. According to the Protestant *North Amer-*

ican, the "blood of citizens, who in peaceful assemblage were assaulted by an organized band of alien or naturalized ruffians, has been shed, unarmed and unprepared men were shot down in the streets like dogs, for daring to assemble to consult over the interests of their native land."[71] In the account by the Philadelphia *Christian Observer*,

> The native Americans uttered no threats, and had done nothing to provoke a hostile movement. . . . Had they been disposed to molest the Roman Catholics, they were strong enough on the 4th to have burnt every church in the city, and put down the whole military force of the country. But no one dreamed of violence from them. Why then was a Roman priest and his brother permitted to collect in their place of worship the implements of death? . . . Was not this proceeding calculated to produce distrust in the police, and confirm the belief that the foreign papists were preparing for the work of murder? . . . In Persia, the arts of these Jesuits are at length understood, and they are expelled from the country,—while our politicians are so wise as to caress them for their votes, and thus encourage them in their schemes to create disorder and riot.[72]

What is noteworthy is not the vehemence of Protestant outrage—Protestant lives lost in the conflicts far exceeded Catholic ones—but the associations it fixes between "Protestant" and "American." While the dismantling of that association had been the aim of Catholics in the debates leading up to the riots, the resulting Protestant deaths eroded the force of Catholic dissent and left the Protestant-American equation the stronger for what ensued as the relative silence of Philadelphia Catholics on the episode and the claims that gave rise to it. In the weeks that followed the July riots, the *Christian Observer* magnanimously extended the blessings of American liberty to Catholics in precisely the language they had rejected in refusing conversion to a "national religion" by means of a "National Protestant Education":

> We wish them [the Roman Catholics] to enjoy the same religious liberty, the same protection, that we enjoy. . . . But when they come to our shores, we wish them to . . . have their minds imbued with *American* principles. We wish them to be *Americanized*, if we may use that term, instead of . . . act[ing] over again, scenes of turmoil in which they have too often been prominent in the old world."[73]

After the riots, members of the Philadelphia Board of Controllers who had proposed initial concessions to Catholic demands for curricular change backed down, electing instead to preserve the Protestant status quo. But the specter of Catholics as stealthy if silenced enemies of the Protestant religious consensus remained: in 1846, two years after the riots, a general assembly of the Presbyterian Church met in Philadelphia and declared as its aims to "keep the Bible open" and to battle "universalism (atheism), Unitarianism (a dead religion), Fourierism (free thinking), and Romanism, the most subtle and dangerous of them all."[74]

NATIONAL REFORMATION AND THE DANGERS OF DISSENT

Conflicts over Bible-reading exercises that escalated to violence in Philadelphia were more quietly sustained in Cincinnati in the 1840s and 1850s and revived as objects of national attention following the dislocations of the Civil War. The Cincinnati Bible "wars" narrowly missed erupting into bloodshed, and their effect over several decades was to draw moderate voices into the debate, which culminated in the 1872 decision of the Ohio Supreme Court to remove the Bible from the public school curriculum. The Cincinnati episodes are worth remarking not only for their role in securing a fragile legislative precedent for non-Protestant redress, but for the ways in which these religious controversies displaced regional, ethnic, and racial tensions within a nation struggling to accommodate both continuing waves of immigrants and newly emancipated slaves.

As one of the most populous and religiously heterogeneous cities to the west of the Protestant east coast establishment and just north of slave-holding strongholds to the south, Cincinnati became a charged locale in a discourse of national unity that was increasingly punctuated from mid-century on by calls to strengthen the white Protestant presence beyond the North Atlantic states. Lyman Beecher's manifesto on Protestant education, *A Plea for the West*, was delivered as a sermon in Boston but penned at Lane Seminary in Cincinnati, which was even then divided over the Presbyterian Church's failure to articulate a coherent antislavery position. In Beecher's *Plea*, however, "slavery" figures not as the system of racial bondage that would throw his seminary into disarray and galvanize members of his own family to the abolitionist cause, but instead as the spiritual unfreedom of Catholics, in this account a "dark minded, vicious populace," a "reckless mass of infuriated animalism" driven west by despotic priests who kept them in the condition of "slaves, slaves in body and mind."[75] While sectarian Protestant mission schools were founded in the West for the purposes of evangelizing Indians and, in Utah, of weaning children from Mormonism,[76] advocates of public, tax-supported, compulsory schools in the West increasingly won adherents by appealing to fear of the Catholic presence. The Vermont minister George Campbell, for example, warned in a sermon that the "grasping demand of their priests and bishops, for a portion of [the] Protestant school fund" could lay waste (by "chains and dungeons," "force and fire") "our free institutions, both in Church and State," unless ground be gained from the "crowds of Catholics, of priests, and bishops, sent out by the Pope and emptied upon our shores . . . even upon the shores of the Pacific."[77]

Bible-centered public schools emerged in Cincinnati as an instrument for the control of Catholic and other unruly "crowds." According to an 1838 law governing the establishment of public schools in the city, "the habits, manners, and morals of the pupils are to be strictly guarded. . . . In addition to parental authority, and the example and admonition of teachers, the moral restraints and obligations of the Bible are to be inculcated as a means of securing good behavior."[78] In 1842 Catholic parents, under the leadership of Cincinnati Archbishop John Purcell, delivered to the Cincinnati School Board a version of the same charges that Catholic parents in the Atlantic states had made, namely, that their children were forced to read the King James Bible and exposed to anti-Catholic sentiments in textbooks. Eight years earlier Purcell had toured the state to inveigh against "sectarian *free-schools*, which the children of poor Catholics frequent for the purpose of learning to read, and where, under the pretext of Charity and to the grievous abuse of that sacred virtue and name, the fountains of spiritual life are poisoned and those unsuspecting children have *tracts* placed in their hands."[79]

Objections from Purcell and Catholic parents in Cincinnati ultimately issued in a resolution from the School Board inviting Purcell to point out the offensive passages in textbooks and providing for the release of Catholic pupils from Bible-reading exercises if their parents so authorized.[80] The resolution was diluted, however, by Protestant school leaders who continued over the next decade to insist, against Catholic objections, that the King James Bible was nonsectarian and so suitable for all pupils. As the *Ohio Educational Monthly* editorialized in 1853, the "simplicity and beauty of its style," the "important information it furnishes," the "purity of its moral code," and the "preciousness of the salvation it discloses" made the Bible ideal as a textbook.[81]

The inflammatory coverage of Protestant-Catholic conflicts in the Cincinnati press made it remarkable that violence did not ensue there, as it had in Philadelphia. In 1844, the *Western Christian Advocate* issued a rallying cry against "papal priests":

Were [they] to become incendiaries, and set fire to our city, their agency would be far less pernicious to its true interests than a successful effort to withhold the Bible from our youth. . . . [A]ll who love God, or regard the welfare of the country, should understand the nature of this warfare. For *it is a blow aimed at the republican institutions and liberties of this country.* . . . [B]anish the Bible, and we will have a populace prepared to re-enact, in this peaceful land, the scenes of blood and devastation, which have marked the progress of revolution in Spain, Mexico, and the South American republics.[82]

Later that year, following the election of the Democrat James Polk, the Whig-controlled Cincinnati *Gazette* bitterly complained that "the victory of the Loco Focos is not that of Americans but a triumph of Irishmen and Germans over Americans. . . . We are compelled to use bullets, if need be, in defense of our country, before we can use the ballot, as partakers of its welfare. We are soldiers before we are free men, while an alien is made a free man before he is a soldier."[83]

A decade later, in 1853, violence was again narrowly averted when the visiting Archbishop Gaetano Bedini of Rome was burned in effigy by a crowd of two thousand Protestant marchers, who advertised on placards their intention to burn the residence of Archbishop Purcell, where Bedini was staying.[84] As Peter D'Agostino observes, Bedini's American visit "crystallized Catholic loyalty to the symbols of papal Rome" in the wake of Pius IX's triumphant return from exile after the fall of the independent Roman Republic in April 1849.[85] Before coming to America, Bedini had been assigned by the Vatican to oversee the defeat of the liberal rebellion in Spain, an involvement that earned him the nickname of the "Bloody Butcher of Bologna" among the rebellion's supporters at home. While Catholic immigrants saw in the pope's humiliation and exile a mirror of their own experiences of alienation in an often hostile new land, American Protestants (among them Margaret Fuller, William Lloyd Garrison, and Horace Greeley) vigorously hailed the rebellion that would have secularized the Papal States and destroyed the Vatican's temporal power. ("So deeply rooted in every American heart is the love of liberty," declared the American consul Nicholas Brown in Rome, that Americans would "at once hail with joy the independence of the Roman Republic.")[86] As a symbol of the Roman Republic's defeat, Bedini's visit to Cincinnati revitalized Catholics' spiritual allegiance to the "Eternal City" and gave urgency to the Protestant project of portraying as dangerously *un*-American those whose more deeply imagined community lay beyond national and temporal borders.

Catholic objections to Bible-reading exercises in Cincinnati schools over the decade preceding the Bedini incident had elicited from the School Board in 1852 a majority report affirming that the King James Bible belonged in common to all Christians, and scolding Purcell for failing to accept the 1842 resolution as sufficient. The report noted further that the introduction of various translations, namely the Douay Bible used by Catholics, would result in chaos. Purcell fueled the controversy in an 1853 pastoral letter arguing that if the public school system remained unwilling to divest itself of its Protestant biases, Catholics would be obliged to seek public funding for their own schools. In 1848 Catholic schools educated slightly more than two thousand Cincinnati pupils, a figure that would double by 1860 and more than double again by 1869.[87] Catholic schools occupied a middle ground between public and private schools, since they were supported in part by donations of parents who could afford to make them, but open also at no cost to the children of the poor. Purcell argued that these Catholic "free" schools relieved the burden of public schools, and therefore that "if they [Catholic parents] now demand their share of the school fund, in proportion to the number of their children, or the amount of their tax bill, they exercise but the right of every freeman. And if they value their privileges as American citizens they will assert them, in the way pointed out by the Constitution, in the selection of candidates who will fairly represent the wishes and requirements of their constituents."[88]

Purcell's attempts to win public funds for Catholic charity schools failed, and few Catholic candidates were then elected to the School Board or to other public offices. But the system of Catholic schools continued to grow, prompting a renewal of Protestant charges that the clergy-driven Catholic populace was intent on undermining the city's civic institutions. In the wake of Purcell's pastoral letter, meanwhile, residual Catholic objections to the Protestant content of public education were framed in the Protestant and secular press as stealthy attempts to divert public funds to sectarian Catholic schools, and so to keep Catholic and Protestant children alike from the "light and purity of evangelical religion."[89]

With the arrival of greater numbers of immigrants in Cincinnati over the next two decades, however, non-Protestant representation on the School Board did increase, so that the Board counted among its members in 1869 two Jews, ten Catholics, eighteen professing Protestants, and ten "others," either nominal Protestants or men with no religious affiliation.[90] In that year, a newly elected Catholic member, F. W. Rauch, sought bipartisan support for a plan that would merge the city's public schools with its Catholic charity schools. Rauch was able to win endorsements from prominent Catholics, including the Archbishop's brother, Father Edward Purcell, who saw the merger as potentially strengthening Catholic education. Rauch's proposal also won support from Protestants attracted to the prospect of bringing Catholic children under the authority of public schools by an act of legislative incorporation, and who perhaps also hoped that a merger would put an end to the growth of a de facto two-party system in Cincinnati in which, if immigration trends continued, they seemed destined to emerge as the weaker.

But Rauch's plan also drew criticism from both sides. The Protestant editor of the Cincinnati *Gazette* referred to the proposal as a "Jesuitical scheme on foot,"[91] while Archbishop John Purcell and other Catholic clergy maintained that Catholic schools could never be put under civil power. In what may have been an effort either to defer the Rauch proposal indefinitely or else to eliminate an obstacle to its acceptance by Catholics, another Board member, Samuel Miller (who professed no religious outlook) proposed an alternative resolution that prohibited "the reading of religious books, including the Holy Bible . . . in the Common Schools of Cincinnati, it being the true object and intent of this rule to allow the children of the parents of all sects and opinions, in matters of faith and worship, to enjoy alike the benefits of the Common School fund."[92] Miller's resolution passed by a vote of 22–15, with all of the Catholics voting for and a majority of Protestants voting against.[93]

The Cincinnati *Enquirer* correctly predicted that the passage of the resolution would "provoke a renewal of the excitement, and active efforts to obtain a re-establishment of the Bible-reading rule."[94] Over the next three years, the vote in favor of the Miller resolution not only galvanized the pro-Bible forces in Cincinnati, but also polarized the terms of a debate that, in the original resolution, were not always clearly resolvable along Protestant-Catholic lines. Soon after the Miller resolution was passed, thirty-seven Protestants sought an injunction to block its implementation, and their case was heard in Cincinnati Superior Court in late 1869. Lawyers for the Board, which had passed the Miller resolution, argued that the Bible was a sectarian book and, further, that to identify Protestant Christianity with the common law of the United States was to abridge the civil rights of the non-Protestants who made up roughly half its citizens. For their part, the plaintiffs who opposed the ban on Bible reading argued that to defer to Catholics on the issue was effectively to establish the Catholic religion in the schools. Lawyers for the plaintiffs argued further that Protestant Christianity *was* the common religion of the land, and that Bible reading in the public schools was therefore necessary for the common good.[95]

In February 1870, ten weeks after the case had been argued, a majority of the Superior Court justices found in favor of the pro-Bible plaintiffs, holding that the King James Bible was indeed nonsectarian, but also that religion was necessary to the interests of the state and therefore that the schools could not be secularized. The ruling thus made an explicitly Protestant civil religion the middle ground between sectarianism and secularization, a ground that, according to the Superior Court, the School Board was bound by the Constitution to defend.[96]

Although none of the lawyers who argued on behalf of the School Board in the Superior Court was Catholic, and support for the Miller resolution had been narrowly bipartisan, representations of the Bible wars in the national press tended to portray them as squarely divided along Protestant and Catholic lines. This was so even when they blurred the issues on both sides. In its front-page coverage of the trial, for example, the *New York Times* asked a lawyer for the Board to frame the Catholic side of the debate. According to the *Times*, the lawyer, Stanley Matthews, "said he had no doubt the Catholics held precisely the same views that were held by the gentlemen on the other side,—that the state should provide religious instruction. They [the Catholics] now wanted to secularize schools; afterward they would try to strike a bargain with [the Protestants]. . . . [T]hey would say, let us divide the school fund and give our children the religious instruction we think is right, and you give yours."[97]

The February 19, 1870 issue of *Harper's Weekly*, printed just as the Superior Court was handing down its decision in favor of the pro-Bible plaintiffs in Cincinnati, reinforced the message of the *New York Times* coverage—that Catholics sought to remove the Bible from public schools only in order to win state funds for their own—even as it made no direct allusion to this particular case. Instead it juxtaposed two images by the political cartoonist Thomas Nast. In the first, denominated "Europe," Queen Victoria and other monarchs and statesmen righteously preside over the severing of a banner into halves marked "church" and "state" while a caricatured assembly of disgruntled Catholic leaders cowers in one corner. In the second image, "America," a crowd of unruly priests and bishops dip their hands into bags marked "public school money" while the figure of Liberty (shackled to a ballot box marked "fraudulent votes") looks on helplessly and a coarse-looking woman in a cross-emblazoned dunce cap stitches the severed pieces of a banner marked "church" and "state" back together.

Read side by side, these two images repeat the earlier warnings of Beecher's *Plea*, which was that a foreign Catholic hierarchy, routed from Europe, was now establishing its dominion in the United States. While the haphazardly restitched banner in the second image looks like the severed banner of the first, however, closer inspection reveals it to be a makeshift map of the United States, on which the cities of New York, Cincinnati, and San Francisco are imprecisely aligned on the tear along which "church" and "state" are awkwardly rejoined. If the cartoon suggests that these are cities in which Constitution-defying Catholic immigrants stand to win the balance of power, it also hints that a mangled United States can only be the result if the reconstitution of the Union proceeds on terms that favor them.

That a Catholic-Protestant divide might stand in for other axes of difference was suggested by a second Thomas Nast cartoon that appeared in the same magazine a week later. This cartoon aligns three images in a vertical display. The uppermost image ("Our Common Schools as They Are") depicts a circle of children of assorted, visually representable races, religions, and nationalities—a black child, a Chinese child, a child in tar-

© 1999 HARPWEEK®

Figure 2. *Church and State* by Thomas Nast. "Mr. Nast's powerful and striking cartoon . . . tells its own story too well to require much explanation" (*Harper's Weekly*, 19 February 1870). Image courtesy of Harpweek.

tan plaid—who join hands in a circle on the grounds of a building marked "Common School." The image at the bottom of the page ("Our Common Schools . . . as They May Be") depicts a similarly diverse group of children now at violent odds—swarthy Jewish and Irish boys exchanging blows, a black boy pulling a Chinese boy's queue—against a backdrop of crowded buildings marked "Methodist school," "Episcopal school," "low church," "high church" "Jewish," "Roman Catholic," "African," "Chinese," "German," and "French" schools. In the image dividing these two, the blindfolded figure of Justice stands mute as a public school's coffers are emptied to enrich the Roman Catholic school just opposite. Although the accompanying text again makes no mention of the Cincinnati decision, it does urge attention to the dangers of what it calls "unsecularization," which it can only depict in the same way that the lawyers for the pro-Bible plaintiffs in Cincinnati portrayed the Miller resolution, that is, as the concession of the public schools to Catholic interests.[98]

In 1872, two years after the Superior Court decided in favor of the Cincinnati plaintiffs, the case was appealed to the Ohio Supreme Court, which this time found unanimously in favor of the School Board, ordering that the lower court's ruling be reversed and that the resolution banning Bible reading in Cincinnati schools be upheld.[99] Protestant school leaders thenceforward focused their efforts on supplying a "moral" education in lieu of a specifically religious one. Among the texts that remained in use in Cincinnati schools were the ubiquitous McGuffey readers, of which Lyman Beecher attested that "their religion is *unsectarian* true religion—their morality the morality of the Gospel."[100] To replace the Bible exercises, Cincinnati school leaders introduced in 1875 a system of moral instruction known as the "Memory Gem" method, in which texts on the soul's immortality, the mercy of God, and the cultivation of benevolence, obedience, and thrift were memorized and recited.[101] For their part, Catholic leaders in Cincinnati now turned their attention to bringing as many Catholic pupils as possible into church schools, and to strengthening their explicitly Catholic mission. Elsewhere, Protestant educators enlisted the secularizing currents in public education in their efforts to keep the character of the public schools broadly Protestant. In 1884, for example, a professor at the denominationally Baptist Pacific University urged the Oregon State Teachers' Association to retain Bible reading in Oregon public schools on the grounds "there *must* be a *religious* basis to our educational system. . . . This *does not* involve either cant or sectarianism. It involves the recognition of certain *facts* and *laws* relating as closely and as scientifically to our moral nature as the laws of physical attraction and chemical affinity do to the objects of sense."[102] So successful were Protestant efforts to demonstrate the compatibility of the Bible with increasingly secular education that individual states continued into the twentieth cen-

© 1999 HARPWEEK®

Figure 3. *Our Common Schools as They Are and as They Might Be* by Thomas Nast. "The dangers that threaten [our common schools] in the way of unsecularization, and the diversion of a large portion of the common school funds for the support of sectarian schools, are happily and only too truthfully foreshadowed in Mr. Nast's admirable composition . . . which requires no comment to enforce its warning admonitions" *Harper's Weekly*, 26 February 1870). Image courtesy of Harpweek.

tury to pass laws *requiring* Bible reading in public schools: Pennsylvania in 1913, Delaware and Tennessee in 1916, Alabama in 1919, Georgia in 1921, Maine in 1923, Kentucky in 1924, Florida and Ohio in 1925, and Arkansas in 1930.[103]

• • •

The Thomas Nast cartoon of the fully integrated public school classroom, from which the religious difference of Catholic pupils has been banished in favor of more iconic forms of otherness, is worth returning to for its overlaying of religious, racial, and national difference at a moment when the nation was struggling to accommodate both non-Protestant immigrants and emancipated slaves. If the cartoon's recasting of the difference of Catholicism as the variously racial, religious, and ethnic diversity of a heterogeneous population worked in part to splinter Catholicism's monolithic otherness, it subtly functioned also to consolidate the specter of an unmanageable pluralism internal to American Protestantism. To blame Catholics for the threatened disintegration of a common American culture was to displace fears of what Emerson saw as the logical end of Protestant individualism, which was a separate church for each believer.[104]

At the same time, the image shows a Protestantism that actively solicits diversity both as an accessory to and a demonstration of its own vaunted coherence. In fact, the African American, Native American, and immigrant children pictured in the image of "Our Common Schools as They Are" were unlikely to have been in public schools in 1870; they were more typically on waiting lists because of overcrowding in urban schools, in parochial or racially segregated schools, or truant because of pressure on them to work. Non-Anglo Protestant children who did attend public schools, moreover, continued to see themselves reflected in textbook representations that more closely resembled the stereotyping at work in Nast's threatening image of "unsecularization."[105] Like the incorporation of the conventions of the travelogue into mid-century editions of the King James Bible, however,[106] the idealized Nast image of a racially and religiously integrated public school points to the emerging self-conception of Protestant elites as connoisseurs and sponsors of difference, a view that figures the white Protestant heritage as uniquely equipped to allow for the enlightened appreciation of cultural diversity. By this logic, the "tolerance" the cartoon figures as emanating from the public school to Catholics, Jews, African Americans, Chinese, and others is not a natural reflection of human equality, but rather a function of the Protestant benevolence on which it depends. This accommodation of non-Anglo Protestants into the implicitly Protestant nation signals the strength of the Protestant center, its resistance to dilution across a religious spectrum, as well as its assimilative range across the same spectrum. Nast's image shows a public school that welcomes diversity as a guest whose presence reflects at once the generosity of the host culture and the flattering desire of the newcomer for inclusion within an implicitly superior structure.

Catholics who protested the use of the King James Bible in schools registered a different notion of collective identity and a different conception of America than the one that offered to "tolerate" them by forcing their accommodation to putatively Christian (and at the same time religiously neutral) norms. This dissent was organized by a largely English-speaking and politically astute population whose lands had not been confiscated, who were not enslaved, and who presumably did not see themselves as mouthpieces for the past and present grievances of Indians, Chinese, African Americans, or others pictured in the Nast cartoons. By muting that dissent at critical moments of national formation, however, supporters of a Protestant public school system could erase the specificity of religious difference as an obstacle to a unified America, and thereby assume on the part of all religious, racial, and immigrant outsiders to America a form of longing that only the implicitly Protestant center was empowered to convert to belonging.

Chapter Four

CONVERSION TO DEMOCRACY:

RELIGION AND THE AMERICAN RENAISSANCE

NINETEENTH-CENTURY attempts by Catholics and others to remove the King James Bible from the public school curriculum were derided in the national press both as "secularizing" (for promoting godlessness) and as "unsecularizing" (for introducing sectarianism). Such characterizations suggest at once how resourceful and how vexed were efforts to maintain the Protestant "consensus" as the invisible, organizing center of American democratic culture. In the 1870 Thomas Nast cartoons that commented obliquely on Cincinnati's Bible-reading cases, the multicultural circle in which children of visibly different groups join hands mutes the specificity of Catholic-Protestant conflict by imaging the public school as a robustly democratic space, one in which all religions, races, and nationalities are amply accommodated. But Nast's portrait of the religious, racial, and ethnic harmony that allegedly characterizes "our common schools as they are" also depicts a democracy so fragile as necessarily to be undone (as the companion image of balkanization makes clear) by any challenge to the model of tolerance proffered by its controlling center. Unable to represent the degree to which Protestant culture is itself inwardly riven by racial, doctrinal, gender, class, and regional differences, the image of balkanization displaces those fractures onto the vivid hostilities that arise among Catholics and Jews, immigrants and ex-slaves released from centralizing Protestant authority. Subject to that center, conflicts resolve themselves as easily as schoolyard games; loosed from it, the "margin" disintegrates in the chaos of its own incompatible differences, leaving the still-invisible Protestant center magically intact. In these images democratic space, as the intersection of varying claims made by Americans of different religions, races, and ethnicities, can be represented as a cozy, nonconfrontational pluralism, or it cannot be represented at all.

As Nast's rendering of the populations most needful of a Bible-based education makes clear, American Protestantism in the middle decades of the nineteenth century constituted its Others not only as religiously but also and simultaneously as racially different.[1] The difference of the immigrant and nonwhite pupils is also given spatial and temporal form in the primitive and Old World costumes donned by new arrivals to the Americanizing precincts of the common school. In this way Nast's common school reproduces the developmental geography the Unitarian Theodore Parker describes in *Social Classes in a Republic*: of the world's "inferior nations," Parker says, "some are inferior in nature, some perhaps behind us only in development; in a lower form in the great school of Providence—negroes, Indians, Mexicans, Irish, and the like."[2] Nast's image promises that the Protestant common school will, like Parker's "great school of Providence," graduate pupils fit to become Americans, however lengthy their stay in the probationary "lower forms."

But Nast also conscripts the difference of the nonwhite and immigrant pupils to his depiction of the America they are being schooled to join. As the ground on which black join hands with white, Old World with New, Nast's common school portrays a radiantly multicultural America achieved through the exemplary accommodation of otherness, or, more precisely, through the conversion of religious, racial, and ethnic diversity into the materials for a new, inclusively American sensibility whose hallmarks are progress and tolerance. America, in Nast's depiction, is "everyone," a visual echo of Thomas Paine's formulation that "the cause of America is, in a great measure, the cause of all mankind,"[3] and an anticipation of Newt Gingrich's "Central Proposition" of American history: "There is an American Civilization. It is diverse and multiethnic, but it is, in fact, one civilization."[4]

Indeed, Nast's circle of clasped hands evokes any number of ways that America's greatness has been imagined by its cultural spokesmen: as the "indissoluble bond" that, for free-market economists following the Civil War, secured the mutual flourishing of capital and (often black and immigrant) labor;[5] alternatively, as the embodied, eros-driven democracy envisioned in Whitman's "The Sleepers" ("The Asiatic and African are hand in hand, the European and American are hand in hand")[6] and given voice in Ishmael's desire, in *Moby-Dick*, to "squeeze hands all around" with the *Pequod*'s multiracial crew;[7] or, differently again, as the dreamt-of freedom, prophesied by Martin Luther King Jr., of "all God's children, black . . . and white . . . Jews and Gentiles, Catholics and Protestants" to "join hands" and sing songs of deliverance;[8] or yet again, as the hands-across-the-border multiculturalism of Walt Disney's (or the World Bank's) small world, after all.

The extreme political lability of so iconic a depiction of democracy alerts us to the uses to which diversity may be put in the interest of promoting a unitary culture. In the Nast images diversity management is made the task, specifically, of a Bible-centered public education, delivered under Protestant but avowedly nonsectarian auspices, and opposed to the allegedly antidemocratic designs of Catholic educators, parents, and clergy. Rendering a religious conflict over Bible reading in graphic scenes of racial, ethnic, and class antagonism, however, the Nast cartoons attest less to the immediate occasion for defending this Protestant program than to its extraordinarily ambitious scope. Those who argued for the centrality of the Protestant Bible to public schooling vested in public education a power that prominent nineteenth-century evangelicals located in the gospel itself, which was, in Harriet Beecher Stowe's words, "to break down all those irrational barriers and prejudices which separate the human brotherhood into diverse and contending clans."[9] Such formulations credit the Christian story with power not only to change hearts, but in so doing to induce spiritual and moral conformity among otherwise diverse populations: "In every age and climate, with every variety of habit, thought, and feeling, from the cannibals of New Zealand and Madagascar to the most enlightened and scientific minds in Christendom," wrote Stowe, "one feeling, essentially homogenous in its character and results, has arisen in view of this cross."[10] From such a perspective, what is at stake in Protestant-Catholic conflicts over Bible reading is whether public schools will be free to continue such a program of acculturation to U.S. citizenship in the name of Christian nurture, and whether Christian nurture is sufficiently powerful to manage social differences potentially more intractable than disagreements over which version of the Bible is appropriate for use in schools.

PROTESTANT SOCIALIZATIONS AND LITERARY DEMOCRACY

Christian Nurture was the title liberal Congregationalist theologian Horace Bushnell gave to his influential 1847 treatise on evangelical education, a refutation of Calvinist notions of infant depravity and a handbook, in part, for replacing an impersonal and potentially coercive mode of family government with what Richard Brodhead names a regime of "disciplinary intimacy." In this model of childrearing, home becomes a haven of Christian love, tender elicitations of loyalty to family norms obviate the need for stripes and harsh words, and parental authority becomes incontrovertible in the measure that it becomes invisible, assuming the benign form, in Bushnell's words, of "a kind of silent, natural-looking power."[11]

Christian Nurture belonged to an outpouring of antebellum child-focused writings that elaborated this disciplinary model and championed its claims to universal validity. Nast's image of the Bible-centered common school overthrown by sectarian interests, in which pupils of "Roman Catholic," "Jewish," "Chinese," "African," and other schools come to blows, echoes the cautionary scenes that figured prominently in this literature, which warned that children deprived of a legitimate Christian upbringing would resort to violence outside the home. Such arguments advanced the cause of common schools by underscoring the compensatory role of education in converting these potential ruffians, drawn from beyond the ranks of the Protestant middle class, into republican citizens. The "silent, natural-looking power" of the common school—Protestant, public, Bible-based—was, says Brodhead, its "power to break in upon the quite different acculturation systems of other American cultures and deliver their children to training on a now 'universal' plan: the public school recast, at that moment, in the middle class's disciplinary image."[12]

A number of antebellum programs for "Shaping a Protestant America," in Winthrop Hudson's phrase,[13] mirrored this disciplinary philosophy of total nurture. Horace Mann's formulation of the common school's aims—to "fold to its cherishing bosom" children "cursed by vicious parentage"[14]—reappears in the programs of novelists, missionaries, and social reformers for the literal or metaphoric adoption of poor, foreign, and nonwhite children into middle-class Christian homes.[15] Urban evangelical ministries took shape in this period as what one pastor called "*a system of organized kindness* . . . which, by touching people on physical, social, and intellectual sides, will conciliate them and draw them within reach of the gospel."[16] Such concerted intimacies, tendered in the name of Christian love, also furthered the extension of U.S. power abroad. According to an 1843 congressional report prepared by John Quincy Adams for the House Committee on Foreign Relations, the people of the United States had a more legitimate interest than any other country in the island nation of Hawai'i thanks to the efforts of American missionaries, who had claimed it "by a virtual right of conquest, not over the freedom of their brother man by the brutal arm of physical power, but over the mind and heart by the celestial panoply of the gospel of peace and love."[17]

Literature comes to join this cultural configuration of discipline-through-love, Brodhead suggests, insofar as antebellum literary production installs the activity of *reading* at the heart of the nurture-centered home and school, and as novels themselves come increasingly to take up the office of abolishing crudely coercive disciplinary regimes: flogging in Melville's *White Jacket*, public shaming in *The Scarlet Letter*, or slavery in *Uncle Tom's Cabin*.

An alternative, gender-focused tradition of scholarship on domestic and sentimental fiction suggests a different relationship between antebellum literature and the socialization of children on evangelical models. The circle of prominent evangelical women reformers at mid-century included a number of bestselling novelists—among them Harriet Beecher Stowe, Susan Warner, Lydia Maria Child, and Catharine Maria Sedgwick—who also published widely as experts on issues of home and family. Jane Tompkins's *Sensational Designs* famously champions this literature as resonating more closely than did the works of the "great" (male) writers of the period—Hawthorne, Emerson, Melville, Poe, Thoreau—with the social and emotional forces "that nineteenth-century readers actually encountered in their lives." Tompkins contends that antebellum works centered on the Christian home and family belong properly to the canon of representative American literature because "the one great fact of American life during the period under consideration was, in Perry Miller's words, the 'terrific universality' " of the evangelical Protestant revival.[18]

For Brodhead, by contrast, the philosophy of loving nurture belongs not to a religious movement but to "the quite particular middle-class world . . . that coalesced around this socializing strategy in the antebellum years"; evangelical Protestantism was but "one of its constituents." Locating disciplinary intimacy not in a particular religious movement but instead in the defining activities of the emerging middle class enables Brodhead to bring writers like Melville and Hawthorne into this social and literary mix together with domestic reformers and sentimental novelists like Stowe, Warner, and Sedgwick. The disciplinary strategies of the new middle class fostered not only the creation of subjects ruled by the commands of love and conscience, Brodhead contends, but also the "creation of the normative": "At a time when it was in no sense socially normal, the new middle class world undertook to propagate itself as American 'normality.' "[19]

But how might so astute a critic as Tompkins (or Perry Miller, for that matter) have come by the conviction of middle-class evangelicalism's "terrific universality" in the antebellum period? Put another way, how is it that, as it appears, a "quite particular middle-class world" managed to propagate not only a class identity but also a religious identity as normative? I wish to press this question not only to draw out a set of normally unspoken connections between religion and class, but also to underscore how, in its alliance with the emergent middle class, a particular strand of Protestant Christianity was able to render itself unspoken, to become "a kind of silent, natural-looking power."

One could argue, of course, that terms like "Protestant," "Christian," and "evangelical" are far too encompassing to describe any cultural formation with precision, least of all a particular class. What the Protestant Christianity of the nineteenth century most shares with the middle class, however, is just this quality, as Stuart Blumin puts it, of being "elusive precisely because it is pervasive."[20] Indeed, the power of such terms as "Protestant" and "middle-class" may most lie in their flexibility and breadth of reference, their apparent ability to unite all "average" Americans and at the same time to give quite specific content to this "average." The term "Christian" in nineteenth-century writings, for example, names a broad range of spiritual and social configurations hardly restricted to the white American middle class, even as "Christian" can function at the same time to indicate the specific concerns of this class, as in the full title of Catharine Beecher and Harriet Beecher Stowe's *The American Woman's Home, or, Principles of Domestic Science; being a Guide to the Formation and Maintenance of Economic, Healthful, Beautiful, and Christian Homes.* "Christian" by turns broadcasts and conceals its exclusions—just as, in this title, do "American" and "Woman."

The separate-spheres ideology elaborated in works like *The American Woman's Home* (and reproduced in much critical reflection on nineteenth-century texts) invisibly tethers religion to class, moreover, by framing specifically Christian and middle-class concerns in an allegedly universal vocabulary of gender. Because, as Michael Gilmore suggests, the new social formation that was the middle class declared itself principally through its "gender arrangements" and "the separation of public and private spheres," scholars have tended to see in nineteenth-century writing "not economic struggle but a clash of gender styles, not a confrontation between social groups" but the displacement of one set of gender norms by another.[21] In its usual iterations, the ideology of separate spheres assigns the work of social and domestic welfare to women, freeing the public sphere from networks of obligation that would hamper the virile exercise of market competition. Even when they show how this new distribution of authority provides the economic and affective architecture of the white middle class, however, scholars have rarely foregrounded the consequences of these changes for outsiders to this class, except as these others figure as beneficiaries of middle-class largesse.[22]

Thus even those who have focused on class in their readings of antebellum literary texts have frequently elided the context of class struggle in which those texts whose "cultural work" it is to elicit consent to middle-class dominance must necessarily operate. In the same way, scholars who highlight the importance of religion to the formation of the middle class, and its expression in gender arrangements and other social forms encoded in nineteenth-century texts, have tended by omission to endorse the particular religious culture such texts often tirelessly promote over and against competing alternatives. Tompkins, for example, notes the "monumental effort" undertaken by white evangelical Protestants within the emerging North Atlantic middle class to "convert the entire nation and eventually the entire world to the truths of Protestant Christianity." Even so, she characterizes this movement—a quite specific cultural campaign with obvious designs on lands west and south, on slaves and free blacks, on native peoples, Catholics, Mormons, and immigrants—simply as "Christian" and as representing "the nation's most cherished religious beliefs."[23]

Mary Ryan's classic study of the origins of the middle class in antebellum Utica, New York also attests to the ease of translating a particular religious culture into a national norm. In her preface to *The Cradle of the*

Middle Class, Ryan points out that while the public records preserved in Utica offered a "veritable treasure trove of historical sources" for reconstituting the region's "family history," almost no record survived of the experiences of the town's immigrant, nonwhite, and non-Protestant communities, 40 percent of its inhabitants at mid-century. Reluctantly excising all references to this non-Anglo Protestant population, Ryan discovered that only in that way could she "spotlight . . . the emergence of a definable middle class." The Utica that emerges in this selective framing so powerfully illuminates, at the local level, "general social conditions and developments" that it becomes, for Ryan, the municipal equivalent of "one of Hegel's world-historical individuals."[24]

Such findings as Ryan's that it was middle-class Protestants almost exclusively who produced and circulated the tracts, minutes, reform writings, and other literature from which historians have drawn inferences about "general social conditions and developments" in antebellum America urge a reconsideration of a pervasive paradigm in American literary studies, which keys American literary history between the Revolutionary and Civil Wars to the progress of American democracy.[25] In her suggestive and wide-ranging *Revolution and the Word*, Cathy Davidson links "the democratization of the written word" in this period to the developments Nathan O. Hatch collectively names "the democratization of American Christianity."[26] In "a common effort to pull down the cultural hegemony of a gentlemanly few," Hatch writes, Americans "on all fronts began to speak, write, and organize against the authority of mediating elites, of social distinctions, and of any human tie that did not spring from volitional allegiance."[27] According to Davidson, the emergence of a distinctively American literature belongs to this movement, beginning in the late eighteenth century, "toward a reassessment of the role of the 'average' American and a concomitant questioning of political, ministerial, legal, and even medical authorities on the part of the citizens of the new nation."[28] Since, however, her evidence suggests that this consciousness-raised "average" American was produced by the Great Awakenings, the proliferation of evangelical tracts, and the promotion of Bible reading, "average" must also mean average, typical, or normal as produced within this Protestant cluster of cultural forms.[29]

Unpacking this cluster, moreover, yields a picture of democratization in which hegemony and resistance are intricately intertwined. Tompkins argues that the sentimental literature that locates "the power to save the world" within the middle-class home and its "closet devotions" reflected that dimension of nineteenth-century experience that was "shaped conclusively by the revival movement."[30] Yet the emphasis on "home" as the site for the cultivation of Christian feeling, whose radiation outward effects the redemption of the social world, conspicuously defused revivalistic energies that might have unsettled either the separate-spheres model or the cultural authority it secured for the white middle class. As Laurence Moore suggests, eighteenth- and early nineteenth-century revivals and camp meetings were marked by a "carnivalesque quality of role reversal."[31] The evangelical summons to redeem the world from sin and injustice made saving faith, rather than status or property ownership, the means of participation in a transformed world. These liberating aspects of evangelicalism elicited radical critiques of the social order from those who might otherwise have remained voiceless, creating fluidity between denominational boundaries and roles, between genders, classes, and races, between public prayer and transformative inner experience. At camp meetings, which encouraged spontaneous exhortations, white and black women, slaves and other poor and struggling people joined clergy in delivering stinging rebukes of the status quo. To see an otherwise "bold and courageous" gentleman "turn pale and tremble at the reproof of a weak woman, a little boy, or a poor African" wrote one new convert; "to see him sink down in deep remorse, roll and toss, and gnash his teeth . . . who can say the change was not supernatural?"[32]

The revival movement drew its energies from beyond established white churches and their internal hierarchies; the support of slave converts, for example, had been critical to the survival of "new method" evangelism, and the incipient religious antislavery movement was in large part a product of their participation. Indeed, what was "new" about the evangelicalism brought to the mainland colonies by John and Charles Wesley, unleashing the Great Awakenings, were elements that English Protestant missionaries had tried unsuccessfully to purge from slave (and Indian) religion during two centuries of African and European presence in the New World. These included lay preaching, open-air religious meetings, and sudden, spontaneous conversions, often accompanied by full-body "shouts," all of which became staples of subsequent evangelical revivals.[33]

For the most part, however, religious exchanges across race and class lines were gradually obscured or denied as white evangelical Christianity sought to maintain its "purity." In the North as well as the South, the increasing African American presence in American Protestantism—in numbers, theology, and styles of worship—meant stronger segregation measures. By the middle of the nineteenth century, white evangelical churches had largely abjured their working-class and nonwhite origins and become venues of respectability for their now largely middle-class constituencies. Where black congregations continued to be marked by dancing shouts and trancelike forms of possession, white congregations called for restraint, associating these forms with "lower" races.[34]

In the same measure, the middle-class white women energized by the revivalistic summons to social critique were chastened into less destabilizing arrangements.[35] Bushnell's *Christian Nurture*, which helped to fasten these women's attentions on family and home, was written in part to urge Christians toward a more "constant" piety than that evinced by the "strenuous and fiery" conversions characteristic of religious revival, a mode of awakening that suggested a religion "of conquest rather than of love."[36] Charging the domestic sphere with the task of redeeming the world from injustice, the middle-class ideology of loving maternal nurture further muted the socially disruptive potential of revivals by figuring populations outside of the white middle class no longer as agents but solely as beneficiaries of evangelical reforms.

If more restrictive definitions of middle-class women's roles were one result of this redirection of revivalism's social currents, the sentimental novel was another. This was so not only because narratives of Christian benevolence on behalf of those deemed bereft of normative families and normative homes afforded middle-class women a public stage to engage from the confines of the private sphere, but also because such narratives provided a venue for ministers who rejected revivals as means of reaching a mass audience.[37] The establishment of Bible and tract societies, the first organized efforts to evangelize through print on a massive scale, created technologies that allowed for the cheap production of fiction, and tract publishers soon capitalized on the accessibility of fiction by making stories rather than doctrine the subject of mass-produced evangelical literature. "Story-hunger in children is even more urgent than bread-hunger," wrote Henry Ward Beecher in the novel *Norwood*, a meditation on the poverty of theology and the greater resources of narrative for Christian faith.[38] Earlier Calvinist prohibitions against fiction had vested the novel's threat in its "oriental" or "Romanish" difference from Protestantism, or in its power to bring down the authority of the pulpit.[39] The softened, story-driven Protestantism championed by this fiction's defenders, in contrast, muted potential opposition by articulating its interests in popular narratives that voiced a seemingly unified national will.

A signal difference between nineteenth-century Protestant religious fiction in England and America, David Reynolds observes, is that while the former belonged to an effort to weigh competing denominational alternatives, the latter was devoted to making American Protestantism increasingly nonsectarian. As Edward Everett Hale noted, English writers ignored "the generous spirit which exists in America between Christians of different names."[40] Nonsectarian piety was a clear desideratum of a nation avowedly devoted to religious freedom and one amenable to the aims of authors and readers whose reassessment of the "average" generated critiques of ministerial authority and sectarian narrowness. As Moore points out, no line between religious and nonreligious literature would distinguish separate markets for antebellum fiction. What he and others identify as the secularization of American print media, a set of processes by which religion was diffused though various "culture industries," had the effect of making Protestant Christianity at once less internally diverse, more normative, and less separable from everyday life.[41]

The intricate work of rendering antebellum cultural production at once more Christian and less identifiably "religious" was closely bound up with what Karen Halttunen identifies as the middle-class impulse to shape all social forms into expressions of sincere inner feeling.[42] Stowe, for example, famously claimed of *Uncle Tom's Cabin* that "God wrote it." Her shrewd appeal to the novel's divine authorship invited readers and literary arbiters to judge the book by the highest available standards for assessing the value of novels at a crucial stage in their emergence as a "democratic" cultural form—their artlessness, transparency, and resonance with self-evident truths. Tolstoy classed *Uncle Tom's Cabin* with the "highest" form of art, which he called "Christian art," distinguished by its ability to unite all persons with God and with one another, as opposed to the sectarian effects of those works that promote "church superstitions" and "patriotic superstitions," "exclusive feelings . . . which do not unite but divide men."[43]

In this view, the value of Stowe's novel and of all true "Christian" art is its power to render Christian religious identity continuous with democratic civil identity. The "great principles of democracy," affirmed Stowe and Catharine Beecher in *The American Woman's Home*, "we conceive to be equally the principles of Christianity."[44] Or as Melville wrote, praising Hawthorne, "no American writer should write like an Englishman, or a Frenchman; let him write like a man, for then he will be sure to write like an American. . . . [W]e should refrain from unduly lauding foreign writers, and, at the same time, duly recognize the meritorious writers that are our own;—those writers, who breathe that unshackled, democratic spirit of Christianity in all things, which now takes the practical lead in this world, though at the same time led by ourselves—us Americans."[45] For Melville as for the Evangelical United Front, "the unshackled, democratic spirit of Christianity" renders America a transcendent nation, where denominational, racial, class, even national differences dissolve in the light of its world-historical mission.

Avowed evangelicals would frame this process in more emphatically Christian terms: in the devotional serial *The Christian Diadem*, for example, Stowe describes "the interior life" as "a state in which the mind is so bent and absorbed by the love of Christ, that all inducements to worldliness lose their power, and the mind becomes as indifferent to them as a dead body to physical allurements." Must not this state become, Stowe continues, "the common experience of all Christians before Christ can subdue the world?"[46] If, in contrast, Melville's "democratic spirit of

Christianity . . . that takes the lead in the world" almost demands a lower-case C, this difference in tone shows how subtly the "democratization of Christianity" could proceed. In being "democratized," Christianity is rewritten *as* democracy, shuttling its specificity while retaining its normative power.

Gendering Religion

Gender, indeed, would seem to be the *only* difference that continues to signify for Melville's abstracted American who "write[s] like a man," just as it is gender most saliently that marks Stowe's affiliation with what Tompkins recuperatively calls "the *other* American Renaissance." According to Tompkins, F. O. Matthiessen's classic *American Renaissance* enshrined Melville, Hawthorne, Emerson, Whitman, Poe, and Thoreau for their "refus[al] to be taken in by the pieties of the age," granting them representative status to the exclusion of authors who "wrote to educate their readers in Christian perfection."[47] Tompkins aims her polemic not only at the resilient critical paradigm established by Mathiessen, but also at Ann Douglas's denigration of the evangelical countertradition for its "feminization"—sentimentalization, trivialization—of American culture. Tompkins's and subsequent revaluations of this tradition have done little, however, to challenge American literary historians' habitual layering of the sentimental, the feminine, and the Christian. In the wake of Tompkins's project, the rescue of the sentimental narrative has most often taken shape as the restoration to the American literary canon of women's voices and women's concerns, and only incidentally of middle-class evangelical voices or concerns, as though this strain of Christianity were simply the cultural camouflage under which female power moves into public discourse.

Recent, welcome critiques of the separate-spheres model as masking differences of race, class, region, and sexuality have thus far largely failed to highlight its *religious* exclusiveness, an omission which, as much as the continued performance of the separate-spheres model in criticism, under-writes a tacit Protestant bias in American literary and cultural studies.[48] Taken together, the "two" American Renaissances—Tompkins's senti-mentalists and Mathiessen's virile skeptics—set the boundaries of reli-giousness in nineteenth-century America as degrees of visible Christian commitment. From Cooper's Leatherstocking tales to *Walden* to *Huckle-berry Finn*, representative male narratives of rebellion typically associate women with the "sivilizing" yoke of Christianity and men with more expansive freedoms, including the freedom of ostensibly subversive reli-gious or theological innovation. If in *Moby-Dick*, for example, the Bible is broken open to become the raw materials of narrative, women's fictions are more likely to include edifying scenes of Bible reading or to interpolate Bible lessons.[49] Appeals to biblical faith testify to women writers' sincerity and respectability, much as the revision or rejection of biblical faith—"The scent of these arm-pits is aroma finer than prayer," declares Whitman, "This head is more than churches, bibles and all the creeds"—signals men's "authenticity."[50]

At the same time, the shared concerns of these authors are often concealed by what Lora Romero calls "the antebellum era's own habit of conceptualizing authority and rebellion through the representational matrix of middle-class gender norms."[51] Canonical works by male writers often enact one half of the pattern by which the Protestant middle class is made, as novels of close-knit bonds of love between family members enclosed in the domestic sphere enact the other: *Walden*, "Self-Reliance," or *Moby-Dick* are, in part, about men whose mode of production engages them in the challenge of living self-sufficiently apart from women and children.[52] The difference is not simply one of (masculine) "autonomy" versus (feminine) "relationality," however; one is hard-pressed to imagine a different function for the spermaceti-squeezing scene in *Moby-Dick*—where Ishmael, overcome with love for his shipmates, feels himself bathed in "the very milk and sperm of kindness"[53]—than to claim affective feeling as the terrain of men as well as mothers, even of those men who conspicuously distance themselves from women and from the civilizing radius of female influence.

Neither the maintenance of separate, gendered spheres in U.S. literary history nor more recent scholarship that questions that division, moreover, considers the way the "spheres" conventionally demarcate a set of works distinguished largely by the degree to which the Christian values championed in one register have rather seamlessly been transmuted into democratic values in the other. Indeed, the "classic" works of nineteenth-century American literature have characteristically been valued for just those capacities—the extension of fellow feeling across races and classes, the incorporation of vernacular and subaltern voices, the embrace of outcasts (Melville's "meanest mariners, and renegades and castaways")[54]—that, in their association with evangelical Christianity, are derided (or recuperatively championed) as feminine or sentimental.[55] To distinguish such writings as belonging to separate spheres, or to competing American Renaissances, both polarizes a relatively narrow spectrum of nineteenth-century cultural production and exaggerates that spectrum, making it stand in for the whole. But it is precisely the "whole," of course, that these works seek to represent in the breadth of their democratic address. Stowe's evangelical melting pot, in which the discernment of Christ within makes "one blood [of] all the nations of men," was called by other writers simply "America," "a teeming Nation of nations," in Whitman's words, where, as Emerson supposed, "the energy of the Irish, Germans, Swedes, Poles, and Cossacks, and all of the European tribes—and of the Africans, and of the Polynesians,—will construct a new race, a new religion, a new state, a new literature."[56]

Antebellum works that turn their gaze on non-Christian (or nonwhite Christian) religious practice typically bring religious otherness within Christianity's expansive fold—in Lydia Maria Child's *Hobomok*, for example the blessings of the Christian God radiate equally "on distant mosques and temples," "on the sacrifice heap of the Indian, and the rude dwellings of the Calvinist"[57]—or else deploy these forms of otherness to indict Christianity's failures of inclusiveness, as Melville does in charging Christian missionaries with violent assaults on native religious freedoms in *Typee*. Amy Kaplan has called attention to the way the antebellum culture of sentiment serves in part to construct the boundaries of the national by distinguishing domestic from foreign space, even as its cultivation of the domestic as the sphere of elevating "feelings" and "influences" promotes an expansive sense of mission that extends beyond national borders. Thus a key function of Christian nurture within *The American Woman's Home* is to enable "Christian families" to gather about them "Christian neighborhoods . . . [so that] ere long colonies from these prosperous and Christian communities [may] . . . go forth to shine as 'lights of the world' in all the now darkened nations."[58] By contrast, more canonical American Renaissance writers often invoke "darkened nations" and "savage" man to expose, and occasionally to redeem, what Melville called white Christian culture's "civilized hypocrisies and bland deceits," or Whitman the "hollowness" and "hypocrisy" signaled in the ability of "churches, sects, etc. . . . [to] usurp the name of religion."[59]

Evangelical Protestant missionary activity in the middle decades of the nineteenth century, however, was also committed to the regenerative potential of "natural" man. The earliest literature of the American Board of Commissioners for Foreign Missions (ABCFM), founded in 1810, insisted that all nations hungered after truth as much as did Christian America, however warped their desires by the distortions of false belief. In alliance with movements in middle-class Protestantism that made natural development (rather than the imposition of structure) the key to Christian life, the ABCFM sought to deliver the world from superstition, inscrutable ritual practice, and other "trappings" of foreign faith. In a speech before the ABCFM, Timothy Dwight, then president of Yale, envisioned a future "when the *Romish* cathedral, the mosque, and the pagoda, shall *not have one stone left upon another, which shall not be thrown down.*"[60] Iconoclastic, anti-institutional energies animated the goal of "carry[ing] light and knowledge in among those who most need it . . . dispers[ing] the clouds of ignorance; and mak[ing] the great body of people intelligent, capable, and worthy of performing the duties of republican freemen."[61] These, in fact, are Whitman's words on the democratizing powers of the common school and the penny press, but they might easily have been those of the ABCFM enthusiast for whom delivery of the gospel "might speedily transform an ignorant, sensual, idolatrous, and selfish community into a nation of intelligent, moral, Christian freemen,"[62] a trajectory as "natural" as the truth of Christianity and one which, once begun, completes itself. Lyman Beecher, in an 1827 report to the ABCFM, offered the hope that within fifty years "every nation may be so far evangelized, as that the work may move onward to its consummation, without extraneous aid."[63]

CONVERSION TO DEMOCRACY

Framed as the removal of artificial and implicitly coercive religious acculturations, the progress both of evangelical faith and democratic faith recapitulates what Philip Fisher calls the "aesthetics of the subtraction of differences" that, in his view, goes to the making of American democratic space as a sphere of mutual intelligibility or transparency.[64] The "subtraction of differences" in the interest of social transparency could proceed as the removal of whole populations—literally, from national space, or ideologically, from national concern—whose alternative modes of social organization or whose histories of subjugation threatened to obstruct the democratic vista.[65] (Thus Melville praises the architect of Indian removal as a model of democratic faith and a living testament to "divine equality"—"thou just Spirit of Equality" "pick[ed] up Andrew Jackson from the pebbles . . . [and] thundere[ed] him higher than a throne!")[66] "Subtraction of differences" could also take place as the illuminating of otherwise opaque subjectivities—as Whitman put it, "carry[ing] light and knowledge in among those who most need it." Consciousness of diversity liberates, says *Leaves of Grass*, yet Whitman can rejoice in a free play of identities—Yankee girl, Brooklyn rough, half-breed, slave—only by negating diversity of consciousness: "I celebrate myself and sing myself, / And what I shall assume you shall assume. . . . If [my thoughts] are not yours as much as mine they are nothing, or next to nothing."[67]

The desideratum of mutual intelligibility across a spectrum of racial, regional, and other differences—"How can it be difficult to know another," asks Fisher, "if all 'assume' the same?"[68] —is itself closely linked to a Protestant model of religious conversion that figures regeneration as a movement from darkness to the light of truth, confusion to clarity, imprisonment to freedom. "We assume the pity of our readers," Stowe wrote in a devotional work published shortly after *Uncle Tom's Cabin*, "and our aim will be to raise them, instrumentally, to higher attainments in the spiritual life . . . until, bursting the shackles that bind them, and rising out of the slough of earthiness in which they are sunk, they come up to that high measure of evangelical sanctification, which the voice of scripture and the exigencies of a dying world alike demand of them."[69] In its literary versions, such emancipatory new birth often brings with it a transforming awareness of the incommensurability of any single form of religious life to the universality of the deity or to the brotherhood of man. "I felt a melting in me," reports Melville's Ishmael; "No more my splintered heart and maddened hand were turned against the wolfish world. This soothing savage had redeemed it."[70] Ishmael's love for Queequeg, who, as Carolyn Karcher notes, "telescopes Polynesian, American Indian, African, Islamic, and even Christian features and customs,"[71] moves him, fittingly, to enlarge on his "particular Presbyterian form of worship" and embrace the "magnanimous God of heaven and earth— pagans and all included."[72]

The framing of conversion as deliverance from fractiousness and spiritual narrowness into an expansive space of freedom maps the religious experience of evangelical Protestants onto the secular goals of American democracy.[73] Insofar as this model of conversion as individual or communal emancipation assumes and underwrites a democratic culture, it opposes the liberating experience of normative conversion not only to the unregenerate state of the unconverted but also to the necessarily suspect experience of the differently converted, whose religious trajectories lead them away from the American mainstream. Such conversions were typically rendered as a propagandistic imposition of limits rather than as the spontaneous awakening to enlightenment. "Can we endure the thought of having our children enslaved by the Church of Rome," asked Theodore Dwight in *Open Convents*, "and forced contrary to the Light of their Minds . . . to comply with all its idolatrous superstitions?"[74] Polemical literature on Mormonism, framed into the twentieth century as "the Islam of America," depicted converts as powerless before quasi-occult forces.[75] Mormon leader Joseph Smith "exerted a mystical magical influence over me" says a heroine of Maria Ward's sensational *Female Life Among the Mormons*, "a sort of sorcery that deprived me of the unrestricted exercise of free will."[76]

David Brion Davis points out that "the ultimate peril" of Mormons, Catholics, and Freemasons in antebellum America "was always conceptualized as 'slavery,' " suggesting "a deep-seated guilt over the expansion of Negro slavery at a time of widening freedom and opportunity for white Americans."[77] The habit of representing illegitimate or aberrant conversion as enslavement continued well after the Civil War, however, as the continuing popularity of narratives of captivity to Mormons, Catholics, Indians, and religiously "foreign" purveyors of sexual vice—"Jew traders," "Polish Jewesses," "Italians masquerading under Irish names"[78]—amply attests. Even the awakening to abolitionism, framed as conversion from darkness to the light of truth, could erase the singularity of racial bondage. Consider Elizabeth Cady Stanton's testimony in an 1860 speech to the American Anti-Slavery Society: "In the darkness and gloom of a false theology I was slowly sawing off the chains of my spiritual bondage, when for the first time, I met Garrison in London. A few bold strokes from the hammer of truth, I was free! . . . [A] doubting soul suddenly born into the kingdom of reason and free thought. Is the bondage of the priest-ridden less galling than that of the slave, because we do not see the chains, the indelible scars, the festering wounds, the deep degradation of all the powers of the God-like mind?"[79] As Stanton's conversion to the truth of "free thought" suggests, such a model could describe the spiritual awakenings of the heterodox as well as the orthodox; in either case, the emancipatory tropes of a liberalizing Protestantism—freedom, inevitability, the clarification of innate inner goodness—control the description of salutary religious change.

What such depictions of normative conversion fail wholly to represent, however, is the loss that even conversion to democracy or "truth" may entail as the movement from one community of tradition to another. When framed as a progression from fragmentation to wholeness or from imprisonment to freedom and enlightenment, conversion describes less the rigors of various newcomers' acculturation to American civil society than it does the "sacred teleology" that consecrates the host culture they must shed very differently constituted beliefs and socializations in order to join.[80] This is a point where conversion to democracy restates what Fisher calls "the central matter of American education" in the nineteenth century: "to bleach out . . . differences [of language, culture, and religion] in the act of producing 'typical' American children."[81]

Seen in this light, the idealized portrait of the common school in Thomas Nast's 1870 cartoon reveals the workings of a sympathetic nationalism whose instrument the sentimental novel and other forms of democratic literary address had by then become.[82] That image shows children who are, but for their iconically magnified differences, *like* the white Protestant pupil—few black or Chinese students actually attended public schools in 1870, but they are nonetheless imagined to be happily present in the cartoon's representation of the diversity it righteously solicits. The opposing image shows children who are quite unlike public school pupils, indeed are not public school pupils at all, since they attend the competing institutions—the "Roman Catholic school," "Jewish school," "African school," "Chinese school," and so on—depicted in the background.

Nyack College
Eastman Library

These children are most unlike the implicitly Protestant common school student *not* in their racial or ethnic difference, however, since these are what the first image shows the common school confidently able to manage. Their crucial difference from the common school pupil lies rather in their internal differences, their incompatible religious beliefs and understandings of democracy. If this image shows the dangers to the nation of resistantly opaque inner lives (signaled by racial and ethnic markers), the first illustrates the means by which democratic union is secured by implicit interventions on feelings and interior states.[83]

Nast's American microcosm of the democratized common school not only homogenizes the differing inner worlds of non-Protestants, moreover, but also conspicuously removes them from their larger historical communities. The Catholic child is represented not with other Catholics, the Jewish child not with other Jews, and so on; each child appears instead as part of an expansive and assimilative Protestantism. No child who has made this transition from foreign to democratic faith appears, however, to be menaced by the divided loyalties or fractious isolation he might well be expected to experience as one who has explicitly been severed from the collective life of a particular tradition. Instead, this state of alienation obtains only *outside* the circle of American/Protestant solicitude, where those who continue to assert communal identities other than American and Protestant are represented as rejecting the extension of community on democratic terms. Within that circle, competing spiritual and social worlds are erased, and only the iconic difference of the non-Protestant child is retained to confirm the extension of Protestant tolerance. Religious, ethnic, and racial conflict gives way to the aesthetic appropriation of otherness, and communal institutions are subordinated to a spirituality of inward illumination found not (or not only) in churches but in schools, novels, and the hearts and minds of adherents.

Coda: The Uses of Otherness

The model of conversion as inevitable, progressive, and emancipatory, a movement away from division and toward clarity and singleness of purpose, belies the complexity of religious change, whether that change takes place as a sudden or gradual transformation in the life of an individual or as the incremental adjustments of middle-class Protestant culture to the rapidly expanding America with which it claimed to be coextensive. If the vaunted multiculturalism of the Nast images exaggerates the actual diversity of the common school system in the later nineteenth century, it also subtly registers historical changes in the character of American Protestantism. These changes, in large part the result of the white Protes-

tant mainstream's encounter with other religions and with nonwhite Christians, also shaped the course of nineteenth-century literature as white Protestant preaching moved from pulpit to narrative and as nonwhite Christians gained access to print culture.

Although Robert Baird's *Religion in America* classed all non-Christian and marginally Christian faiths among the nonevangelical religions he disparaged, the northeastern, established religions he favored had since the late eighteenth century followed a liberalizing course thanks in part to the influence of writers, among them prominent defectors from mainline Protestantism, who turned to non-Christian religions to register their critique both of Calvinist strictness and of dissension among the various strands of Christianity to which it gave rise. David Reynolds has detailed the ways in which the "Oriental tales" condemned from the pulpit in the late eighteenth and early nineteenth centuries provided their authors as well as their audiences "a convenient camouflage for satirizing orthodoxy and promoting tolerance."[84] In Royall Tyler's *The Algernine Captive*, for example, the New England Presbyterian Updike Underhill learns from his Muslim captors the "gentle precepts" of Islam, among them the "Unity of the Deity" and the infinite mercy of God. In Samuel L. Knapp's *Ali Bey*, a Muslim proselytizer in New England (where he initially lives undiscovered, disguised as a Frenchman) discovers a Christianity "weak, divided, and multitudinous" yet opening along its fault lines "a door to the healthful breeze of truth."[85] In these orientalized representations, Muslims ultimately figure negatively, as enslavers and spies. Although it is Christians who are ostensibly converted, not to Islam but to a gentler and more accommodating Christianity, these narratives also subtly pry their despotic Muslims away from the unifying energies of Islamic faith, now abstracted from its social and human contexts in order to be better assimilated to the strand of Protestant liberalism it inspires.

Such gestures, which drew on the teachings of non-Christian religions while ultimately subordinating them to a form of American religion rendered more expansive by their influence, were repeated throughout the nineteenth century. New England Transcendentalism, whose critiques of dogmatic, institutional forms of Protestantism extended well beyond its original locus among Boston's Unitarian elite, was inspired by its adherents' readings in Buddhism and Hinduism, including Emerson's of the *Bhagavad Gita* and Thoreau's of the *Lotus Sutra*. Encounters with non-Christian religions also contributed to New Thought, mind cure, and other new religious movements of the nineteenth century, whose devotees frequently advocated a form of pan-religious unity that extended the liberal Protestant consensus to include not only America but the entire world. In the extravagant (if somewhat self-annulling) claim of the sometime—Christian Scientist Emma Hopkins, for example, "the remarkable

analogies of the Christian Bible, the Hindu Sacred Books, Egyptian Ancient Teachings, Persian Bible, Chinese Great Learning, Oriental Yohar,
Saga, and many others, show that the whole world has had life teachings
so identical as to make them all subjects for respectful attention and investigation by the thoughtful of our age."[86]

Closer to home, black and Native American spiritualities powerfully
influenced white Protestant culture in ways that gradually if unevenly dis-
lodged the religious hegemony of New England's Calvinist elite. To argue
that the extension of Protestant Christianity to Indians and African
Americans delivered many of these new Christians to what Jon Butler
calls a "spiritual holocaust" is, importantly, to call attention to the oppressive contexts of many black and Indian conversions and to the violence done to the converts' former belief systems and spiritual communities.[87] But such an argument also risks undermining the spiritual and
political agency of these converts, and diminishes the intricacy of what
were, by and large, neither forced nor unthinking assents to, but rather
critical appropriations of, their new faith. What Albert Raboteau calls
"slave religion"—an amalgam of traditions and practices carried over
from Africa, the revisionary Christianity of black churches in Northern
cities, and the religion of Southern white churches—gave involuntary immigrants from different cultures a shared vocabulary and united them in
a common struggle for justice within an environment that offered few
other resources for maintaining dignity amid ongoing violence, pain, and
degradation.[88] Conversion also represented a survival strategy for Indians
whose communities had suffered critical losses. While some Indians
whose communities had been weakened by disease and U.S. territorial
expansion banded with members of other tribes in similar circumstances,
others chose conversion to Christianity as, in part, an alternative to the
loss of cultural and kinship identity that resulted from fusions with other
tribes. "By accepting the Christian minister . . . as the functional equivalent of a native shaman, and by giving traditional meanings to Christian
rites, dogmas, and deities," James Axtell argues, "Indians ensured the
survival of native culture by taking on the protective coloration of the
invaders' religion."[89]

Conversion to Christianity, together with the accession to English literacy it accompanied for some, also provided nonwhite converts with the
resources for calling their white Christian counterparts to confront the
claims of their shared faith.[90] The black abolitionist Maria Stewart, for
example, used her status as a Christian convert to address "the great and
mighty men of America" on common moral ground. "Are not [black
men's] wives, their sons, and their daughters, as dear to them as the white
man's?" Stewart asked. "Certainly, God has not deprived them of the
divine influences of his Holy Spirit, which are the greatest of all blessings,

if they ask him. Then why should man any longer deprive his fellow man of equal rights and privileges?"[91] Other literate, nonwhite Christians found opportunities in print to criticize the unjust practices of whites they saw as Christian only in name. "I do not hesitate to say that . . . the prayers, preaching, and examples of those pretended pious," wrote Pequot Indian and Methodist convert Willliam Apess in his 1836 *Eulogy on King Philip*, "ha[ve] been the foundation of all the slavery and degradation in the American colonies toward colored people." (By "colored," as Karim Tiro demonstrates, Apess designated Indians, African Americans, and on at least one occasion, Jews.) Apess added: "[W]e might suppose that . . . Dr. Mather, so well versed in Scripture, would have known his work better than to have cursed any of God's creatures."[92]

For nonwhite Christians to speak *as Christians*, as in these examples, was implicitly to engage in strategic acts of consensus *and* dissent by invoking a common faith as the grounds for their critique of its white adherents' practices. Of course, such critiques came not only from nonwhite Christians who could read and write English; the deployment of scriptural vocabularies by a largely and forcibly illiterate slave population enabled the black prophetic tradition that emerged from slavery to function as a kind of oral Torah, challenging and expanding the scriptural rhetoric of mainstream churches.[93] In the experiences of nonwhite Christians who articulated their dissent in writing, however, literacy served the dual function of bringing them further into the fold, as socially recognized beings in a world where shared scriptural and narrative forms (e.g., the spiritual autobiography) could be appealed to and circulated, *and* of positioning them, as critics, outside of that center where whiteness, Christianity, and access to the Word were neatly aligned.

The intricately layered subject positions and corresponding narrative strategies of nonwhite Christians who called white Christian culture to account would seem to install these forms of address squarely within an American literary tradition prized for its "dissonan[ce]" and hybridity, its faithfulness to moments of "struggle" and "conflict" between ideologies and cultural positions.[94] According to Leo Marx, such features make *Moby-Dick*, *Huck Finn*, and *Leaves of Grass*, among other works in the American Renaissance canon, "brilliant studies (and expressions) of 'heteroglossia.' " Echoing Bakhtin, Marx argues that the dialogic, "vernacular" style of such works, their incorporation of social and regional dialectal speech and underground ideological discourses, constitutes "not simply a style, but a style with a politics in view": the "apprehension of equality as an ultimate good," and the democratic extension of freedom "*from* the oppression of society" and "*to* establish . . . egalitarian community."[95]

According to Marx, the mere incorporation of black and dialectal regional voices in the great "vernacular" works of nineteenth-century American literature—for example, *Democratic Vistas'* "graft[ing]" of workers' "slang or local song or allusion" to "American poetic expression"—made possible a "national style" that affirmed an "egalitarian faith so radical that we can scarcely credit it today."[96] But different dialogisms, and correspondingly different articulations of freedom and authenticity, structure the address of nonwhite Christian witness and the more canonical literature of democracy. A rather different project than Whitman's of "grafting literacy onto orality," in Harryette Mullen's phrase, animates the writings of Sojourner Truth and Harriet Jacobs, who focus "on a continuum of resistance to oppression available to the illiterate as well as the literate."[97] The narrative requirements for Melville's portrayal of "discursive democracy" may result, as readers have noted, in *Moby-Dick*'s distinctive "polyphony" of voices and genres, its "conflict of fictions" and "double-voiced discourse" that by turns appropriates and undermines authoritative speech;[98] but a different conflict of fictions and a differently double-voiced discourse marked slave testimony that registered the censoring presence of white readers, or spirituals that conveyed coded information on escape from white oppression. In Marx's and like celebrations of American literary democracy, it appears that only by being carried into new, white-authored contexts can such forms as the spiritual or the slave testimony, now enclosed within "Song of Myself," *Huck Finn*, or *Uncle Tom's Cabin*, unambiguously signal freedom.[99]

"Democratizing" incorporations of the voices of racial, regional, and class others characterize not only the established canon of American Renaissance writing but also the works of sentimental and domestic authors. In either context, these incorporations of otherness tend to reinscribe a religious/secular fault line that also demarcates the gendered literary spheres to which these works have traditionally been assigned. That is, male writers of the American Renaissance will typically appeal to the authenticity of the vernacular for their implicit critique of Christianity— Whitman's "little healthy rudeness," Huck's decision to "*go* to hell"[100] — while sentimental and domestic authors are more likely to invoke the vernacular in the voices of ardent, "natural" Christians who make revisionary claims on the social order. This difference reflects a divergent set of responses to the revival movement and to the social retrenchments within middle-class Protestant culture that followed. As evangelical congregations disowned their working-class and nonwhite origins in their bid for middle-class respectability, canonical American Renaissance writers retrieved these cast-off voices to argue middle-class Christianity's failings, while sentimental and domestic writers recurred to a model of Christianity that contained multitudes.

Elizabeth Stuart Phelps's *The Silent Partner,* for example, shows the workings of an intricate dynamic in American evangelicalism, in which the discovery of common life in Christ enables middle-class women to identify across class and race lines, even as the trope of equality in Christ promises that the injustices of class and racial division can be overcome, finally, only through divine intervention. In the novel, the improbable friendship between the wealthy mill owner's daughter Perley Kelso and the orphaned factory worker Sip Garth (who, though white, is also repeatedly described as "black," "brown," or "dark") awakens Perley not only to the miseries of wage slavery, embodied in Sip, but also to her own curtailed freedoms as an upper middle-class woman whose flourishing, in the logic of the novel, depends as much as does Sip's on the caprices of men who profit from the factory system. In the course of the novel, Sip becomes a street preacher while Perley, redeemed from her unfeeling social insularity by way of spiritual identification with the working-class Sip, devotes herself to benevolent activities on behalf of the poor.[101]

This was the trajectory of many middle-class evangelical women who experienced a newfound autonomy in periods of revival, but who ultimately chose to retreat from radicalism in return for social rewards unavailable to those who defiantly continued to preach. For evangelical women whose impulses toward transcendence of their gender- and class-bound roles were ultimately thwarted by the sanctions of middle-class respectability, sympathetic identification with race and class others—"I feel it would be delightful to spend my life teaching the heathen," as Mrs. Mary Mathews wrote to Mrs. Charles Finney in 1831[102]—could serve as a conduit for forbidden desires, a mode of recapturing the liminality of the revival while containing its disruptive potential, a way of participating vicariously in the "age of the common man."

Cathy Davidson argues that the sentimental novel's implicit readers, as well as its writers, were those women for whom novels provided a space for dissenting from those features of white Protestant culture they as women experienced as oppressive.[103] The sentimental novel's promise of a more expansive identity for its implicitly white, Christian, middle-class, and female audience largely resided, moreover, in the presence in its pages of outsiders to this audience, who could voice political and spiritual claims on the broader culture in ways that the novel's intended readers might as themselves be reluctant to own.[104] What the sentimental novel nevertheless *cannot* readily incorporate is the residue of these other subjects' resistance to the sympathetic interventions the novelist purports to exercise on their behalf. A feature of the "rhetoric of selective, socially differentiated understanding" that marks African American and other outsider narratives has often been, as Doris Sommer argues, "an unyielding response to the liberal embrace": "[W]ritten from clearly drawn positions on a chart where only the powerful center can mistake its specificity for universality . . . 'marginal' or 'minority' texts draw boundaries around that arrogant space."[105] Moments of resistance to "the liberal embrace" include Frederick Douglass's silence, in his *Narrative*, on the details of his escape from slavery, or Harriet Jacobs's refusal of emotional identification with the white reader of *Incidents in the Life of a Slave Girl*: "O reader, can you imagine my joy? . . . No, you cannot, unless you have been a slave mother."[106] For a reader like Stowe, however, whose *Key to Uncle Tom's Cabin* registers the profound and ostensibly authenticating debt of her novel of slavery to slave testimonies themselves, such rejections of democratic transparency instead become "lures" to empathy, invitations "to fill in . . . the constitutive gaps" these texts make visible by "assimilat[ing] oneself into the other's culture, just as the other has had to work at negotiating mainstream English."[107]

In *Uncle Tom's Cabin* and elsewhere, Stowe forecloses the possibility of such resistance by figuring the power of sympathy, the capacity to feel *with* others and to know their hearts, as a special quality of blackness. The "freedom" of even enslaved blacks, for Stowe, was their "naturalness," their capacity to feel and love deeply in ways that ostensibly transcend the barriers of race and servitude.[108] In an essay called *Repression*, Stowe argued that "it is natural, Christian, that we fight against the reserve inherent in our Anglo-Saxon nature. . . . We can educate ourselves to it, if we know and feel the necessity; we can make it a Christian duty, not only to love, but to be loving."[109] Eva may teach Topsy to "be good" by loving her, but it is more typically white characters (and audiences) who find liberating life lessons in *Uncle Tom*'s examples of a *slave's* love— for Christ, for family and children, for fellow slaves, for white mistresses and masters.[110]

• • •

American literature differed from European belles-lettres, Larzer Ziff argues, precisely to the degree that U.S. writers "yielded to their untidy America" and conceded that "democracy meant the end of high literature as the world knew it."[111] If American literature's hallmark, as Giles Gunn proposes, is its exemplary "imagination of otherness," and if that imagination, as Philip Fisher suggests, "is democratic in that it experiments with the extension of full and complete humanity to classes of figures from whom humanity has been socially withheld," it would seem that what this imagination of otherness most magnifies is less the scope of humanity than the importance of that sector of Americans with whom "full and complete humanity" is here identified.[112] And if its "devotion to the possibilities of democracy," in F. O. Mathiessen's phrase,[113] is what decisively severed the American literary tradition from the English, that commitment paradoxically furthered the assessment that America is nowhere *more* English than in its power to embrace diversity, to accommodate potentially conflicting positions. Emerson, enumerating America's defining English traits, approvingly quoted Emmanuel Swedenborg: "For the English nation, the best of them are in the centre of all Christians, because they have interior intellectual light. This appears conspicuously in the spiritual world. This light they derive from the liberty of speaking and writing, and thereby of thinking."[114]

In the section titled "Race" in *English Traits*, Emerson joined America to the "British Empire" on the grounds that America's "foreign element, however considerable, is rapidly assimilated."[115] Englishness, according to Emerson, is strong by virtue of its composite character: "Everything English is a fusion of distant and antagonistic elements . . . but collectively a better race than any from which they are derived."[116] *English Traits* ends, of course, in a vision of a weakened England and a transfer of its assimilative strengths to Emerson and his countrymen on "the Allegheny ranges" and "the capes of Massachusetts . . . [by] my own Indian stream."[117] The vaunted power of the heirs of this "mother of nations"[118] to draw energy from a racially and religiously diverse population allies their imagination of democracy to the manifest destiny of the Empire whose command America now assumes: "The English derive their pedigree from such a range of nationalities, that there needs sea-room and land-room to unfold the varieties of talent and character."[119]

PART TWO

Secular Fictions

Chapter Five

FROM ROMANISM TO RACE:

UNCLE TOM'S CABIN

SIMON LEGREE's taunting invitation to "join [his] church" reminds us that the novel routinely credited with abolishing slavery relied for at least part of its force on anxieties surrounding religious conversion.[1] While conversion as the emotional surrender to clarified faith under one or another form of Protestantism remained the norm when Harriet Beecher Stowe was writing *Uncle Tom's Cabin*, as many as seven hundred thousand Americans did join the Roman Catholic Church as converts in the nineteenth century. The middle third of the century also saw the arrival of nearly three million Catholic immigrants, whose perceived intemperance, sexual license, and conspiratorial designs on American institutions animated white Protestant preaching and political action more consistently than did the evils of slavery or racism.[2] That slavery eventually (if barely) displaced "Romanism" as the primary object of American Protestant attentions in the mid-1850s is thanks in large part to *Uncle Tom's Cabin*, whose antislavery arguments draw broadly on a more long-standing anti-Catholic rhetoric for their structure, imagery, and sensational appeal.[3]

This argument will be unremarkable to readers of Jenny Franchot's *Roads to Rome: The Antebellum Protestant Encounter with Catholicism*. Taking the measure of an extraordinary range of texts, including nativist polemics, salacious convent-escape narratives, and the literary works of American Renaissance writers, Franchot argues for the recovery of Roman Catholicism as a "competing voice at the heart of (and on the excluded edges) of antebellum Protestantism." Catholicism, Franchot writes, "performed an integrative function crucial to New England's pursuit of national primacy," with the unintended consequence of an "eventual disintegrative impact, for the attack on Roman Catholicism, in its enumeration of Rome's suspicious charms, often led to an uncomfortable recognition of"—and occasional attempts to remedy—"the spiritual deficiencies and psychological pressures of Protestant culture."[4]

A quick look at publishers' lists, plenary addresses, and journals in American literary and cultural studies would suggest that most students of nineteenth-century America would sooner argue this thesis in racial than religious terms: black voices sound from the center as well as the excluded edges of popular culture, literature, and politics; encounters with African Americans lead to Euro-American self-critique and cultural revitalization; and slavery emerges as an issue of national primacy in response to black challenges to white notions of acceptable social and individual morality. As Shelley Fisher Fishkin writes at the end of *Was Huck Black?*, "Understanding African-American traditions is essential if one wants to understand *mainstream* American literary history."[5] The point is well taken; as Henry Louis Gates has remarked, segregation "is as difficult to maintain in the literary realm as in the civic one."[6] But Fishkin's characterization of white imitative responses to black culture as yielding a kind of luscious jambalaya—"jazzy and improvisational, unpredictable and serendipitous, dynamic and tricky"—risks missing the ways in which dominant power is mobilized in gestures of empathy, improvisation, and imitation.[7] Huck is not, as she suggests, just "signifyin" when he tells his Willie Horton story about Jim; differentials of power govern the ways in which black and white voices, like the flavors in Huck's culinary "barrel of odds and ends," get "swapped around."[8] Moreover, while such projects might in some sense "deconstruct . . . 'race' as a meaningful category,"[9] as Fishkin puts it, they also reinforce the sense that race has historically been the *only* meaningful category in American cultural history, or that religious vocabularies for thinking about difference have left no mark on an avowedly but unevenly secular culture.

Eric Lott reminds us that "blackface songs and skits incorporated Irish brogues and other ethnic dialects, with absolutely no sense of contradiction; blackface, bizarrely enough, was actually used to represent *all* ethnicities on the antebellum stage prior to the development of ethnic types."[10] Eighteenth-century Anglo-America tended more typically to represent its various Others not as black or blackened, however, but as Catholic or Catholicized. In 1741 the supposed leader, later hanged, of an alleged African American plot to burn New York City and murder its white inhabitants was described in Philadelphia papers as a "Romish Priest."[11] In 1776, British aggressions by a "Popish king" were read by white American Protestants as attempts "to stir up the Negroes in the midst of us, to cut our throats at unawares, and to let the Savages and Roman Catholicks like bloodhounds at our backs."[12] "Rome" was furthest from the Protestant elect and so, paradoxically, closest to the Protestant in need of saving grace. The evangelical John Wesley, in moments of self-abasement, could go no lower than to claim kinship with Catholicism: "A murderer convict I come / My vileness to bewail; / By nature born a son of Rome, / A child of wrath and hell." A few stanzas down in the same Methodist hymn comes a more expansive instance of Christlike largesse: "Heathen, and Jews, and Turks, may I / And heretics embrace; / Nor e'en to Rome the love deny / I owe to all the race."[13]

Today, of course, the cultural divides across which that subjectivity-enlarging "embrace" is extended are unlikely to be imagined in exclusively religious terms. Franchot points to a mid-nineteenth-century "shift in the elaboration of cultural difference from religion to race," a movement whose first trajectory, she suggests, "serve[d] the mandates of racial purity, dedicated to the aligning of whites (Catholic or Protestant) against native [nonwhite] cultures," and whose "second, conflicting trajectory serve[d] the dictates of class anxiety, the stratification of New England society into various Protestant masters and Irish Catholic subordinates."[14] Put another way, the racializing of a Protestant religious vocabulary created "whiteness" as a category that might strategically cross religion and ethnicity in the interests of national unity, while also being capable of assigning different ethnic and religious groups to separate races. Thus Catholics might join Protestants in defining their Americanness against the foreignness of nonwhite others, even as many of the post–Civil War discourses that supported the equation of whiteness with Americanness sought to withhold both not just from African Americans but from Catholics, Jews, and all non–Northern European immigrants.[15]

In part, the displacement of threatening otherness from religion onto race calmed fears of instability occasioned by conversion. The beguiled Protestant virgin might enter a "black nunnery" as a Catholic convert; the white woman, in the cultural imaginary of Jim Crow America, is in no similar danger of *becoming* black, whatever her vulnerability to the conspiratorial energies of black sexuality.[16] At the same time, just as the most marked episodes of antebellum anti-Catholicism took place against a backdrop of Gothic revival architecture, a thriving industry of Protestant tourism to Catholic Rome, and the rise of the novel and other cultural forms long condemned as "Romanish" by New England Calvinism, so also the dynamics of attraction and disavowal that structured white interactions with blackness, as Lott has argued, supported and were supported by Jim Crow. The remapping of cultural difference from religion onto race preserved anti-Catholicism's mandate that the Other's otherness be contained while remaining available for appropriation, that lines of difference be emphatically *there* but also open to strategic traversals.

But how does a Protestant vocabulary of religious otherness become a secular vocabulary of racial otherness? More specifically, how does "blackness" come to name what, to use a phrase of Edward Said's, had been the "battery of desires, repressions, investments, and projections" formerly and elsewhere signaled by "Catholicism"?[17] Occasionally in *Uncle Tom's Cabin* (the "Mediterranean" St. Clare plantation scenes, for example), the same habits of description will accommodate slaveholders as easily as slaves, as though Catholic, Southern, and African modes of the exotic and erotically charged were equally useful for setting against a white New England Protestantism marked by industry, thrift, and emotional reserve.[18] But even the imagined rescue, under Protestant auspices, of slaves from (a Catholicized) slavery proved opportune for relodging Catholicism's meanings in "blackness." Stowe and like-minded abolitionists sought not only to free slaves but also to strengthen them in the forms of Protestant Christianity.[19] To evangelize the slave, in this model, was to secure not only his conformity to a recognizable spiritual path but also his commitment to the work ethic (witness the roster of industrious free black laborers that ends *Uncle Tom's Cabin*) and to the preservation of the bourgeois family (if often only as its servant; think of the sequels for Topsy, Eliza, and their models in the *Key*). In this version of the trajectory from slavery to freedom, however, the assimilation of emancipated slaves into the spiritual, economic, and familial structures of Anglo-American Protestantism left an unassimilable bodily difference. And within a white Protestant culture long engaged in constituting itself against the magnified corporeality of a Catholic Other, the embodied otherness of free black persons—read not only as the real or imagined difference of color but as the putative physical *excess* of their lived relation to worship, work, and home—could not fail to signify within the terms of an existing vocabulary of attraction and repulsion, fear and desire.[20]

If, as I argue, *Uncle Tom's Cabin* sheds light on this transformation, it is not because Stowe made Rome her particular enemy in this or other works; indeed her ironic and temperate references to Catholicism seem designed to moderate the militant anti-Catholicism of her father's *Plea for the West* or her brother Edward's *Papal Conspiracy Exposed*. Rather, the very ordinariness of Stowe's religious attitudes ("not exceptional but representative," as Jane Tompkins has said of *Uncle Tom's Cabin*) make them more likely agents of cultural formation than Edward or Lyman Beecher's vitriolic attacks.[21] The visibility of late twentieth-century efforts to "restore" Stowe's novel to the literary canon notwithstanding, no text in American literary history has been as *relentlessly* canonical—as widely translated, as diversely commodified, as enduringly iconic—as *Uncle Tom's Cabin*.[22] The thousands of pirated editions, lampoons, and stage productions, which proliferated even before the novel had finished running in serial form, indexed sectional and class frictions leading up to the Civil War, which was itself read, by Abraham Lincoln among others, through the lens of *Uncle Tom*.[23] The power of the novel to reach unprecedented numbers of people—it was the first American novel to sell a million copies—resulted in the reprinting of earlier works by Stowe, and vastly enlarged the audience for her nonfiction and subsequent novels, which were typically compared, often unfavorably, to *Uncle Tom's Cabin*.

In this sense, discussions of American cultural change in the latter half of the nineteenth century, as well as of Stowe's career in its entirety, are largely discussions of the afterlife of *Uncle Tom's Cabin*. It was, as Emerson is said to have put it, "the book that encircled the globe." Its ocean-crossing—one might say, imperialist—career was established in Britain, where it initially had a far larger run than in the United States. This was thanks in part to the status of copyright law in the mid-nineteenth century, which made it cheaper for British publishers to print American works (and vice versa), but also to Stowe's careful nurturing of her English readership and to the "reciprocal moral surveillance" that bound white North Atlantic Protestants in shared projects of expansion and reform.[24] It is largely as a self-consciously Anglo-American production that I read *Uncle Tom's Cabin* and its role in translating the discourse of "Romanism" into a discourse of race.

ROMANISM AT HOME

Appeals to transatlantic Anglo-Saxon solidarity that sustained the anti-slavery efforts of American evangelicals and the imperial projects of Victorian Britain were also central to anti-Catholic sentiments in British America and to nineteenth-century revivals of anti-Catholicism on both sides of the ocean. When Stowe compares the slave's unpaid labor to the tortures of the Inquisition (403–4),[25] or Lyman Beecher, in a different register, charges the Catholic Church with bringing "debasement and slavery to those who live under it,"[26] both signal their debt to an Anglo-American narrative of freedom that set Protestantism, the Hanoverian succession, and love of liberty against Catholicism, the Jacobites, and "slavery," a noun that enjoyed a long career as a metaphor for endangered self-government at a time when few colonists went on record as being troubled by racial bondage

Slavery could be seen in the Roman Catholic doctrine of transubstantiation, which elicited Jonathan Mayhew's defense of "the common rights of seeing, hearing, touching, smelling, tasting; all which popery attacks and undermines . . . and would take . . . from us, as a means of making us dutiful sons, or rather wretched slaves of the church."[27] Slavery was also the message to be read in the territorial realignments that followed the Seven Years' War; in a 1765 broadside the Philadelphia printer Benjamin Mecom warned of "the infernal Monster, called slavery," who "will first persuade you to sin and then send you to the pope of degenerate *Rome*, for absolution. . . . Behold slavery afar off! he bends his Course this Way from Louisiana!"[28] A 1774 *Address to the People of Great Britain by the Continental Congress* described "Catholic emigrants from Europe" as "fit instruments in the hands of power, to reduce the ancient free Protestant Colonies to the same state of slavery with themselves."[29]

In the rhetoric of the British colonies on the cusp of Independence, the "power to reduce us to slavery" was variously imagined as belonging to the Pope, the French and Spanish colonies, the British crown, or all three.[30] In 1773, toleration by the British government of a Roman Catholic bishop in Quebec met with accusations by Massachusetts republicans that Parliament had appointed "courts of Inquisition . . . as arbitrary, and terrable [sic] as those under the Pope's Jurisdiction."[31] The closing of Boston Harbor by the British in 1774 brought forth an advertisement for the *Master-Key to Popery*, a book "highly necessary to be kept in every Protestant family in this country; that they may see to what a miserable state the people are reduced in all arbitrary and tyrannical governments, and be thereby excited to stand on their guard against the infernal machinations of the British ministers, and their vast *host* of tools, emissaries, etc., etc., sent hither to propagate the principles of Popery and Slavery, which go hand in hand as inseparable companions."[32]

Although American vocabularies Catholicizing Britain were briefly revived during the War of 1812, the effect of transatlantic Protestant discourses thereafter was to downplay the two nations' conflicts and to emphasize their shared religious values and commitment to reform.[33] This was especially the case among evangelical antislavery activists.[34] Following the lead of the British Presbyterian George Bourne, the anti-Catholic author and abolitionist whose *The Book and Slavery Irreconcilable* led to his election to the board of the American Antislavery Society, career abolitionists in Britain came increasingly to America to continue the successes of the antislavery movement at home. Both Arthur Tappan, president of the American Antislavery Society, and Theodore Dwight Weld, the Lane Seminary rebel whose *Slavery as It Is* guided Stowe in writing *Uncle Tom*, reported being converted to abolition by British evangelicals; in 1837 Tappan wrote to the British abolitionist George Thompson to ask that Britain stand with the North in imposing on the South "the moral embargo of the civilized world."[35]

Among Protestant antislavery activists in both countries the anti-Catholic impulse was widely shared.[36] The splintering of the transatlantic Evangelical Alliance over slavery in 1846 cemented Anglo-American antislavery bonds that had been nurtured in a context of shared opposition to the Oxford movement, Irish emigration to England and the United States, and the expansion of Catholic missionary efforts.[37] One British abolitionist explained the existence of American slavery by pointing out that the Roman Catholic, who "condemned a Protestant to be burned alive" and delighted in torturing "the follower of Mahomet or Manu," had nothing worse in store for the African: "when it occurred to the Spaniards, that the tropical regions of the new hemisphere . . . might perhaps be profitably cultivated by seizing Negroes in Africa, and transporting them to America, the cruelty or the injustice of thus treating the Negro was not an element in the deliberation."[38] For their part, antebellum Anglo-Protestants often made England the enemy of all tyranny, slave or Catholic. To the American anti-Catholic Nicholas Murray, England was the "open and noblest antagonist of the Vatican in the earth";[39] to abolitionist Charles Sumner, there was "no power . . . so fixed [as England] beyond the possibility of retreat or change in its opposition to Slavery, whatever shape it may assume."[40]

At least some of the shapes that slavery could assume were legible in the terms of a long-standing linkage between Catholicism and captivities of various kinds. The British edition of George Bourne's voyeuristic convent exposé *Lorette, or the History of Louise, Daughter of a Canadian Nun, Exhibiting the Interior of Female Convents* identified whites in slave states as hereditary Catholics; Bourne's *Picture of Slavery in the United States of America*, meanwhile, likened slave quarters in the American South to "the dungeons of the Popish Inquisition."[41] Weld's *Slavery as It Is* begins by comparing self-described Christian slave owners to Louis XIV, who, "when from the English channel to the Pyrenees the mangled bodies of the protestants were dragged on reeking hurdles by a shouting populace," continued to proclaim himself "His most *Christian* majesty."[42]

The Catholicizing of slaveholders by British and Northern evangelicals preserved the illusion of a unified Protestant America even as Southern Protestants had "virtually seceded from their national communions," as Eugene Genovese puts it, over the issue of the biblical judgment of slavery.[43] For Northern antislavery Protestants like Bourne and Horace Mann, the literalism of Southern Protestants who read divine sanction in scriptural references to slavery could be viewed as "Jesuitical ingenuity of corruption" and the failure to bring the letter of the law, "Protestant fashion, to the test of individual judgment and conscience."[44] The "Jesuitical" leanings of Southern churches, according to Bourne, directly licensed the "multiform incests, polygamy, adultery, and other uncleannesses" that kept the slave states in the condition of what Bourne, together with Wendell Phillips and Garrison's *Liberator,* referred to as "one vast brothel," a term Bourne and others also routinely applied to the Catholic Church and its convents.[45] The brothel, whose immoralities (like slavery's) disrupt both home and marketplace, made a fitting marker for the religious faith that Edward Beecher and others spoke of as "the great whore."[46] The Bible verse routinely affixed to convent escape narratives and other anti-Catholic tracts—"Come out of her my people, that ye be not partakers of her sins, and that ye receive not of her plagues" (Rev. 18:4)—was also the proof text of the Garrisonian "comeouter" movement, which appealed to Protestants whose churches welcomed slaveholders to separate themselves "from a contaminated religious body."[47]

A more genteel Northern rhetoric framed the opposition between Prot-estant New England and a discursively Catholicized South as the battle of Puritan versus Celt (or Cavalier), the latter "impulsive, impassioned, tending strongly toward a sensuous ritual and centralized priesthood and empire," but providentially capable of becoming "Americanized in time, if only we let him be."[48] In this view, represented by James Russell Lowell, among others, anti-Catholicism could be chided for deflecting attention from the more pressing task of abolishing slavery, which "exercise[d] a more complete spiritual tyranny than ever the pope did in the palmiest days of his power." "How long will it be," Lowell asked, "before we are able to see as clearly the atrocities which are daily erected before our eyes as those which have been dead and buried for centuries?" At the same time, since slavery and "Popery" were "co-partners . . . in sham," Lowell declared it impossible to "encourage resistance against the one without stimulating it also against the other," a view that secured the demise of slavery in the providential defeat of an allegedly "dead and buried" Ca-tholicism. "The fanaticism of the Abolitionists," Lowell wrote, "has re-tarded emancipation, just in the same way that Luther retarded the Refor-mation. . . . [S]lavery has nothing behind it but the sheer precipice, nothing before it but the inevitable retributive Doom."[49]

Within Stowe's own family, responses to Catholicism ran from vituper-ative censure to genteel "tolerance" to imitative (if finally disavowed) de-sire, and drew varying degrees of association between the Roman church and slaveholding culture. According to Charles Beecher in *The God of the Bible Against Slavery*, "*Any* system . . . which darkens the mind, and tends to prevent repentance, and faith, and holy living, must in the highest degrees incur the wrath of God"; since "[a]ll Protestants admit this princi-ple as applied to Romanism[,] consistency requires them to admit it as applied to slavery."[50] Edward Beecher was converted to antislavery by the murder of Elijah Lovejoy, the abolitionist martyr and unwavering anti-Catholic whose torch Beecher carried as manager of the Illinois Anti-Slav-ery Society and as author of *The Papal Conspiracy Exposed and Protes-tantism Defended in Light of Reason, History, and Scripture*.[51] Catharine Beecher, though acknowledging Catholicism as a "false and slavish faith," routinely compared herself to a Mother Superior, referred to Protestant single woman teachers as Sisters of Mercy, and based her expanded con-ception of motherhood (which extended even the single woman's influ-ence from home and family to school, hospital, and nation) on the model of convents and their concentric networks of activity and support.[52]

The most singularly anti-Catholic of Stowe's immediate family was, of course, her father. Lyman Beecher's *Plea for the West* portrayed American Catholics as a "poor, uneducated, reckless mass of infuriated animalism" ruled by "an absolute spiritual dominion in corrupt alliance with political despotism—displaying their perverting power and acting out their own nature."[53] *A Plea for the West* was based on sermons delivered in Boston on August 11, 1834 and widely credited with inciting the destruction of the Ursuline convent at Charlestown by a Protestant mob the following night. Inflamed by warnings of Catholicism's sinister designs on Protestantism, patriotism, and female purity, the working-class rioters dragged unclothed convent pupils from their beds to effect their involuntary "escape," tore down walls in search of the convent's alleged prisoner, and pulled the bodies of five dead nuns from their coffins before burning the convent to the ground. Beecher later contended that "not an individual in the mob, probably, heard the sermon or knew of its delivery"; his avowed ignorance of the Protestant rioters allowed him to direct his censure toward the (unsuccessful) Catholic efforts for redress: "Has it come to this, that the capital of New England has been thrown into consternation by threats of a Catholic mob, and that her temples and mansions stand only through the forbearance of a Catholic bishop?"[54]

Stowe's response to outbreaks of anti-Catholicism in her family was typically to mock their stridency, if not their general sentiment. While Lyman Beecher railed against the beast of papacy from his pulpit at Lane, Stowe won praise from Bishop Purcell of Cincinnati for the comparatively mild depictions of Catholicism in her *Geography for Children*. She urged Henry Ward Beecher's Indiana congregation to welcome the single Protestant woman teachers who had dared to take on the Jesuits—"one bright well-trained free born Yankee girl is worth two dozen of your nuns who have grown up like potatoe [*sic*] sprouts in the shades of a convent"—yet she also cheerfully nicknamed the Beecher family domicile the "Presbyterian nunnery." Though not above berating Jesuit educators or broadcasting the haplessness of Irish Catholic servants, Stowe increasingly poked fun at Protestant vigilance, caricaturing those who formed "Committee[s] of Supervision" for the inspection of convents, or who viewed the communal rituals that drew her to the Episcopal Church as "only an insidious putting forth of one paw of the Scarlet Beast of Rome, [which] . . . if not vigorously opposed . . . tooth and claw, would yet be upon their backs."[55]

Stowe's moderation on Catholic questions might usefully be viewed as a way of negotiating a troublesome gender terrain. As Anne Norton notes, the antebellum Protestant ascription of femininity to the Catholic Church assumed forms "ranging from rape to the image of the woman armed."[56] Lovejoy, for example, warned of "the stealthy, cat-like step, the hyena grin, with which the 'Mother of Abominations' was approaching the Fountain of Protestant Liberty, that she might cast into it the poison of her incantations."[57] Although "respectable" anti-Catholic writings were widely read by women and men in both England and America, more lurid narratives were sometimes addressed (at least overtly) to men alone:

one 1852 advertisement warned that "Ladies and Youth [were] positive-ly prohibited" from attending a lecture titled "Popish Confession and Priestcraft Exposed," since "some awful disclosures [would] be made."[58]

The allusion was to Maria Monk's *Awful Disclosures of the Hotel Dieu Nunnery*, professedly the autobiography of a self-styled "escaped nun" that had by 1852 sold over three hundred thousand copies. Monk's narra-tive, in fact largely the work of George Bourne and other Protestant cler-gymen, identified a Catholic or Catholicized femininity both with the "Mother of Abominations," in the person of a carnal Mother Superior, and with the duped vulnerability of the young postulants, many of them converts, whom the Roman church had reduced to the condition of prosti-tutes and slaves. Protestant responses to the Ursuline convent riot, which contributed notoriety to Monk's book, similarly staked the range for a nativist understanding of femininity between what a Maine editorial called the "defenceless[ness]" of victims in need of Protestant protection and rescue, on one hand, and on the other the dangerous independence of the Mother Superior, whom Charlestown citizens, marking the first anniversary of the riot, planned to parade in effigy and riddle with bul-lets.[59] Stowe's genteel anti-Catholicism, which mocked the nuns as well as their Protestant detractors, allowed her to sidestep an ideology of gen-der that was typically elaborated with reference to the presumed threat of immigrant assaults on Protestant freedoms, and that vested sexual dan-ger and the concomitant requirement of passivity not only in women but in a despised alien population.

THE REFORMATION OF SLAVERY

Against rumors of foreign Catholic conspiracy, more moderate Protestant voices affirmed that "[o]ur country is safe enough, if we instruct the whole people, especially the immigrant portion of them . . . in the true principles of government, teach them the differences between intelligent liberty and mere licentiousness, [and] place in their hands the Bible and the constitu-tion of the republic."[60] Since the primary sites for the cultivation of "intel-ligent liberty" were the Protestant home and common school, education for American citizenship fell increasingly to Protestant mothers and teach-ers. In Stowe's *Geography for Children*, for example, tranquil scenes of reading and prayer in Protestant New England offset violent images of "heathen" and Catholic countries.[61] In this lavishly illustrated children's book, Spaniards torture Mexicans, Hindus burn their widows alive, and American Indians nail their infants to the wall. While a blue-eyed New England girl learns to read at the knee of her pretty schoolteacher, her dark-skinned counterpart in Catholic Portugal watches as her family is swallowed alive in the Lisbon earthquake. To the first image, the caption reads: "See what a pretty schoolhouse that is; see that sweet looking lady with a book!" To the second: "See the hands and arms of her brother who is trying to escape from the pit. . . . There are dreadful noises coming out of the earth, mingling with the shrieks and cries of the distracted people."[62]

The book the New England children are learning to read is evidently a Bible, the "reverence" for which, along with "good schools" and "industrious habits," distinguishes the "descendants of the Pilgrim fathers" from other contenders for citizenship. Wherever the Bible is unknown, Stowe's *Geography* asserts, "females are despised and cruelly treated," and "there is no such thing as liberty." Stowe's *Geography*, reprinted after the success of *Uncle Tom*, keys Bible reading to the cultivation of myriad freedoms, including those of women, slaves, conscience, and the market; thus "no people in the world have been more prosperous in every kind of business than those in New England, for God always makes those most prosperous who are most obedient to his laws in the Bible."[63]

In addition to nations "where the Bible is not known at all," Stowe's *Geography* discusses "Roman Catholics or papists": "They believe that [the pope] cannot make mistakes about anything in religion, and that he has a right to tell them what to believe and what to do. . . . They believe in the Bible, but generally are not allowed to read it." The position of the American South in this text is analogous to that of Catholic countries: impoverished or else enervated by wealth, nominally Christian yet oppressively hierarchical, ignorant, and Bible-poor. Spain, for example, "cursed" by the wealth it plundered from Mexico and Peru, "has no schools for the common people, the Bible is not allowed to be read by them, and their rulers are oppressive and unjust." Nor can "common schools . . . flourish in the slave states, because the white people live so far apart on their plantations, and the colored people are not allowed to learn to read." In Catholic Italy, where "people have few schools, are not allowed to have the Bible, and are oppressed and neglected by most of their rulers," they "[i]n consequence . . . are much degraded, and the greater portion lives in indolence and vice." So also white inhabitants of slaveholding states, "seeing that labor is disgraceful, become shiftless and indolent, and their children grow up in indolence and sloth."[64]

Stowe's *Geography* was typical of antebellum textbooks in its endorsement of Protestant imperial aims: Christianity now contends with fatalistic Turks, debased Chinese, and African Moors who buy white slaves from Barbary pirates, but "[i]f all men read the Bible and would obey it perfectly, this would be a delightful world indeed."[65] Stowe's portrait of evangelization included slaveholding populations among the "nations" whose redemption was prefigured not only by the exodus and conquest, or the resurrection of Christ, but also by what one history textbook called the "rais[ing] up [of] the immortal Luther" to deliver a Catholic Europe "buried," "like Chaldea of old . . . in sin, in ignorance, in superstition, and in idolatry."[66] Occasionally, Northern evangelicals figured the entire union as an unredeemed nation for harboring slavery within it.[67] More typically, as in *Uncle Tom's Cabin*, the South alone is likened to the heathen nations, and Protestant free soil, whether in Britain or Ohio, to the promised land (446, 91). Defending her graphic depictions of Southern violence in *Uncle Tom*, Stowe wrote in the *Key* that "when our missionaries first went to India, it was esteemed a duty among Christian nations to make themselves acquainted with the cruelties and atrocities of idolatrous worship, as a means of quickening our zeal to send them the gospel."[68]

Applied to the South, the evangelical discourse of "heathen nations" effectively rendered slaves and their owners continuous in their difference, potentially figured as both religious and racial, from the Protestant North. As American anti-Catholic vocabularies could be directed simultaneously against two national Others, a foreign despotic power and a resident immigrant population, so antislavery discourses could find their targets in both the slave power (according to Salmon P. Chase, a "distinct, independent, aristocratic power in the government, naturally opposed to the temper and spirit of our institutions") and the slave population (according to Stowe's *Key*, "a class degraded by servitude, ignorant, indolent, deceitful, provoking, as slaves almost necessarily are, and always must be").[69] The charge that the domestic slave trade had, as Horace Mann put it, "converted the slave states into another Africa" censured the South for its blackness as well as its immorality and excluded slave states from what Nicholas Murray, commending the "advancing influence of Protestantism" represented by the extension of Anglo-American power at home and abroad, called the "white spots on the moral map of the world."[70] Thus both the British magazine *Blackwood's* and the American *National Era* could look past antiblack and anti-Catholic rioting in the North to contrast "the moral power of Boston, thrilling with peace, to the violence of New Orleans and St. Louis."[71]

New Orleans, home of Augustine St. Clare, offered itself to the Northern imagination as a microcosm of the unredeemed world. According to *The Manhattaner in New Orleans*, it was "the Calcutta of America," an apt "locality for a congress of nations."[72] *New Orleans as It Is*, written on the model of Weld's *Slavery as It Is*, represented the city as "a living spectacle of almost every nation, kindred, and tongue."[73] In the terms of a cultural narrative known in *Uncle Tom's Cabin* to visiting cousin Ophelia and her neighbors in Vermont, New Orleans—Catholic and Latin rather than Protestant and Anglo-Saxon—was as remote from New England as the "Sandwich Islands, or anywhere among the heathen" (188), a place where "men of all nations" (386) mingled blood as well as tongues in their various careers as Sabbath-breakers, drunkards, slave traders, and whoremongers. It was Catholic moral laxity that resulted, according to chapter titles in *New Orleans as It Is*, in all manner of "Illegitimate Families," "Concubinage," "Kept Mistresses," and "Amalgamation."[74]

Are the St. Clares Catholic? A number of readers infer that they are, despite the complicating circumstances of cousin Ophelia's Calvinism (presumably shared by St. Clare's New England father), of his Huguenot mother, or of Ophelia and Marie St. Clare's joint attendance at the Protestant church where a Dr. G. preaches proslavery sermons.[75] Yet the St. Clares are surely discursively Catholicized, even in the attribution of no religion to their household (211, 217–18):[76] St. Clare's enervation and fondness for poetry and drink, his wife's vanity and scheming passivity, the sensuous gardens and interiors of their home, the statuettes, pictures, and trinkets in Eva's room: all are familiar figures in the lush and dangerous landscape of "Catholicism" as constituted in the Protestant North.[77] Perhaps the nominal Protestantism of this household is meant to invite a mutual recognition between Northern antislavery Sinclairs and Southern slave-owning St. Clares that a less equivocal Romanizing of the South would obstruct. At the same time, Stowe's attribution of a Catholic identity (if one finally narrowly evaded) to the New Orleans St. Clares frees her desire to represent slave owners in their best light from too-contaminating sympathies. As St. Clare's Huguenot mother could sweetly sing the Latin hymns of the Mass while apparently remaining unconverted by them, so Stowe's own rendering of the South's ambivalent allures might be, like her assessment of Longfellow's in *Evangeline*, "dyed rich" in foreign "cathedral . . . tints," but loyal finally to the "strong dominant colors" of New England home.[78]

Uncle Tom's Cabin positions both slaves and slaveholders as citizens of the Catholicized "nations" of the South. If turbaned Topsy and the plantation's Mediterranean architecture strike the Yankee Ophelia as equally "heathenish" (278), Tom has an innate appreciation of his French- and Spanish-influenced surroundings, he being, qua Negro, an "exotic of the most gorgeous and superb countries in the world" (195). Tom presides majestically over his duties at the Moorish plantation like the "Bishop of Carthage" (212), that is, like his master Augustine's patron saint; he loves Eva with the reverence of a Catholic for his icons, "gaz[ing] on her as an Italian sailor gazes on his image of the child Jesus" (302).

If slaves and slaveholders alike partake of the sensuous pleasures available to Catholics and other "exotics," however, they are also equally vulnerable to Romanism's instability and poisonous excesses. The malevolent energies of this household's unlocalizable Catholicism threaten to pull Eva's statuettes and faithful credulity dangerously near to Legree's "witch things" (432) and Cassy's "partial insanity" (466),[79] the beautiful strains of *Dies Irae* (363) to the sinister cadences of Virgil's "*informis, ingens, cui lumen ademptum*" (379), or interracial affections (whose display Ophelia disdains) to the sexual exploitation of slaves by their masters.[80] In its darker aspects, Catholicism no longer figures that to which slaves are instinctively drawn but that from which they are providentially ordained to escape: Stowe compares George Harris to an unsung Kossuth, and runaway slaves to refugees from Catholic Austria.[81]

In the South as elsewhere in the heathen world, the providential Christianizing of the nations depended on Bible literacy. In North Atlantic evangelical circles, the distribution of Bibles was made the key to ending both slavery and Romanism: the aim of the abolitionist "Bibles for Slaves" campaign was to "publiciz[e] the refusal of southerners to allow slaves the spiritual comfort of the Bible," thus assimilating the white South's withholding of literacy from slaves to the desires of Catholic immigrants to have their children excused from Protestant religious exercises in public schools.[82] In *Uncle Tom's Cabin*, Eva hatches a plan to introduce common schools to the South, where slaves would learn to "read their own Bible, and write their own letters, and read letters that are written to them" (310). Reading, according to the dying Eva, is the key to heaven, to becoming Christians and "angels forever" (338), and if Eva's reading lessons win no new converts, her pupil Tom's tireless bodying forth of scripture ("all the moral and Christian virtues bound in black morocco, complete" [179]) eventually bring the "ignorant heathen" (585) on Legree's plantation, even the "savage men" Quimbo and Sambo (482), to the cause of Christ.

Beyond Bible-ignorance, intemperance, Sabbath-breaking, and the urge to "mutilate our common schools," antebellum Protestant discourses frequently charged Catholics with assaults on domesticity.[83] In Maria Monk's narrative, nun, prostitute, and child-murderer become the overlapping markers of femininity loosed from Protestant motherhood. Others cautioned that no Catholic priest recognized Protestant marriages as valid, and might consider any woman not married in the Roman rite legitimate sexual prey. Catholicism's dirty secret, like slavery's, was its designs on the family.[84] Endless probings of Catholic "secrecy" generated still further readings of Catholic antidomesticity: whether in the moral decay of its institutions, the darkness of mind that descends on those seduced by its doctrines, or the beguiling exteriors and corrupt recesses of its convents and confessionals, Catholicism is strongly associated with disorderly interiors, an association to which Stowe gives surprisingly literal expression in her representations of Catholics as terrible housekeepers.[85]

Uncle Tom's Cabin reproduces Catholicism's disordered interiors as slavery's disordered interiors. Legree lives among the ruins of overcivility, his surroundings, like Cassy's past, a cautionary tale of thriftlessness, sensuality, and excess. The word Stowe applies most often to Cassy—a Catholic who seems to Tom "an embodiment of the temptation with which he had been wrestling" (419)—is "wild": her history is "wild, painful, and romantic" (409), her spirit "wild [and] unsettled" (462), her "wild eyes" (419) lit by the "lurid fires" (462) a "wild and peculiar glare" (461). Often Cassy's wildness tends toward "raving insanity" (431); at other moments "wildness" names the immense and menacing power of a New Orleans *voodooienne*: "'Dog!' she said [to Legree], 'touch *me*, if you dare! I've power enough, yet, to have you torn by the dogs, burnt alive, cut to inches! I've only to say the word!' " (411).

Beginning in the 1840s, reports of voodoo in New Orleans, by then a prestigious center (along with Haiti and Cuba) of Afro-Catholic religious syncretism, appeared among the evidence cited by anti-Catholic writers for the familiar argument that Protestantism alone was truly Christian, and the Roman church a corruption whose members—"Popish Cannibals, God-Makers, and God-Eaters"—were naturally attracted to the ritual forms of "savage" peoples.[86] The suggestions of voodoo in *Uncle Tom's Cabin* also anticipate the Know-Nothing conspiracy theory that Catholic interests would succeed in annexing Cuba, Haiti, and Brazil to Mexico, making the larger part of North America Catholic and black.[87] But the threat that the considerable resources of African American spirituality, already well used by white evangelicals, might slide irretrievably to the side of the rival church looms only fragmentarily before Cassy's "wildness" turns finally toward the innocent and spiritually arable, the blank slate of the heathen ripe for Christian conversion.

Cassy's story repeats a trajectory familiar from the captive nun's tale. With the plantation as carceral cloister and Legree as lecherous priest, convent-educated Cassy incarnates both of the problematic femininities given voice in the genre of convent "rescue."[88] Cassy's crazed vulnerability recalls the emotionally disturbed Ursuline novice Sister Mary John, the "Mysterious Lady" of Boston newspaper accounts whose reputed plight—"detained in th[e] Convent against her will . . . immured in a dungeon and there cruelly treated"—was a subject of Lyman Beecher's inflammatory sermons.[89] At the same time, Cassy in her autonomy resembles the Charlestown Mother Superior Mary St. George, "the sauciest woman I ever heard talk," according to one of the riot's perpetrators, who claimed she had only to say the word for Bishop Fenwick of Boston to unleash thousands of angry Irishmen on the mob.[90] By the novel's final chapters, however, Cassy takes her place as a "devout and tender Christian" mother (500), the escaped nun (or beguiled convert) soothed and returned to the domestic hearth. Even as Legree is credited with the intuitive knowledge that slavery begins, and is sustained, as an assault on motherhood, so Cassy's redeemability is signaled earlier in the novel by her recognition of domesticity as the path of freedom from Catholic captivity. "I wanted only one thing," she says of the man whose mistress she'd been in New Orleans, "I did want him to *marry* me" (424). The novel's ending restores Cassy to the scene of her domestic happiness, alongside child and grandchild "in a small, neat tenement, in the outskirts of Montreal" (497).

Canada has a special resonance within American anti-Catholicism: the convent exposés of Maria Monk and George Bourne were set there, and the Ursulines whose Charlestown convent was destroyed were forced to flee there. The Canadian setting of Monk's and other popular convent narratives both distanced and magnified the threat of Catholicism to Anglo-Saxon culture in the United States by demonstrating that Catholic power could flourish even in territories ruled by the British crown.[91] The future of Canada—French or British? Catholic or Protestant?—was vocally contested on both sides of the border.[92] While U.S. Catholics looked to Canada as their spiritual ally, antislavery Protestants like Lowell advocated the annexation of Canada as a way to "reduce slaveholders to a more odious and contemptible minority." Far from alienating the British, according to Lowell, admitting Canada to the Union would in fact strengthen "the ties of ancestry and of a common past, so rudely snapped between the Mother Country and the Thirteen Colonies." As Lowell envisioned it, the annexation of Canada and the consequent intensification of Anglo-Saxon antislavery sentiment in the United States (despite the "very perplexing" presence of the "French element") promised to reunite the Mother Country, England, with the "Daughter it had disinherited and disowned."[93]

The mother-daughter reunion of Cassy and Eliza (Cassy and George, recall, have managed to "pass" into freedom as Creole French and Spanish, respectively) figures more ambiguously for the Anglo-Saxonizing of the Union: if George can, presumably, wash the Catholicizing burnt cork from his face once in Canada, still the imperializing aims of Stowe's Protestant America require his further removal to "glorious Africa," and its reclamation by this "Christian patriot" not as "an Elysium of romance, but . . . *a field of work*" (504). On one hand, the radiant domesticity of this family's tidy quarters in Montreal helps to displace the Catholic foreignness of a New World city renowned for its Romish Indians, haunted convents, and awful disclosures. On the other, as a stop en route to a Protestant black Africa, their sojourn in Montreal imaginatively removes Catholics beyond national borders and former slaves beyond national concern. Conversion, martyrdom, the globalization of the work ethic: these were the solutions of the popularly appointed "Martin Luther of slavery."[94]

LOVE OF FREEDOM AND THE ANGLO-SAXON RACE

Shortly after finishing the novel Stowe left for England, where she had sent advance copies of *Uncle Tom* to antislavery spokesmen, and on whose soil (including its colonies) it had by the end of 1853 sold ten times more copies than were sold at home.[95] English readers, for their part, were eager to claim Stowe's novel for English literature and that literature's global career. According to the British editor of *The Christian Diadem*, Stowe's "sanctified genius has secured for her more than a British, or even European fame—for the name of Harriet Beecher Stowe will be known and loved and honored wherever, and as long as, our language and our literature exist."[96] *Uncle Tom's Cabin*, according to the *Westminster Review*, which only "a few months ago was appearing as a *feuilleton* of a weekly newspaper in the states" was now a "part of the history of two mighty nations, influencing their feelings, and through them surely, though indirectly, their actions."[97] In England, according to Clare Midgeley, the visiting Mrs. Stowe quickly came to symbolize white missionary power "to bring freedom and Christianity to grateful black slaves," a "racially based power" that crossed gender and class lines.[98]

In America, meanwhile, the novel and its author continued to rise in national prominence as Stowe's earlier works were reprinted and *Uncle Tom's Cabin* took to the stage. William Lloyd Garrison wrote of a staged version of *Uncle Tom* that "it was a sight worth seeing, those ragged, coatless men and boys in the pit (the very material of which mobs are made) cheering the strongest and the sublimest anti-slavery sentiments. . . . I wish every abolitionist in this land could see this play as I saw it, and exult as I did that, when haughty Pharisees will not testify against slavery, the very *stones* are crying out!"[99] On her return from England, Stowe told the Duchess of Sutherland, she used money from the penny offering (a collection taken up by British women to offset Stowe's losses from unauthorized British editions of *Uncle Tom*) to block the Nebraska bill, the substance of which nevertheless passed into law as the Kansas-Nebraska Act on May 26, 1854.[100]

Remarkably, given the intensity of Free-Soil agitation between 1853 and 1856, the fastest-growing political party during this period was not the antislavery Republicans but the anti-Catholic Know-Nothings. As Michael Holt has suggested, to "many in the North, the major threat in 1854 was not that the presence of black slaves might keep them out of Kansas and Nebraska, but that the presence of immigrant Catholics in the East might force them to go there."[101] A Methodist press put out at least three books on the Inquisition in 1855, claiming that this was "the kind of information which the American people stood much in need of just now."[102] The *Master Key to Popery*, marketed eighty years before as a gloss on British aggressions against the colonies, was revived in 1854 and became a bestseller in Boston, where a Nunnery Investigation Committee was convened the same year.[103] Andrew Cross's 1856 *Priests' Prisons for Women* defended Maria Monk's narrative as fact and asserted that nuns were "*slaves*," or worse than slaves, since their "treatment is such as the hardest slaveholder would be unwilling that his slaves should undergo."[104]

If, as Garrison suggested, the *Tom* shows made abolitionists of the mob, that "mob" ranged itself also against Ireland and Rome. Temperance, anti-immigrant, and public school platforms, all anti-Catholic, were also people's platforms, anticlerical and populist; Republicans contending for nativist loyalties fronted the 1856 Free-Soil (and Lincolnesque) candidate J. C. Frémont as "a new man—fresh from the people and one of . . . the people themselves."[105] The Know-Nothing Massachusetts Governor Harry J. Gardner blamed Catholics and "foreigners" for Frémont's defeat, as did, bitterly, Stowe.[106]

The new resonance with which events of the 1850s invested a more entrenched anti-Catholic vocabulary is audible in Know-Nothing Thomas Whitney's 1855 declaration that in "a word, American Republicanism is FREEDOM; Romanism is SLAVERY!"[107] The perceived hospitality of *Uncle Tom's Cabin* to Know-Nothing and anti-Irish sentiments was suggestively indicated by a Missouri political cartoon showing Stowe "fattening up a baby for a Know-Nothing sacrifice," as also by the *Irish American*'s wry take on the *Tom* shows, "Mrs. Stowe in Cork."[108] Stowe would have known of the Irish-black connection in minstrelsy from her years in Cincinnati, a center of blackface innovation during that time; readers noted how closely the black characters in *Uncle Tom* were to minstrel types even before they were embodied in blackface on the stage.[109]

Associations between Irish and black proved awkward for white abolitionists, whose anti-Irish sentiments won support from both the "people" at home and the British overseas. Fears that Irish rebellion in Britain might foment slave rebellion at home prompted Lowell to ask, in the *Anti-Slavery Standard*, that "any American favorer of Irish rebellion explain to us the moral distinction between Ireland and South Carolina. . . . [A]ll that we ask of the friends of Ireland is that they should be consistent, and make no chromatic distinctions between white slaves and black." Lowell ignored his own warning a few months later when in the same paper he reminded those who compared the "Irish laborer and the slave" that the former's condition was the result (not of British indifference or policy) but of potato rot, "a calamity whose approach was not calculated in the almanacs," and that were the diet of the slave similarly depleted all comparison "to his poor brother over the ocean, would be put out of the question."[110]

If the inhabitants of Catholic Ireland could be likened to slaves, however, they were also like the Confederate South; as Charles Sumner put it, if "Ireland were in triumphant rebellion against the British Queen, complaining of rights denied, it would be our duty to recognize her as an Independent Power; but if Ireland rebelled, with the declared object of establishing a *new* Power . . . then it would be our duty to spurn the infamous pretension, and no triumph of rebellion could change this plain and irresistible necessity."[111] Irish Catholics could be compared to slaves or to the Confederacy; put another way, they could be likened to African Americans or figured as their tormentors, and it was the latter characterization that Northern Protestants deployed to court British support back to their side after the dislocations of the Trent Affair in 1861. In "England and America," a speech delivered in Manchester in 1863, Henry Ward Beecher posed and answered the question of how the prejudice that made black persons "a race odious by oppression" came to exist: "It was on account of the multitude of Irishmen who came to the states (cheers and interruption). . . . I bear witness that there is no class of people in America who is so bitter against the colored people, and so eager for slavery, as the ignorant, the poor, uninstructed Irishman."[112]

Beecher's warm welcome in cotton-poor and recently South-leaning Manchester was prepared by Stowe's wartime *Reply to the Affectionate and Christian Address of Many Thousands of Women in Great Britain and Ireland to their Sisters the Women of the United States of America,* which stirred mass meetings and tilted British opinion back toward the Union.[113] Thomas Bayley Potter, the president of the British Union and Emancipation Society who introduced Beecher to the Manchester audience, likewise framed the relation between the two nations as one of kinship; Beecher's visit, he hoped, would be a means of "bind[ing] together in peace *the two great representatives of the Anglo-Saxon race—England and America . . . [that] being one in race, language, religion, and love of freedom,* they may thus lead the van of civilization, and bid defiance to the shocks which jealousy or suspicion might bring upon them."[114]

The following year, a British diplomatic appeal for peace between North and South similarly removed non-Anglo-Saxons from both nations: "We are of the same race, and many of you are our brothers. . . . We ask you . . . is it not time to cease the cruel war in which you are engaged? . . . Compare the course pursued by the south now and the colonies in 1776 . . . and we think you will discover many striking resemblances."[115] That mapping of Anglo-American brotherhood onto the prospective North-South reunion meant that the rebuilding of America could proceed under the sign of what an 1868 bestseller christened *Greater Britain,* "a conception . . . of the grandeur of our race, already girdling the earth"; America, according to this conception, "offers the English race the moral dictatorship of the globe."[116]

From Romanism to Race

In the providential imagination that reads history as the gradual triumph of Anglo-Protestant culture in North America, to Catholicize slavery is to preordain its demise in the Reformation's defeat of Romanism. As deviations from providential history, slaves and slavery (like Catholics and the Church) belong together to a moribund past superseded by a triumphal Christian present. The abolition of race slavery, in this model, clears the way for further projects of Protestant expansion, which require the specification and defeat of other captivities: "Our day has seen a glorious breaking of fetters," Stowe wrote in her preface to Frances Stenhouse's *"Tell It All": The Story of a Life's Experience in Mormonism*, "the slave-pens of the South have become a nightmare of the past; the auction-block and the whipping-post have given place to the church and school-house, and the songs of emancipated millions are heard throughout our land. May we not then hope that the hour is come to loose the bonds of a cruel slavery whose chains have cut into the very hearts of thousands of our sisters—a slavery which debases and degrades womanhood, motherhood and the family?"[117] In Stowe's *House and Home Papers*, begun during the war, "slave" had already come to be the position occupied by the insufficiently industrious New England homemaker cursed with Irish Catholic help: "She who can once put her own trained hand to the machine in any spot where a hand is needed never comes to be the slave of a coarse, vulgar Irish woman. . . . [T]he old New England motto, *Get your work done up in the forenoon*, applied to an amount of work that would keep a common Irish servant toiling from daylight to sunup."[118]

If slavery was to be condemned in all its forms, however, both "blackness" and "Catholicism" were for Stowe the sites of more reluctant disavowals. As Lott has suggested, blackness became for antebellum whites a prime locus for "the religious appreciation of the emotions that came with the decline of Calvinism."[119] In her avowed attraction to the sensuous spirituality of American slaves, Stowe seems indeed to have numbered herself among those who, as the travel writer Frederika Bremer put it, "have felt an Africa of religious life, and who might have produced glorious flowers and fruits" had their spiritual awakenings "not been smothered by the snow and the grey coldness of conventionality."[120] Yet not only Africa but also Rome seemed to offer Stowe temporary, sheltering warmth from what, in *The Minister's Wooing*, she called "snow-banks of cold Puritan preciseness."[121] "The Yankee race," she lamented, "will never rest until everything antique and poetic is driven out of that world."[122] The antique and poetic could be retrieved, for Stowe, at her Mandarin, Florida retreat, which reminded her of Catholic Sorrento; in her devotion to the Virgin Mary and her mining of Catholic apocrypha for her later religious works; or in what Marie Caskey calls her "yearnings toward Catholicism" as well as her "determination to claim as Protestant whatever features of late medieval Catholicism were most praiseworthy."[123]

In her introduction to Charles Beecher's *The Incarnation: or Pictures of the Virgin and Her Son*, Stowe suggested that the proper use of Catholic pleasures by Protestant readers was homeopathic: the book's object was "to reproduce the sacred narratives" in images as vivid as any "borrowed from some antiquated engraving or old church painting, the fruit of monkish revelry or of artistic inspiration." Protestants so supplied, she said, would be spared the need for "the strains of a Byron, or the glowing pictures of a Bulwer or a Sue."[124] *Uncle Tom's Cabin*'s appreciation for the Catholic and black "exotic" over the "colder and more correct" austerities of New England Protestantism follows a similarly homeopathic logic. The voluptuousness of St. Clare's plantation, Cassy's wild autonomy, the Negro's "passion for all that is splendid, rich, and fanciful" (195): all are indulged in order eventually to be renounced or reformed, as though the exuberant disorder of Dinah's kitchen, however warm and accommodating in contrast to Ophelia's rigid "order and system" (249) would, left to itself, lead entropically to Legree's plantation, where the family exists only as concubinage, and which hasn't a kitchen at all.[125]

That Catholicism's sacramental aesthetic ("sensuality"), celibate communities ("perversion"), and alternative subjectivities ("slavery") could ever have been assimilated, under the heading of threats to the family, to the socially and economically sanctioned rape and breeding of slaves and the forced separation of slave families suggests something of the vexed self-definition of the institution whose functions nineteenth-century theorists of domesticity felt themselves continually called to elaborate and exalt. Indeed, with white middle-class men commuting to work, their wives buying goods instead of making them, and black and immigrant servants increasingly available to look after declining numbers of children, what's a family for?[126] Or as Stowe and Catharine Beecher put it in their *American Woman's Home*, "What . . . is the end designed by the family state which Jesus Christ came into the world to secure?" It is, they answer, "to provide for the training of our race to the highest possible intelligence, virtue, and happiness . . . with chief reference to a future immortal existence."[127] Moreover, since "a state is but an association of families . . . there is no reason why sister, wife, and mother should be more powerless in the state than in the home."[128]

What is remarkable about this vision of "home" is its dependence on the contributions of religious and racial others it ultimately excludes. Together with the literature of the eternal living room popularized by Elizabeth Stuart Phelps, where heaven becomes the site of "another family gathering and a better family worship,"[129] Stowe and Beecher's rendering of immortality as an extension of the "family state" finds its sources not only in the Catholic conviction of the community of the dead and the intercession of saints, but also in the West African (and later Afro-Christian) notion of the afterlife as a "homecoming" for a family of spirits.[130] One might note other cultural debts in this model, as Jane Tompkins puts it, of "the kingdom of heaven on earth as a world over which [white] women exercise ultimate control"—to the female prophetic tradition in black preaching, for example, or to Catholicism's alternative conception of female vocation. The Beecher/Stowe "blueprint for colonizing the world in the name of the family state under the leadership of Christian women" (Tompkins again) requires, however, that the Christian family state's racial and religious mixtures be either segregated and hierarchized or else tracelessly absorbed.[131] As the state comes more and more to resemble the kingdom of heaven, heaven comes more and more to look like the racially stable, middle-class home. What's a family for? The work of the family, in this view, is the spiritualization—both the heightening and the strategic erasure—of race.[132]

In the project of elaborating the meanings of racial otherness from the resources of a more long-standing discourse of religious otherness, Catholics obviously fared differently than emancipated slaves. American Catholics pressed their assimilationist claims as the most numerous members of the pool of European ethnics from (if not precisely for) which "whiteness" was created.[133] If this realignment made racial sameness the basis for joint Protestant-Catholic assertions of national unity, it also subtly racialized the class division between the Protestant middle class and their Catholic servants. "The mistresses of American families, whether they like it or not," Stowe wrote in *House and Home Papers*, "have the duties of missionaries imposed upon them by that class from which our supply of domestic servants is drawn." Where the scheming papist or the "female jesuit" had required drastic psychic, spiritual, and moral rewiring, the lowly Irish girl need only be trained in the ways of middle-class domesticity; so "missionized," her religious life takes its place alongside her mistress's as separate but (more or less) equal: "In speaking of the office of American mistresses as being a missionary one, we are far from recommending any controversial interference in the religious faith of our servants. . . . [T]here is a real unity even in opposite Christian forms; and the Roman Catholic servant and Protestant mistress, if alike possessed by the Spirit of Christ

. . . cannot help being one in heart, though one go to mass and the other go to meeting."[134]

The relative ease of assimilating Catholics under the heading of "Christian" and European ethnics under the heading of "white" contrasted sharply with the difficulty of bringing emancipated slaves under the third of these overarching signifiers, "American." Stowe gave voice to this difficulty in *Woman in Sacred History,* one of a number of nineteenth-century narratives about biblical women intended for a white, middle-class, Protestant, and predominantly female readership.[135] Although Stowe had moved away from her colonizationist solution to slavery by the time this book appeared, the chapter titled "Hagar the Slave" retrospectively finds scriptural precedent for the vision of slave repatriation that ended *Uncle Tom's Cabin.* In the later text, Hagar's "unseemly exaltation" on finding herself pregnant by the patriarch Abraham anticipates her failure of comportment when, after the birth of Ishmael, she learns of Sarah's miraculous pregnancy: "A mother who had known the blessedness of motherhood would have rejoiced when the mistress who had done so much for her was made so joyful. . . . But the dark woman and her wild son are of untamable elements. They can no more become one in spirit with the patriarchal family than oil can mix with water."[136] Motherhood, the redemptive point of identification between slave and free women in *Uncle Tom's Cabin,* here becomes the wedge between Hagar and Sarah:

> When the weaning feast is made, and all surround the little Isaac, when the mother's heart overflows with joy, she sees the graceless Ishmael mocking; and instantly, with a woman's lightning prescience, she perceives the dangers, the impossibilities of longer keeping these aliens under the same roof,—the feuds, the jealousies, the fierce quarrels of the future. "Cast out this bondswoman and her son," she says, with the air of one accustomed to command and decide; "for the son of this bondswoman shall not be heir with my son."[137]

"Mothers," however, are here empowered not only to cast out slaves but to relate to them as benevolent rescuers. To the aid of the "[p]roud, hot-headed, ungoverned slave girl" comes the maternal presence of "God, in whose eyes all human beings are equal, and who looks down on the boiling strifes and hot passions of all of us below, as a mother on the quarrels of little children in the nursery."[138] The slave's rescue becomes the pretext for the consolidation of race; Hagar, like George or Topsy, is liberated by the divine maternal presence into what is not yet but is on its way to becoming "her own country" (505): "For this was the world's infancy, and each character in the drama represented a future nation for which the all-Father was caring."[139]

"Nation," here, is interchangeable with both religion and race. God guides Hagar and Ishmael to the Arabian desert, the birthplace of Islam. Sarah's son Isaac becomes, via the providential re-sorting of the blood-lines of slaves and masters, and some supersessionary sleight of hand, the progenitor not primarily of Jews but of Christians: "As a skillful husband-man, bent on perfecting a certain seed, separated it from all others, and grows it by itself, so the Bible tells us that God selected a certain stock to be trained and cultivated as the sacerdotal race. . . . Out of this race in its final outcome and perfected flowering was to spring forth Jesus, spoken of as the BRANCH of this sacred tree."[140] As *Uncle Tom's Cabin* had argued for emancipation as the answer to slavery's racial mixtures, producing in the novel's final pages a list of "full-black" and "three-quarters black" Cincinnati wage earners as proof of the "capabilities of the race" (517–18), so the divine segregation of slave and master in *Woman in Sacred History* produces the "strongly marked" Arab "race" and secures the purity of the Christian "race," "a race selected, centuries before, from the finest physical stock in the world."[141]

Equating the "flowering" of the "Christian era" with the establishment of Anglo-American culture, *Woman in Sacred History* locates Christian flourishing in the containment of Islam, the supersession of Judaism, and the withholding from non-Anglo-Saxon Christians of the mantle of the "sacerdotal race."[142] It also insists that such formations—the slavish Ori-ental, the Jew whose arrogance is his refusal to leave the historical stage, and the racial entitlement of Anglo-Saxon Christianity—coexist under the banner of a divinely modeled pluralism, for the "ear of the All-Father is as near to the cry of the impetuous, hot-tempered slave, and the moans of the wild, untamable boy, as to those of the patriarch."[143] Divine indif-ference to race becomes the source and stabilizer of racial difference: "For the formation of this [Christian] race, we see a constant choice of the gentler and quieter elements of blood and character, and the persistent rejection of that which is wild, fierce, and ungovernable. Yet it is with no fond partiality to the one, or antipathy to the other, that the Father of both thus decides."[144]

The category-generating resources of "race" occasionally moved Stowe and her contemporaries to taxonomic frenzies: by way of introducing Frederick Douglass in *Men of Our Times*, in a passage that names no fewer than six different "races" that fall under the broader classification of "white," Stowe insisted that neither is "the black population of America . . . one race," but rather "a mixture torn from tribes and races quite . . . dissimilar." "The Mandingo has European features, a fine form, wavy, not woolly hair, is intelligent, vigorous, proud, and brave. The guinea Negro has a coarse, animal head, is stupid, dirty, cunning. Yet the argument on *Negro* powers is generally based on some such sweeping classification as takes the guinea Negro for its type."[145]

However productive of typological profusion, and whatever its resources for setting a Frederick Douglass in closer relation to the European than to the "guinea Negro," the remapping of social difference from religion to race made "blackness" the site of a host of traits formerly signaled by "Catholicism," with "whiteness" inheriting from Protestantism the privilege of needing never to speak its name.[146] Antebellum anti-Catholicism's thematics of captivity, conspiracy, and corporeal excess licensed a way of thinking about race later in the nineteenth and into the twentieth centuries as fixed and bounded, or as dangerously elusive, present even when invisible, or as evolutionarily keyed to degrees of bodily appetite and restraint.[147] For a generation and more preceding the Civil War, a white Protestant discourse whose concerns included, say, rape, violence, imprisonment, undisciplined fertility, mismanaged homes, failures in education, and failures of self-government was as invested in lodging these fears in Romanism as Reconstruction-era and later (and hardly now exhausted) versions of the same discourse have been in attaching them to blackness. At the same time, and in some of the same mouths, "blackness" names a well of sexiness, spiritual and psychic resilience, and alternative aesthetic consciousness routinely tapped to reinvigorate a still denotatively "white" American culture. The long-standing habit of figuring first one then the other formation (Catholicism, blackness) as a threat to, and occasional refuge from, the legacy of Protestant individualism, and the more recent failure to authorize the possibility for legal redress of racial discrimination on any but individual terms, belong to the same history.[148]

● ● ●

Close to the time of Stowe's death in 1896, the Supreme Court handed down its landmark separate-but-equal decision in *Plessy v. Ferguson*, lynching was at its height, and the rise of the New Negro had begun to be charted against nostalgic depictions of winsome plantation darkies in postcards, minstrel shows, and other national cultural forms.[149] Stowe's will offered further testimony to the remarkable ability of cross-racial sympathies and identifications to coexist with their containment. In her will, according to Joan D. Hedrick's biography,

> Stowe distributed to her surviving children her most valued possessions. To Charles she gave the silver inkstand given to her by the women of England and the bound volumes of the half a million signatures collected by them for the "Affectionate and Christian Address." To Hatty she gave "the large silver waiter given to me by the women

of England" and to Eliza "the silver cake basket given to me by the women of England." Had Georgiana lived, she would have inherited the gold bracelet given her mother by the Duchess of Sutherland, now inscribed with the date of the Emancipation Proclamation.[150]

All of Stowe's most valued possessions came to her as a result of her authorship of *Uncle Tom's Cabin*. The promise, daring, and presumption of Stowe's acts of ventriloquism and self-extension across racial lines, authorized by an imperializing white Protestantism, here resolve into domestic heirlooms having a distinctly attenuated relation to slavery (in fairness, the Duchess's gold bracelet *was* cast in the form of a slave's shackle), and evoking as this family's mother not only Harriet Beecher Stowe but also "England," elsewhere described by Stowe as "the mother of us all."[151]

This legacy consolidates the Stowe family in the image of an Anglo-America expunged of blackness that inspires the repatriation fantasies indulged in both *Uncle Tom's Cabin* and *Woman in Sacred History*. But the deep, now dynastic embeddedness of *Uncle Tom's Cabin* in this American Woman's Home points also to the need to keep blackness perpetually at home in white America, as testimony to the nobility and largesse of its extension of Christian sympathy to former slaves.[152] From this vision of a piously unified America, the difference of Catholicism has fallen away, disappeared or been subsumed under the cover of an increasingly unmarked Christianity, which now requires a language of race to name the difference at its heart.

Chapter Six

MARK TWAIN AND THE AMBIVALENT
REFUGE OF UNBELIEF

IN 1983 A BLACK ADMINISTRATOR at the propitiously named Mark Twain Middle School in Fairfax, Virginia produced an edition of the *Adventures of Huckleberry Finn* from which the words "nigger" and "hell" were removed. John H. Wallace urged that Twain's novel be "*listed as racist and excluded*" from middle and high school classrooms, and intended for his altered version to be used only in schools where it remained required reading. Arguing that the experience of being made to read *Huckleberry Finn* aloud could be "devastatingly traumatic" for black pupils, Wallace insisted that those pupils not be forced by "so powerful an institution as the school" to "tolera[te] . . . 'ironic' or 'satirical' reminders of the insults and degradation heaped upon their ancestors."[1]

Predictably, Wallace's attempt to banish *Huck Finn* from the classroom drew outcries from across a political spectrum. Russell Baker hoped that students would never be taught to "misread Twain as outrageously as Mr. Wallace has" in finding depictions of the "dishonesty, dumbness, and inhumanity of blacks."[2] Christopher Hitchens portrayed those who challenged the novel's fitness for schoolchildren as "know-nothings," "noise-makers," and "neurotics."[3] And George Will, who elsewhere describes American literary critics who take up questions of race as "forces . . . fighting against the conservation of the common culture that is the nation's social cement," praised *Huckleberry Finn* against "ninnies" like Wallace who remain deaf to the book's lessons on "freedom understood in a distinctively American way, as the absence of social restraints, and obedience to the promptings of a pure heart."[4]

In the shorthand of Wallace's adversaries, to criticize *Huck Finn* was to criticize America. As Jonathan Arac points out in *Huckleberry Finn as Idol and Target*, *Huck*'s champions over the last several decades have tended overwhelmingly to reiterate the cold war–era consensus on the novel's exemplary Americanness that had secured its privileged place in the curricula of most American junior high schools by the mid-1950s. In Arac's reading, those who would rescue *Huck Finn* from objections to its racist epithets and depictions shore up the political function conferred on the book after World War II, which was to provide in the friendship of

Huck and Jim an image of America at its democratic best. Perversely, the narrative of democracy it was the book's new function to endorse *required* the continued repetition of the word "nigger," since this is what allowed the book's defenders to contend, in Arac's gloss, that even though Huck's "society was racist, he was not, and so 'we' are not. For African Americans to challenge this view is to challenge 'us' just where 'we' feel ourselves most intimately virtuous, and it is also to challenge Mark Twain, and thereby the America he 'quintessentially' represents." (Arac adds that he has "never seen so much use of the term 'quintessentially' as in claims for the Americanness of *Huckleberry Finn*.")[5]

If Wallace's suppression of the racial epithet spoken 211 times in *Huckleberry Finn* registers dissent from a notion of Americanness persistently identified with Mark Twain—"the America we like best," as a *New Yorker* piece on Twain once put it, "sounds like him"[6]—what then about the word "hell"? Those who have weighed in on the controversy begun by Wallace (whom the editors of a set of African American responses to *Huckleberry Finn* describe as "strongly religious" and raised in a Pentecostal Christian church) have said very little about his editing out of this word, a decision about which Wallace, too, has remained mostly silent.[7] Alongside his fierce indictment of the book's depiction of its black characters, Wallace's objection to Huck's use of the word "hell" is admittedly puzzling, since Huck's decision to "*go* to hell,"[8] we recall, settles his moral quandary over whether to reveal Jim's whereabouts to his owner or to reject his culture's church-sanctioned reading of Jim as human chattel.

In this sense Huck's resolve to "*go* to hell" and "steal Jim out of slavery" (835) would seem to parallel Twain's own revolt against a white Christian culture where church bulletin boards advertised slave auctions and where sermons licensed their listeners to hold other human beings in bondage or, following Emancipation, to terrorize them into a captive docility. *Huckleberry Finn* thus takes its part in what Stanley Brodwin describes as the "Enlightenment mode of attack on institutional religion" Twain undertook in order to "liberate a spiritually enslaved humanity."[9] "No god or religion can survive ridicule," Twain wrote; no "church" or kindred "fraud" can "face ridicule in a fair field and live."[10] Accepting an honorary degree from Yale University in 1888, Twain declared that the "one serious purpose" of all humor was "the deriding of shams" and the "laughing of stupid superstitions out of existence," and that "whoever is engaged in this sort of warfare . . . is the natural friend of human rights and human liberties."[11]

That Twain played *Huckleberry Finn*'s agonizingly protracted "escape" sequence for laughs on his lecture tours might appear to compromise this view of the humorist as invariably the friend of human liberties, though we can't know whether the laughter at such performances was elicited by the minstrel-show trappings of Jim's plight or, more uncomfortably, by what Eric Sundquist calls Twain's "penetrating critique of the collapse of Reconstruction ideals" embedded in the "charade of Jim's mock liberation."[12] But perhaps what is subtly voiced in Wallace's move to strike the word "hell" from the novel, and so to uncouple what he calls Huck's "sacrilegious[ness]" from his bungled and belated "freeing" of Jim,[13] is a protest against Twain's comic and emancipatory view of secularization: a reminder that the "Enlightenment mode of attack" on religion was not in and of itself liberating for all Americans, nor was deliverance from what Twain called the "hundred fretting chains" of an oppressive deity to be equated with the deliverance of slaves from bondage.[14] Nor, one suspects, was freedom from the alleged debilities of their religious lives the freedom most cherished by the black pupils being integrated into all-white public schools just as *Huckleberry Finn* was becoming entrenched in the curriculum.[15]

NATIONAL IDENTITY AND CIVIL RELIGION

Twain too, I suggest, came uneasily (and unevenly) to question the emancipatory power of unbelief, though his more tentative writings on spiritual matters resist the kind of adulation given *Huck Finn* by readers like Arthur Schlesinger Jr., for whom the "human struggle against the absolute in the finest scene of the greatest of American novels"—the scene, of course, that culminates in Huck's decision to "*go to hell*"—sums up "what America is all about."[16] In Twain's own day this sense that the "human struggle against the absolute" could claim a distinctively American pedigree found voice in the speeches of Robert G. Ingersoll, the gifted orator and professed atheist who attracted huge crowds by debating fundamentalist ministers, consecrating war memorials, and preaching a gospel of America's greatness. Ingersoll fashioned the oft-repeated charges of antebellum evangelicals against Calvinist doctrines of predestination and infant damnation—their propensity, as William Ellery Channing put it, to "degrad[e] man into a chattel slave of power" and nurture "a slavish spirit of fear"[17]—into blunter instruments for use against religion in all its forms. "Is it a small thing," Ingersoll asked, "to unbind the martyr from the stake; break all the chains; put out the fires of civil war; stay the sword of the fanatic, and tear the bloody hands of the Church from the white throat of Science? Is it a small thing to make men truly free?"[18] Ingersoll insisted that "[t]here can be but little liberty on earth while men worship a tyrant in heaven," but also, happily, that tyranny had been all but dethroned in the separation of the New World from the Old. In Ingersoll's narrative of national deliverance, America's distinctive brand of freedom lay in the secularizing energies of its founding, for in their passage from the Old World to the New "men whose flesh had known the chill of chains" were freed from "scepters and titles and crowns," and "the prejudices and feuds of Europe faded slowly from their hearts."[19]

Twain found Ingersoll tremendously compelling and praised his speeches as "the supreme combination of words that was ever put together since the world began."[20] Among his admirers Ingersoll also counted Henry Ward Beecher and other evangelicals, despite their commitment to spreading the Christian gospel and Ingersoll's to silencing it. From the standpoint of patriotism the alliance was shrewd, since the alleged enmity between evangelical Christianity and Ingersoll's brand of unbelief tidily set the boundaries for an emerging religious consensus on the meaning of America. Like his evangelical counterparts, Ingersoll envisioned human history in millennial terms, substituting the revelation of human self-sufficiency for the progressive realization of the kingdom of God on earth. To "oppose" their points of view, as Ingersoll and his Christian interlocutors did, was to posit a spectrum of American religion extending from evangelical Christianity to a thoroughly secularized Protestantism, a spectrum that accommodates varying (though not all) degrees of Protestant Christian commitment while rendering alternative religious worlds un-American or invisible. Ingersoll and his evangelical rivals may have disputed the question of whether the Bible and Christianity were friends of liberty, justice, and enlightenment—for Ingersoll they surely were not—but not whether *America* was the friend of liberty, justice, and enlightenment, nor whether these values, framed within the Protestant-secular continuum in ways that made them unnecessary even to define, should carry the day. In Ingersoll's version of American exceptionalism, Americans wave the "wand of progress" that "touches the auction block, the slave-pen, [and] the whipping-post" and "write[s] upon the eternal dome, glittering with stars, the grand word—freedom."[21]

This is the national-religious imagination at pains to safeguard *Huckleberry Finn* and Mark Twain as American icons. What commentators began in the 1950s to call American civil religion, a devotion to the nation's sacred ideals that allegedly transcends denominational alliance, emerges from the Protestant-secular continuum and renders it coextensive with American identity. In his landmark *Protestant, Catholic, Jew,* Will Herberg wrote that the "great mass of Americans identify themselves [as Protestant, Catholic, or Jewish] to establish their social location once they have really sloughed off their immigrant foreignness"; at the same time, he made clear, to be any of these without having also accommodated oneself to the secularized Protestantism that governs American public culture was to remain insufficiently American.[22] Thus Lionel Trilling, a Jew and *Huck Finn*'s decisive canonizer within the academy, won entrance into an American university culture otherwise closed to him, in Arac's reading, by "redefin[ing] the relation of a book to our nation at a key moment in history," enlisting *Huck Finn* in the 1950s to prove the superiority of America's democratic faith over the coercive designs of enemy regimes.[23] And when subsequent challenges to *Huck Finn* have been condemned as "censorship," that charge has carried overtones not only of antidemocratic leanings but also of immoderate or too-public religiosity, an association that John Wallace's Pentecostal faith no doubt confirmed for his detractors.

In this way Twain's own religious skepticism tends to bolster the civic piety that makes a national shrine of *Huckleberry Finn*. In 1885, Twain wrote to his friend Charles Warren Stoddard in response to the latter's announcement of his conversion to Catholicism: "You must not make the mistake of supposing that absolute peace of mind is obtainable only through some form of religious belief; no, on the contrary, I have found that as perfect peace is to be found in absolute unbelief. I look back with the same shuddering horror upon the days when I believed, as you do upon the days when you were afraid you did not believe. Both of us are certain now, and in certainty let us rest."[24] The epitaph on Twain's memorial in Hannibal, Missouri—"his religion was humanity, and a whole world mourned for him when he died"[25]—salutes this unbelief as democratic and emancipatory, the faith of a "hilarious image-breaker," as Bret Harte called Twain,[26] whose iconoclastic impulse directed itself against all "royalties, nobilities, privileges and . . . kindred swindles" that have an enslaving God-concept at their heart.[27]

Against this reading of what Brodwin calls Twain's "secular comic reflex,"[28] however, a dimmer view, solidified in much biographical criticism, finds Twain's increasingly caustic pronouncements on human nature and the cosmos to signal both a personal and an artistic unraveling. In this reading, the scattered, dreamlike, occasionally "nightmarish" quality of Twain's later writings charts the descent of embittered pessimist who ultimately surrendered to the "unrelenting despair" of spiritual and social nihilism.[29] These later works include a number of writings that take up the themes of (to draw on the bookstore vernacular) "religion and the occult," among them the fragmentary *Mysterious Stranger* manuscripts and the unfinished satirical narratives *Three Thousand Years among the Microbes* and *The Secret History of Eddypus, the World Empire*. These works are seldom mentioned when Twain's "quintessential" Americanness is invoked, for their very directionlessness would seem to breach the paradigm that continues to hallow *Huckleberry Finn* as what a 1957 *New York Times* editorial, taking issue with the NAACP's cautionary stance on the book's use in schools, called a "great document in the progress of human tolerance and understanding."[30]

RELIGION AND RACE: ALTERNATIVE ENGAGEMENTS

Susan Gillman argues that the growing murkiness of Twain's later writings, rather than intimating his personal dissolution, might more usefully be seen to mirror the baffling complexity of the racial issues that Twain, determined to expand the "limited rhetorics" of race available to him, risked artistic failure to comprehend.[31] I would add that the same drift toward fragmentation and uncertainty shows Twain struggling also with the equally limited rhetorics of religion available to him from within the civil-religious consensus. Nothing, evidently, could ring truer for many American readers than Huck's decision to go to hell to free a black slave, to defy in one turn a religious threat and the social injustice it allegedly supports. What gives the moment its clarity, in part, is the neatness with which a set of either-or choices about race and religion apparently align: Huck rejects a coercive Christianity for a do-it-yourself apostasy, the law and custom of slavery for the riskiness of outlawed freedoms, the privileges of white America for solidarity with black.

In being so starkly juxtaposed, however, these dichotomized rhetorics of religion and race reveal their limitations. Of the alleged oppositional pairs—belief/unbelief, slavery/freedom, black/white—none is stable and belief/unbelief perhaps least of all, since dissent from Christian belief (itself, needless to say, a diversity) might take the form not only of resolute or wavering unbelief but also of varying degrees of allegiance within a vast range of alternative faiths. This variety makes Twain's vaunted antipathy toward "religion" much harder to track than assessments of Twain as simply an agnostic or atheist would suggest. Indeed from the earliest of his *Alta California* journalism to the *Mysterious Stranger* manuscripts and beyond, Twain's writings show a fascination with religions that resist being plotted along the trajectory from Protestant conviction to its absence. These include the new religions of the nineteenth-century United States, among them Mormonism, spiritualism, and Christian Science; the Old World faiths of Catholicism, Judaism, and Islam; the Asian religions encountered in *Following the Equator*; and the "heathen" belief systems of Hawai'ian natives, American Indians, and black slaves.

These alternatives to mainstream Christianity blur the distinction between religion and race by including categories of subjects whom Twain represented as both (and inseparably) religiously and racially marked.[32] Unevenly accommodated within the landscape of American civil religion, these positions beyond the Protestant-secular continuum put questions to the conventional reading of Huck's apostasy as a clear strike in favor of racial equality. For example: If Christianity is inevitably tainted by association with slaveholding (as *Huckleberry Finn*'s total silence on

Christian abolitionism would seem to suggest),[33] where outside of Christianity might resources for freedom be found—in the nonreligious or in the differently religious? Can religious identity be discarded as easily as Huck does his when it lies closer to race, as in Twain's renderings of Jews, Arabs, American Indians, and others, or does the proximity of religion and race in such cases suggest that race itself might be differently construed? What happens, moreover, when secular values (civic piety, say, or scientific "proof") reveal themselves to be as hostile to racial justice as any constraint of dogma, religious custom, or sect? This last question becomes especially acute, for if institutional religion could easily be made the target of Twain's zeal for exposing "shams" and "superstitions," neither humor nor outrage could as readily undermine these secular values' increasing presumption to legitimacy, or reveal their complicity in the forms of injustice Twain sought to redress.

That so much of Twain's later, more obscure writing on loosely religious themes remained unfinished suggests, in part, what wrestling with these questions looks like. But Twain also engages such questions in earlier and better known works, including the *Tom Sawyer–Huck Finn* sequence and *Pudd'nhead Wilson*, the narratives most often invoked in discussions of Twain and race. Religion seldom features in these discussions, perhaps because the same agnosticism that leaves racial questions provocatively unresolved in Twain's writings would seem to position him, less ambiguously, as what one critic calls a "casebook representative of the Gilded Age that produced Robert G. Ingersoll."[34] Critics who do consider Twain's religious views have tended to frame them in the terms of an Ingersoll-style binary between belief and unbelief, setting these at the ends of a spectrum that, whatever spiritual shades of grey it accommodates, nevertheless aligns belief with recognizably Protestant conviction rooted in Calvinist absolutes. In this schema, Twain's early departure from the ranks of Christian believers yields a secular worldview variously figured as freeing or privative but dogged in either case by the pressures of an incompletely exorcised Presbyterian conscience. Such a reading explains Twain's late "dark" determinism as "a dogma of absolute necessity that fitted his childhood Calvinism,"[35] and, perhaps implicitly, attributes the alleged retreat of his later works from the liberatory promise of *Huckleberry Finn* to the contaminating "traces" left by Presbyterianism and the "moral sense" through "all the years of his adult 'emancipation.' "[36]

Twain's own reflections on Christianity by turns resist and recapitulate this binary framing, revealing his share in what Ralph Ellison called "the white American's Manichean fascination with the symbolism of blackness and whiteness."[37] In some contexts, "blackness" or "darkness" signals outsidedness to Christianity, for good or, occasionally, for ill. "I am 'dark' yet," Twain wrote to Olivia Langdon, prior to their marriage, of the rewardlessly "dim . . . grop[ings]" that constituted his first and only adult attempt to become a Christian;[38] more than three decades later he addressed one of his anti-imperialist writings to the colonial subject "Sitting in Darkness" who might yet be spared the "glass beads and theology, maxim guns and hymnbooks" of the Christian emissaries of American imperialist policy.[39] Twain gives racial content to the "darkness" of his failed conversion; as a child, he wrote, he was "playmate to all of the niggers, preferring their society to that of the elect."[40] Elsewhere, however, Twain aligns blackness not with a wistful or salutary distance from Christian redemption but with particularly resilient, legitimate, and alluring forms of Christian faith, like Roxy's in *Pudd'nhead Wilson*, whose "piety was no sham, but strong and sincere," and which survives, as Huck's does not, her construction of an alternative moral world in which stealing from slave owners constitutes no "sin that God would remember against h[er] in the Last Great Day."[41] Twain's own attempt to "grope blindly" through the "dark[ness]" to Christian conversion, moreover, was also in effect a conversion to the Langdons' abolitionism, a position he had much earlier appeared to deride as "niggerism."[42] "Darkness" remained for the later Twain a marker of the "despised and bastard sect[s]" of Christians who, like the Langdons, had broken with their churches' sanction of slavery,[43] even as it also signaled the depravity of a "Christendom" "besmirched" in "pirate-raids" on subject peoples in China, South Africa, and the Philippines.[44]

In these reflections, American Christianity and whiteness, never precisely continuous, manage inevitably to implicate one another in what are almost always mutually compromising ways. Not surprisingly, then, "foreign" religions intrigued Twain in part for appearing to offer a recourse from whiteness and an alternative rhetoric of race. Thus in *Following the Equator*, the travel book that followed *Pudd'nhead Wilson*, whiteness identifies Twain as "Christian" by association with his "English [and] American" companions, while India's multiple religious worlds make a vivid rainbow of color out of "black and brown skins." The subcontinent's "brilliant colors" include its "masses of . . . complexions" no less than its "Oriental conflagrations of costume," a point Twain makes clear in proposing to mount a "hideous exhibition" of "Christian" clothing against "Indian splendors," in which "Christians" suffer the "added disadvantage of the white complexion." Against the stiffness of "Christian hats and clothes," the fluidity of Indian dress, all "rich and exquisite minglings and fusings," seems to extend to the racial and religious otherness it marks. The brilliantly dyed garments that slip from the "lithe, half-covered forms" of Ceylonese men and women—"silk-thin, soft, delicate, clinging"—prompt in Twain the desire, at once erotic and spiritual, to abandon his implicitly Christian clothing and the Christian women companions among whom he feels "ashamed." "I wish I were a *chuprassy*," he writes in Bombay, a "turbaned big native" in "robes of fiery red."[45]

IMAGINED COMMUNITIES

Following the Equator suggests that a change of religion, here a departure from Christianity, might be as easy as a change of clothes, as mysterious and enlivening as a redirection of sexual desire, and as momentous as a change of race. Elsewhere in Twain's writings, however, the possibility of movement from one religious identity to another is just what retracts the promise of self-transcendence, for it suggests spiritual fraud as well as a deadening sameness across traditions. The Immaculate Conception, for example—the Roman Catholic doctrine that Twain, like most of us, conflates with the biblical story of the virgin birth—"had been worn threadbare before we adopted it as a fresh new idea. . . . The Hindus prized it ages ago when they acquired Krishna by the Immaculate process. The Buddhists were happy when they acquired Guatama by the same process. . . . The Greeks of the same period had great joy in it. . . . The Romans borrowed the idea from Greece. . . . We got it straight from heaven by way of Rome." Or again, "It is another case of begats. What's his name begat Krishna, Krishna begat Buddha, Buddha begat Osirus, Osirus begat the Babylonian deities, they begat God, he begat Jesus, Jesus begat Mrs. Eddy."[46] Twain famously sought to expose Mary Baker Eddy as a fraud on the scale of the Immaculate Conception; in *Eddypus, the World Empire*, "Eddypus" names the former United States, now a "tyrannical politico-religious" regime formed by the merger of Christian Science and the Roman Catholic Church. If the impulse toward religious cross-dressing in *Following the Equator* suggests a brilliant constellation of spiritual, sexual, and racial freedoms, the male clerics who disguise themselves as versions of Mary Baker Eddy in *Eddypus* do so only to further "the most insolent and unscrupulous" religious imposture to "dominate . . . a people since the palmy days of the Inquisition."[47]

At such moments in Twain's writing, the full spectrum of religious possibility contracts to the opposition between unbelief and blind credulity, between the stringency of secular truths and the "elaborately masked and disguised artificialities" purveyed by "*all* religions" (and "most philosophies").[48] Disguise, of course, may be the most resonant and protean of tropes in Twain's oeuvre, where instances of cross-dressing, blackface, infants switched in their cradles, and more fantastic metamorphoses provide occasions both for the ruthless debunking of shams and for the unlikely transcendence of oppressive fact. Likewise the religious imagination, in Twain's depictions, offers access to new modes of being, now transparently as imposture, now as relief from real injustice. "The spirit has no nationality," Twain wrote of his subject in his notes for *The Personal Recollections of Joan of Arc*,[49] the "luminous" child whose dream-driven identity shifts carried her "above the limitations and infirmities of our human nature."[50] In *Tom Sawyer* and *Huckleberry Finn* this heightened spiritual mobility of childhood confronts the limitations and infirmities of race, affording both a means of eluding the confinements of antebellum white Christianity and an especially egregious case of bad faith.

Shape-Shifting on the Mississippi

"If Tom has a religion," Alfred Kazin suggests, "it is the superstitions known only to boys and the negro slaves they have borrowed them from."[51] But the religion of *Tom Sawyer*, the book Twain called a "hymn,"[52] is really the religion of "enchantment" that brings white boys into communion not only with slaves but with those forms of life the town's Protestant congregation casts at ever widening remove in its prayers for "the church, and the little children of the church; for the other churches of the village, for the village itself . . . for poor sailors, tossed by stormy seas; for the oppressed millions groaning under the heel of European monarchies and oriental despotism . . . [and] for the heathen in the far islands of the seas."[53] Allying himself with Jim in choosing to "*go to* hell," Huck rejects a set of local customs that had never sat well on him before now; much earlier in the novel Huck declared his desire to go to the "bad place" (626) because there was no room in heaven for his other spiritual companion, Tom Sawyer. Tom is most Huck-like in his restless resistance to "siviliz[ing]" (912), an induction both religious and racial. Conscripted into attendance at Sunday school, Tom reluctantly scrubs his face and whites up: "the clean territory stopped short at his chin and his jaws, like a mask; below and beyond this line there was a dark expanse of unirrigated soil" (30).

To the "clean territory" of white adult Christian norms (where, Twain wrote near the end of his life, the minds of Protestant children were in fact inevitably "soiled" and "defile[d]" by the Bible),[54] *Tom Sawyer* opposes the racially indeterminate spaces of an idealized antebellum childhood, like the town pump where "white, mulatto, and negro" (16) children converge, or the "virgin forest of an unexplored and uninhabited island" (90) where Tom, Huck, and Jo Harper "go . . . into savagery" (111) and darken their naked bodies with mud. Tom fantasizes about running off with the Indians, returning a "great chief" and stalking into Sunday school "hideous with paint" (60); he abandons his short-lived career as a cadet of temperance to become a blackfaced minstrel ("the first of all the negro minstrel shows came to town, and made a sensation; Tom and Jo Harper got up a band of performers and were happy for two days" (139–40).

Tom's aversion to whitewashing marks his kinship with the unwashed Huck, who "came and went, at his own free will. He slept on doorsteps in fine weather and in empty hogsheads in wet; he did not have to go to school or to church, or call any being master or obey anybody; he could go fishing or swimming where and when he chose"(45). "We are descended from desert-lounging Arabs," Twain wrote in *Roughing It*, "and countless ages of growth toward perfect civilization have failed to root out of us the nomadic instinct."[55] Their shared compulsion to escape fixed dwellings aligns Tom and Huck with cultures Twain figured as stalled on the civilizing path; not just Arabs but also, say, American Indians, from whom the "nomadic instinct," Twain declared in *Innocents Abroad*, could never "be educated out . . . at all."[56] Huck's and Tom's wanderings do bring them into the company of Injuns and A-rabs, and if these figures, together with Jim's character's "violation of our conception of adult maleness," in Ralph Ellison's assessment,[57] signal Twain's complicity with nineteenth-century anthropological notions of "savage" peoples as an "infant race,"[58] they also suggest a different view of race—not a presocial category aligned with evolutionary stages of human development, but instead a form of social identity that, like religion, infants and children are unevenly acculturated *to* in the process of becoming adults. Writing of newspaper reports of the slaughter of Moro men, women, and children by American soldiers in 1906, Twain would say that "they were mere naked savages, and yet there is a sort of pathos about it when the word 'children' falls under your eye . . . and by the help of its deathless eloquence color, creed, and nationality vanish away."[59]

The spatial correlative to Tom's imagination, which chafes at the confinements of white Christian identity, is the river, a dreamlike space both "mulatto" and "profan[e],"[60] whose "folk are a race apart and not like other folk,"[61] and where Huck and Jim produce a version of Genesis from which the scattering of nations and the punishment of Ham are conspicuously lacking (742). *Life on the Mississippi* figures the river as the preferred destination of boys seeking "mysterious lands and distant climes" (257), who revel in "riotous powwow[s]" (258) and the "glittering notoriety" (120) of sun-darkened skin: "cows and horses would suggest [to him] the circus," Twain wrote of the Tom Sawyeresque riverboat pilot with whom he apprenticed; "the transition from the circus to the menagerie was easy and natural; from the elephant to equatorial Africa was but a step; then of course the heathen savages would suggest religion" (309). By the early chapters of *Huckleberry Finn*, however, the "enchantment" that brings Tom into the company of circuses and elephants and heathen savages has begun to impress Huck with "all the marks of a Sunday school" (638). The river, like Tom's imagination, is indeed a space of self re-creation, but the transformations that Jim and Huck undergo there—Jim into a "sick Arab" and Huck into a girl, several different boys, and finally into Tom Sawyer—are less instances of enchantment than strategies for survival in the world of slavery that Tom's imagination renders invisible, or worse, the materials of romance.

It is, of course, the backdrop of sleepy slaveholding village Christianity that gives Tom's adventures their exotic charge; he needs the church and the Sunday school to make his entrance as a sun-darkened Indian or the "Black Avenger of the Spanish Main" (60). And what prolongs Jim's captivity in *Huck Finn* is not only the romantic resonance of his plight for Tom (who likens Jim to "one of them prisoners at the bottom dungeon of the Castle Deef, in the harbor of Marseilles" [863]), but also his appeal to the homespun evangelical sensibilities of Jim's captors in the "nonnamous letter[s]" he sends as their "Unknown Friend" who has lately "got religgion" (888–89). Christian hypocrisy licenses Tom's cruelties to Jim and makes them heroic, much as Theodore Roosevelt, whom Twain would call "the Tom Sawyer" of the twentieth century, "always showing off," could authorize the massacre of six hundred Moros in the Philippines and still be "idolize[d]" by a nation whose "feeling about its president . . . or its religion" was all "procured at second hand."[62] If Tom's desire to cast off whiteness and Christianity makes him like the raceless and creedless Moro children, it also aligns him with the president who praised their executioners. No more than Roosevelt's heroic "skirmishes" do Tom's engagements with exotic populations constitute an alternative to white Christian America's perpetrations of injustice, since the counterworld of Tom's restless imagination—with its pirates, Arabs, Indians, and Spanish monks who elude the "captivity and fetters" (42) of white Protestant culture—is also the world that provides all the materials for Jim's reenslavement.

INNOCENTS AT HOME

Tom Sawyer's career illustrates the difficulty Twain faced in imagining sustained alternatives to the "sivilizing" complex of Christianity, whiteness, and slaveholding that Huck Finn is ever in flight from, even as "lighting out for the [Indian] Territory" (912) only conveys Huck more deeply into American civilization's imperializing heart. To note this is to trouble civil-religious assessments of *Huckleberry Finn*. Victor Doyno, for example, applauds the book's "nativist" politics and explains Tom Sawyer's "racially based contempt for Jim" as the result of the "enslavement" of an "average American boy" to "European notions" and "foreign values."[63] Roger Salomon contrasts the "true romance" of the "American folk hero," represented by Huck, to Tom's "perpetuation of a foreign mythology on alien soil.[64] By the close of *Huckleberry Finn*, however, the register of the "foreign" and its potentially enslaving mythologies have blurred indistinguishably into the local settings that produce folk heroes and average American boys.

This is also the landscape of *Pudd'nhead Wilson*, where a tour that includes Dawson's Landing's Methodist, Presbyterian, and Baptist churches impresses the visiting Italian Capello twins only as a repeat of "some fifteen or sixteen hundred thousand previous experiences of this sort in various countries of Europe" (951), and where the twins' own foreignness ("Italians, how romantic! Just think ma—there's never been one in this town!" [944]) secures their warm welcome in the Missouri village from which their religious difference all but disappears. If *Huckleberry Finn* strives mightily to align racial freedom with a principled dissent from Protestant culture, *Pudd'nhead Wilson* seems instead to depict its slaveholding village's Protestantism as having absorbed all possible alternatives. The novel's opening "Whisper to the Reader" sets its composition in Italy, where Twain's earlier travels elicited extensive commentary on the curiosities of its inhabitants' religion, and Twain was in fact steeped in Catholic history as he worked intermittently on *The Personal Recollections of Joan of Arc* while writing *Pudd'nhead Wilson*. But although the Capello twins descend from Florentine nobility, their hereditary Catholicism, which would otherwise stand out clearly against the town's Protestant religious landscape, is nowhere remarked.

Instead, religious difference in Dawson's Landing is refracted along two familiar dividing lines: a black-white racial axis that sets the "colored Methodis[m]" (926) of Roxy's slave religion away from the mainstream Christianity of Dawson's Landing's white inhabitants, and a Protestant-secular axis that separates Christian belief from the Free Thought professed by David (Pudd'nhead) Wilson and Judge York Leicester Driscoll. The erasure of the Capello twins' Catholicism leaves the Protestant-secular axis undisturbed: Angelo and Luigi join a white Christian congregation and the fledgling Freethinkers, respectively. The town's racial binary is slightly less accommodating of the twins, who blur the color line as Mediterraneans, though separately they are described as one "brown" (1001) and the other "fairer" (945).

No "hymn" to antebellum white boyhood, *Puddn'head Wilson* is instead a deeply cynical look at racial identity and its constraining conventions in the period both of its antebellum setting and its 1894 composition. Central to the story's unfolding is the "one-drop rule" according to

which a single known black ancestor makes a person black even when
visibly white, as in the case of the Driscolls' mulatto slave Roxana and
her infant son Chambers. Left to raise both the Driscolls' newborn and
her own when her mistress dies in childbirth, Roxy secretly acts to free
Chambers by switching the babies in their cradles. The exchange goes
undetected until Roxy's now-grown son, raised as the white heir Tom
Driscoll, murders his supposed uncle using a knife stolen from the Capello
twins. The murderer is identified by the eccentric gentleman lawyer
Pudd'nhead Wilson, who, never having tried a legal case, devotes himself
instead to what the townspeople call his "black-magic arts," among them
the collecting of fingerprints. (Twain read about fingerprinting in the early
1890s, before its establishment as a forensic science.) His catalogue of the
townspeople's fingerprints allows Wilson to vindicate the twins by proving that the murderer was Tom and, more fantastically, to reveal that Tom
is actually the "black" Chambers.

The Tom-Chambers cradle switch originated as a subplot within an
earlier short story called "Those Extraordinary Twins." In the earlier narrative the Capello twins are brought to trial on the charge of kicking Tom
Driscoll, but the jury can reach no verdict as to which of the two is guilty
since in this version the brothers are conjoined ("Siamese") twins who
share control of a single pair of legs. Twain eventually separated the two
stories by what he called "a literary Cesarean operation" and separated
the twins in *Pudd'nhead Wilson*.[65] (He botched the second of these operations slightly, leaving traces of the twins' conjoinedness in passages that
appear to have been imported from the story into the novel unedited.)[66]
What the twins are doing in the novel at all, beyond supplying the plot
device of the stolen knife, is unclear, though some critics have found in
the twins' conjoined status in the earlier narrative a symbol of the racial
indeterminacy it is Pudd'nhead Wilson's dubious achievement to "resolve" in the later one. In the novel, by this reading, the twins' separate
but still-entangled selves embody the spectacular moral failure of separate-but-equal and the incoherence of the one-drop rule that creates dis-
crete racial categories only by acknowledging the race-mixing it is its function to deny.[67]

If the twins persist in the novel as a kind of psychic residue, a repository
of Twain's ambivalent experience of the racial divide, they likewise carry
a burden of religious ambivalence by signaling the inadequacy of the only
spiritual divides acknowledged in Dawson's Landing. In *Pudd'nhead Wilson* the twins' religious otherness disappears into Dawson's Landing's
spiritual landscape, with its neat separation of religious alternatives by
race (black or white) and by the presence or absence of Protestant conviction. In the earlier story, however, the twins' peculiar embodiment makes
it literally impossible for them to stand on either side of the Protestant-

secular divide. "Whenever Luigi had possession of the legs, he carried Angelo to balls, rum shops, sons of liberty parades, horse races, campaign riots, and everywhere else that could damage him with the party and the church; and when it was Angelo's week he carried Luigi diligently to all manner of moral and religious gatherings, doing his best to regain the ground he had lost before. . . . [A]s a result of these double performances, there was a storm blowing all the time . . . a storm of frantic criticism of the twins, and rage over their extravagant, incomprehensible conduct."[68]

Twain based "Those Extraordinary Twins" on the Italian Tocci brothers, "a youthful Italian freak—or freaks . . . on exhibition in our cities."[69] The freakishness that in the short story renders the twins extravagant and incomprehensible to both the town's Christians and its Freethinkers is preserved in some of the novel's hastily imported passages, as when Luigi and Angelo tell of being "placed among the attractions of a cheap museum" (947) or are derided by the townspeople as "side show riff raff, dime-museum freaks" (1017). Extraordinary bodies and their display also figure prominently in association with European Catholicism in *Innocents Abroad*, where disfigured and dismembered bodies preserved as relics attract credulous pilgrims to the shrines and chapels Twain described as "clap-trap side-shows and unseemly impostures of every kind."[70] (The twins' name, Capello, means "chapel" in Italian.)

If the exoticism of Italian Catholicism, in Twain's imagination, renders bodies extravagantly, at times uncomfortably present, more conventional strains of Christianity seem to cause bodies (and their attributes of race and sexuality) to disappear. Thus in *Following the Equator* another set of religious exotics, Bombay's "Parsee women—perfect flower-beds of brilliant color" recall the black slave women of Twain's boyhood, while missionary Christianity washes the color from Ceylon's "Christian black girls, Europeanly dressed" who become the "duplicates" of Twain's English and American companions.[71] "The first thing a missionary teaches a savage is indecency," Twain wrote in his notebook; "he makes him put clothes on"[72]—a fate evaded, Twain observed, by the Kanaka women of the Sandwich Islands, "dark, gingerbread colored beauties" whose eager desire to "fornicate," as he put it, made them unsalvageable by the Christian missionaries sent to convert them.[73] Likewise in Twain's own voicing of cross-religious desire—his penchant for singing black spirituals "just as though all of the sorrows of them Negroes was upon 'im,"[74] his impulse to shed his colorless "Christian" clothes for the brilliant robes of a Hindu servant, or his confessed wish at times "to be a [Catholic] priest's slave . . . & duck my head & crook my knee at a painted image & glide out again with my immortal part refreshed"[75]—to depart from Anglo-Saxon Protestantism is potentially to arrive at a more keenly felt embodiment and more fully awakened senses, even at the cost of personal or social debility.

The invisibility of the twins' religious otherness forecloses a more complete rehearsal of these forms of spiritual desire in *Pudd'nhead Wilson*, where religious difference narrows to the opposition between white and black Christianity, on the one hand, or between Christianity and secular Free Thought, on the other. If one burden of the novel is to trouble the line dividing white and black, however, so the difference between believers and unbelievers also proves unreliable, at least in the response of either to questions of race. Although two of the town's most prominent citizens, Judge Driscoll and Pembroke Howard, were "a free thinker and . . . a strong and determined Presbyterian," respectively, "their warm intimacy suffered no impairment in consequence. They were men whose opinions were their own property." The intimacy of the two men, whose property includes slaves as well as their differing opinions on spiritual matters, resides in their membership in the "aristocracy" of Old Virginia and joint adherence to its higher laws. "These laws required certain things" of a man "which his religion might forbid—then his religion must yield— the laws could not be relaxed to accommodate religions or anything else" (985–86).

Indeed, if Catholicism's positive valence in Twain's imagination sets it apart from a world where spiritual eccentricities yield to convention, the effect of its negative valence is to Catholicize Dawson's Landing in just those qualities that make for its initial adoration of the European twins. In *Life on the Mississippi*, Twain praises the revolution that "broke the chains of the *ancien regime* and of the church," making "abject slaves" into "freemen," and then laments that revolution's undoing by a revival of "medieval chivalry silliness": "Then comes Sir Walter Scott with his enchantments, and by his single might checks this wave of progress, and even turns it back, sets the world in love with dreams and phantoms, with decayed and swinish forms of religion, with decayed and degraded forms of government, with the sillinesses and emptinesses, sham grandeurs, sham gauds and sham chivalries of a brainless and worthless long-vanished society." Thanks to Scott, "the genuine and wholesome civilization of the nineteenth century is curiously commingled with the . . . Middle-Age sham civilization and so you have practical, common-sense, progressive ideals . . . mixed up with the duel, the inflated speech, and the jejune romanticism of an absurd past that is dead, and out of charity ought to be buried. . . . It was Sir Walter that made every gentleman in the South a Major or a Colonel, or a General or a Judge. . . . For it was he that created rank and caste down there. . . . [H]e is in great measure responsible for the war" (500–501).

The charges against Walter Scott are those Twain elsewhere brings against the Catholic Church: introducing "inherited dignities and unearned titles" and "taint[ing]" even "American blood" with "reverence for rank and title."[76] In *Pudd'nhead Wilson* the Catholic "taint" extends even to secular faith: as the Freethinker Judge Driscoll and the Presbyterian Pembroke Howard are equally devoted to the religion of aristocracy, so the Freethinker David Wilson and the European twins are equally adept in the "occult arts" that *A Connecticut Yankee in King Arthur's Court* associates with pre-Reformation Christianity and whose effect here is to sell Tom Driscoll into slavery. Until Wilson's courtroom victory, his interest in the "black-magic arts," with their whiff of foreignness, earns only ridicule from his neighbors: "Wilson's got a scheme for driving plain widow-glass out of the market by decorating it with greasy finger-marks, and getting rich by selling it at famine prices to the crowned heads over in Europe to outfit their palaces with" (974). The twins, however, whose own history calls up "dim and awful associations with gilded courts and stately ceremony and anointed kingship" (948), recognize the value of Wilson's "magic arts" from their acquaintance with the "strange sights and strange customs" of other worlds: "We have seen something of palmistry in our wanderings, and know very well what astonishing things it can do. If it isn't a science, and one of the greatest of them too, I don't know what its other name ought to be. In the Orient—" (976). If the twins' approval locates Wilson's clandestine arts among what *A Connecticut Yankee* figures as "the powerfulest enchantment[s] known to the princes of the occult arts in the land of the East,"[77] where magical thinking blocks both democratic and scientific progress, *Pudd'nhead Wilson* vindicates the twins' assessment of Wilson's "black-magic arts" as "science." Wilson's "miraculous" ability to prove Tom Driscoll's "true" racial identity, Twain affirmed in a letter to his editor, was "quite thoroughly and scientifically examined by Mr. Galt" and remains within the "the bounds of his ascertained facts."[78] ("Mr. Galt" was Sir Francis Galton, who pioneered the study of fingerprinting but who was primarily celebrated in America as the spokesman for eugenicist theories of protection from white racial decay through immigration and miscegenation.)

Near the end of his life Twain wrote that the deafness of religion to scientific facts kept believers in the condition of "lay slaves" beholden to outmoded and punishing doctrines.[79] In *Pudd'nhead Wilson*, however, neither Galton's "science" nor its liberation from foreign religious superstition in the hands of the freethinking Wilson is sufficiently powerful to end slavery or to reform the "jejune . . . middle-age sham civilization" that is Dawson's Landing. Nor, since its effect is to shore up the "fiction of law and custom" (925) that fixes identity first as racial and then as only either black or white, can Wilson's courtroom victory accommodate the kinds of fluidity embodied in the confusion of Tom and Chambers and elsewhere associated with Negro spirituals, Old World mixtures, or Hindu dress. If Wilson's science rewrites "black-magic arts" as "established facts" that expunge hidden blackness from Dawson's Landing, the novel ends in retreat from this clarified secular space, as the Italian twins return to Europe, Roxy to her "colored" church, and Twain to the Catholic mystery of *Joan of Arc*.

MUDDYING THE SACRED WHITES

"Protestant ruminations on the Eternal City" Stephen Rachman observes of nineteenth-century American travelers' accounts of Rome, are typically "questions of dirt."[80] This is true of *Innocents Abroad*, with its attention to the "rags and vermin" of Italy's beggars, the "jeweled frippery" of its churches, and the ubiquitous reliquaries and catacombs with their reminders of death-in-life—the blood of martyrs preserved in a supposed state of "miraculous liquefaction," curving vines and flowers fashioned by monks from human bones—that link the ostentatious church and its unwashed subjects in a single register of corruption and decay.[81] Dirt and decay, indeed, mark not only Rome but all religious cultures outside of what *Innocents Abroad*, written as Twain was both launching his career as an American man of letters and vying for acceptance in his wife's Presbyterian family, gamely called the "true religion—which is ours."[82] Constantinople is clotted with lepers; Arab children suffer "all the distempers that are bred of indolence, dirt, and iniquity"; the Holy Land presents the "usual assemblage of squalid humanity" who remind Twain of American Indians in being "infested with vermin . . . the dirt caked on them till it amounted to bark."[83] Such descriptions—similar ones appear in Twain's letters and journalism of the time[84]—conflate religious, national, and racial otherness in contaminating opposition to the normative Protestant Christianity Twain here briefly entertained as "true."

Sander Gilman suggests that Twain habitually linked dirt and disease with exotic religions because he needed to separate his own white, Christian, American identity from that of Jews and other foreigners.[85] By the last decade or so of his life, however, dirt and disease had come to signal less the threatening otherness of "foreign" religions than the moral corruption of what Twain in 1900 called the American "religion" of patriotism.[86] Five years after his conversion to anti-imperialism in the face of U.S. expansion in the Philippines—"I am [an 'anti-imperialist']," he told the *Chicago Tribune* in 1900, "A year ago I wasn't"[87]—Twain began *Three Thousand Years among the Microbes*, in which germ-nations battle among themselves to colonize (in a "high policy" of "Benevolent Assimilation") the diseased body they take to be their universe.[88] In *The Secret History of Eddypus*, also from this period, America "wipe[s] its feet upon the Declaration" and proceeds to make "the sly and treacherous betrayal of weak republics its amusement, and the stealing of their land and the assassination of their liberties its trade."[89] Without losing sight of the Russian massacre of Jews, Leopold II's "murder, mutilation . . . [and] rapine" in the Congo, or the crushing of the Boers by the British in South Africa, Twain's anti-imperialist writings explicitly criticize U.S. policy not only for its extension of the doctrine of Manifest Destiny into Hawai'i, Cuba, Puerto Rico, and the Philippines but also for continuing injustices within its borders. Having "imported [its] imperialism from monarchical Europe," Twain wrote, the United States now "Americaniz[es] Europe" by instructing it in the arts of "poisoning the world for cash" and "work[ing] the widow and orphan for profit."[90] (It is when "foreigners" become "Americanized" and not vice versa, Twain wrote, that they "los[e their] ancient sympathies for oppressed peoples struggling for life and liberty.")[91]

America's transformation from republic to empire prompted comparison with ancient Rome, whose "material prosperity" and "spreading dominion"—"not fortunate glories" but "a disease and freighted with death"—tell "exactly our own history over again." This is so, Twain wrote, because the human race "never changes": "In the course of ages it has built up several great and worshipful civilizations," each "bearing deadly gifts which looked like benefits and were welcomed, whereupon the decay and destruction of each of these stately civilizations has followed."[92] The eponymous narrator of *The Chronicle of Young Satan* renders a similar verdict: "Man is made of dirt—I *saw* him made. I am not made of dirt. Man is a museum of disgusting diseases, a home of impurities; he comes to-day and is gone to-morrow, he begins as dirt and departs as stench; I am of the aristocracy of the Imperishables. And man has the *Moral Sense*."[93]

The Chronicle of Young Satan, Schoolhouse Hill, and *No. 44: The Mysterious Stranger* form the manuscript fragments of a novel Twain worked on from 1897 onward without completing. Each of the three *Mysterious Stranger* manuscripts features a trickster in the form of an adolescent boy, a nephew of Satan, who travels across continents and centuries to impart his shape-shifting powers to a select few (characters much like Tom and Huck, as it happens) while pointing always to the poverty of human striving and the inevitable decline of religions and civilizations. One of the more intriguing attempts to explain "44," the name of the Mysterious Stranger figure in two versions of the narrative, looks back to the Levin brothers in Hannibal, who belonged to the first Jewish family Twain ever knew: together the two boys were called "Twice Levin—twenty-two." Jewishness was the Levins' most distinctive trait in Twain's memory of them, making 44 doubly Jewish, because twice 22.[94] Such a link between Jewishness and the dark angels of the Mysterious Stranger manuscripts plays on a number of long-standing tropes: the Wandering Jew, the hoary antiquity of the Jews, the Jew in league with the devil. (The devil was a sympathetic figure in Twain's imagination: both the Jews and the devil were Christianity's scapegoats, the contributions of neither to civilization given their due.) And as Jews and other religious foreigners in Twain's depictions manage often to escape the black/white racial divide, so 44 and his counterparts assume different racial and national identities at will: Young Satan becomes a Hindu magician; "Quarante-quatre" in *School-house Hill* shifts easily between languages and dialects; 44 appears as a black man to play a Jew's harp and sing "Buffalo Gals" and "Sewannee River," music "silken dress and a white face and white graces would have profaned."[95]

To my ear, the name 44 also recalls the numbered mud islets Twain tells of learning to navigate in *Life on the Mississippi* ("bowling down the bend above island 66. . . . *Mark* twain!" 310–11). They were numbered rather than named because they constantly changed shape and location and made the course of the Mississippi "as dissolving and changeful as if it had been a mountain of butter" (278); Twain remembered one that threw the river into particularly vexing angles as "Devil's Island" (399). Like the stereotypically ancient Jew ("clothed," Twain wrote, "in the damp and cobwebby mold of antiquity"),[96] the river marks the passage of centuries, as *Life on the Mississippi* notes, by tracing the progress and decline of civilizations along its banks (e.g., 230–32). At the same time that Jewishness and the river are steeped in histories of slavery and imperialism, moreover, both also remain mysteriously aloof from those histories, Jewishness in being the "immortal" faith Twain exempted from the predatory decadence that corrupted other cultures and religions,[97] the river in passing through territories "stolen and re-stolen 500 times,"[98] yet inducing in its "majestic, unchanging sameness" a "symbol of eternity" (391) remote from human striving. And as the Mysterious Stranger figures and the Jew in Twain's imagination dissolve the boundaries of racial and national identity, so the river's numbered islets play "havoc with boundary lines"—one moment a "man is living in the State of Mississippi," the next he's "subject to the laws of the State of Louisiana" (228). That is, one could be legally black one moment and white the next, now slave and now free, subject now to U.S. and now to French-derived laws, all depending on the evanescent accretions of mud the river churns up in its course.

What is strange then, is Young Satan's insistence that unlike his audience he is *not* made of dirt, that he is of the "aristocracy of the Imperishables," since he and his counterparts in each of the *Mysterious Stranger* manuscripts stand in the same shifting relationship to history and identity as do the muddy Mississippi and the "dirty" Jews. In 1907 Twain wore his by-then customary white suit to a banquet at London's Savage Club, to which he had been elected an honorary member three decades before, and delivered nearly the same assessment as Young Satan's of his listeners: "When I find myself in assemblies like this, with everybody in black clothes, I know I possess something that is superior to every one else's. Clothes are never clean. You don't know whether they are clean or not because you can't see. . . . I am proud to say that I can wear a white suit of clothes without a blemish for three days. . . . I do not want to boast. I only want to make you understand that you are not clean."[99] In one of Twain's earliest public appearances in the white suit—at a White House reception, no less—he told reporters that it was the "uniform of the American Association of Purity and Perfection," to which he himself was "the only man in the country eligible" to belong.[100]

While the white suit would become identified with Mark Twain as indelibly as the *Adventures of Huckleberry Finn*, the memorable dress belongs to a period of largely forgotten production, speculative narratives that break off without finishing and polemics that went unpublished in Twain's lifetime. And if the singular white suit stands in ironic contrast to the spotty literary output, it remains at least as difficult to read. Obviously, unreliably, the white suit projects a white persona: in *Pudd'nhead Wilson*, we recall, the infant slave Chambers becomes the white slave owner Tom Driscoll by being dressed in his master's "holy" clothes, his white Sunday gown (937, 930). In his white linen or silk-lined flannels Twain must have reminded audiences of the rajas who, according to *Following the Equator*, wrested the control of India from "Hindoo and Mohammed rulers" and "establish[ed] British superiority there."[101] In *Following the Equator*, written just as the United States was launching the imperialist career that would soon eclipse Britain's, Twain confessed that his own and his Anglo-Saxon companions' white "Christian" clothes were in fact "a lie": "they are on us to expose us, to advertise what we wear them to conceal"; "they are . . . a pretence that we despise gorgeous colors"; "yes, our clothes are a lie. . . . [T]hey are the ugly and appropriate outward exposure of an inward sham and a moral decay."[102]

In *Pudd'nhead Wilson*, the "lie" of white Christian clothing enables Roxy's son to grow up "a white gen'l'man en rich" (966), though unable to forget "the 'nigger' in him" (969) from the moment the truth of his birth is revealed. In a manuscript passage Twain eventually rejected, Tom Driscoll "loathed the 'nigger' in him, but got pleasure out of bringing this secret 'filth,' as he called it, into familiar and constant contact with the sacred whites."[103] In pronouncing his White House and Savage Club audiences "unclean" Twain makes the white suit an invisible reproach to *these* sacred whites, to what in his "Greeting to the Twentieth Century" he calls the "stately maiden named Christendom," who "return[s] bedraggled, besmirched, and dishonored from pirate-raids in Kiao-Chou, Manchuria, South Africa, & the Philippines, with her soul full of meanness, her pocket full of boodle, and her mouth full of pious hypocrisies. Give her soap and a towel, but hide the looking-glass."[104]

If the spectacularly unblemished white suit would seem to distance Twain from an ensoiling "Christendom," however, it offers no comparable exemption from "whiteness." In "The Stupendous Procession," another of the unfinished narratives from Twain's white-suited period, modern nation-states parade with symbols of their territorial conquests, whiteness trumpeting its own ability to contain, as it were, all colors. America, the last and largest in the procession, marches with banners that pointedly revise the Declaration of Independence—"All white men are born free and equal"; the Fourteenth Amendment—"white slavery shall no longer exist where the American flag floats"; and the "Battle Hymn of the Republic"—"Christ died to make white men holy; he [Abraham Lincoln] died to make white men free."[105]

Complicating the gesture of the white suit even further is Twain's insistence that he chose to wear white because in fact he loved colors. In his early public appearances in the white suit Twain likened it to the "splendid dress" of the middle ages: "gorgeous, glorious, gaudy costumes—then we could wear colors!" Elaborating for reporters, he asked: "Why not adopt some of the women's styles? They always have beautiful fabrics, splendid colors, and, moreover, women's clothes are always pretty."[106] Twain indulged fantasies of gender crossing in the fragmentary dream narratives he was writing at the time; his desire to wear splendid colors is the desire, Susan Gillman suggests, to render gender identity permeable. But it seems equally the desire to escape the identity the white suit itself became a component of: Twain the exemplar of Americanness, the icon of American civil religion.

In this sense the flamboyant white suit asks to be read as a kind of WASP drag, a symbol whose entangled referents include both white, American, Christian identity and the alternative identities that *Following the Equator* renders in the medium of extravagant dress. The pointedly nonflamboyant clothes that identify Twain and his white American companions as "Christian" in that book make their national and racial identity continuous with religious identity, though religious identity of a rather contentless sort. Twain is Christian only insofar as he is also white and American, all default identities within the imaginary landscape of American civil religion. *Following the Equator* also follows a civil-religious imaginary in figuring this "Christian" identity as first and foremost a voluntary one, a matter of consent (which can, as in Twain's case, be withheld) and not of descent, as is presumably the case for the racialized religious exotics of the Old World or Far East. *Following the Equator* connects the civil-religious imagination to the imperial imagination of otherness in its suggestion that the person for whom religion is insepara- ble from "religious freedom," from the cherished, supremely American right to pick and choose, also enjoys a privileged, nonreciprocal access to the mysterious worlds of those for whom religion lies closer to race, in the variously liberating and confining precincts of embodiment. At the same time, *Following the Equator* exposes fantasies of unbridled access to these exotic worlds as faintly ridiculous, politically ominous, and finally impossible desires. The passage that identifies white Christian clothing as the "lie . . . that we despise gorgeous colors" continues:

> [W]e do love brilliant colors and graceful costumes. . . . [W]e go to the theater to look at them and grieve that we can't be clothed like that. We go to the King's ball, when we get a chance, and are glad of a sight of the splendid uniforms and the glittering orders. When we are granted permission to attend an imperial drawing-room we shut ourselves up in private and parade around in the theatrical court-dress by the hour, and admire ourselves in the glass, and are utterly happy; and every member of every governor's staff in demo- cratic America does the same with his grand new uniform—and if he is not watched he will get himself photographed in it, too.
>
> The last little brown boy I chanced to notice in the crowds and swarms of Columbo had nothing on but a twine string around his waist, but in my memory the frank honesty of his costume still stands out in pleasant contrast with the odious flummery in which the little Sunday School dowdies were masquerading.[107]

The "dowdies" are the black mission-schooled pupils whose dress matches that of the American tourists among whom Twain is "ashamed to be seen," prompting his exonerating confession that in fact "we do love" the Orient's brilliant colors and the racial and religious variety they mark.[108] All he can offer as evidence of that love, however, are instances of imperial pageantry that give the lie to American democracy. To forego—as much as to uphold—the "pretense that we despise gorgeous colors" is to find oneself on the imperialists' side of the divide.

At once camouflage and scarlet letter, the white suit advertises Twain's "quintessential" Americanness, in all of its intricately knotted tensions and evasions. In 1906 Twain wrote to his publisher that he wanted to wear all colors, but resigned himself to white. "I can't bear to put on black clothes again," he wrote; "I wish I could wear white all winter. I should prefer, of course, to wear colors, beautiful rainbow hues. . . . I should like to dress in a loose and flowing costume made all of silks and velvets resplendent with stunning dyes."[109] No comparable sense of am- bivalence or renunciation inheres, it would seem, in the image of the white-suited Twain that has for a century been instantly recognizable in the visual media of American consumer culture, including advertisements for life insurance, cigars, resorts, banks, and package tours of the world. Most "devote a corner to two boys on a raft," Louis Budd observes of these displays of the "white-color-coded" Twain; "surely he is still reminiscing about them."[110] An iconic national memory of freedom flourishes just where the author avowed limitation; the civil-religious myth of Mark Twain fills and overfills the space he ceded to identities he could not assume, narratives he could not finish, varieties of experience he could not enter.

SECULARISM, FEMINISM, IMPERIALISM: CHARLOTTE PERKINS GILMAN AND THE PROGRESS NARRATIVE OF U.S. FEMINISM

HOW MIGHT a theory of secularization serve to unite the seemingly disparate discourses of feminism and racial imperialism? This is a question that might fruitfully be put to a promising departure in the writing of U.S. women's history, which has sought to place the American women's movement in the latter nineteenth century within the contours of a broader, social-evolutionary discourse of civilization. In *White Women's Rights: The Racial Origins of Feminism in the United States*—which can stand in for much of the best of this work—Louise Newman calls attention to the ways that nineteenth-century appeals on behalf of women's rights drew strength from and furthered a range of "civilizing missions and imperial projects" by which the United States extended its power over so-called primitive peoples at home and abroad.[1] The evangelical Christianity of the emergent white middle class, with its gendered spheres of home and world, proved especially amenable to such alliances: the assumption that Protestant Christianity was the most advanced religion, in relation to which others were primitive, allowed evangelical women to take part in the "civilizing" operations of empire, associated with men, without appearing to depart from their appointed sphere, associated with Christianity. Women who identified the cause of women's rights with the superiority of Western, Christian civilization—in part through the shrewd deployment of a vocabulary that kept the implicit degradation of non-Western, non-Christian women in view: the harem, the seraglio, foot-binding, child-marriage, suttee—commanded all the authority of the West's imperial reach even as their access to public, institutional forms of power remained quite limited.[2] As we saw in the domestic writing of Catharine Beecher and Harriet Beecher Stowe, for example, the duties of the Christian housewife to her home and family serve the larger purpose of enabling "Christian families" to gather about them "Christian neighborhoods . . . [so that] ere long colonies from these prosperous and Christian communities [may] . . . go forth to shine as 'lights of the world' in all the now darkened nations."[3] Reconceived as part of a broader civilizing mission, domestic ideology could in turn be made to serve the emancipatory ambitions of white, middle-class, Protestant women. Since "a state is but an association of families," insisted Stowe, "there is no reason why [woman] should be more powerless in the state than in the home."[4]

Implicit in the task of recovering a history of cooperation between movements to expand women's freedoms, on the one hand, and movements to consolidate Anglo-Saxon domination, on the other, is a call to redress that history by disentangling feminism from imperialism in the present, as far as possible. If the historical articulations between women's rights and U.S. imperialism are clearest in the realm of religion, however, this is also where the required work of *dis*articulation would seem to be all but done, since the terrain on which white, middle-class women managed most successfully to enlarge their political and social authority in the nineteenth century—evangelical Christianity—is also the terrain from which American feminism in its second and third waves has most concertedly retreated in its efforts to constitute itself as genuinely progressive. Which leaves a question that needful interrogations of the social-evolutionary paradigm in U.S. feminist history have so far neglected to ask: what happens to the forms of racial imperialism encoded within the progress narrative when feminists lay claim to that narrative in the name of secularism?

I pursue this question by looking at the career of American activist, social theorist, poet, and fiction writer Charlotte Perkins Gilman (1860–1935), a career that now includes a burgeoning of feminist scholarly interest in Gilman that gained critical mass in the 1970s and has yet to abate. Nor was Gilman unsung in her own day: Upton Sinclair called her "America's most brilliant woman poet and critic"; William Dean Howells praised her "wit flashing from profound conviction," and figures as diverse as Woodrow Wilson, Eugene Debs, and George Bernard Shaw quoted her verse from memory.[5] Gilman lectured throughout the United States and Europe and published in all five novels, eight books of nonfiction, and close to two thousand essays, stories, and poems. Her writings were translated into several languages and used in college courses in her lifetime; much of her work has since been reissued and is widely taught in women's studies and American literature courses today.[6]

Gilman's longevity—she began writing in the 1880s against the still-trenchant ideology of woman's domestic sphere—makes her a useful index not only to U.S. feminism's successive waves but also to the ways an avowedly secular academic feminism both announces and obscures its debt to an implicitly Protestant narrative of emancipation. This is the narrative that—for example—enabled pioneering women's rights activists like Elizabeth Cady Stanton not only to wield the language of "slavery" to join their own demands for greater freedom to the abolitionist cause, but also to mobilize a well-worn vocabulary of "priestcraft" to describe their oppression under patriarchy. Recall Stanton's 1860 speech to the American Anti-Slavery Society: "In the darkness and gloom of a false theology I was slowly sawing off the chains of my spiritual bondage, when for the first time, I met [abolitionist William Lloyd] Garrison in London. A few bold strokes from the hammer of truth, I was free! . . . [A] doubting soul suddenly born into the kingdom of reason and free thought. Is the bondage of the priest-ridden less galling than that of the slave, because we do not see the chains, the indelible scars, the festering wounds, the deep degradation of all the powers of the God-like mind? . . . No the mission of this Radical Anti-Slavery Movement is not to the African Slave alone, but to the slaves of custom, creed, and sex; and most faithfully has it done its work."[7]

Setting aside, for a moment, the stunning erosion of the singularity of racial bondage even in this supposed account of strengthened commitment to abolition: Stanton's narrative of her deliverance into the kingdom of free thought veers only slightly from the more conventional nineteenth-century script by which the emancipatory tropes of a liberalizing Protestantism guide the experience of evangelical Christian conversion. Nor is it far from Stanton's born-again experience to the consciousness-raising encounters that galvanized a second wave of U.S. feminist activism a century later. By that time, however, a certain "squeamishness about religious faith," as Ann Braude puts it, had set in among feminist historians, who muted the impact of religion on the American women's movement in apparent deference to the assumption that "religious women suffer from false consciousness and that their allegiance to patriarchal organizations makes them incapable of authentic work on behalf of women." In a new introduction to her now-classic *Radical Spirits: Spiritualism and Women's Rights in Nineteenth-Century America*, Braude describes her effort "to draw religious history and women's rights into a common narrative" as "the most difficult 'sell' of the book's goals."[8]

From this perspective, Gilman—the rebellious grand-niece, as it happened, of Catharine Beecher and Harriet Beecher Stowe—would seem to be the pivot on which American feminism turns itself from a Christian into a secular enterprise. This, indeed, is why she is revered. As a typical assessment has it, Gilman's "first book, *Women and Economics* . . . turned Aunt Catharine Beecher on her head by locating the home as the place of women's oppression, " while "her last work [*His Religion and Hers*] . . . repudiated the entire Beecher clan and their religion."[9] That celebratory sense of rupture between Gilman's secular vision and her evangelical Christian inheritance in fact belies what her writing more insistently records as continuity, a continuity whose racial dimension, as we'll see, gives an implicit historical coherence both to Gilman's model of a post-Christian America and to the feminist genealogy of which she forms a cherished part.

Despite her enormous productivity and considerable renown, Gilman believed she suffered from a chronic condition of "nerve bankruptcy" brought on by the depression that followed the birth of her daughter Katharine in 1885 and by the effort to maintain a semblance of domestic life during four years of a disappointing marriage to Walter Stetson. By Gilman's reckoning this weakness cost her twenty-seven years, "a little lifetime in itself, in which with my original strength of mind, the output of work could have been almost trebled."[10] The perception of curtailed and damaged "output" was especially agonizing to Gilman in light of her conviction that it was *work* that fueled the evolutionary advance of each generation over the last and that all one truly owed one's forebears—including in Gilman's case the celebrated Beechers—was "to be better than they were."[11] In this sense the *appearance* of rupture between Gilman's secular vision and her evangelical Protestant heritage is no accidental effect; indeed it seems that the entire point of Gilman's first and most acclaimed book, *Women and Economics*, was to subject to devastating social-scientific critique the ideology of woman's domestic sphere her Beecher aunts had promoted in works like *Principles of Domestic Science* and *The American Woman's Home*.

Having read little on the subject of economics and operating with only the "vaguest" recollection of what she had read,[12] Gilman wrote *Women and Economics* in six weeks, pausing to consult just two sources. One was biologists Patrick Geddes and J. Arthur Thomson's 1889 *Evolution of Sex*, which posited a metabolic basis for sexual difference—in brief, men spend energy; women store it. The other was sociologist Lester Frank Ward's 1888 essay "Our Better Halves," which advanced his "gynaeco-centric" theory of civilization: "Accepting evolution as we must," wrote Ward, we need to acknowledge that "woman *is* the race, and [that] the race can only be raised up as she is raised up."[13]

Nineteenth-century domestic ideology had depicted the Christian family circle, overseen by women, as capitalism's salvific counterpart: pious, nurturing, morally regenerative, and sealed from the corrosive energies of the market. *Women and Economics* begins from the premise that this hallowed division of gendered spheres is in fact a survival from cave-dwelling days, having come into being as soon as primitive men began to keep women forcibly confined for sexual purposes rather than fight other men for access to whatever women happened to be around. Defenseless in the face of this arrangement, women came to depend entirely on attracting the men who would keep them, with the result that women evolved as a degenerate species specializing in "sex functions." Men, meanwhile, developed the political and cultural systems that made them "human, far more than male" and set them "thousands of years in advance of the female," whose condition of dependence left her stalled at the evolutionary stage of "a savage in the forest."[14] As Gilman reiterated in *The Home: Its Work and Influence*: "In all this long period of progress the moving world has carried with it the unmoving home; the man free, the woman confined; the man specialising in a thousand industries, the woman still limited to her domestic functions."[15]

Gilman insisted that the enclosure of women in the home in fact thwarts progress not only for them but for men as well, since mothers necessarily transmit their regressive characteristics to their male and female children, and so keep "alive in us the instincts of a savage individualism which we should otherwise have well outgrown."[16] The solution she proposes is to socialize the domestic sphere, making its duties of childcare, cooking, and cleaning the responsibility not of mothers but of whole communities. Only in this way could women pursue their talents beyond the home and so evolve into fully civilized human beings. For Gilman the progress of humanity quite literally proceeds as women's work, since only the liberation of women's activity from the domestic sphere could remove the conditions of "arrested development, primitive industry, and crippled womanhood" that bind even civilized nations to a savage past.[17]

Clarifying proof that the domestic sphere *could* be "open[ed] to the blessed currents of progress that lead and lift us all" was to be found, for Gilman, in the realm of religion,[18] where strangling pressures and received ideas slowly but inevitably dissolve in the light of truth. "In place of the dark and cruel superstitions of old time, with the crushing weight of a strong cult of priests, we have a free and growing church, branching steadily wider as more minds differ, and coming nearer always to that final merging of religion in life which shall leave them indistinguishable."[19] Religion could be plotted on an evolutionary spectrum, with its dark and superstitious forms at one end and its enlightened disappearance (into "life") at the other. As Gilman explained, "[p]rimitive man bowed down and fell upon his face before almost everything, whether forces of nature or of art. To worship, to enshrine, to follow blindly, was instinctive with the savage." In contrast, the "civilized man has a larger outlook, a clearer, better-ordered brain. He bases reverence on knowledge, he loses fear in the light of understanding. Freedom and self-government have developed him."[20] That such an advance in religion furthered the cause of women's emancipation could go without saying. Human beings were made "to grow—to develope [*sic*]—to follow the radiant line of progress which [God] has set before us; lit with truth and built on Law; and that path is not to be followed by rite and ceremony, by sacrifice and abasement, by any arbitrary behavior assumed as especially pleasing to the distant Deity; but by the Virtue and uplifting of our common business—by the work which we do in the world! . . . That is the reason why housework is not sufficient for a sex."[21]

After writing several books, each of which returns to a version of this theme, Gilman in 1909 began a journal, *The Forerunner*, as a venue "to publish and edit myself and preach."[22] The "social philosophy" to be set forth in the journal, she wrote, "may be summarized under several heads":

> A. As to Human Life in general: That . . . it is as "natural" as any lower form, is governed by natural law and has at work upon it the same Lifting Force, often called God, which has developed all life forms, has brought us so far on our way, and is still pushing upward in us.
>
> B. As to Pain and Sin: That our visible difficulties and distresses are not inherent, not necessary, but merely due to our misconceptions, and may be easily and swiftly outlived as soon as we understand them.
>
> C. As to Religion: That the main error in all religions is in their demand for a fixed and absolute belief, a habit paralyzing to the human mind.
>
> D. As to God: That the force called God is the truest thing there is; a ceaselessly acting force, to which we are all welcome, always. There is no anger in it, no punishment, no need to be praised and placated or importuned with prayers. . . . In living in accordance with this ever present force we live naturally and follow the rules of social evolution.

And so on through P ("As to Progress"), Gilman listed the convictions she set herself to expound in the journal's seven-year run, writing every word of copy herself.[23] *The Forerunner* ultimately folded for lack of subscribers, and by the time of Gilman's death in 1935 all her books were out of print.

Obscurity proved comparatively brief. In 1956 the now-eminent historian Carl N. Degler sought to redress what he called "a neglect in American intellectual history difficult to explain" by writing "Charlotte Perkins Gilman on the Theory and Practice of Feminism," an essay that placed Gilman among the resources for a second wave of feminist scholarship in the 1960s and 1970s.[24] The revival of interest in Gilman during this period came largely from newly minted feminist scholars who by their own accounts felt marginalized by the neglect of women in American literary and cultural history and who found in Gilman a model for turning personal struggles into political ones. For many in this group the value of newly discovered stories like Gilman's "The Yellow Wallpaper," whose protagonist "was questioning marriage and motherhood in the interest of her need for some greater fulfillment," lay in the fact that the discovery came, as one critic put it, "at a time when we were posing the same questions about our own lives."[25] Feminist critics who "read [their] own li[ves]"[26] into Gilman's fiction typically buttressed their readings with now-familiar details drawn from Gilman's biography, including the break-up of her parents' marriage in Gilman's childhood, leaving her mother in poverty and deteriorating health, and Gilman's tenacity in securing an education through a home reading course when it was clear there would be no money for college (despite her only brother's being sent to MIT). Also frequently recounted were Gilman's own unsatisfying marriage and emotional collapse, her widely criticized decision to separate not only from her husband but from their child, whom she gave to Stetson's care, and the hunger for paternal approval that followed her into relationships with mentors like William Dean Howells and the sociologist Edward Ross. In what emerged from this era of scholarship as an established refrain, "women's experience" supplied Gilman's perennial themes, which one critic lists as "the absolute necessity for women to do 'meaningful work' outside the home; the stultifying oppression of patriarchal culture; the suffocating effects of the nineteenth-century doctrine of the 'woman's sphere,' the impossible 'double-bind' experience[d] by the women artist, and the depression and emotional breakdown which often result."[27]

EVOLUTIONARY FEMINISM

What commentary Gilman's view of religion has elicited, then or now—most readers have found it entirely unremarkable—would seem to support Braude's observation that among feminist historians the assumption that "religion and feminism are opposing forces in American culture" holds untroubled sway.[28] A quick sampling: one critic celebrates the ways Gilman "gleefully attacked the . . . religious manifestations of the Western 'master narrative'";[29] another feels "glee" at Gilman's having "repudiated the most sacred institutions of her time and ours: marriage, motherhood, home, religion";[30] a third (tempering the antic joy) suggests that Gilman's feminism emerges directly from her "rejection of religious authority," and that her "religious and moral struggle," in turn, "was connected with [her] struggle against the submissiveness, dependency, and suppression of self inherent in the Victorian conception of femininity."[31]

What might explain this exuberant embrace of Gilman as the paradigmatic secular feminist, the one who threw off the enslaving yoke of religion once and for all? Put another way: what other investments might the move to erase religion from U.S. feminist genealogy—a move evidently facilitated by Gilman's example—serve to obscure?

Inextricably bound up with Gilman's narrative of religious progress was a companion narrative of racial progress. Race, indeed, is the thorn on which Gilman's still-buoyant reputation as a feminist foremother has recently come to snag: although most of her readers persist in attributing her "stray" racist or anti-Semitic remarks to historical or psychological exigencies, a few have begun to insist that Gilman's critique of patriarchy relies for its power, in our day as in hers, on the identification between white women and backward races that runs through nearly all of her nonfiction works.[32] *The Home: Its Work and Influence*, for example, revisits the primal scene of *Women and Economics*, the sequestering of women so that men could become fully human. Surveying industrial advances over millennia ("Where . . . [once we] chewed and scraped the hides, wove barks and grasses . . . now the thousand manufactures of a million mills supply our complex needs and pleasures"), Gilman lights her rhetorical gaze on the contemporary middle-class home and finds there a woman who cooks, keeps house, and cares for children. "[W]hat! Has the world stopped! Is history a dream? Is social progress mere imagination?— *there she is yet!* Back of history, at the bottom of civilisation, untouched by a thousand whirling centuries, the primitive woman, in the primitive home, still toils at her primitive tasks. . . . [W]hat iron weight of custom, law, religion, can be adduced in explanation of such a paradox as this? . . . By what art, what charm, what miracle, has the twentieth century preserved *alive* the prehistoric squaw?"[33]

The comparison between the bourgeois housewife and the primitive "squaw" implicitly empowers the former insofar as its suggestion of equivalence is meant to mobilize Gilman's audience of implied readers to change. Gilman's poem "Two Callings," for example, warns that to serve "the Home" and not "the World" is to cast one's lot among "the squaw— the slave—the harem beauty."[34] The message is that the woman Gilman addresses may and should elect to serve "the World" even as her primitive counterpart remains choicelessly bound to "the Home." That is to say, primitive women remain bound to the primitive stage of development Gilman always associates with her notions of home. For while enclosure in middle-class homes rhetorically makes white women into primitives, the women who appear in Gilman's writings as squaws, Negroes, or immigrant peasant stock typically do not have such homes from which to be emancipated, and indeed their labor in other women's homes often provides the means of these other women's "humanization."

Thus Gilman ranks women of different cultures on an ascending scale. "Here are five mothers, equally loving. One is a Hottentot. One is an Eskimo. One is a Hindoo. One is a German peasant woman. One is an American and a successful physician. Which could do most for her children?"[35] This way of framing a question ostensibly about childrearing shows the influence of Victorian anthropologist Edward Burnet Tylor, whose *Primitive Culture* was one of the books in the home study program to which the haphazardly educated Gilman devoted herself at age eighteen. "The educated world of Europe and America," Tylor proposed by way of introducing his "rough scale of civilization," could readily measure "progress and retrogression" by "simply placing its own nations at one end of the social series and savage tribes at the other, arranging the rest of mankind between these limits according as they correspond more closely to civilized or savage life." Criteria for the classification of the stages of "culture, or civilization" include "the presence or absence, high or low development of the . . . arts [and] . . . scientific knowledge, the definiteness of religious belief or ceremony, the degree of social organization, and so forth. . . . Few would dispute that the following races are arrayed rightly in order of culture: Australian, Tahitian, Aztec, Chinese, Italian."[36]

Gilman would seem to be extending Tylor's evidence for the ranking of culture stages to include the opportunities a given culture affords its mothers to provide for their children. At the same time, she insists that no surfeit of maternal care can alter or compensate for the deficiencies of a low culture stage. "The young of the human race require for their best development not only the love and care of the mother, but the care and instruction of many besides their mother. So largely is this true that it may be said in extreme terms that it would be better for a child to-day to be left absolutely without father or mother of any sort, in the city of Boston, for instance, than to be supplied with a large and affectionate family and be planted with them in Darkest Africa."[37] And lest the young Bostonian's advantages be perceived as "merely" cultural, Gilman argues that were one "buying babies, investing in young human stock . . . a sturdy English baby would be worth more than an equally vigorous young Fuegian," since given "the same training and care, you could develop higher faculties in the English specimen than in the Fuegian specimen, because it was better bred. . . . Education can do much; but the body and brain the child is born with are all that you have to educate."[38]

Which was not to say that lower races were incapable of being "raised." Gilman's "Suggestion on the Negro Problem," for example, straightforwardly assigns races "A" and "B" to evolutionary status 10 and 4, respectively, to pose the question of how race A "can best and most quickly promote the status of race B." To remedy the Negro's "present status"— "widely dissimilar and in many respects inferior," and "to us a social injury"—Gilman proposes that black men, women, and children should be "taken hold of by the state" and assigned to compulsory federal labor camps. Having made domestic labor the province of primitive races, Gilman could then solve the "Negro problem" and liberate white women from housework in a single stroke: "A training-school for domestic service might be part of each stationary base; and individuals could be sent from this on probation as it were—perfectly free to remain out in satisfactory home service, or to improve their condition as they were able. In case of unsatisfactory service they should be reenlisted—and try some other form of labor."[39] Needless to say, Gilman nowhere recommends a comparable policy of conscription for white women, whatever residual primitivism now obstructs their ascent to evolutionary stage 10, nor does she distinguish between black women and black men at evolutionary stage 4. As Gail Bederman suggests, the entire point of Gilman's project "was to create an alternative ideology of civilization in which white women could take their rightful place alongside white men as full participants."[40]

Gilman's alternative ideology of civilization, moreover, was mapped onto a rather conventional ideology of secularization, narrated through the characters of the primitive and the modern, and routed through the structures of Christian teleology, now rewritten as chapters in the story of Western "progress." With college beyond her financial reach, Gilman embarked at eighteen on a reading program of works she judged useful to the degree that "they showed our origin, our lines of development, the hope and method of further progress."[41] The list included William Boyd Dawkins's *Cave Hunting* (1874), James Fergusson's *Rude Stone Monuments in All Countries* (1872), William E. H. Lecky's *History of European Morals, from Augustus to Charlemagne* (1859), John Lubbock's *Prehistoric Times as Illustrated by Ancient Remains* (1865) and *The Origin of Civilization and the Primitive Condition of Man* (1870), George Rawlinson's *The Five Great Monarchies of the Ancient Eastern World* (1862–67), and E. B. Tylor's *Researches into the Early History of Mankind and the Development of Civilization* (1865), in addition to his *Primitive Culture* (1871).[42] Faithful to the contours of the colonial narrative that enabled them, these books added "primitive man" to the story of Western civilization, not only as the starting point of the modernizing trajectory through which the West defines itself, but also as its static counterpart, as that which does *not* progress.

It was in relation to this imagined primitive counterpart that ostensibly universal definitions of religion (like the vague nostrums of Gilman's *Forerunner*) first emerged in eighteenth-century Europe. As Talal Asad points out, the Renaissance encounter of European explorers with so-called primitive and oriental peoples created a two-pronged theological challenge for European Christianity, which was to square human diversity with the Mosaic account of creation and to square foreign belief systems with revealed Christianity's unimpeachable truths. The Enlightenment solution to the dilemma of difference, racial and spiritual, was to recast Christianity in light of the universal morality it allegedly augurs—the "*one religion*," as Kant put it, "which is valid for all men and at all times"—and then to plot all peoples and religious practices in progressive relation to this one, essential religion, as distinct from its phenomenal forms. Henceforth, Asad suggests, the Christian story of redemption, told in ways that sought to accommodate the heathen peoples encountered in colonial expeditions, could give way to a secular narrative of European world hegemony, told in developmental terms.[43]

This is the narrative to which Gilman sought to restore "woman." At about the time she began her reading course in evolutionary history and anthropology Gilman created what she called her own religion, "based on knowledge."[44] Even so, she continued to value her Judeo-Christian heritage as an enduringly supersessionary one: the Jew, she observed, refuses to evolve past the "tribal stage"; the status of women in America is higher than in "Romanist" Italy or Spain because Protestantism is "wider and deeper" and "more human" than Catholicism.[45] As the ultimate chapter in this progressive history, the "merging of religion in life" to which Gilman looked forward both parallels and extends the movement of Western women from savage to civilized conditions. Christianity, Gilman believed, was a central factor in the relative freedoms of white Western women in comparison to women of other races and cultures, which is why in her view its specific truth claims so easily do, and must, give way to Enlightenment critique even as its emancipatory trajectory remains unbroken. In this sense Gilman's secular faith in "knowledge" completes the path of reform begun in Christianity with the fulfillment/abolition of the Jewish law in Christ. Let "scientific truths annul the folly of ancient religious falsehood," Gilman wrote in "The Labor Movement," the prizewinning 1892 essay that launched her public career, "and erase from our minds the thought that labor is a curse." The "feeling that to labor is to admit inferiority," she argued, is a relic of primitive times, a "Hebrew idea, held in common with all early races," whose "weight with us is due to our receiving it as a religious truth."[46]

Twenty-four years later, as the *Forerunner* drew near the end of its run, Gilman reiterated her views:

Don't worry about God.

God is *there* working all the time, not angry or jealous or any of those things the limited intelligence of those ancient Hebrews discredited him with, but a steady lifting force. . . .

Cast out of your mind the trailing, sticky remnants of early misbelief. . . .

Do you not see the pathetic egotism of those early Hebrews in imagining their special God[?] . . . [W]e never shall have a decent uplifting religion till we first dissociate it from the utterly derogatory ideas we have been taught were "sacred," and second associate it with the rest of the laws of the universe.[47]

Gilman's last major theoretical work, *His Religion and Hers: A Study of the Faith of Our Fathers and the Work of Our Mothers*, argued that religion as currently practiced did not guide human beings in their main social duty, race improvement. As a contemporary explained in a glowing review, "She sees heaven not as a place, but as a race condition. . . . [She remains] serenely intent, unshakably insistent that all arts, all religions, shall bend to the religion of a race ascent to a perfected peace."[48] It matters little whether by race improvement Gilman meant the perfection of the white race or of the human race; to "improve" in this scheme meant always to be sloughing off the trailing, sticky remnants of outmoded religions and backward races.

The intertwining of these narratives of religious and racial progress has largely escaped scrutiny even by those who call Gilman's racism to account. And no doubt Gilman's notion of "decent, uplifting religion" is partly to blame, for its apparent contentlessness renders it unremarkable and even benign in contrast to the pointed specificity of her portrait of white Europeans as a superior race. But it is precisely the bland universalism of Gilman's religious vision that sets her safely ahead of Jews and other "early races" on the civilizing scale she brought to bear on her program for change. Gilman's project of merging the gendered spheres of "home" and "world" shifts the axis of subordination from gender to race, closing a gulf between white women and men by insisting that the more salient divide is the one separating women and men at the highest evolutionary stage from the women and men beneath them. In a similar way, her project of merging the erstwhile separate (and gendered) spheres of "religion" and "life" puts emancipated women on modernity's side of the gulf it fixes between the secularizing West, on one side, and less evolved religious cultures, on the other.

The path of disappearance by which religion comes eventually and inevitably to shade into "life," moreover, seems equally to have made this narrative's racism invisible to all but a handful of critics as anything more than a sign of Gilman's times, at worst an eclipse of visionary zeal. Thus a fairly standard apology has it that Gilman's "racist, anti-Semitic, and ethnocentric ideas . . . [must] reside primarily in the psychological realm, because the racist and nativist views she held did not fit with the vision she espoused of radical social and political transformation."[49] For Gilman's champions, indeed, holding fast to her all-encompassing vision of progress in which "things are all marching together"[50] seems to have made her racist opinions that much easier to jettison for being so clearly out of step. Even as it lies at the center of her vision of feminism as an evolutionary movement, then, Gilman's racism is routinely sacrificed without apparent loss to that vision, since only in the context of a feminism that evolves can Gilman's views on race be dismissed as a backward lapse or a psychological block, a snare of past mistakes to be smoothed and set right for progress to continue.

In this way Gilman's racial progressivism—her commitment to a model of social progress through racially graded evolutionary stages, now reflexively disowned as retrogressive and racist—persists undisturbed in the form of a similarly structured religious progressivism, in which reformed Christianity trumps all of its more or less tribal antecedents and rivals before blurring benignly into a universal secular. Perhaps the self-righting, self-transcending mechanism that allows race to disappear from feminist history requires this blurring for its continued demonstration.

HERLAND: THE IMPERIAL SECULAR

Consider what happens to religion and race in Gilman's *Herland*, originally serialized in the *Forerunner* in 1915, jubilantly hailed as a "lost feminist utopian novel" on its republication in 1979, and continuously in print ever since.[51] *Herland*'s claim to canonical status within second- and third-wave feminism as well as its story line appeal equally, it would seem, to utopian fantasies of the American women's movement as a coherent, pristine, and unbroken narrative of progress.[52]

The novel's eponymous setting is a nation populated only by women. Early in the book the American male sociologist who stumbles into this all-female domain helpfully observes that, though landlocked somewhere in South America, its inhabitants were unmistakably of "Aryan stock, and were once in contact with the best civilization of the old world" (54). What has secured the Herlanders' racial purity over centuries, we learn, was the abrupt demographic shift that took place two thousand years before the story opens. At that time, shortly after the male citizens of what was then a "bi-sexual" nation left their harem-bred women and slaves to fend off savage incursions from below, a volcanic eruption sealed off Herland's only mountain pass. "Very few men were left alive, save the slaves; and these now seized their opportunity, rose in revolt, killed their remaining masters even to the youngest boy . . . intending to take possession of the country with the remaining young women and girls" (54–55). In a gamely mimetic act of revolt, the Aryan women and girls immediately rise en masse to slay their "brutal conquerors" (55) preferring to die out rather than reproduce with racially inferior men. The remaining slave women forge a tenuous—at any rate, temporary—solidarity with the white women who, no longer confined to sexual and domestic service,

grow so rapidly in self-sufficiency that one among them eventually ac-
quires the miraculous ability to induce pregnancy by force of will. Her
offspring are similarly gifted, so that the all-female nation that comes into
being as a result—the women conceive only girls—is literally "[o]ne family, all descended from one mother," "a new race . . . [of] ultra-women,
inheriting only from women" (57).

The ultra-women's superiority is not only racial but also, inseparably,
religious. The novel is structured largely through conversations between
the intrepid sociologist, Van, and his plucky Herlander companion Ellador, each educating the other on the history and culture of their respective
worlds. When the conversation first turned to religion, Van reports, Ellador "made a sort of chart, superimposing the different religions as I described them, with a pin run through them all, as it were; their common
basis being a Dominant Power or Powers. . . . It was not hard to trace
our human imagery of the Divine Force up through successive stages of
bloodthirsty, sensual, proud and cruel gods of early times to the conception of a Common Father with its corollary of a Common Brotherhood.
This pleased her very much, and when I expatiated on the Omniscience,
Omnipotence, Omnipresence, and so on, of our God, and of the loving
kindness taught by his Son, she was much impressed" (109–10). The Herlanders' religion, Van learns, had followed a similar trajectory. Inhabitants of the original nation worshiped "a number of gods and goddesses;
but [after the disappearance of men] they lost all interest in deities of war
and plunder, and gradually centered on their Mother Goddess altogether.
Then, as they grew more intelligent, this had turned into a sort of Maternal Pantheism" (59), the personal deity giving way to an uplifting spiritual
force. "Their great Mother spirit was to them what their own motherhood
was—only magnified beyond human limits. That meant that they felt beneath and behind them an upholding, unfailing, serviceable love—perhaps it was really the accumulated mother-love of the race they felt—but
it was a Power" (111–12).

Van notes that the Herlanders' religion had no name, no domain apart
from the culture of their nation as a whole, and no rituals beyond parades
and civic pageants, "as much educational as religious, and as much social
as either. But they had a clear established connection between everything
they did—and God. Their cleanliness, their health, their exquisite order,
the rich peaceful beauty of the whole land, the happiness of the children,
and above all the constant progress they made—all this was their religion" (114–15). Van sums up Herland's religious virtues as "all that we
call 'good breeding' " (114): "You see they were Mothers, not in our sense
of helpless involuntary fecundity . . . but in the sense of Conscious Makers
of People" (68). A Herland elder tells Van that "we have, of course, made
it our first business to train out, to breed out, when possible, the lowest

types" by preventing some women from becoming mothers—women with "bad qualities," or women who desire to give birth out of a "disproportionate egotism" (82). For the "lowest" people reproductive desire amounts to "a brute passion, a mere 'instinct,' a wholly personal feeling"; for the race mothers of Herland "it was—a religion" (68).

Lest the fabulous conceit of an all-female utopia obscure the novel's function as a blueprint for change in Gilman's America, consider *Herland*'s debts to Edward Bellamy's *Looking Backward: 2000–1887*, the extraordinarily influential novel that gave rise to the progressive social movement known as Nationalism. Gilman began her public career in Nationalist publications and Nationalist clubs, which proliferated into the early 1890s against a backdrop of growing European and Asian immigration, rapid industrialization and economic depression, and the northern migration of southern black labor. This is the world that *Looking Backward*'s protagonist leaves behind, lapsing into a coma in 1887 and waking in the year 2000 to find the nation transformed into a paradise of peace and plenty. The change was accomplished, he groggily but patiently learns as the novel creaks onward, by the reforging of national citizenship as the condition of belonging to a single "family, a vital union, a common life."[53] Characters in the new world of the novel marvel that differences of wealth and education among Americans could once have opened gulfs as wide as those that divide races, divisions now but dimly perceived at the horizon of the global federation that determines policy toward "backward races" in far-off lands.[54] In contrast to its lengthy digressions on how the new, familial model of nationhood obliterates class distinctions, *Looking Backward* is silent on how national composition is to be made racially uniform, except to point out that among American women of the future, selective breeding takes precedence over passion or romantic love. In the new America of the novel "women sit aloft as judges of the race and reserve themselves to reward the winners. . . . Their feeling of duty in this respect amounts to a sense of religious consecration. It is a cult in which they educate their daughters from childhood."[55]

In this sense Herland's politics are Nationalist from the moment of its founding insurrection, which is why Ellador instinctively recognizes who the real Americans are on her subsequent travels with Van. Accompanying Van to the United States in *Herland*'s sequel *With Her in Ourland*—which even more patently brings *Herland*'s lessons to bear on the twentieth-century United States—Ellador observes that "Your little old New England towns and your fresh young western ones, have more of 'America' in them than is possible—could ever be possible—in such a political menagerie as New York. . . . New York's an oligarchy; it's a plutocracy; it's a hierarchy; it reverts to the clan system with its Irishmen, and back of that, to the patriarchy, with its Jews."[56] The description repeats what Ellador has apparently learned of "Judeo-Christian" history from Van, faithfully setting Jews behind Catholics and Catholics behind the enterprising Protestant settlers of the English-speaking New World. Within the larger narrative of the *Herland* saga, however, Protestant Americans— Van shrugs that he is "as much [Christian] as anything" (109)—recognize their own backwardness in relation to Herland's religion of race motherhood, the "most practical, comforting, progressive religion [Van] ever heard of" and the "more Christian" than his, he concedes, for needing never to be named as a religion at all (115). In *Herland* family and religion, nation and race form a single, all-inclusive sphere: "All the surrendering devotion our women have put into their private families, these women put into their country and race" (95). Religious subjectivity disappears into a radiant national subjectivity, its invisibility inseparable from its expansionist drive.

THE NEW AMERICAN WOMAN'S HOME

In this sense *Herland* continues the legacy of Protestant domestic reform that Gilman is valued, in large part, for appearing so roundly to subvert. Far from repudiating "home" and "religion," Gilman sought instead to dissolve the walls of separation that shut each off from the rest of national life. In this she follows the plotlines of her Beecher aunts' *The American Woman's Home*, whose final chapters extend the homemaker's duties out from and beyond her own family circle. Beecher and Stowe suggest that the "homeless, helpless, and vicious" would be better cared for in the embrace of the "loving Christian family" than in institutions; they argue that the "woman in the sacred retreat of a 'Christian home'" is best prepared to undertake the "divine labor" of redeeming the "lost and wandering" of the world.[57] The cultivation of the home as a space of centrifugal moral energies promotes an expansive sense of mission that extends beyond the home to the "homeless, helpless, and vicious" at its doors and beyond national borders to "darkened nations" in need of evangelical light. In this way Stowe and Beecher reimagine the world as the Christian home writ large; at the same time, the boundaries of both home and nation remain intact insofar as the project of Christianizing the world first requires that the American woman's home be Christian.

Gilman differed most from her aunts' model of domesticity in urging that housewives' duties be outsourced to institutions (like communal nurseries) rather than that the social duties now undertaken by institutions (like the care of orphans) also be made theirs. But the vision of home as a centrifugal national entity remains the same. "They had no exact analogue for our word *home*" we learn of the Herlanders, "any more than they had for the Roman-based *family*"; their devotion to one another "broaden[ed] to a devotion to their country and their people for which our word 'patriotism' is no definition at all. . . . They loved their country because it was their nursery, playground, and workshop—theirs and their children's" (94). For Gilman the sphere of the domestic, dismantled in its function as a "sacred retreat" from the public sphere, survived most crucially in its function as a bulwark against the foreign.[58] Even as she continued to represent the private home as a primitive relic whose demands deflect women from the more pressing task of advancing the race, she increasingly appealed to a rhetoric of the home's autonomy and the sanctity of the family in order to fortify national boundaries. "Our country is our home," Gilman insisted in "Is America Too Hospitable?"; "Any man who wants to turn his home either into an asylum or into a melting pot is,—well, he is a person of peculiar tastes."[59]

Two ways, then, in which Christianity "returns with a vengeance," in Ranu Samantrai's phrase,[60] to Gilman's post-Christian America. One is through the rendering of all but Euro-Protestant national subjects as interlopers within the secular space of freedom. For Gilman, America's policy toward "swarming immigrants" within and beyond its borders was a matter of maintaining the "distinct national character"—"a flexible progressiveness, an inventive ingenuity, a patience and broad kindliness of disposition"—that "the American people, as representing a group culture, brought with them from England and Holland and Scandinavia." And since not all nations have reached the democratic stage, it "would be far more helpful to the world if we could make such clear advance alone as to set all nations to imitating us, rather than to mix our physical stock and clog the half grown 'body politic' with all manner of undemocratic peoples."[61]

What Gilman took to heart from *The American Woman's Home* was not only its blueprint for empire but also the equivalence it insists on between "the principles of Christianity" and "the great principles of democracy."[62] The Christian spirit that radiates from the American Woman's Home to its outlying, heathen terrain Gilman rewrites as the superior democratic sense that distinguishes the American people from the "undemocratic peoples" over whom they nevertheless enjoy the near-limitless influence that Stowe and Beecher accorded to Protestant motherhood. This is why Ellador knows just how to diagnose and to manage the struggles among warring nations she encounters for the first time on leaving Herland. "Anything more like the behavior of a lot of poor, little, underbred children it would be hard to find, quarrelsome, selfish, each [national entity] bragging that he can 'lick' the others—oh you poor dears! How you do need your mother! and she's coming at last!"[63]

A second way that Christianity returns to patrol the sites of its disappearance is through the enforcement of gendered bodily disciplines—
namely compulsory heterosexuality and motherhood—that ensure the racially pure reproduction of that normatively Euro-Protestant, (post-)
Christian America.[64] As Gilman wrote of "the power and purpose of the
mother sex" in *His Religion and Hers*: "Whatever qualities she finds desir-
able she can develop in the race, through her initial function as a mother—
selection. This is her duty as a sex function, and her duty as a member of
a great race."[65] The American woman's "duty as a member of a great
race" is also "her" religion of the book's title, the liberating, dogma-free
corrective to all "androcentric religions" whose enslaving doctrines
would keep her at the level of "the crippled Chinese lady or the imprisoned odalisque."[66]

•   •   •

Gilman's champions have yet to find her religious views anything but
freeing, and even those few who thoroughly limn the dependence of Gilman's feminism on her narrative of racial progress have left her narrative
of religious progress largely unremarked. But why, beyond the desire to
combat antifeminist religious agendas, would feminist scholarship welcome such a trajectory? It would appear that what makes Gilman's supersessionary model of religion fail to rankle in the way her supersessionary
model of race has finally begun to do is also what accounts for the more
widespread difficulty of engaging religion as a category of analysis in contemporary cultural and feminist studies.[67]

The difficulty is nothing if not complex; here I pick out just two strands
of the knot, as I see it. One has to so with the ways the concepts of "religion" and the still more sacrosanct "religious freedom" have been constituted in the United States. The rule of government noninterference in (or
tolerance of) religion required that religion be largely relegated to the
interior space of personal belief in exchange for protection from coercive
intervention by the state.[68] And when religion is seen as interior, spiritual,
and subjective and not also as social, embodied, and historical there is
little more to be said, not least because the constitution of religion as
belief seems to make religion a matter of individual choice in ways that
race, for example, appears not to be. As Laura Levitt points out, however,
the framing of religious identity as wholly discretionary is itself a Protestant framing, one that bends all forms of religious affiliation to the volun-
taristic model of the Protestant congregation.[69] So too the construction of
religion as belief tallies with the aims and needs of a Protestant "priesthood of believers" far more neatly than it does those traditions and communities for which religious belonging means differently. Under the re-

gime of tolerance, moreover, whether religious, racial, or otherwise, "choice" often amounts to no more than the choice to accede to the conditions under which tolerance will be granted. Hence Gilman's suggestion that the solution to the "Jewish problem" is for Jews to simply leave off being Jews.[70]

Another strand of the difficulty—speaking of tolerance—is that the disciplines of women's and gender studies are so comparatively new, their place at the table so contested, that there is considerable reluctance among academic feminists to disturb the narrative that promises, breathtakingly, to include us. Never mind that seventy million Americans get the Christian Coalition's voter guide and a mere six thousand subscribe to *Signs*: secularism (we tell ourselves) makes us feminists into citizens of the university, the universe, the expansive realm whose claims to universality really must be universal, as opposed to the similar claims of religions, which secularism exposes as particular.[71] Further testimony to our sense of precariousness, our scramble for limited shelf space in the academy, comes in the way that in-house attempts to subject U.S. feminist history to critical scrutiny seem inevitably to take the form of canon debates: if we expose—and expunge—a white racist like Gilman, we get to add a black abolitionist, perhaps a lesbian Jew. But of course tidying this history, cleaning up the story of feminism we wish to tell, goes hand in hand with failing to see Gilman's racism as anything but a blind spot, a dark corner from which the progress narrative of secularism promises to deliver us.

A reason, then, for keeping Gilman on the reading list may be to lay bare the seemingly disparate trajectories that converge in her career, and so to trouble the binary between a supposedly progressive secularism and a supposedly regressive religion between which feminists tend to imagine ourselves as urgently needing to choose. We do well to note that the same binary, its terms differently weighted, is invoked by religionists quite at odds with avowedly feminist agendas; as Braude points out in her call for including religion in the story of the nineteenth-century women's movement, "secular feminism" is the watchword of progressive feminists and religious conservatives alike.[72] That the Christian right not only rails against a secular culture that permits feminism to flourish but couches its message in the lingua franca of religious freedom, however, might suggest that there is more to be done than simply to restore religion to the story of U.S. feminist beginnings, since such a restoration by itself does little to undermine the narrative of religious progress implicit in the invocation of feminism as a secular enterprise.

The religion/secularism binary at once assumes and conceals a teleological relation between its terms, which is why so many of Gilman's readers celebrate what they take to be her—and implicitly, U.S. feminism's—decisive break from an ostensibly backward religious inheritance, even as Gilman herself routinely equated the "line of social evolution" with "the line of Christianity."[73] Rather than modeling the rejection of an outmoded religious past, Gilman's example might help us instead to begin to see those places where Christianity and secular reason belong to the same constellation of knowledge and power. Gilman worked assiduously to find points of entry *into* this regime, undeterred by its impasses and blind turns, blazing a trail, as they say, for U.S. feminists to follow. But the map she left might be equally useful for finding a way out, or at least for thinking differently about the terrain on which we now stand. Such an effort yields the possibility of a secular feminism that would see various religious feminisms not simply as pieces of a past to be overcome, but as potential allies in dissent from a vision of progress in which, as Gilman saw it, religious difference would disappear into a single religion known simply as "Living and Life,"[74] and a particular model of Western, Christian civilization would realize its dominance by becoming, at long last, invisible.

Chapter Eight

F. SCOTT FITZGERALD'S CATHOLIC CLOSET

IN A LUMINOUS ESSAY on F. Scott Fitzgerald and the Jazz Age, Mitchell Breitweiser suggests that Fitzgerald's gift for rendering that epoch lay in his ability not only to get the details just right but to make even the most localizing of details seem to burn with the brightness of national energies, to participate sacramentally, as it were, in the nation itself. Fitzgerald's America, Breitwieser writes, "is where the Eucharist couples with the commodity fetish," the author's "spiritual and libidinal nationalism appropriating the emotional and theoretical energies of his Roman Catholic upbringing" to bestow "the kiss of worth on objects that . . . partake of [America's] splendor by expressing it symbolically." So too with Fitzgerald's most radiant characters: "Insofar as a person is a living seismograph of the idea, a pure register of abstract national content," that person is truly vital and alive; "insofar as he is particular—a person with projects, worries, tics, pleasures, and sorrows, all of them inflected by ethnicity, religion, class, gender, parental neurochemistry, and so on," he takes his place in what *The Great Gatsby*'s narrator Nick Carraway figures as a devitalized world of dust and ashes, "an outpost in which the rhythms of the capital have long since been forgotten."[1]

In an equally luminous reply to Breitwieser, Thomas J. Ferraro counters that if "Nick's absolutist distinction between infinite grace and foul dust is also Fitzgerald's then Fitzgerald is every bit as much a Jansenist as the adolescent protagonist in his short story 'Absolution' "—which was to have been *Gatsby*'s prologue before Fitzgerald decided on publishing it separately. In that story, a "spoiled Communion" and subsequent encounter with a disturbed parish priest launch Rudolph Miller/Jimmy Gatz beyond the parched Dakota wheat fields of his privative Catholic upbringing and toward "something ineffably gorgeous somewhere that had nothing to do with God."[2] "But 'Absolution,' " Ferraro rightly points out, "is mighty suspicious of sexually repressive, casuistic interpretations of the dispensations of God's grace," with the result that "the novel Fitzgerald wrote from this tellingly neglected tale"—*The Great Gatsby*—puts into play "a less bounded, more generous sacramental economy than Nick is able or willing" to articulate. It's "Nick's own tic of midwestern gentility of tone, innuendo, and misdirection," says Ferraro, "that tempts us to accept that idealist discourse of transcendent symbolism—which I read as a secularization of the *Protestant* theory of the eucharist, and which I think the novel undercuts. Just witness those shirts."[3]

The shirts in question, of course, are those Jay Gatsby produces for Daisy Buchanan's "well-loved eyes" one rainy afternoon on West Egg, a scene that follows the creakily staged impromptu that brings them together for the first time since Gatsby had been a penniless army officer briefly stationed in Daisy's Louisville five years before the novel begins.[4] The awkward "tea" at Nick's place earlier has since moved on to a tour of Gatsby's mansion that wends through music rooms and galleries and "period bedrooms swathed in rose and lavender silk" (60) before stopping at Gatsby's dressing room at the top of the house. Moving from room to room, Nick observes, Gatsby

> stared around at his possessions in a dazed way, as though in [Daisy's] actual and astounding presence none of it was any longer real. Once he nearly toppled down a flight of stairs . . .
>
> After his embarrassment and his unreasoning joy he was consumed with wonder at her presence. He had been full of the idea so long, dreamed it right through to the end, waited with his teeth set, so to speak, at an inconceivable pitch of intensity. Now, in the reaction, he was running down like an overwound clock.
>
> Recovering himself in a minute he opened for us two hulking patent cabinets which held his massed suits and dressing-gowns and ties, and his shirts, piled like bricks in stacks a dozen high.
>
> "I've got a man in England who buys me clothes. He sends over a selection of things at the beginning of each season, spring and fall."
>
> He took out a pile of shirts and began throwing them, one by one, before us, shirts of sheer linen and thick silk and fine flannel, which lost their folds as they fell and covered the table in many-colored disarray. While we admired he brought more and the soft rich heap mounted higher—shirts with stripes and scrolls and plaids in coral and apple-green and lavender and faint orange, with monograms of Indian blue. Suddenly, with a strained sound, Daisy bent her head into the shirts and began to cry stormily.
>
> "They're such beautiful shirts," she sobbed, her voice muffled in the thick folds. "It makes me sad because I've never seen such—such beautiful shirts before." (60–61)

Nearly every critic in pursuit of the "Catholic element" Fitzgerald told his editor the novel would contain has paused to comment on this scene, if only to belabor the apparent obviousness of its "sacramental" resonance.[5] But given that Gatsby has amassed his wardrobe (no less than his reproduction Merton College Library down the hall) with the goal of fitting in among moneyed WASPs like the Buchanans, just what could be said to be recognizably Catholic about "those shirts"? Ferraro's finely calibrated reflections on the *competing* sacramental imaginations at work in the novel—Gatsby's versus Nick's—would seem to lodge Gatsby's "Catholic" luster just this side of Nick's Midwest-to-Ivy "Protestant" polish, in its mirror, as it were: think how closely both Jay Gatsby and F. Scott Fitzgerald have become identified (as has John Fitzgerald Kennedy) with what continues to pass for a distinctively *American* style of dress and demeanor, a style that flashes WASP more legibly than any (other) ethnoreligious marking.[6] Fitzgerald's dapper alter ego Amory Blaine in *This Side of Paradise*—in whose honor some Princeton friends proposed to Scribner's an "exhibit of Fitzgeraldiana," including the "first Brooks suit worn by Fitzgerald," the "first yellow silk shirt worn by Fitzgerald at the beginning of his great success," and a "mirror"[7]—is pointedly, though priest-haunted, "not even a Catholic";[8] so keen was Fitzgerald to distance himself from the Irish Catholic provincialism of his own upbringing that he had even his army uniforms made by Brooks Brothers.[9] "When the time had come for him to wear good clothes," Fitzgerald wrote of his protagonist Dexter Green in "Winter Dreams," an earlier working through of Gatsby's rise, "he had known who were the best tailors in America, and the best tailors in America had made him the suit he wore this evening. . . . [H]e knew that to be careless in dress and mannerism required more confidence than to be careful. But carelessness was for his children. His mother's name had been Krimlisch. She had been a Bohemian of the peasant class and she had talked broken English to the end of her days. Her son must keep to the set patterns."[10]

To find the novel's all-but-submerged "Catholic element" in Gatsby's closet, then, is also to discover that the closet holds a good deal more than clothes. This "more" includes some queer energies, to be sure—we needn't revisit the more gossipy strains of Fitzgerald biography, or even the question of what actually happens between Nick and Mr. McKee, to be struck by the fact that it's Nick who delivers the sensuous goods on Gatsby from beginning to end. The soft rich folds that muffle Daisy's sobs give a sensuous form as well to the novel's mingled undercurrents of corruption, grandeur, longing, and loss: we never really do find out where Gatsby's money comes from, nor why even Nick should hear the "aching, grieving beauty" (59) in Daisy's voice just now, but at least some of what spills from the closet in this scene would seem to be the tangled emotions that come with discarding, incompletely, one identity for another. In Gatsby's case, the edifice of bricklike shirts now tumbling into disarray points to his deconstruction and precarious reconstruction of "home," his shame in relation to the family of origin he's disowned—the Gatzes were "shiftless and unsuccessful farm people"(65)—and shame too, perhaps, in the disowning. But if the closet is where shadow selves go hiding, it's also where the

Figure 4. "The twelve pages of ads for Ralph Lauren's clothes stand out as by far the most appealing, likeable, and even interesting thing in the whole 294 pages [of the inaugural issue of the revived *Vanity Fair*]: even the rather unbelievable picture of the young man (Princeton, Class of '20) who clearly, knowing he is beautiful, does not worry that he may be damned; his left hand caressing his right knee, his deep gaze that of a man who does not need a mirror to look timelessly on himself" (Henry Fairlie, "The Vanity of *Vanity Fair*"). Ralph Lauren, né Ralph Lifshitz, rose to prominence after designing the costumes for the 1976 movie version of *The Great Gatsby*. Photo courtesy of Polo/Ralph Lauren Corporation.

brighter materials of artifice are stored, and one effect of Gatsby's gorgeous wardrobe and "elaborate formality of speech" (32), each a notch campier than Dexter Green's tailored suits and "set patterns," is to keep always in view how *performative* are Gatsby's efforts at belonging.

Identity-as-performance, unspoken desires layered in unspoken losses, corruption in the service of an apparently untarnishable ideal, a reveling in sensuous display: the themes mobilized in the novel's closet scene all take their places in a Catholic constellation that manages also to be secular—not much "religion" here—without being at all self-effacingly Protestant-secular. In the artful reading of Paul Giles, Catholic ideology resonates secularly in the novel in two ways: first in its meditations on the power or efficacy of symbolic transformations of various kinds, and second "in its inclination toward becoming a parody of the American dream." The novel's "strangely 'literal' symbolism," suggests Giles, shows the workings of an "inherited Roman Catholic analogical mindset," nourished on the mysteries of incarnation and transubstantiation, whose impulse, in Marian Ronan's lovely phrase, is to "imbricate the transcendent with the ambiguous, nonsensical things of this earth,"[11] to wed unutterable vision to perishable breath. And that "sense of corruption and idealism being symbiotically entwined," says Giles, also describes the novel's "ambivalent narrative mode" that shuttles between parodic distance and rapt, desirous contemplation in its rendering of the world it describes. The tension between parody and less ironic imitative desires, moreover, reproduces the ambivalence with which variously assimilated American Catholics confronted the American dream in the 1920s, a time when, Giles points out, the Catholic Church was itself deciding whether its well-being in the United States "was best served through resistance to that dream or cooperation with it."[12]

The "Americanism" debate among Catholic theologians in the early decades of the twentieth century turned on the question of whether the church should nurture its sense of separation from the American cultural mainstream or else move toward assimilating itself more seamlessly within it. In this sense the Americanism controversy continued a more long-standing debate over "modernism," condemned by Pius X in a 1907 encyclical as the corruption of Catholic teaching and practice by corrosive, secular rationality. In its ostensibly antimodern mode the Catholic Church, following Aquinas, stood aloof from the American glorification of wealth, even as it built the most costly, ornate, and elaborate of its U.S. cathedrals (like St. Patrick's on Fifth Avenue, New York) with the donations of a mostly Irish immigrant population of low-wage servants and laborers.[13] And although the desire for American-style "respectability" was, as Delores Liptak puts it, "one of the postbellum legacies which happily befell more and more of the American Irish,"[14] the neo-Thomist vision of pristine, organic coherence imaged in the cathedrals they helped to build (and reproduced in an increasingly regimented ecclesial and lay culture) strove to separate, as "substance" from "accidents," a pure, unified Catholicism from the contaminating evils of the modern, secular—read American—world.[15]

Like Daisy's voice, then, the question on either side of the Americanism debate would seem to be full of money: ought the church to promote the free and easy commerce of its members with secular optimism and capital, or should it remain the glittering refuge of impoverished immigrants seeking escape from the pressures of Protestant materialism?[16] Eventually that distinction lost its edge, for as William H. Halsey points out, the rigid neo-Thomist ideology that emerged triumphant from the modernism and Americanism debates not only sheltered American Catholics from the cultural and moral complexity they identified with the modern, secular world, but did so in a house that looked remarkably like the one their Protestant neighbors had recently abandoned. While nineteenth-century immigrant Catholics struggled to broker their various paths into an increasingly fragmented American culture, their middle-class Protestant counterparts, as we have seen, projected a remarkably coherent, resilient, and counterfactual vision of American Protestant unity. If the First World War heralded the end of this era of Protestant optimism, however, the sparkling clarity of neo-Thomist ideology provided a way for newly respectable American Catholics to resist their own encounter with the dislocations of modernity, and in this sense to inherit the protective cloak of nineteenth-century American Protestant "innocence."

For immigrant Catholics whose passage to middle-class respectability was eased by the clear, rigid distinctions supplied by neo-Thomist categories, the universe appeared moral and rational, and a Catholic education became a stepping-stone to gentility.[17] Ironically, then, aggressive devotion to their erstwhile "foreign" faith had by the early twentieth century joined light skin and spoken English as keys to the assimilation of Irish Catholic immigrants into American society. The neo-Thomist ideology that insulated them at once from institutional self-critique *and* critique of the Protestant ethos of capitalist individualism they rapidly adopted enabled the Irish to become, as the saying has it, the most Catholic of Americans and the most American of Catholics. And this Irish ascendancy ultimately "resolved" the Americanism debate by making the commitment to maintain Catholic distinctiveness inseparable from the commitment to pursue the American dream.[18]

"American Catholic innocence," in Halsey's phrase, deployed neo-Thomism's pleasingly architectonic worldview as a bulwark against the moral and cultural ambiguities of modernity, including those ambiguities that beset the path of American Catholic assimilation. This is the world of Fitzgerald's "Absolution," where the "smooth boards" of the Miller kitchen are "yellow and clean as wheat," where the home fires burn in the hearth at the center of the house and "tins fitted into tins like toys" (191) and where a child's sip of water before Holy Communion incurs a savage beating. Rudolph Miller's father, who bloodies his son for failing to observe the requisite pre-Eucharistic fast, had arrived in Minnesota-Dakota country "with the second wave of German and Irish stock" and become a local freight agent whose "two bonds with the colorful life were his faith in the Roman Catholic Church and his mystical worship of the Empire builder, James J. Hill. . . . For twenty years he had lived alone with Hill's name and God" (190).

The historical James J. Hill was the dazzlingly wealthy railroad tycoon known to Fitzgerald since boyhood as the owner of the most spectacular house in the Fitzgeralds' hometown of St. Paul, Minnesota. Under the leadership of the Americanist Archbishop John Ireland, who denounced the immigrant labor strikes of the 1890s and declared the Catholic Church to be "the great [bulwark] of social order and law,"[19] the Lutheran frontier town of St. Paul had become a bastion of gentility for upwardly mobile Catholics like Fitzgerald's family, or those with aspirations to mobility, like Rudolph Miller's. Little wonder that in his brief appearance in *The Great Gatsby*, Carl Miller/Henry C. Gatz arrives for his son's funeral with his son's childhood copy of *Hopalong Cassidy* in hand, eager to prove to Nick that Gatsby's journey to the glittering mansion on West Egg began in devotion to the work ethic penciled on its flyleaf: Rise from bed at 6, Study electricity and needed inventions, "Read one improving book or magazine a week" (116), and so on.

"Absolution" puts a different beginning to Gatsby's rise. On one level, "Absolution" is a story about "leaving" the church, as much Fitzgerald's as Rudolph Miller's, with whom he shared a history of lying in the confessional, a penchant for gilded apostasy followed by pangs of conscience, and the childhood conviction that he was not his parents' son. "Not believing I was the son of my parents" is one of Rudolph's honest confessions and one more lightly recounted than the sins against purity ("with two boys and a girl") that stick in his throat with the memory of "a strange, romantic excitement"; indeed Rudolph's sin of pride and other "less shameful fallings away" are relayed as "airily" as his answer to the priest's question, coming at the end of this particular interview, of whether he has told any lies: "Oh no Father, I never tell lies" (186–88).

> For a moment, like the commoner in the king's chair, he tasted the pride of the situation. Then as the priest began to murmur conventional admonitions he realized that in heroically denying that he had told lies, he had committed a terrible sin—he had told a lie in confession . . .

He must fix this now—it was a bad mistake—but as his teeth shut on the last words of his prayer there was a sharp sound, and the slat was closed.

A minute later when he emerged into the twilight the relief in coming from the muggy church into an open world of wheat and sky postponed the full realization of what he had done. Instead of worrying he took a deep breath of the crisp air and began to say over and over to himself the words "Blatchford Sarnemington, Blatchford Sarnemington!"

Blatchford Sarnemington was himself, and these words were in effect a lyric. When he became Blatchford Sarnemington a suave nobility flowed from him. Blatchford Sarnemington lived in great sweeping triumphs . . .

He was Blatchford now for a while as he strutted homeward along the staggering road, but when the road braced itself in macadam to become the main street of [the town], Rudolph's exhilaration faded out and his mind cooled, and he felt the horror of his lie. God, of course, already knew of it—but Rudolph reserved a corner of his mind where he was safe from God, where he prepared the subterfuges with which he often tricked God. Hiding now in this corner he considered how he could best avoid the consequences of his misstatement.

At all costs he must avoid communion the next day. (188–89)

Instead his father's blows in reprisal for the attempted ruse—the sip of water—so embitter Rudolph that he proceeds to take communion anyway, "deep in mortal sin" and with a "dark poison"(195) in his heart. Before scruples again overtake him, sending him to the priest's private study to unburden his conscience, Rudolph experiences a moment of "maudlin exaltation" in knowing that "an invisible line had been crossed": "[H]e had become aware of his isolation—aware that it had applied not only to those moments when he was Blatchford Sarnemington but that it applied to all his inner life. Hitherto such phenomena as 'crazy' ambitions and petty shames and fears had been but private reservations, unacknowledged before the throne of his official soul. Now he realized unconsciously that his private reservations were himself—and all the rest a garnished front and a conventional flag. The pressure of his environment had driven him into the lonely secret road of adolescence" (194).

What is remarkable about the transformed awareness this passage records is that the line crossed in the moment of self-discovery does anything but separate Rudolph's "real" self from its facades, since artifice controls the presentation of self before and after, within and without. And this effect is only heightened in the subsequent interview with his confessor, which springs Rudolph from the story's tense enclosures, so the Latin heading for this section of the tale would suggest, like an arrow soaring toward God (*Sagitta Volante in Dei*).[20] It's here that the ill priest with "nerves . . . strung thin" and "cold watery eyes" (196) and an inordinate, oppressive awareness of Rudolph's pubescent beauty manages to express, in words that become increasingly "inarticulate and heartbroken" (198) before giving way to a choked, dying prayer, something of what Ferraro calls the "more generous sacramental economy" of *The Great Gatsby*.

> [Rudolph] had finished telling his sin to Father Schwartz. . . . He knew that as long as he was in the room with this priest God would not stop his heart, so he sighed and sat quietly, waiting for the priest to speak. . . . [But the priest] could not remember now what it was he should say. . . .
>
> For a moment longer the silence persisted while Rudolph waited, and the priest struggled to remember something that was slipping farther and farther away from him, and the clock ticked in the broken house. Then Father Schwartz stared hard at the little boy and remarked in a particular voice:
>
> "When a lot of people get together in the best places things go glimmering."
>
> Rudolph started and looked quickly at Father Schwartz's face.
>
> "I said—" began the priest, and paused, listening. "Do you hear the hammer and the clock ticking and the bees? Well, that's no good. The thing is to have a lot of people in the centre of the world, wherever that happens to be. Then"—his watery eyes widened knowingly—"things go glimmering."
>
> "Yes, Father," agreed Rudolph, feeling a little frightened.
>
> "What are you going to be when you grow up?"
>
> "Well, I was going to be a baseball-player for a while," answered Rudolph nervously, "but I don't think that's a very good ambition, so I think I'll be an actor or a Navy officer."
>
> Again the priest stared at him.
>
> "I see *exactly* what you mean . . . You look as if things went glimmering," cried Father Schwartz wildly. "Did you ever go to a party?"
>
> "Yes, Father."
>
> "And did you notice that everyone was properly dressed? That's what I mean. Just as you went into the party there was a moment when everyone was properly dressed" . . .
>
> Rudolph found himself thinking of Blatchford Sarnemington.
>
> "Please listen to me!" commanded the priest impatiently. "Stop worrying about last Saturday. Apostasy implies an absolute damnation only on the supposition of a previous perfect faith. Does that fix

it? . . . [T]hey have lights now as big as stars—do you realize that?—
I heard of one light they had in Paris or somewhere that was as big
as a star. A lot of people had it—a lot of gay people. They have all
sorts of things now that you never dreamed of."

"Look here"—He came nearer Rudolph, but the boy drew away.
. . . "Did you ever see an amusement park?"

"No, Father."

"Well, go and see an amusement park." The priest waved his hand
vaguely. "It's a thing like a fair, only much more glittering. Go to one
at night and stand a little way off from it in a dark place—under
dark trees. You'll see a big wheel made of lights turning in the air . . .
a band playing somewhere . . . and everything will twinkle" . . .

Father Schwartz frowned as he suddenly thought of something.

"But don't get up close," he warned Rudolph, "because if you do
you'll only feel the heat and the sweat and the life." (196–98)

The "heat and the sweat and the life" are what Rudolph *does* want to
feel, at least some of the time—even in confessing his "immodest thoughts
and desires" his pulse races with the thought of "hard-eyed incorrigible
girls" (188)—and one senses that the priest's hedging at just this point
("don't get up close") has something to do too with the "failure to achieve
a mystical union with our Lord" (184) that he places at the core of his
killing sadness. But the absolution the strange conversation nevertheless
effects puts Rudolph's sin of lying in the confessional on a continuum
with other forms of heroic self-presentation—the "impression of moral
resiliency" (185) the priest manages to summon from the depths of his
melancholy, the effect of contrition Rudolph musters to salve his father's
murderous temper, or Blatchford Sarnemington's suave nobility, chan-
neled at critical moments of spiritual duress—and reveals that corner of
his mind where Rudolph fashions his subterfuges, safe from God, to have
been the space of benediction all along.

All this talking seemed particularly strange and awful to Rudolph,
because this man was a priest. He sat there, half terrified, his beautiful open eyes wide and staring at Father Schwartz. But underneath
his terror he felt that his own inner convictions were affirmed. There
was something ineffably gorgeous somewhere that had nothing to
do with God. He no longer thought that God was angry at him about
the original lie, because He must have understood that Rudolph had
done it to make things finer in the confessional, brightening up the
dinginess of his admissions by saying a thing radiant and proud. At
the moment when he had affirmed immaculate honor a silver pennon
had flapped out into the breeze somewhere and there had been a
crunch of leather and the shine of silver spurs and a troop of
horsemen waiting for dawn on a low green hill. (198)

Toward a Catholic Secularism

The either-or logic of Rudolph's Catholic boyhood had forced a choice between the church's sheltering strictures and the "something ineffably gorgeous somewhere that had nothing to do with God." But God doesn't stay out of this picture for very long, and one suspects that in fleeing his Jansenist upbringing Rudolph Miller/Jimmy Gatz remains somehow within a Catholic frame, much as the adolescent Fitzgerald, abandoning St. Paul's lace-curtain Irish provincialism for prep school and then Princeton in the glamorous East, discovered there an urbane, European-inflected Catholic subculture that, he later recalled, made "the church of my youth a dazzling, golden thing."[21]

The attraction was largely one-sided, for the church of his youth tended to excoriate Fitzgerald when it failed to dismiss him entirely: angry and "heartbroken" American Catholics upbraided Fitzgerald for his portrayals in "Absolution" and the earlier "Benediction," a story set in a Jesuit seminary; the Jesuit periodical *America* sized up *This Side of Paradise* as "a fair example of our non-Catholic colleges' output."[22] Such responses suggest how narrow in the 1920s was the permissible range of self-criticism among U.S. Catholics, for whom religious devotion had become the unlikely key to their assimilation into American culture. "It's too much for me," Fitzgerald complained to his sometime-mentor, the Irish poet Shane Leslie; "It seems that [Catholics abroad] can write anything but an American had better have his works either pious tracts for nuns or else dissociate them from the church as a living issue."[23]

Laura Levitt calls attention to the situation of Jewish immigrants in the later nineteenth and earlier twentieth centuries, for whom religious observance likewise became the path of assimilation into American culture under the banner of religious "tolerance."[24] Immigrants who experienced their Jewishness far less as a form of worship or belief than as the layering of distinctive modes of being—national, ethical, political, intellectual, gendered, sexual, linguistic, familial, gustatory, and otherwise—found little space for these secular forms of Jewish identity in the United States, where Jewish arrivals from Europe were asked to be synagogue-based in order to be Jews.[25] In this way Judaism took its place in the American religious landscape by becoming, for the first time in its history, a voluntary religious organization on the model of the Protestant congregation. As Joseph L. Blau commended this new Judaism in "What's American about American Jewry?": "The term 'Protestantism' describe[s] that movement in religion in general (not only Christianity) which allows of a multiplicity of conclusions."[26] Jewish immigrants found this Protestant landscape of denominational pluralism hospitable above all to those who engaged their Judaism as a mode of religious practice and belief. Secular

Jews—as opposed to unmarked "nonbelievers"—had little purchase on this terrain.

Fitzgerald joined the ranks of lapsed or nonpracticing Catholics in his early twenties, leading a number of critics to conclude that a thinly veiled nostalgia for the vividness of childhood faith is what gives his writing its distinctive cast—its persistent overtones of longing, of defeatism tinged with grandeur, of hard-won equilibrium always at the point of being lost.[27] One might even argue, following a suggestion of Jenny Franchot's, that what drives Fitzgerald's narratives is the perpetual need to reconstitute lost belief in the displaced form of the glittering, sensuous objects that mark its absence: Anthony Patch's elusive millions, Amory Blaine's erotic conquests, Gatsby's shirts.[28] The problem with such readings is that Fitzgerald never engages Catholicism as a transparent confession of *belief*, even in childhood—on the contrary; in Rudolph Miller's case, confession is where a certain theatricality *begins*.

I would suggest that Fitzgerald was shaped far less by the impossibility of remaining a believing Catholic than he was by the challenge of remaining a *secular* Catholic, of recovering Catholic difference as something richer and more variegated than a difference of belief.[29] Put another way, what Fitzgerald identified as the particularly American difficulty of writing something other than pious tracts while still engaging Catholicism as a living issue would seem to be the difficulty of sustaining an alternative to an observant Catholic vision of America that would not disappear into an unmarked, Protestant vision of America. To draw on a distinction made by Edward Said, this would be a secularism undertaken not as a habitual majority practice but as a willed minority practice,[30] a refusal equally of a Protestant-secular trajectory given as seamless and of a Catholicism that functions best as a mechanism for passing into the dominant culture under the mantle of religious tolerance. One direction such a Catholic secularism might take—and over the course of Fitzgerald's career, I believe, does take—is toward engagement with new ways of being American, with forms of otherness that call to account a culture of "pluralism" that most readily embraces diversity in the form of a marketplace of private religious faiths.[31]

Before going further, a caveat: if it is undoubtedly true that, as Giles puts it, the adult Fitzgerald was "an apostate who came to despise what he thought of as the piety and the bigotry" of the rising Irish Catholics he'd grown up among in St. Paul, it is no less true that he was caught up in their paradoxes.[32] And if Fitzgerald made the boorish racist Tom Buchanan the cautionary emblem of the moneyed white America that assimilating Irish Catholics sought assimilation into, it's also occasionally difficult to separate, in *The Great Gatsby* and elsewhere, Tom Buchanan-style invective from its parodic critique. One senses often in Fitzgerald's vision a kind of internal fracturing, whereby one, recognizably Catholic frame for organizing experience breaks up under pressure of another no less Catholic. So, for example, a finely honed apparatus of Catholic bigotry and homophobia is undone by a more generous economy of presence—and frequently enough, vice versa; a sexual code that fits erotic need to the imperative of racially pure reproduction is unsettled by another in which reproduction simply doesn't figure—and where *no* sexuality, as it happens, has the approval of a final imprimatur. As Tom Ferraro puts it, the greatest personae in American literature tend to embody "*both* pronounced trajectories within the national symbolic—including ethnoreligious and sociosexual disenfranchisements, the impress of industrial finance and consumer capitalism, the forces of internal and external colonizations—*and* the critique of such trajectories simultaneously."[33] Or as Fitzgerald famously observed in the confessional narrative of his emotional breakdown at thirty-nine, "the test of a first-rate intelligence is the ability to hold two opposed ideas in the mind at the same time, and still retain the ability to function."[34]

Balancing Acts

To "retain the ability to function," Fitzgerald went on to say in "The Crack-Up," meant to balance "the sense of the futility of effort and the sense of the necessity to struggle; the conviction of the inevitability of failure and still the determination to 'succeed'—and, more than these, the contradiction between the dead hand of the past and the high intentions of the future."[35] Fitzgerald accepted that high-wire act as a kind of genetic inheritance. Struggle, determination, and the "high intentions of the future" described his mother Mollie McQuillan Fitzgerald, devoutly Catholic and (in her son's eyes) uncouth, who came from "straight 1850 potato-famine Irish who prospered with the rising Middle West."[36] The "dead hand of the past," meanwhile, lay heavily on his enervated father Edward, a landless aristocrat and Confederate sympathizer whose string of business failures made the family entirely dependent on his wife's new money. "I am half black Irish and half old American stock with the usual exaggerated ancestral pretensions," Fitzgerald told the writer John O'Hara, who'd asked how he managed to "do the 'climber' so well." "The black Irish half of the family had the money and looked down upon the Maryland side of the family who had, and really had, that certain series of reticences and obligations that go under the poor old shattered word 'breeding.' . . . so if I were elected King of Scotland tomorrow after graduating, Magdalene to Guards, with an embryonic history that tied me to the Plantagenets, I would still be a parvenu. I spent my youth in alternately crawling in front of kitchen maids and insulting the great."[37]

The tension between parvenu vigor and antibourgeois languor was not only etched in Fitzgerald's psyche but also built into the curriculum of the Newman School, Fitzgerald's prep school and the model for Amory Blaine's St. Regis in *This Side of Paradise*. One of a handful of prep schools for the American Catholic elite at the turn of the century, Newman taught students both to value Catholicism's glorious European past (and with it the difference of their own worldliness vis-à-vis Protestant America) *and* to pass smoothly into the upper echelons of the Protestant establishment by gaining admission to the Ivy Leagues. Thus Newman students learned subtly to look down on environments they were in the same measure being groomed to blend into: Amory's mentor and confidante Monsignor Thayer Darcy commends St. Regis to him as "a gentleman's school," where "democracy won't hit you so early. You'll find plenty of that in college" (24).[38]

Begun as what Fitzgerald called a "somewhat edited history of me and my imagination,"[39] *This Side of Paradise*, like "Absolution," records its protagonist's passage from "a small enclosure into a great labyrinth" (231), a translation of spiritual sensibility from the narrow register of certainty to the more alluring and confounding haunts of mystery, even as the setting of Amory Blaine's conversion is, conspicuously, Princeton University and not the Roman Catholic Church. Nor is Amory the son of Fitzgerald's parents: in the novel, Stephen Blaine apparently succumbs to Edward Fitzgerald's listlessness and ennui by all but disappearing from the space of Amory's activity and awareness, while coarse Mollie Fitzgerald is reborn there as the languid, diaphanous, and vaguely European Beatrice O'Hara Blaine, a lapsed Catholic and critic of the lamentably "bourgeois quality" of American Catholicism who was "quite sure that had she lived in the shadow of the great Continental cathedrals her soul would still be a thin flame on the mighty altar of Rome." Beatrice "maintained an enchantingly wavering attitude" toward her faith since "discovering that priests were infinitely more attentive when she was in the process of losing or regaining" it (8). Amory's spiritual father in the novel is Monsignor Darcy, a priest once drawn to the flickering flame of Beatrice's faith-turned-erotic-lure and a barely fictionalized rendering of the charismatic Monsignor Sigourney Fay, the Newman trustee and later headmaster whose brilliant, intimate, and narcissistic letters to Fitzgerald, copied nearly verbatim, contributed long passages to *This Side of Paradise*.

Biographers describe Father Fay as a "fin-de-siècle aesthete" of considerable appeal, "a dandy, always heavily perfumed" who introduced the teenaged Fitzgerald to Oscar Wilde and good wine, a man of irresistibly "infectious charm" who loved "to gossip and tell stories which he punctuated with high-pitched giggles."[40] Innuendo of this sort, less winking if no harder to miss, circulates in and around *This Side of Paradise* most indicatively in the figure of Oscar Wilde himself: Wilde supplies one of the book's two epigrams; early critics noted, without specifying, the novel's atmosphere of "Wildean decadence"; Amory's Princeton is where "magnificent, exquisite" men exchange knowing invitations to "come up to the room" and read *The Picture of Dorian Gray* (47).[41] To be sure, the novel is as packed as any of Fitzgerald's fiction from this period with football games and debutantes and Ivy League dances, but it's easy to gather from such scenes that just as one could not render the world of youthful WASP privilege as ardently as Fitzgerald did and be entirely contained by it, so neither could one be as keen an observer of the mating rituals by which that world is reproduced and be entirely identified with them, either. In *This Side of Paradise* Catholicism and gay or potentially gay recognition become organizing schemes for one another through the Wildean vector of "worldliness." Consider the scene where Amory goes for the first time, on Beatrice's suggestion, to meet Darcy:

> Monsignor Darcy's house was an ancient, rambling structure set on a hill overlooking the river, and there lived its owner, between trips to all parts of the Roman Catholic world. . . . Monsignor was forty-four then, and bustling—a trifle too stout for symmetry, with hair the color of spun gold, and a brilliant, enveloping personality. When he came into a room clad in his full purple regalia from thatch to toe, he resembled a Turner sunset, and attracted both admiration and attention. . . . He was intensely ritualistic, startlingly dramatic, loved the idea of God enough to be a celibate, and rather liked his neighbor.
>
> Children adored him because he was like a child; youth revelled in his company because he was still a youth, and couldn't be shocked. In the proper land and century he might have been a Richelieu—at present he was a very moral, very religious (if not particularly pious) clergyman, making a great mystery about pulling rusty wires, and appreciating life to the fullest, if not entirely enjoying it.
>
> He and Amory took to each other at first sight—the jovial, impressive prelate who could dazzle an embassy ball, and the green-eyed, intent youth, in his first long trousers, accepted in their own minds a relation of father and son within a half-hour's conversation.
>
> "My dear boy, I've been waiting to see you for years. Take a big chair and we'll have a chat. . . . [H]ave a cigarette—I'm sure you smoke. Well, if you're like me, you loathe all science and mathematics" . . .
>
> They slipped briskly into an intimacy from which they never recovered. (23–24)

The hazard in tracking the seductive current of innuendo in such passages to the place where we discover, say, a gay Monsignor Darcy, a gay Amory, or a gay Fitzgerald is that the ends of such a pursuit would seem to be inscribed in advance by the desire to separate sensibilities that may in fact be far less extricably meshed. And just as surely as Fitzgerald's career records the ambient, dogging pressure to repel charges of his own homosexuality by stabilizing and restabilizing the needful opposition between heterosexual and homosexual definition, it also manages on occasion to deflect that pressure with surprising agility and grace. Such moments often cluster in the neighborhood of "innuendo" itself, where the closet that would wall off presumably separable identities is both implied and closest to being dissolved.[42] The guarded expressions of feeling in Fay's letters, for example, convey a teasing provocation as much as the need of a secret code, still less a fear of being unrequited or misunderstood (e.g., "There are deep things in us and you know what they are as well as I do . . . a terrible honesty at the bottom of us, that all our sophistry cannot destroy, and a kind of childlike simplicity that is the only thing that saves us from being downright wicked").[43] After reading a draft of *This Side of Paradise*, Fay wrote Fitzgerald with some suggestions for altering his fictional persona and urged that "when we write one another, we ought to think of the possibility of the other person someday publishing that letter."[44] It's hard to separate, here, the impulse toward safety from the impulse toward self-display, to decide whether this counts as a plea for discretion or else an attempt to nurture a shared exhibitionist tendency toward even more fabulous heights of expressiveness.

Nor do we "know what it means" that Fitzgerald not only dedicated *This Side of Paradise* to Sigourney Fay but also projected his reverberant magnetism into *The Great Gatsby* by making Sigourney and Fay into family names for Jordan Baker (via Aunt Sigourney Howard) and Daisy Fay Buchanan, women whose iconically WASP appeal also and as ostentatiously certifies Nick's and Gatsby's desires as heterosexual. What can at least be inferred is that "heterosexuality" and "homosexuality" are for Fitzgerald intricately co-implicated—as for that matter, and in much the same way, are Fitzgerald's shimmering WASP America and glittering Catholic Church.

Let me say here, if it even needs to be said, that I have no interest in determining the "truth" of Fitzgerald's relationships with men, no wish to keep faith with the forensic project by which Fitzgerald's more scrupulous biographers deny his homosexuality on the basis of there being (surprise!) no incontrovertible proof of it. My concern, rather, is in how affective possibilities, fantasies, and dilemmas that exceed the bounds of a normative heterosexuality find in Catholicism a resource for their forbidden representation, as well as in how religious subjectivity, itself so resistant to representation in other than propositional statements of belief, borrows from the register of the erotic for its own visibility as a sign and experience of alienation or belonging.

"A Gaudy, Ritualistic, Paradoxical Catholicism . . ."

Consider the resonance of *Princeton*, in and beyond *This Side of Paradise*, as a figure equally and sometimes interchangeably of WASP/hetero assimilation and Catholic/gay excess. Fitzgerald's conditional acceptance to Princeton after a mediocre performance at Newman was and remained for him a cherished ticket to the inner circles of an East Coast Protestant elite. Under Monsignor Fay's tutelage, however, Presbyterian Princeton— where Amory's "ghost of a code" is "a gaudy, ritualistic, paradoxical Catholicism," whose "prophet was Chesterton, whose claquers were such reformed rakes of literature as Huysmans and Bourget, whose American sponsor was Ralph Adams Cram, with his adulation of thirteenth-century cathedrals" (112)—became in some ways a *more* Catholic environment for Fitzgerald than Newman had been, largely because it nurtured an intellectual and cultural worldliness lost in Newman students' pursuit of acculturation via athletics, namely football (a trajectory perfected at such schools as Notre Dame).

At the same time, Fitzgerald genuinely revered football as the sign of something quintessential to Princeton, which he claimed to have made his college of choice after its stunning victory in the 1911 Princeton-Harvard game.[45] "At Princeton, as at Yale," Fitzgerald wrote in the 1927 essay "Princeton," "football became, back in the nineties, a sort of symbol . . . at first satisfactory, then essential and beautiful."[46] As a "sort of symbol," the public face of his college years, football in Fitzgerald's fiction often signals a world of effusive heterosexuality, where Ivy League games matter not least as stops on various debutantes' tours of marriageability, or as preludes to the erotic frisson of the postgame cotillions—think of Edith and Gordon in "May Day" or Minnie and Basil in "Basil and Cleopatra." Ruminating in drunken sleep near the end of *This Side of Paradise*, Amory describes his amorous conquests as though they formed an all-star collegiate gridiron lineup: "No desire to sleep with Jill, what would Alec see in her? . . . Own taste the best; Isabelle, Clara, Rosalind, Eleanor were all-American" (227).[47]

After being made to leave Princeton for failing grades, as Fitzgerald nearly was, Amory concludes that life is a ruined football game (232), but it's hard to know whether the restless sense of loss Fitzgerald would come to associate with Princeton—"only when you tried to tear part of your past out of your heart, as I once did," he wrote in the essay "Princeton," "were you aware of its power of arousing a deep and imperishable love"—was bound up more in the "all-American" world of bowl games and wealthy debutantes or in what "Princeton" mysteriously alludes to as the "host of more intimate things that are now as blurred and dim as our cigarette smoke or the ivy on Nassau Hall that last night."[48] During a semester of academic probation Fitzgerald wrote what he called his first "mature" story, "The Spire and the Gargoyle," which describes this Princeton-on-its-way-to-being-lost not as the football game that sidelines Amory but as something more closely resembling a monastery. Reworked portions of the story appear in *This Side of Paradise*:

> The night mist . . . clustered about [Princeton's] spires and towers, and then settled below them, so that the dreaming peaks were still in lofty aspiration toward the sky. . . . The Gothic halls and cloisters were infinitely more mysterious as they loomed suddenly out of the darkness, outlined each by myriad faint squares of yellow light. . . . Evening after evening the senior singing had drifted across the campus in melancholy beauty, and through the shell of [Amory's] undergraduate consciousness had broken a deep and reverent devotion to the grey walls and Gothic peaks and all they symbolized as warehouses of dead ages.
>
> The tower that in view of his window sprang upward, grew into a spire, yearning higher until its uppermost tip was half invisible against the morning skies, gave him the first sense of the transiency and unimportance of the campus figures except as holders of the apostolic succession. He liked knowing that Gothic architecture, with its upward trend, was peculiarly appropriate to universities, and the idea became personal to him. The silent stretches of green, the quiet halls with an occasional late-burning scholastic light held his imagination in a strong grasp, and the chastity of the spire became a symbol of this perception (49–50).

Stadium and cloister: in one constellation Fitzgerald's Princeton stands for America, Protestantism, and heterosexuality; in the other, Princeton summons images of Europe or Ireland, Catholicism, and queer sexuality, bachelorhood, or celibacy.[49] Often in Fitzgerald's Princeton stories the difficulty of moving in both of these worlds at once, or the felt imperative of keeping them separate, expresses itself in a certain tendency toward either-or thinking. Among the men in his class, for example, Amory distinguishes the "spiritually married" who conform to convention from the much smaller group of the "spiritually unmarried" who pursue an inner calling at the expense of money, power, and success (238), a distinction given national and religious shading in an earlier short story, "Sentiment and the Use of Rouge." That story began in a letter Fitzgerald wrote his

Maryland cousin Ceci Taylor—the model for the Madonna-like Clara in *This Side of Paradise*—as he contemplated being called to the front in World War I. "Updike of Oxford or Harvard says 'I die for England' or 'I die for America,' " Fitzgerald wrote to his cousin; "Not me—I'm too Irish for that—I may get killed for America—but I'm going to die for myself."[50] "Sentiment and the Use of Rouge" gives these lines to a wounded Irish soldier bickering with his English counterpart in their dying moments on a battlefield in France. The Irishman, O'Flaherty, murmurs Hail Marys amid gibes at "Updike just out o' Oxford" and the "damned Luther" of the English and insists that he "may get killed for me flag, but I'm going to die for meself." His death leaves his English companion in the trenches to confront the poverty of his own "Y.M.C.A. God" as opposed to O'Flaherty's God of "fear and love." In an odd, strained reach, the story's "Irish" critique of Anglo-Saxon culture links the latter's threadbare spirituality ("you pass from life in the name of your holy principles, and hope to meet in Westminster") with the lax morality of the rouged English girls, who reason that "Young men are going to get killed for us.—We would have been their wives—we can't be—therefore we'll be as much as we can."[51]

In another story written at Princeton, "The Ordeal," a flash of heterosexual revulsion saves a wavering seminarian for the priesthood. The story frames what Fitzgerald in his notebooks called the "choice between God and Sex"—"If you choose both, you're a smug hypocrite; if neither, you get nothing"[52]—as the crisis of a Jesuit novice preparing to make vows at a moment "when the world seemed gloriously apparent and the monastery vaguely impotent." The man ultimately decides in favor of the monastery, but not before a disorienting experience in the hot, incense-heavy chapel where he prays. "Afterwards he could never describe it except by saying that some undercurrent had crept into his prayer, something unsought, alien. . . . He felt himself alone pitted against an infinity of temptation." Temptation takes the form of a Blatchford Sarnemington–like tableau: "Art, beauty, love, and life passed in a panorama before him, exotic with the hot perfumes of world passion. He saw struggles and wars, banners waving somewhere, voices giving hail to a king—and looking at him through it all were the sweet sad eyes of [a] girl who is now a woman." The man "tremble[s] in the void" for "a minute, an eternity" until finally "something snap[s]," altering his vision and confirming his vocation: "They were still there, but the girl's eyes were all wrong, the lines around her mouth were cold and chiseled and her passion seemed dead and earthy."[53]

Then there's the peculiar episode in *This Side of Paradise* where, as an early review put it, "a chorus girl named Axia laid her blond head on Amory's shoulder and the youth immediately rushed away in a frenzy of terror and suffered from hallucinations for forty-eight hours. The explanation was hidden from us. It did not sound altogether characteristic of Princeton."[54] The events begin when Amory alone among the group of Princeton friends gathered at Maxim's in New York City notices a pale, middle-aged man staring from another table. Eventually the Princeton group ends up in a call girl's apartment, where a nervous Amory announces his intention to leave and immediately worries about sounding "priggish" to his classmates. From this point on in the scene, heterosexual squeamishness comes to look strangely like homosexual panic: just when "temptation cre[eps] over [Amory] like a warm wind" on the woman's couch he inexplicably sees the staring man from Maxim's, noticing with special horror his "virile pallor," "nervous hands," and "unutterably terrible" feet (101–2). In flight from the apparition Amory runs into an alley, only to confront a second specter, a pale face "distorted with a sort of infinite evil" (104). Amory recognizes the face as belonging to the "exquisite" (47) Dick Humbird, a beloved classmate whose death in a car wreck Amory had witnessed several scenes back. There Amory's gaze had likewise been drawn to his dead friend's feet: "He looked at the shoe-laces— Dick had tied them that morning. *He* had tied them—and now he was this heavy white mass. All that remained of the charm and personality of the Dick Humbird he had known—oh, it was all so horrible and unaristocratic and close to the earth" (79).[55]

The Devil episode, as Fitzgerald called it, was drafted early in his work on the novel and survived all revisions, despite its strangeness; Amory describes the experience as one to which he "never succeeded in giving an appropriate value, but which, nevertheless, haunted him" for years afterward and "drowned" out the "envy and admiration" (99) he felt for certain of his classmates at the time. The scene precedes Amory's showy ruminations on his "all-American" taste in women,[56] much as the news of his suspension from Princeton prompted Fitzgerald that night for "the first time . . . [to hunt] down the spectre of womanhood that, for a little while, makes everything else seem unimportant."[57] That theatricalized display of heterosexual desire in the wake of a crucial recasting of homosocial bonds was repeated after the death of Father Fay. "This has made me nearly sure that I will become a priest," Fitzgerald wrote to Shane Leslie on hearing the news of Fay's death in 1919; "I feel as if in a way his mantle had descended upon me—a desire, or more, to someday recreate the atmosphere of him."[58] Instead Fitzgerald immediately abandoned his calling to the priesthood in favor of his grail-like pursuit of Zelda Sayre, the Alabama debutante whose "sexual recklessness," as he put it years later, provoked him to spasms of contrition and remorse.[59] Fitzgerald's letters from this period link his supposed dissipation into (hetero)-

sexuality with his loss of religious faith. "You're still a catholic," he wrote to a childhood friend at the time, "but Zelda's the only God I have left."[60]

BENEDICTION

If Princeton-as-stadium represented a world of heterosexual WASP entitlement whose loss Fitzgerald most lamented for never having been fully admitted to it in the first place, Princeton-as-monastery would seem to represent an alternative world Fitzgerald mourned less for its incomplete acceptance of him than for his own incomplete—complex, difficult, fragmentary—rejection of it. Negatively, both Catholicism *and* other-than-heterosexual desire could be experienced as sites of a double-edged loss, reminders at once of an ineluctable outsiderhood, on the one hand, and of attachments denied, disowned, or "forgotten" on the path to assimilation, on the other. If we understand melancholia, with Freud, as what remains of unfinished mourning, of losses ungrieved and displaced because never fully owned up to *as* losses, we have a clue to the brooding sense of sadness, failure, and regret that so fills Fitzgerald's retrospective accounts of his marriage and early success.[61] (Sixteen years into their flawed, fraught, but surprisingly tensile marriage, for example, Fitzgerald continued to describe his relationship with Zelda as "one of those tragic loves doomed for lack of money, and one day the girl closed it out on the basis of common sense.")[62] The social traumas Fitzgerald's stories tend obsessively to replay—"The whole idea of Gatsby," he once explained, "is the unfairness of a poor young man not being able to marry a girl with money. This theme comes up again and again because I lived it"[63]—might be seen in this light to conceal, by their compulsive reiteration, other griefs that could thereby persist unacknowledged. The narrative of being always the "poor boy in a rich boy's school,"[64] for example, the outsider to "America" in its Princeton-WASP mode, could take up and hide within it also a sense of alienation from his abandoned Catholicism, even as Fitzgerald would blame Catholicism for his feelings of inferiority and shame.[65] So too Fitzgerald's narratives of erotic regret, always outwardly given as the loss of the girl, could take up the unspoken weight of other, disavowed desires, even as Fitzgerald would eventually, bitterly, pin his "loss" of Zelda on her suspicions of his homosexuality.[66]

All the more stunning, then, that Fitzgerald managed to mediate so deftly between the two registers—WASP/heterosexual, Catholic/queer—in a story like "Benediction." "Benediction" rewrites "The Ordeal," dividing its protagonist's experiences now between two characters: Kieth, a warm and intelligent Jesuit priest wholly devoted to his calling, and his younger sister Lois, beautiful, impulsive, polished, and vain, whom Kieth hasn't seen in over a decade but whose exploits he's begun to follow in the society pages since her well-publicized debut a year or so before the story opens. The occasion for their visit is a rendezvous Lois waveringly decides to keep in the city of Kieth's seminary, the setting for most of the story. The romance appears by some unspoken standard unworkable; Lois's lover has written urging her to come to Wilmington even though the two "can't marry" and she does, letting him know in a telegram of her plans to visit her brother in the seminary before their assignation.[67]

If the much sought-after Lois, wealthy, petulant, and bored with the "*inconvenien[ce]* [of] being a Catholic . . . as far as morals go" (395) can in these ways stand in for Zelda Sayre, Kieth and his brothers in the monastery would seem to represent the world that his dogged pursuit of Zelda, begun after Fay's death and his departure from Princeton, obliged Fitzgerald to leave behind. The monastery of "Benediction"—not "technically" a monastery "but only a seminary; nevertheless it shall be a monastery here despite its Victorian architecture or its Edward VII additions or even its Woodrow Wilsonian, patented, last-a-century roofing" (383)— images a world where "Princeton" goes on forever, where the kinds of relationships with the kinds of men Fitzgerald knew there continue into middle age and beyond, where there is no returning to a world beyond its gates in which marriage is expected and required, and where, significantly, even a coarse Irish initiate might find his flourishing, might belong as naturally to this landscape as the leaves of a tree:

> [A]s a great mellow bell boomed the half hour a swarm of black, human leaves were blown over the checker-board of paths under the courteous trees.
>
> Some of these black leaves were very old with cheeks furrowed like the first ripples of a splashed pool. Then there was a scattering of middle-aged leaves whose forms when viewed in profile in their revealing gowns were beginning to be faintly asymmetrical. These carried thick volumes of Thomas Aquinas and Henry James and Cardinal Mercier and Immanuel Kant and many bulging notebooks filled with lecture data.
>
> But most numerous were the young leaves; blond boys of nineteen with very stern, conscientious expressions; men in their late twenties with a keen self-assurance. . . .
>
> There were many Americans and some Irish and some tough Irish and a few French, and several Italians and Poles, and they walked informally arm in arm with each other in twos and threes and in long rows, almost universally distinguished . . . for this was the Society of Jesus, founded in Spain five hundred years before by a tough-minded

soldier who trained men to hold a breach or a salon, preach a sermon or write a treaty, and do it and not argue. (383–84)

Kieth had entered this world sixteen years earlier, and in the story his account of his call to the priesthood proceeds very much as a grace-filled coming-out narrative, unhampered by lingering misgivings or regrets.[68] In "Benediction" the vocational crisis of "The Ordeal" is transferred instead to Lois, the shallow debutante, who, like the earlier story's protagonist, experiences a kind of existential vertigo in the incense-heavy chapel. On regaining her bearings, flooded suddenly with "a warm peace," Lois feels "oddly broken and chastened, as if someone had held her stripped soul up and laughed" (394).

"Benediction" ends ambiguously, it remaining unclear whether a second telegram Lois tears up moments before sending in the story's final scene—"This is in the way of a permanent goodbye. I should suggest Italy" (398)—had signaled her disciplined rejection of a vaguely illicit affair or else a pert send-off of the lover who could afford to lick his wounds in Europe but not to support her in the manner to which she believes herself entitled. Nor is it certain that ending the affair was the result her brother had prayed for, kneeling at the pietà on the monastery grounds long after Lois's departure. The conventional reading of "Benediction" is that Lois's conversion experience in the monastery chapel didn't quite take, and that after leaving the chaste domain of Kieth's influence she returned to her own sexual recklessness and her presumably married lover. But the lover is never quite marked off as married, and Kieth is hardly a passionless ascetic. "Benediction" describes monastic life as one of deeply embodied commitments and pleasures ("out behind was the farm where half a dozen lay brothers were sweating lustily as they [worked] . . . to the left, behind a row of elms, was an informal baseball diamond where three novices were being batted out by a fourth, with great chasings and puffings and blowings" [383]), and Kieth looks forward with great warmth and tenderness to the day he might hold Lois's children on his lap.

A better reading, to my view, is that the experience in the chapel—also rendered with great sympathy—strips Lois of the cool indifference that had her trifling with a man who loved but could not yet support her, much as Zelda had only recently broken down and agreed to marry Fitzgerald, then in the first flush of his success, for what he must surely have hoped were more than financial reasons.[69] In this reading the prospective, still precarious triumph of heterosexual passion at the end of "Benediction"— Lois keeps her rendezvous rather than send her impoverished or otherwise unsuitable lover away—transfers to their connection, and so to Fitzgerald's pursuit of Zelda, the imprimatur of Kieth's unswerving commitment to his calling, as though Fitzgerald were seeking the benediction of Father Fay and his Princeton companions in "mellow monasticism"[70] in choosing in favor of what the protagonist of "The Ordeal" ultimately rejects.

Possible Worlds

Fitzgerald counted "Benediction" among his best stories—an appraisal not widely shared by his critics, who tend to fault the cheapness of its ostensible O. Henry–like ending.[71] To my reading the absence of narrative tension comes instead in the too rigidly drawn characters of Lois and Kieth, who come too cleanly to embody alternative worlds—WASP America and Catholic cloister, heterosexual desires and other desires— that were anything but easily separable for Fitzgerald. Lois and Kieth come newly to know and to cherish one another in the course of the story, but from the moment the seminary gate clangs shut behind Lois their lives remain distinct, with each wanting nothing of the other's world except for the other to have it. If a closed door finally divides "Protestant" and "Catholic" sensibilities in "Benediction," however, the kinds of knowledge that pass between *The Great Gatsby*'s "Protestant" and "Catholic" protagonists, Nick and Gatsby, seem instead to require what Eve Sedgwick calls an "open mesh of possibilities, gaps, overlaps, dissonances and resonances, lapses and excesses of meaning" through which the constituent elements of both sexual and religious identity "aren't made (or *can't* be made) to signify monolithically."[72]

Fitzgerald cut away the narrative of Gatsby's Catholic boyhood and published it separately as "Absolution" out of a desire, he said later, to "preserve the sense of mystery."[73] The novel never explicitly identifies Gatsby as Catholic—a colorless Lutheran minister presides at his funeral—yet traces of his expunged religious heritage surface, for example, in the way his iconicity plays off of Nick's more "scriptural" mediations. Nick steps in on occasion to remind us that he's also writing the story he tells ("Reading over what I have written so far . . ." [37]), noting that at Yale he'd been "rather literary" (3). Gatsby, meanwhile, never bothers cutting the pages of books in his faux-Gothic library, which, Nick expertly observes, exist only for show. Attentive readers have likened Gatsby to a Catholic priest—"dispensing holy waters, consecrated food and other elements of the sanctified life to whatever aspirants he can gather around him," as Giles Gunn puts it[74]—and Nick's narrative does assimilate Gatsby to two of Fitzgerald's fictional priests, imputing to Gatsby both the glimmering vision of Father Schwartz in "Absolution" (Nick remarks that Gatsby's "place looks like a World's Fair" [53], noting earlier that his parties were run by "rules of behavior associated with an amusement

park" [27]) and the sartorial resplendence of Monsignor Darcy, flamboyant in his purple regalia like a Turner sunset.

Gatsby also shares Darcy's ambient sympathy, the quality that, as
Amory put it, had made him feel "safe when [Darcy] was near" (233).
Just that sense of having been secretly understood and radiantly approved
is what fastens Nick onto Gatsby, whatever his protestations: Gatsby had
"one of those rare smiles," Nick observes, "with a quality of eternal reassurance in it. It faced—or seemed to face—the whole external world for
an instant, and then concentrated on *you* with an irresistible prejudice in
your favor. It understood you just as far as you wanted to be understood,
believed in you as you would like to believe in yourself, and assured you
that it had precisely the impression of you that, at your best, you hoped
to convey" (32).

No such ameliorative gaze meets *Gatsby*'s desire not to be taken as a
fraud or imposter, however, and in this sense Gatsby's closeted Catholicism—closeted insofar as his background is suppressed—reveals itself as
much in Gatsby's longing to "pass" as it does in his incorrigible outsiderhood, his glittering, extravagant otherness. To the degree that Gatsby
returns Nick's fascination, his interest would seem most to lie in Nick's
flawless performance of what Donna Haraway calls the "god-trick," the
practice by which members of privileged social groups come to occupy a
seemingly "unmarked class" beyond class, race, sexuality, or ethnicity;
an invisible space into which "competing groups long to disappear."[75]
It's this that allows Nick to "melt . . . indistinguishably" (118) into the
American continent on the westbound trains of his youth, or Daisy Fay,
having "given" herself to Gatsby in Louisville, to "vanish . . . into her
rich house, into her rich, full life, leaving Gatsby—nothing" (99).

And yet Gatsby, it seems, has never entirely appreciated the lesson of
the "invisible cloak of his uniform" (99) that first allowed him to pass
into Daisy's world as an impoverished army officer years before; even
when Daisy's professed dislike for the carnival atmosphere of his parties
has him dimming the lights of his mansion like Stella Dallas trimming the
flounces from her more garish frocks, Gatsby wants a *lot* more than
merely to blend in. Much has now been made of Gatsby's "blackness":
the fact that, according to the books Tom's been reading (like *The Rise
of the Colored Empires* by "this man Goddard" [9]) Gatsby isn't entirely
white, or that the disclosure of his renewed affair with Daisy prompts a
litany from Tom that ends in predicting "intermarriage between black
and white" (86).[76] As Fitzgerald was writing *Gatsby* popular works of
racist pseudo-science (like *The Rising Tide of Color* by Lothrop Stoddard)
sounded alarms on an America that was becoming less and less Euro-
Protestant and native-born, yet to judge from the names on Gatsby's notorious guest list (40–41), it's just these troublesome "new" Americans who

come in droves to Gatsby's "overpopulated lawn" (44).[77] In this sense Gatsby's "blackness" might be said to mark the more general forms of otherness he elicits, the kinds of heterogeneity to which he is host. Here is Nick on his first ride in Gatsby's outlandish car:

> The city seen from the Queensboro Bridge is always the city seen for the first time, in its first wild promise of all the mystery and beauty in the world.
>
> A dead man passed us in a hearse heaped with blooms, followed by two carriages with drawn blinds, and by more cheerful carriages for friends. The friends looked out at us with the tragic eyes and short upper lips of southeastern Europe, and I was glad that the sight of Gatsby's splendid car was included in their somber holiday. As we crossed Blackwell's Island a limousine passed us, driven by a white chauffeur, in which sat three modish negroes, two bucks and a girl. I laughed aloud as the yolks of their eyeballs rolled toward us in haughty rivalry.
>
> "Anything can happen now that we've slid over this bridge," I thought; "anything at all . . ."
>
> Even Gatsby could happen, without any particular wonder. (45)

There's more than sex, I would hazard, to what one critic calls the "sexual drama of Nick and Gatsby":[78] if Gatsby's bungled desire is for invisibility, for the god-trick, for "the Platonic conception of himself" (65), Nick's is for abundant presence, for the carnival-like *ekklesia* of Gatsby's overpopulated lawn, for the "inexhaustible variety of life" (24). Gatsby's love for Daisy, all theatricality and flourish, enacts the desire for WASP America, for the girl, green breast and green light; Nick's attraction to Gatsby, all hedges and circumspection, barely hinted at and barely contained, suggests other desires, other Americas. Each wants, it appears, what the other seems effortlessly to embody, yet neither can entirely relinquish his own more obdurate patternings in the end. Nick's last word on Gatsby—in effect, that his hopeless dream of loving Daisy was the equally hopeless dream of belonging to a world where houses are known for generations by a family name—would seem to constitute an affirmation of Tom Buchanan's America and of the closed circle of "breeding" in whose name Tom exposes Gatsby as "black" on the basis of his illegitimate desire for Daisy.[79] So too Nick's final insistence that he "disapproved of [Gatsby] from beginning to end" (103) implies a disavowal of any desire of his own that exceeds the logic of the family name, the regulating schema of monogamous, racially pure heterosexuality by which Tom Buchanan's America is reproduced.[80]

Except that the novel never really supports that view of coherence: Nick heads back to the rolling plains of the Middle West to wash his hands of the mess and feel unutterably aware of his identity with America once more, then proceeds to write a book about the man he could scarcely tear his eyes from that summer or his thoughts from since. Flickers of credulity aside, Nick knows that Gatsby is desperately trying to pass, that his glamorous persona shows every sign of having come from "skimming hastily through a dozen magazines" (44). And yet despite himself Nick sees—cannot stop seeing—"something gorgeous" in Gatsby and in a life lived as "an unbroken series of successful gestures" (1).

The question of whose America Nick's narrative is finally "for"—Tom Buchanan's, on one hand, or Gatsby's, on the other—has prompted competing appraisals. For some readers, Gatsby's failure to pass into the economic and familial structures of WASP entitlement pegs the novel as a kind of blueprint for a racially purified America, a "culture [produced] out of race,"[81] "a society utterly responsive to unification by a single design."[82] A raft of other critics, however, find in *The Great Gatsby* a message not of exclusivity but of "tolerance": a paean to the American vision of "unity" and "integration,"[83] a liberating "indictment of the postwar hypocrisy of the American East Coast Establishment,"[84] and a corrective resource for "for overcoming that curious form of spiritual myopia which seems to afflict us as Americans," which is "our insensibility to forms of life, forms of being, other than our own."[85] The latter reading is surely facilitated by a notion of performativity that makes Gatsby's "unbroken series of gestures" the antidote to the essentialism that lies at the heart of Tom Buchanan's America, or Lothrop Stoddard's, "a racialized conception of American identity," as Peter Mallios puts it, "emphatically closed to the idea that nationality might be acquired through cultural performance."[86] The counternarrative ostensibly embodied in Gatsby—"that 'maleness' or 'whiteness' or ethnicity can be performed or enacted, donned or discarded," in Elaine Ginsburg's formulation, promises instead an expansive "space for creative self-determination and agency," a stage on which "to construct new identities, to experiment with multiple subject positions, and to cross social and economic boundaries that exclude or oppress."[87]

And yet to frame race and ethnicity, sexuality and gender as largely or wholly volitional phenomena may only be, as Paul Giles warns, to "celebrat[e] the free and quintessentially American individual," to "testify, in the most traditional manner, to an American power of unfettered liberty and romantic self-invention."[88] In a similar way, to understand Catholicism as primarily performative may finally do no more than resituate Catholic identity squarely within a Protestant landscape of denominational pluralism, one option among others in a free market of religious choices.[89] Eve Sedgwick points valuably here to "the frightening ease with which anything that our capitalist/consumer culture does not figure as absolute *compulsion* (e.g., addiction) it instead recasts as absolute *choice* through the irresistible metaphor of the marketplace."[90] Let's take Nick's ambivalence seriously, then, for the alternative it suggests: the possibility that what goes most deeply to the making of identity—religious, sexual, ethnic, racial—might be in the end, to paraphrase Sedgwick, *neither* essential and unchanging, *nor* free-floating and discretionary, a possibility that, more than the notion of performativity itself, marks a rupture both in the marketplace model of diversity and in the closed circle of Tom's America.

Fitzgerald, we know, could match instances of repugnant racial and ethnic description with the most bullying of his contemporaries (compare Hemingway's "To Have and Have Not"). But he could also create characters who refuse to bow to the reigning order of representation, like the unnamed "negro man" in *The Last Tycoon* who comes to the beach at night to read Emerson,[91] or like Fifi Schwartz, the "ravishing Jewess" in "The Hotel Child," whose allure for the "platoon of young men of all possible nationalities and crosses" who trail in her wake lies not only in her beauty but in the fact that she feels no "insufficiency" in their midst.[92] Even in the description of *Gatsby*'s "modish negroes," condescension and stereotype pull in one direction, the promise of entirely new forms of relation ("anything can happen") in quite another. *Nowhere* in the mix do we find anything like the genteel "tolerance" that Nick especially might be expected to proffer. Already in very early and marginal pieces, something in Fitzgerald's responses to black cultural production anticipates Nick's descriptions of Gatsby and Gatsby's parties, in which an unshakeable cathexis to vitality overpowers the initial revulsion that gives it form. In "The Trail of the Duke," for example, published in his high school literary magazine, Fitzgerald wrote of "bugs . . . gathered around the lights like so many humans at a carnival, buzzing, thugging, whirring. . . . In the flats that line upper New York, pianos (sweating ebony perspiration) ground out ragtime tunes."[93]

In a long manuscript passage later cut from *The Great Gatsby*, Nick describes the experience of hearing "The Jazz History of the World," the musical composition played at the first of Gatsby's parties he attends, immediately after catching his first-ever glimpse of Gatsby himself.

> "The piece is known," [the conductor] concluded lustily, "as Les Epstien's Jazz History of the World."
> When he sat down all the members of the orchestra looked at one another and smiled as tho[ugh] this was a little below them after all. Then the conductor raised his wand—and they all launched into one of the most surprising pieces of music I've ever heard in my life. . . .
> It started out with a weird, spinning sound that seemed to come mostly from the cornets, very regular and measured and inevitable

with a bell now and then that seemed to ring somewhere a good distance away. A rhythm became distinguishable after a while in the spinning, a sort of a dull beat but as soon as you'd almost made it out it disappeared—until finally something happened, something tremendous, you knew that, and the spinning was all awry and one of the distant bells had come alive, it had a personality somehow of its own. . . .

The second movement was concerned with the bell only it wasn't the bell anymore but a muted cello and two instruments I had never seen before. At first there was a sort of monotony about it—a little disappointing at first as though it were just a repetition of the spinning sound but pretty soon you were aware that something was trying to establish itself, to get a foothold, something soft and persistent and profound and next you yourself were trying to help it, struggling, praying for it—until suddenly it was *there*, it was established rather scornfully without you and it seemed to lurk around with a complete self-sufficiency as if it had been there all the time.

I was curiously moved and the third part of the thing was full of an even stronger emotion. . . . [T]here would be a series of interruptive notes that seemed to fall together accidentally and colored everything that came after them until before you knew it new music was introduced and became the theme and new discords were opposed to it from outside. But what struck me particularly was that just as you'd get used to this new discord business there'd be one of the old themes rung in this time as a discord until you'd get a ghastly sense that it was all a cycle after all, purposeless and sardonic until you wanted to get up and walk out of the garden. . . . Whenever I think of that summer I can hear it yet.[94]

Breitwieser takes the discarded passage as evidence that when it came to jazz Fitzgerald really did *get* it, so much so that he must also have understood that to leave the passage in—in the final version of the novel Nick says only that the nature of "The Jazz History of the World" eluded him, because he was arrested by Gatsby's presence just as the band began to play—would have signaled an "exuberant betrayal of the aesthetic norms governing the book in which it would have been enclosed." "To someone as intensely and deeply committed to a sacramental and holistic conception of art and society as Fitzgerald was at this time in his life," says Breitwieser, such a "departure from script" could only "endanger the coherence and recognizeability of the whole."[95]

It may be that what the finished novel offers in place of the excised passage—Nick's lingering reflections on Gatsby's tanned skin, "approving eyes," and the fact that no women ever seemed to approach him

(33)—intimates as much a "departure from script" as his startling and emotionally complex response to "The Jazz History of the World." Certainly Nick's response to Gatsby remains as vexingly alive when the summer is over. But in that case, too, the novel's silencing of a difficult music would seem to go hand in hand with its muting of discordant desire, desire at once for Gatsby and for the irrepressibly "mixed" America that both tempts and tempers Nick's supremely WASP midwestern gentility.

In this sense, Nick's attraction to Gatsby ironically resembles the attraction of the Jesuit novice in "The Ordeal" to the world beyond the Catholic Church's walls, a world whose complexity he finally refuses. There Fitzgerald had written of the "unsought, alien" undercurrent that enters disturbingly into the would-be priest's awareness:

> [I]t seemed to take the form of music. He raised his eyes with a start— far down the dusty road a group of negro hands were walking along singing, and the song was an old song he knew.
>
> > We hope ter meet you in heavan whar we'll part no mo',
> > Part no mo'.
> > Gawd a'moughty bless you twel we
> > Me-et agin . . .
>
> That song was old in his life. His nurse had hummed it through the dreamy days of his childhood. Often in the hot summer afternoons he had played it softly on his banjo. It reminded him of so many things: months at the seashore on the hot beach with the gloomy ocean rolling around him, playing with sand castles with his cousin; summer evenings on the big lawn at home where he chased fireflies and the breeze carried the tune over the night to him from the negro-quarters. Later, with new words, it had served as a serenade—and now—well, he had done with that part of his life, and yet he seemed to see a girl with kind eyes, old in a great sorrow, waiting, ever waiting. . . .
>
> Other music ran now as an undercurrent to his thoughts: wild, incoherent music, illusive and wailing, like the shriek of a hundred violins, yet clear and chord-like. Art, beauty, love, and life passed in a panorama before him, exotic with the hot perfumes of world passion. . . .
>
> Again the music changed; the air was low and sad. . . . For a minute, an eternity he trembled in the void and then—something snapped. They were still there, but the girl's eyes were all wrong, the lines around her mouth were cold and chiseled and her passion seemed dead and earthy.[96]

In "The Ordeal" strange music is silenced in the pat resolution of an either-or dilemma; in *Gatsby* by a more ambivalent narrative reworking. Turn now to a haunting passage in *The Last Tycoon*, Fitzgerald's final work of fiction, left unfinished when he collapsed of a fatal heart attack in his low-rent Los Angeles apartment at the age of forty-four. Here the novel's deeply imagined protagonist, the widowed movie mogul Monroe Stahr, drives home alone through the Hollywood hills after dropping his new love interest, Kathleen Moore, at her rented bungalow:

> Winding down the hill, he listened inside himself as if something by an unknown composer, powerful and strange and strong, was about to be played for the first time. The theme would be stated presently, but because the composer was always new, he would not recognize it as the theme right away. It would come in some such guise as the auto horns from the technicolor boulevards below, or be barely audible, a tattoo on the muffled drum of the moon. He strained to hear it, knowing only that music was beginning, new music he liked and did not understand. It was hard to react to what one could entirely compass—this was new and confusing, nothing one could shut off in the middle and supply the rest from an old score. (113–14)

The passage follows what is surely the deftest *hetero*sexual love scene in Fitzgerald's fiction, an encounter between Stahr and Kathleen that breaks up and begins to unfreeze the pattern of stalled mourning for his wife that until now has had Stahr putting in twenty-hour days at the studio. Later that evening the two walk together on the beach: "little silver fish . . . came swarming in with the tide, and Stahr and Kathleen stepped over them barefoot as they flicked slip-slop in the sand. A negro man came along the shore toward them, collecting the grunion quickly, like twigs, into two pails. They came in twos and threes and platoons and companies, relentless and exalted and scornful, around the great bare feet of the intruders, as they had come before Sir Francis Drake had nailed his plaque to the boulder on the shore" (110).[97]

The "intruders" on this shore are Stahr, the scrappy Jewish street fighter turned industry titan, the mysterious not-quite-ingénue Kathleen, new to Hollywood via the soup kitchens of Ireland, and the unnamed black man who scorns the movies and reads philosophy at night on the beach. This is a markedly different vision of the continent than the one that "flowered once for Dutch sailors' eyes" (121) in the last, elegiac paragraphs of *Gatsby*, the WASP-America-in-the-making that could make no room for Jimmy Gatz.[98] Underscoring that difference in *The Last Tycoon* is the kind of musical epiphany—"nothing one could shut off in the middle and supply the rest from an old score"—that the protagonist of "The Ordeal" struggled mightily *not* to hear, that Fitzgerald ultimately cut from the story of Nick and Gatsby. "Consistency, unity, homogeneity seem to be a danger to [this] music, rather than its redemption," Breitwieser suggests; "the maintenance of an intersubjective contest, conversation, or seduction seems to be the aesthetic task."[99]

• • •

Two years after the failure of *Tender Is the Night* to revive his moribund literary fame, Fitzgerald retreated for several weeks to a North Carolina hotel—"a dollar room in a drab little town"[100]—where he lived on tinned meat and crackers and managed to drill through his writer's block by repeating the mantra, "I can't write stories about young love for the *Saturday Evening Post* because I can't write stories about young love for the *Saturday Evening Post* because I can't write stories about young love for the *Saturday Evening Post* because . . ."[101] What emerged from this period of forced introspection—the "moving about of great secret trunks"[102]— were the "Crack-up" essays ("The Crack-Up," "Handle with Care," "Pasting It Together"), a series of personal revelations so intimate that Max Perkins considered them "an indecent invasion" of Fitzgerald's privacy yet elliptical enough to prompt the suspicion, as Alfred Kazin put it, that "something is being persistently withheld, that the author is somehow offering us certain facts in exchange for the right to keep others to himself."[103] The essays do not show Fitzgerald in his best lights, and they record no single moment of transformation, but they do unflinchingly name, as "parallel experiences" to his emotional collapse a year or so earlier, the two traumas that his fiction would no longer compulsively rehearse: the first was his "failure as a big shot" at Princeton, and the second his rejection by Zelda, a year before their lifelong marriage, on account of his being poor.[104] In this sense they describe the gradual breakdown of a psychic structure—Fitzgerald called it the "hole or bag in which [you] find all the things [you've] ever lost"[105]—by which one set of failures or disappointments, endlessly revisited, could function to keep an entirely different register of experience at bay. From here until *The Last Tycoon*, Fitzgerald's fragmented literary output would hover at thresholds—between "art" and "life," between various enclosures ("The Author's House," "Inside the House," "Strange Sanctuary,") and the leaving of them—as though, having written the last of his debutante stories for the *Saturday Evening Post*, he might now begin to narrate a different coming out.

AMERICAN RELIGION AND THE

FUTURE OF DISSENT

I BEGAN MAKING plans for this book as President Bill Clinton was battling impeachment and finished a draft just as President George W. Bush was elected to a second term. Roughly midway between these events came the September 11 attacks, whose reverberations in our global and domestic policy continue to rob what solace might otherwise be had in the arc of events from the harrowing back to the merely dispiriting. During this time it occurred to me more than once that whatever social capital might remain to left-leaning academics surely ought not to be squandered in calling even the progressive elements of a secularized Protestant culture to account. Why choose this of all moments to put hard questions to cherished liberal narratives about, for example, the separation of church and state, the value of literacy, or the privatization of religious faith (to take three of this book's concerns) when all appear to be under siege from quite other directions?

At the same time, the hegemonic power of appeals to a Protestant consensus in American public life remains, it would seem, as strong than ever: what William Hutchison identifies as the nineteenth-century dynamic of "[religious] pluralism as selective tolerance" made itself felt at the end of 2004, for example, in the various pressures that combined to stifle inquiry into possible voting irregularities before the presidential election results were ratified by Congress, sending a message to all those beyond this election's fragile, "Christian"-inflected consensus to "just behave," in Hutchison's phrase,[1] in the interest of maintaining (at least the illusion of) national unity.

So also in the post–September 11 calls from politicians and pundits for a "Reformation" in Islam, an Islam that would conform to Western expectations of acceptable religion: should we be surprised if such appeals are no longer made by the side of a moderate Muslim leader produced for the occasion, and *all* forms of Islam are now suspect for not looking *enough* like post-Reformation Christianity?[2] Consider the case of the Geneva-based scholar Tariq Ramadan, a self-described Western Muslim who, two weeks before moving to the United States in the fall of 2004 to take up a new post as Luce Professor of Islamic Studies and Director of the Program in Religion, Conflict, and Peacebuilding at the University of Notre Dame, had his visa revoked under the Patriot Act's ample provisions for silencing voices on issues deemed "sensitive" to national security.[3] The fate of Ramadan—prevented from taking leadership of an academic forum devoted to religious conflict, its ramifications, and possible resolutions—suggests how embattled is the public space left for dissent in post-9/11 America, where even the *study* of dissent, conducted under mixed Christian and Muslim auspices, may come to be branded as bordering on the seditious.

A parallel move to constrain a potentially dissonant pluralism in the name of American values may be seen in the broader rhetoric of our current (but strangely eternal) "war on terror" which, as Amy Kaplan points out, "reduces the complex interactions of the United States with the world to a Manichean conflict 'to rid the world of evil,' a definition that evacuates the present moment of politics, history, agency, and struggle."[4] If the rhetoric of perpetual warfare against those who refuse the universal human values embodied by Americans sounds timeless by design, what *is* new is the way the imperial ambitions that undergird this rhetoric have unabashedly taken center stage. As Kaplan suggests, the notion of an American empire has gravitated in the last decade or so from left-wing critique to mainstream policymaking, "business as usual," where talk quite openly revolves around the questions of whether the American empire "is benevolent or self-interested, whether it should rely on hard power or soft power, whether this empire most closely resembles the British Empire or the Roman, and whether it is in its ascendancy or in decline."[5] Though sounded from across a political spectrum, such talk is rarely cautionary or critical (as in the work of those who, like Kaplan, raised the question of American empire in the early 1990s) but instead more typically "celebrates the United States as finally revealing its true essence—its manifest destiny—on a global stage."[6]

The question of empire brings into view a set of connections between this manifest destiny and the Protestant-secular continuum I have sought in this book to elaborate. Janet Jakobsen and Ann Pellegrini suggest that the Christian right develops its political and cultural power "both by drawing on its connection to the Christian aspect (itself supported by mainline Protestantism) of hegemonic Christian secularism and by claiming to be oppressed by the same secularism."[7] (Secularists, meanwhile, might be said to draw on the secular aspect of hegemonic Christian secularism while claiming to be oppressed by its Christian aspect.) Nowhere is this strategic flexibility more apparent than in questions of American global policy. However starkly continuing dispatches from the "culture wars" may portray an America divided into a conservative Christian faction hostile to the secular and a dogmatic secularism at odds with religion, it must be noted that the category of the West readily accommodates *both* of these polarized alternatives when the paradigm shifts from the culture wars between Christians and secularists to the "clash of civilizations" between the West and the rest. The very distinction between the religious and the secular, Peter van der Veer argues, is itself a product of Western imperialism, part of a narrative that drew sharp opposition "between the irrational, religious behavior of the [colonial subject] . . . and rational secularism, which enabled the westerner to rule."[8] A variant of that narrative produces what Winnifred Fallers Sullivan identifies as the "curiously Janus-faced quality" of religion in modernity: "Religion's one face is associated with the irrational, the savage, and the 'other' in a profoundly constitutive way. That face is to be feared and kept separate . . . . [R]eligion's other face is regarded as a primary source of ethical reflection and behavior and is thought by some to be the only source."[9] According to either version of this story, the formation of democratic societies requires that "irrational" religious behavior be banished to the private sphere, on the Protestant model, as a way of containing otherwise intractable and potentially violent conflict between contending worldviews. This is the model to which warnings of a "clash of civilizations" continue to appeal, even if secularists looking out from the West see theocratic assaults on modernity where religionists see godless assaults on the cherished values of Western civilization. It is also the model that Western projects of nation building have traditionally sought to install around the globe.

In the same way that a familiar liberal narrative of Islam—"the Reformation of Islam will arrive as an inevitable byproduct of modernization"—is made to yield up to its more violent and triumphalist counterpart—"Islam will ever remain incompatible with the West's secularized Protestant values"—so also do two versions of U.S. imperialism become mutually supporting and difficult to untangle. In the first, a liberal interventionist narrative sees the United States as uniquely able to redress, even if reluctantly, the failure of backward states and cultures to enter fully into modernity. The United States acts in its own interests and in the interests of those oppressed by the failed states in which they reside, this story runs, when it uses whatever means necessary to bring the blessings of religious liberty, economic freedom, and representative government to those parts of the world that would otherwise remain breeding grounds for violence, human rights abuses, and terrorism. This narrative's calming appeal to freedom, democracy, and their inevitable sway migrates also to its more hawkish counterpart, which urges perpetual aggressions against all those who oppose our universal values and who "hate" the freedoms we hold so dear—witness the hypocrisy of our guarantee of "religious freedoms" to those Muslims violently detained at Guantánamo Bay, without due process and apparently indefinitely.[10] So also the liberal-interventionist narrative that makes it the task of empire to bring benighted populations *into* the blessed circle of humanity might be said necessarily to retract humanity from the very objects of our benevolence, erasing our strategies of dehumanization even when these are on display for all to see. When conversation in my classroom turned to Abu Ghraib in late August 2004, an earnest student raised her hand to urge her peers not be too hard on the U.S. soldiers charged with prisoner abuse; they've been living among the poor brutalized Iraqis, she explained, and know full well that humiliation and torture are all those people understand.

What happens, asks Kaplan, when power long operating in and through denial suddenly proclaims itself openly? On one level, critics of empire might welcome such a development for sparing them the minute and typically thankless task of unpacking its operations from within the coded narratives that conceal them. At the same time, however, the very openness of this new American imperialism seems to deflect criticism from the idea of empire itself, recasting the question of whether and in what sense America is an empire to the question of what kind of empire America ought properly to be. But it may also be the case that the very brashness of the language of empire used in the United States today, which builds so transparently on the fear and grief of September 11, reveals even as it assiduously papers over a sense of weakness and vulnerability at the heart of American notions of manifest destiny. As Kaplan points out, the narrative of empire (particularly in its touchstone British and Roman versions) has always entailed its eventual decline and fall, which is perhaps why the name of empire remained unspoken in U.S. policy for so long. The case against Tariq Ramadan suggests that this new American empire vests the threat of its own undoing not only in oppositional identities but in those hybrid or layered identities—Western Muslim, for example—that resist the categories imposed by the for-or-against mentality so crucial to claims of American invincibility.[11]

Leo Marx points to a "doubleness" at the heart of American episodes of protest and dissent, including the abolitionist, feminist, labor, and antiwar movements: "To mobilize opposition to slavery, egregious forms of capitalist exploitation and injustice, and unjust wars, leaders of these dissident movements affirmed their provisional belief in the idea of America," a stance from which they could both "denounce and defend, confirm and affirm." "It was a compelling means," says Marx, "of exposing the discrepancy between a real and an ideal America or, as Melville put it on the eve of the Civil War, between the world's foulest crime and man's fairest hope."[12] Something of that doubleness is surely to be discerned in the ways that marked religious communities have played transformative roles in American culture: African American churches in the civil rights movement, for example, Catholic and Jewish immigrants in the labor movement, or Christian pacifists in the antiwar movements. Religious "outsiderhood," R. Laurence Moore reminds us, has long been "a characteristic way of inventing one's Americanness."[13]

What such outsiders to the American religious consensus at various points in our history might tell us today is that the model we seek to export in the name of American values, one that attempts to ensure religious freedom and eradicate conflict by confining religion to a privatized sphere, does not even describe the dynamics of our *own* history. Worse still, it hides the violence and coercion that have attended the formation of American democratic space in the guise of the neutrality and universality of the secular. Academics tend to dismiss challenges to this narrative as the retrogressive voices of religionists who clamor for an ever greater share of public power. And not without evidence. Even so, however, our own embrace of a simplified narrative of secularization-as-progress is in part what allows this template to operate as the norm for bringing American values to a benighted world. As the newly emboldened language of empire may yet give new traction for dissent, however, my hope is that our increasingly public discourse of religion might yet clear the way for more nuanced assessments of the contradictions and ideological limitations of the secularization narrative. Such a rethinking of the complex, recombinatory, often volatile exchanges between religions and between religious and secular domains that have in fact characterized our history points also to the possibility of a newly energized and contestatory pluralism, one where appeals to freedom, values, even faith mean more and otherwise than what the loyalty oaths of our present climate would make of them.

NOTES

Introduction

1. Giles Gunn, *The Interpretation of Otherness: Literature, Religion, and the American Imagination*, 13.

2. Gunn, *The Criticism of Culture and the Culture of Criticism*, 5.

3. See, e.g., Paul Tillich, *Theology of Culture*.

4. Robert A. Orsi, "On Not Talking to the Press," 19. For fuller discussion, see Orsi, *Between Heaven and Earth: The Religious Worlds People Make and the Scholars Who Study Them*, especially 177–204.

5. I owe this point to Janet R. Jakobsen and Ann Pellegrini, "World Secularisms at the Millenium: Introduction," 23. Secularism also flourishes in American literary studies and in the humanities more broadly to the degree that we rely on a secular liberal paradigm to avoid divisiveness in the classroom. This paradigm, part of whose work is to render religion a private matter of conscience and belief, has kept religion out of the curriculum of most academic disciplines apart from religious studies; even there, faculty typically provide students a model of detachment and objectivity, the secular scholarly gaze. Whatever the shortcomings of such a model, including its foreclosure of the possibility that committed intellectual exchange among contending positions within a culture of religious pluralism might be cultivated as a positive good, it remains entrenched insofar our tools for engaging religion remain limited to a bland respect for others' deeply held beliefs and a privileging of religion *as* belief, neither of which can safeguard the classroom from the sincere desire of any to proselytize, or to trump evidence presented in class with devout appeals to higher law. Better then (we say) to check religion at the door. For a valuable account of how the inadequacy of public discourse on religion in America within and beyond the academy itself derives from and reflects the dominance of Protestant religious models, see Winnifred Fallers Sullivan, "Diss-ing Religion: Is Religion Trivialized in American Public Discourse?"

6. In an 1852 journal entry headed *Races*, Emerson wrote: "Nature every little while drops a link. How long before the Indians will be extinct? then the negro? then shall we say, what a gracious interval of dignity between man and beast!" (*Journals and Miscellaneous Notebooks of Ralph Waldo Emerson*, 8:54). A later entry: "The dark man, the black man declines. The black man is courageous, but the white men are the children of God, said Plato. It will happen by and by, that the black man will be destined for museums like the Dodo. Alcott compassionately thought that if necessary to bring them sooner to an end, polygamy might be introduced & these made eunuchs, polygamy, I suppose, to increase the white births" (*Journals and Miscellaneous Notebooks*, 8:286–87). Barbara Packer suggests that Emerson's "desire to see black people disappear arose not from irrational prejudice but from [his] despair of seeing them successfully assimilated into a human race [he] needed to see as progressive" (Barbara Packer, "Emerson and the Overgod").

7. The conversion of the Unitarian Anna Baker Ward to Catholicism prompted Emerson to reflect in his journal: "The running into the catholic church is disgusting, just as one is looking amicably around at the culture and performance of young people, and fancying that the new generation is an advance on the last. . . . But in regard to Ward . . . it must be said that there is the eternal offset of the moral principle. . . . *Morals*, it has not yet its first hymn. But, that every line and word may be coals of pure fire, perhaps ages must roll ere these casual wide-falling cinders can be gathered into a broad and stealthy altar flame. 'The mills of God grind slow but grind fine. . . . [T]he Lord is *tedious*, but he is sure'" (*Journals of Ralph Waldo Emerson*, 7:341).

8. Jodi Wilgoren, "Politicized Scholars Put Evolution on the Defensive," *New York Times*, 21 August 2005; Peter Slevin, "Kansas Education Board First to Back 'Intelligent Design'; Schools to Teach Doubts About Evolutionary Theory," *Washington Post*, 9 November 2005; "Ten Commandments Backed by Bush in Court Fight," Bloomberg Media, 8 December 2004, http://www.bloomberg.com/apps/news?pid=10000103&sid=aVq7CjVw_3Zc&refer=us.

9. So nearly have socially conservative Catholics and Protestants come to unite their political interests in the last quarter-century that the category of the Christian Right may now seem to mark no distinction between them. To suggest however with Noah Feldman, most recently, that the "deep divide in American life" is not over religious affiliation but over the appropriate role of religion in politics (*Divided by God*, 6) is potentially to obscure the history by which Protestants have set the terms of this debate. As Winifred Fallers Sullivan puts it, the "modern religio-political arrangement," particularly "in its American manifestation," is largely the product of "protestant reflection and culture." Sullivan continues: "I use 'protestant' not in a narrow churchy sense, but rather loosely to describe a set of political ideas and cultural practices that emerged in early modern Europe in and after the Reformation; that is, I refer to 'protestant,' as opposed to 'catholic,' models of church-state relations. (According to this use, Protestants can be 'catholic' and Catholics 'protestant.') Religion—'true' religion some would say—on this modern protestant reading, came to be understood as being private, voluntary, individual, textual, and believed. Public, coercive, communal, oral, and enacted religion on the other hand, was seen to be 'false.' The second kind of religion, iconically represented historically in the United States, for the most part by the Roman Catholic Church (and by Islam today), was, and still is, the religion of most of the world. Indeed, from a contemporary academic perspective, that religion with which many religion scholars are most concerned has been carefully and systematically excluded, both rhetorically and legally, from modern public space. Crudely speaking, it is the first kind—the modern protestant kind—that is 'free.' The other kind is closely regulated by law" (*The Impossibility of Religious Freedom*, 7–8). The question of how conservative Catholics and Protestants have now come jointly to wield the authority of "true" religion in American public life, all the while pressing their claims in ways that make religion seem anything but private and discretionary, bears thoughtful examination.

10. Against the Bush Administration's "teach the conflicts" approach, the December 2005 decision of Judge John E. Jones III in *Kitzmiller v. Dover Area School District*, which ruled the teaching of intelligent design in Pennsylvania public

schools unconstitutional, and the Clergy Letter Project, in which upwards of ten thousand American clergy have signed their names to a letter protesting intelligent design on theological grounds (Neela Banerjee and Anne Berryman, "At Churches Nationwide, Good Words for Evolution," *New York Times*, 14 February 2006), mark recent, abundantly welcome interventions in a pitched battle by which evolutionary theory and Christian faith continue to be portrayed as conflicting "sides" between which schoolchildren in Kansas will still (as of this writing) be directed by no less an authority than their State's Board of Education to "choose." But the question remains: why, at a moment when religious and religiously tinged conflicts are erupting around the globe and shaping U.S. policy both domestically and internationally, has the discourse on religion and the appropriate education of students for citizenship come to be dominated almost entirely by the issues debated eighty years ago in the Scopes trial?

11. Max Weber, *The Protestant Ethic and the Spirit of Capitalism*, 36. I am indebted to Janet R. Jakobsen and Ann Pellegrini for this reference. See also Jakobsen and Pellegrini, "World Secularisms at the Millennium: Introduction." My debts to their rich discussion of secularism and its entanglements with Protestant Christianity extend throughout this book.

12. Terryl L. Givens discusses this effect in *The Viper on the Hearth: Mormons, Myths, and the Construction of Heresy*.

13. Jakobsen and Pellegrini, "World Secularisms at the Millennium," 8.

14. See, e.g., David D. Kirkpatrick, "Some Democrats Believe the Party Should Get Religion," *New York Times*, 17 November 2004.

15. Catherine L. Albanese, *America: Religions and Religion*, 398, 395.

16. David Hackett, ed., *Religion and American Culture: A Reader*, ix.

17. Hackett, "Gender and Religion in American Culture, 1870–1930" (typescript, 1994), 1. A revised version of this essay was later published under the same title in *Religion and American Culture: A Journal of Interpretation* 5.2 (Summer 1995): 227–57. My thanks to David Hackett for allowing me to quote from the earlier, unpublished version.

18. William R. Hutchison, *Religious Pluralism in America: The Contentious History of a Founding Ideal*, 1

19. Ibid., 3

20. On the "narrative fiction" of Protestant consensus in American religious history, see also Ann Braude, "American Religious History *Is* Women's History," especially 92–96.

21. Andrew Ross, *No Respect: Intellectuals and Popular Culture*, 55–56. I am aware of the argument from many quarters that there has been no theologically, racially, economically, or politically homogenous culture named American Protestantism at any point in our history, that Protestant denominations now numbering in the hundreds are characterized by a diversity that matches or exceeds that of other religious cultures in America, and that public Protestantism, therefore, remains an inadequate paradigm for explaining the character of American public life. My use of Protestantism as a blanket term in these chapters is meant not to minimize the internal complexities of Reformed Christianity but to suggest that conventional depictions of religious "diversity" in American history—Old Lights and New Lights, orthodox and free-thinkers, the settled religions of the establish-

ment and the revivalistic religions of the frontier, the evangelical piety of sentimental women and the stringent skepticism of representative men—misleadingly limit religious difference to a comparatively narrow spectrum. In their care not to portray American Protestantism as a monolith, such representations nevertheless elide non-Protestant or marginally Protestant concerns from national debate. The contraction of much of American religious history to the set of positions taken by white Protestants in relation to one another further obscures what Homi K. Bhabha points to as the power residing in the dominant culture's "repertoire of conflictual positions," the system of dissonances that register not merely internal conflict but also the implicit interrogation of weaker groups (*Location of Culture*, 77). Asked to "speak for Protestantism" in an interreligious conversation on environmental issues, a contemporary theologian responded that she would "do so *in glad protest against and therefore also with* the endlessly self-diversifying, heterogenizing set of Christian traditions variously rooted in the protests of the Reformation" (Catherine Keller, "The Lost Fragrance: Protestantism and the Nature of What Matters," 356; emphasis added). Such assessments of Protestantism's exemplary accommodation of critique, whatever their ambivalence, belong to and further a tradition that aligns Protestantism with democracy and personal freedom, with what a chapter title of Nathan O. Hatch's *The Democratization of American Christianity* proclaims as "The Right to Think for Oneself." Much of my thinking in this book takes its bearings from a challenge Jenny Franchot posed in a footnote to *Roads to Rome: The Antebellum Protestant Encounter with Catholicism*: "I am not aware of any study that satisfactorily theorizes the relation between such religious democratization [as described by Hatch] . . . and the practices of often brutal exclusion involved in the formation of American selfhood" (373–74n30).

22. Cathy N. Davidson, *Revolution and the Word: The Rise of the Novel in America*, vii.

23. Edward W. Said, *Culture and Imperialism*, 15.

24. See Robert Cushman, "Reason & Considerations," in *Mourt's Relation*, 68; Cotton Mather, *Magnalia Christi Americana*, bk. 3, 191

25. *Philadelphia Public Ledger*, 8 June 1844, quoted by Michael Feldberg, *The Philadelphia Riots of 1844: A Study of Ethnic Conflict*, 95.

26. Harriet Beecher Stowe, *The Key to Uncle Tom's Cabin*, 49; Walt Whitman, "Preface 1855, Leaves of Grass, *First Edition*," in *Leaves of Grass and Selected Prose*, 711; Ralph Waldo Emerson, *Complete Works*, 2:133.

27. Catharine E. Beecher and Harriet Beecher Stowe, *The American Woman's Home*, 146–47.

28. Mark Twain, *Adventures of Huckleberry Finn*, 835.

29. Charlotte Perkins Gilman, *The Home: Its Work and Influence*, 5–6.

CHAPTER ONE
LEGIBLE DOMINION: PURITANISM'S NEW WORLD NARRATIVE

1. Christopher Columbus, *Four Voyages to the New World*, trans. and ed. R. H. Major (Gloucester, MA: Peter Smith, 1978), 1–2, quoted by Myra Jehlen, "Why Did the Europeans Cross the Ocean?," 43. "Proving, in this invocation of

sonorous Spanish and snappy standards deployed on an innocent beach," Jehlen writes of this scene, "that when you have the upper hand you can afford to look ridiculous" (43).

2. John Winthrop, *The History of New England from 1630 to 1640*, ed. James Savage, 2 vols. (Boston, 1825), 1:290, quoted by Patricia Seed, *Ceremonies of Possession in Europe's Conquest of the New World, 1492–1640*, 16.

3. John Cotton, *God's Promise to His Plantations*, 5.

4. From a sermon of John Eliot, recorded by Cotton Mather, *The Life and Death of the Reverend Mr. John Eliot*, 23–25.

5. William Bradford, *History of Plymouth Plantation*, 1:106.

6. Edward Johnson, *Wonder-Working Providence*, 231.

7. On these punishments, see Perry Miller and Thomas H. Johnson, eds., *The Puritans*, 1:183–87.

8. Philip Fisher, "Democratic Social Space: Whitman, Melville, and the Promise of American Transparency," 76.

9. Richard L. Rapson, "The Religious Feelings of the American People, 1845–1935," 327.

10. See Catherine Albanese, *America: Religion and Religions*, 396–431; Will Herberg, *Protestant, Catholic, Jew*, 114.

11. Scholars of American religious history have increasingly come to recognize, with David W. Wills, that the accepted narrative of American religious history as one of "tolerance" and "accommodation" necessarily marginalizes the experiences of groups whose historical trajectories remain unassimilable within what Thomas Tweed calls the (allegedly) "whole story" of American religious life populated by "male, northeastern, Anglo-Saxon, mainline Protestants" and "set in public spaces" (Wills, "The Central Themes of American Religious History"; Tweed, *Retelling U.S. Religious History*, 3). As Tweed and others have observed, that narrative, which reflects and is bound up in the broader network of privileges enjoyed by those it describes, is rapidly losing ground to what David Hackett describes as "a multicultural tale of Native Americans, African Americans, Catholics, Jews, and others" (Hackett, *Religion and American Culture*, ix). The potential failing of this new scholarship, however, is its propensity to leave unquestioned the assumption that the history of America's religious development remains a story of "tolerance" and "accommodation" whose laudable goals the new, "multicultural tale" implicitly furthers. Strategies of resistance to forms of power wielded in and by the master narrative will not easily find a place in a new narrative that, devoted to uncovering what the older narrative obscures, but failing to account for the effects of that obscuring on the new subject, asks us only to expand our gaze.

12. To argue that the Puritans made language a tool not only for the conquest of their own unquiet souls but for the subjugation of troubling others is to urge attention to the relationships between Puritan words and Puritan violence, not to make a facile argument about the "oppressive" nature of Christian scripture or of English literacy more broadly. Useful studies of Puritan language, violence, and power include Ann Kibbey, *The Interpretation of Material Shapes in Puritanism*; Jane Kamensky, "Talk Like a Man: Speech, Power, and Masculinity in Early New England"; and Jill Lepore, *The Name of War: King Philip's War and the Origins of American Identity*.

13. Those of us who seek to make sense of Puritanism's religious and cultural legacies inevitably contend with, and are sometimes misread as offering support for, what R. Marie Griffith identifies as "the chestnut of Protestantism as a thoroughly disembodied tradition, its leaders conspiring to eradicate both pleasure and pain in an attempt to rely solely on the cool, rational mind" (*Born Again Bodies: Flesh and Spirit in American Christianity*, 256n21). Griffith's work amply and elegantly contests this assumption. Nevertheless, to turn away from the often volatile juxtapositions of spirit and flesh in American Protestant discourses, with their attendant religious, racial, and national shadings, is to promote a different distortion; indeed, as Griffith's *Born Again Bodies* so compellingly shows, the point to be made about Protestant aspirations toward ever more disciplined embodiment is not that the impulse to spiritualize the flesh upholds an unfashionable metaphysical dualism, but rather that it exalts particular bodies and forms of embodied community over others and often at these others' violent expense.

14. Baxter, *The Saints Everlasting Rest*, 124, 127; Delbanco, *The Puritan Ordeal*, 247–48. The 1647 ordinance that stipulated compulsory instruction in reading for the children of English families in Massachusetts Bay came to be known as the "Old deluder Satan" act for its insistence that it was the Devil's chief object "to keep men from the knowledge of the scriptures" (Nathaniel B. Shurtleff, *Records of the Governor and Company of the Massachusetts Bay*, 2:203). For Puritans, literacy and Bible literacy were inseparable attainments that clothed them in what Charles Chauncey, the second president of Harvard College, called the "*Christian armour to defend themselves from spirituall enemyes*" (Charles Chauncey, *God's Mercy, Shewed to His People . . .*, 3).

15. I am here indebted to Jenny Franchot's discussion of "Protestant Meditations on History and 'Popery' " in *Roads to Rome*, 3–13, especially pp. 6–7.

16. Joshua Moody, *Souldiery Spiritualized, or the Christian Souldier Orderly, and Strenuously Engaged in the Spiritual Warre*, 1:368.

17. John Cotton, *Christ the Fountaine of Life*, 119–20; Miller and Johnson, *Puritans*, 1:61

18. Finding the English Puritan settlers to have grappled with a "language under terrible stress, threatened by migration itself," Delbanco suggests that a critical failure to attend to the recurring strains of inner disquietude, tentativeness, and self-persuasion that distinguish Puritanism's massive literary output has caused readers too hastily to dismiss the Puritans as "the people, *tout court*, 'who massacred the Indians and established the self-righteous religion and politics that determined American ideology' " (Delbanco, *Puritan Ordeal*, 14, 7; quoting J. Hillis Miller's 1986 Presidential Address to the Modern Language Association, *PMLA* 102.3 [1987]: 281).

19. Mark A. Noll, Nathan O. Hatch, and George M. Marsden, *The Search for a Christian America*, 19.

20. The Puritans made little use of notions of race as we would recognize them today, but the connections they drew between spiritual and embodied differences were intricate and pervasive. The terms "heathen" and "savage," habitually used to describe native peoples, signify both sets of difference simultaneously to indicate that the Indians are subhuman or nonhuman: William Bradford, for example, referred to "those vast and unpeopled countries of America, which are fruitfull, and fitt for habitation; being devoyd of all civill inhabitants; there are only salvage,

and brutish men, which range up and down, little otherwise than the wild beasts of the same" (Bradford, *History of Plymouth Plantation*, 1:96–97). On the Puritans and race, see G. E. Thomas, "Puritans, Indians, and the Concept of Race"; Leonard Cassuto, *The Inhuman Race: The Racial Grotesque in American Literature and Culture*, 30–74.

21. Perry Miller, Sacvan Bercovitch, Ann Douglas, Jane Tompkins, and other cultural historians of American Protestantism on whom I rely here and elsewhere have been criticized for remaining "confined within the tradition they seek to comprehend" (Anne Norton, *Alternative Americas*, 5) by conflating American culture with the Anglo-European culture of the eastern seaboard. My interest is not in determining whether such scholarship accurately assesses the influence of New England and the North Atlantic on the national culture but, again, in what it illuminates of the way New England Protestantism made so evidently compelling a case for its own historical and national primacy.

22. Seed, *Ceremonies of Possession*, 19.

23. This point is developed by Richard Slotkin, *Regeneration Through Violence*, 43; and by Michael Rogin, *Fathers and Children: Andrew Jackson and the Subjugation of the American Indian*, 8.

24. Cotton Mather, *Magnalia Christi Americana*, bk. 3, 191.

25. Samuel Purchas, "A Discourse of the diversity of Letters used by the divers Nations in the World . . .," in *Hakluytus Posthumus, or Purchas His Pilgrimes*, 20 vols. (Glasgow: James MacLehose & Sons, 1905), 1:486, quoted by Stephen Greenblatt, *Marvelous Possessions*, 9–10.

26. Robert Cushman, "Reason & Considerations touching the Lawfulnesse of Removing out of England into the Parts of America," 69–70.

27. Chauncey, *God's Mercy, Shewed to His People*, 2–3.

28. Cotton Mather, general introduction to *Magnalia*, unpaginated.

29. John Winthrop, "Reasons to be Considered, and Objections with Answers," 177–88.

30. Seed, *Ceremonies of Possession*, 62–63.

31. Cushman, "Reason & Considerations," 68.

32. This point is made by Cassuto, *Inhuman Race*, 38.

33. Cotton, *God's Promise to His Plantations*, 5.

34. John White, *The Planter's Plea*, 2.

35. Francis Higginson, *New-Englands Plantation*, 1:123.

36. Francis Jennings, *The Invasion of America*, 65. As Jennings points out, Indians were better farmers in many cases than the English, whose more ecologically taxing methods of cultivation sooner exhausted the soil. In the early twentieth century, more than half of U.S. economic production was in plants first domesticated by native peoples and later taken over by European settlers (62–63).

37. John Cotton, "An Enquiry, Whether the Church may not, in the Celebration of the Sacrament, use other Rites," 29. Cotton's authorship of this treatise is the subject of some dispute; see Kibbey, *Interpretation of Material Shapes*, 155–59.

38. This point is made by Margaret W. Ferguson in "Saint Augustine's Region of Unlikeness: The Crossing of Exile and Language," 842; quotation from Cicero's *De Oratore* also on 842.

39. Sacvan Bercovitch, *Puritan Origins of the American Self*, 113

40. William Hubbard, *A General History of New England*, 60.

41. Bercovitch, *Puritan Origins*, 112.

42. Peter Smart, *A Sermon Preached in the Cathedrall Church of Durham, Iuly 7, 1628*, 23.

43. Boston Synod, *A Confession of Faith*, 141–42.

44. John Winthrop, *A Short Story of the Rise, Reign, and Ruine of the Antinomians*, 13.

45. Charles E. Hambrick-Stowe cites these examples in *The Practice of Piety*, 46.

46. John Calvin, *Institutes of the Christian Religion*, 105, 102.

47. Thomas Shepard, quoted in Hambrick-Stowe, *Practice of Piety*, 46. W.J.T. Mitchell writes eloquently of the ways that iconoclasm functions as a key to the formation of godlike, "rational" identity: "An idol, technically speaking, is simply an image which has an unwarranted, irrational power over somebody; it has become an object of worship, a repository of powers which someone has projected onto it, but which it in fact does not possess. But iconoclasm typically proceeds by assuming that the power of the image is felt by somebody *else*; what the iconoclast sees is the emptiness, vanity, and impropriety of the idol. The idol, then, tends to be simply an image overvalued (in our opinion) by an *other*: by pagans and primitives; by children and foolish women; by papists and ideologues (*they* have an ideology; *we* have a political philosophy). . . . The rhetoric of iconoclasm is thus a rhetoric of exclusion and domination, a caricature of the other as one who is involved in irrational, obscene behavior from which (fortunately) we are exempt" (*Iconology*, 113).

48. Thomas Shepard, *A Treatise of Liturgies, Power of the Keyes, and of Matter of the Visible Church* . . . (London, 1653), 61, quoted by Hambrick-Stowe, *Practice of Piety*, 43.

49. John Cotton, *The Powring Out of the Seven Vials*, 152, 150. The imaginative presence of "popery" in the Puritan colonies was sufficiently strong that even dissenters from Puritan strictness denounced it in the terms by which Puritans attacked their enemies; Roger Williams's pamphlet against John Cotton, *The Bloudy Tenent of Persecution*, compared Cotton's desire to secure spiritual uniformity through political force to the tactics of the British monarchy or, worse, of Catholic Europe: "In vain have *English Parliaments* permitted *English Bibles* in the poorest of *English* houses, and the simplest man or woman to search the Scriptures, if yet against their soules perswasion from the Scripture, they should be forced (as if they lived in *Spaine* or *Rome* it selfe without sight of a *Bible*) to beleeve as the Church believes" (1:217).

50. Williams, *A Key into the Language of America*, 131.

51. Mather, *Magnalia*, bk. 3, 191. The Puritan view of Indians as "ruines" belongs to a larger constellation of Puritan perceptions of Indian ritualism and spiritual deficiency. As Mary Douglas observes, when ritual is "defined as a routinized act diverted from its normal function, [it] subtly becomes a despised form of communication. . . . The ritualist becomes one who performs external gestures which imply commitment to a particular set of values, but he is inwardly withdrawn, dried-out and uncommitted" (*Natural Symbols*, 2).

52. William Perkins, *The Whole Works*, 1:642. "Counterfeiting" entailed not only feigning the spiritual authority of the elect, but also concealing distinctions that were imagined to be inborn and unbridgeable. The doctrine of election by free grace made God the arbiter of social as well as spiritual difference; according to John Winthrop in *A Modell of Christian Charity*, "God Almightie in his most holy and wise providence hath soe disposed of the Condicion of mankinde, as in all times some must be rich some poore, some highe and eminent in power and dignitie; others meane and in subjeccion" (in Edmund Morgan, ed., *The Founding of Massachusetts*, 190). In 1634, Massachusetts courts ruled that the "estate or quality of each person" authorized the "perticular rules" of his or her proper dress; those found to "exceed their rankes & abilities in the costlyness or fashion of their apparrill" were judged guilty of hypocrisy (Jane Kamensky, "Talk Like a Man," 23n11). In Mary Rowlandson's captivity narrative, English dress serves Indians as a tool of dissembling: "In that time came a company of Indians to us, near thirty, all on horseback. My heart skipt within me, thinking they had been English-men at the first sight of them, for they were dressed in English Apparel with Hats, white Neckcloths, and Sashes about their wasts . . . but when they came near their was a vast difference between the lovely faces of Christians, and the foul looks of those Heathens" ("A Narrative of the Captivity and Restauration of Mrs. Mary Rowlandson," 148).

53. I rely here on Kibbey's elegant and far-reaching analysis of the connections between Puritan iconoclasm and violence against human others. As she puts it, "because iconoclasm concerned the significance of human beings as material shapes, because it sanctioned material harm, and because it thrived on the confusion between people and objects, the iconoclastic dimension of Puritanism strongly influenced the development of prejudice" (*Interpretation of Material Shapes*, 44).

54. When the Puritan renegade John Oldham was killed off of Block Island by Indians with whom he had dealt violently, Winthrop put Endicott in charge of Puritan retaliations. Winthrop instructed Endicott to put the male inhabitants of Block Island to death, relocate the women and children, and take possession of the island. Endicott went further, burning Indian settlements to ashes and invading mainland Pequot territory without provocation. The treaty violation and violence that ensued culminated in the Pequot War. See Thomas, "Puritans, Indians, and the Concept of Race," 13–14.

55. John Winthrop, letter to John Winthrop Jr., 6 November 1834, in *Letters from New England: The Massachusetts Bay Colony, 1629–1638*, ed. Everett Emerson, 125; *Winthrop's Journal: "History of New England," 1630–1649*, 1:137.

56. Kibbey, *Interpretation of Material Shapes*, 103.

57. John Mason, *A Brief History of the Pequot War*, 14.

58. Increase Mather, *A Brief History of the War with the Indians in New England*, 139.

59. Increase Mather and Cotton Mather, *The History of King Philip's War*, 196–97.

60. The diminution of native personhood also gives rise to the "Indian" as a massed ethnic characterization. By the end of King Philip's War, in which the Puritans waged violence not only against Philip's Wampanoag Indians but also

against their own treaty partners, the Narragansetts, Puritan law gave all English persons power to kill any Indian: "For security of the English and Indians in unity with us," a 1676 Massachusetts ordinance ran, "it shall be lawful for any person, whether English or Indian, that shall find any Indian travelling in any of our towns or woods . . . to command them under our guard and examination, or to kill or destroy them." While the category of "Indians in unity with us" nominally included the native inhabitants of the old "Praying Indian" towns who had remained loyal to the Puritan cause during King Philip's War, the ruling effectively gave all white colonists power over any Indian, Christian or not (Thomas, "Puritans, Indians, and the Concept of Race," 20). On Puritan inabilities to distinguish one Indian from another see Kibbey, *Interpretation of Material Shapes*, 108.

61. Mather, *Magnalia*, bk. 7, 56.

62. Mather, *Brief History of the War with the Indians*, 142.

63. Johnson, *Wonder-Working Providence*, 115.

64. Mather and Mather, *History of King Philip's War*, 208–9.

65. The view that Indians had no language, or that their language was a gestural, literal language without resources for representing a disembodied deity, required enormous psychic energy to maintain. Jonathan Edwards urged against such a view; see Myra Jehlen, "The Literature of Colonization," 81–82. Even so, the assumption that Indians were linguistically challenged, and that verbal deficiencies amounted to spiritual deficiencies, persisted well into the nineteenth century. George Bancroft's *History of the United States* notes as a feature of Indian languages the "absence of all reflective consciousness and of all logical analysis of ideas"; Indian religions, accordingly, include "no conception of an absolute substance, of a self-existent being" (George Bancroft, *History of the United States*, 19th ed. [Boston, 1866], 3:302, quoted in Roy Harvey Pearce, *Savagism and Civilization: A Study of the Indian and the American Mind*, 162).

66. "The Charter of the Colony of Massachusetts Bay in New England, 1628–29," 1:17.

67. Hall, *Cultures of Print: Essays in the History of the Book*, 53.

68. While some Puritans, notably John Eliot, were zealous in their efforts to make "praying Indians" of the colony's native inhabitants, most Puritans approached the task of evangelization with extreme wariness, indifference, or aversion. Ten years passed from the founding of the colony until the evangelization of Indians was mandated by a 1644 court order. Stipulating that conversion was to proceed through the preaching of the Word and not by the sword, Massachusetts courts nevertheless found scriptural authority for sentencing to death anyone, "whether Christian or pagan" who would "blaspheme his holy name, denying the true God, or his creation or government of the world, or shall curse God, or reproach the holy religion of God." The court also levied fines on Indians who persisted in their own spiritual practices, defined as "worship of their false gods or the devil" (Thomas, "Indians, Puritans, and the Concept of Race," 5–6). According to testimonies recorded by Eliot and by Experience Mayhew, Indians who did seek conversion by verbally confessing their depravity and need for grace did so by effectively confessing only to being Indians (William S. Simmons, "Cultural Bias in the New England Puritans' Perception of Indians," 67; see also 67n35). The structure of the Puritan confession of depravity, moreover, became the model

by which Indians were subjugated for their Indianness; King Philip, for example, was made by the Commissioners of the United Colonies to meet with them in 1671 and utter a series of "confessions" whose predictable result was to subject him to English authority. Puritans who wished to see Indians converted to Christianity also tied those conversions to the acquisition of English literacy, less to extend the blessings of Christian deliverance to Indians than to tame them in their resistance to Puritan occupation. John Eliot, one of the few colonists who did learn Indian languages, sought to introduce the Massachuset Indians to English and Christian literacy in order "to convince, bridle, restrain, and civilize them and also to humble them" (John Eliot in Thomas Shepard, "The Clear Sunshine of the Gospel breaking Forth Among the Indians in New-England," 50).

69. Williams, *Key into the Language of America*, 118. Cotton Mather asserted that Indians in Massachusetts Bay recognized the godlike qualities of the Puritans in the same way that the Narragansett Indians did in Williams's account, but also that they remained uncurious as to the "religious" advantage that accounted for the colonists' superiority, a view that allowed him to credit Indians with this flattering assessment of Puritan achievements while preserving them for Puritans themselves: "Tho' they saw a People Arrive among them, who were Clothed in *Habits* of much more Comfort & Splendour, than what there was to be seen in the *Rough Skins* with which they hardly covered themselves; and who had *Houses full of Good Things*, vastly out-shining their squalid and dark *Wigwams*; And they saw this People Replenishing their *Fields*, with *Trees* and with *Grains*, and useful *Animals*, which until now they had been wholly Strangers to; yet they did not seem touch'd in the least, with any *Ambition* to come at such Desireable Circumstances, or with any *Curiosity* to enquire after the *Religion* that was attended with them" (*India Christiana*, 28–29).

70. Mather, *Magnalia*, bk. 3, 193. On Puritan readings of Genesis that posited Indians as remnants of the postdiluvian migrations, and their unwieldy languages as the result of the confusion of tongues that followed the fall of the tower of Babel, see Richard W. Cogley, "John Eliot and the Origins of the American Indians."

71. Roger Willliams reported having done his best "to dig into [the Indians'] Barbarous, Rockie speech" in order to preach to them, without success (*George Fox Digg'd Out of His Burrowes*, 5:464–65.

72. Cotton Mather, *Corderius Americanus*, 11.

73. Efforts to render Indians the obdurately material counter to a Puritan culture of the Word included not only the identification of Indians with a wilderness in need of clearing and planting, but also the suppression of Indian attempts at negotiation. King Philip's War, the Pequot War, and the earlier aggressions by Plymouth authorities against the Wessagussit Indians were all occasioned by English exercise of their "civill right" to occupation, which overcame not only the Indians' "naturall right" to their own lands but also, in the latter two conflicts, the 1634 Massachusetts Body of Liberties that had nominally protected them. In Increase Mather's account of the violence at Wessagussit, Indian complaints that white settlers who had made no provisions for surviving the winter of 1627 had robbed them of their food stores prompted Plymouth officials to declare that "there was no dealing with the Indians (as other nations do one with another)

above board" and to send Miles Standish and his troops in March to "catch them unawares." This Standish did by murdering several of the Indians who complained (*A Relation of the Troubles*, 16). Indian outrage over Puritan occupation and the silencing of that outrage established by the Wessagussit precedent also contributed to King Philip's War. When King Philip (Matacom) met with Lieutenant Governor John Easton of Rhode Island in June 1675 in an effort to avoid war, Easton reported that Philip and his advisors said that "the English ronged them. . . . [A]ll English agreed against them, and so by Arbitration they had much rong; mani Miles Square of Land so taken. . . . [I]f 20 of their . . . Indians testified that and Englishman had done them rong, it was nothing. . . . [N]ow they had no hopes left to keep ani land. . . . English cattell and horses still increased" (John Easton, *A Relaction of the Indian Warre* [hand-copied by H. M. Dexter, 1675], 4–10, quoted by Thomas, "Puritans, Indians, and the Concept of Race" 18–19).

74. Merrill, "Some Thoughts on Colonial Historians and American Indians."

75. Slotkin, *Regeneration through Violence*, 119.

76. Ibid., 147; Bercovitch, *Puritan Origins*, 226–27n8.

77. Patricia Caldwell, *The Puritan Conversion Narrative*, 125.

78. Cotton Mather, *Humiliations Follow'd with Deliverances*, 49–50.

79. These titles of Puritan conversion narratives are given in Bercovitch, *Puritan Origins*, 29.

80. Hooker, *The Application of Redemption*, bk. 9, 5.

81. On metaphors of warfare, excrement, and burning in Puritan spiritual relations, see Bercovitch, *Puritan Origins*, 8–25.

82. Hooker, *The Soules Implantation*.

83. John Cotton, *An Exposition upon the Thirteenth Chapter of the Revelation*, 176. On conversion typology and Puritan land use see also John Owen King, *The Iron of Melancholy: Structures of Spiritual Conversion in America from the Puritan Conscience to Victorian Neurosis*, 13–82. Lucy Maddox notes that Puritan conversion morphology continued to drive westward expansion into the 1850s (*Removals: Nineteenth-Century American Literature and the Politics of Indian Affairs*, 65).

84. Slotkin, *Regeneration Through Violence*, 109–11; Hambrick-Stowe, *Practice of Piety*, 258–63.

85. William Hubbard, *The Present State of New-England . . . to which is Added a Discourse about the War with the Pequods in the year 1637*, 2:78.

86. Jay Fliegelman, *Prodigals and Pilgrims: The American Revolution against Patriarchal Authority, 1750–1800*, 145; Tara Fitzpatrick, "The Figure of Captivity: The Cultural Work of the Puritan Captivity Narrative," 13–16. On resistantly unredeemed captives see James Axtell, "The White Indians of Colonial America."

87. See Robert Pope, *The Half-way Covenant: Church Membership in Puritan New England*; Winthrop Hudson, *American Protestantism*, 10–17; Edmund S. Morgan, *Visible Saints: The History of a Puritan Idea*, 113–38.

88. John Cotton, *God's Promise to His Plantations*, 19

89. Thomas Mayhew in John Eliot and Mayhew, "Tears of Repentance: Or, a Further Narrative of the Progress of the *Gospel* amongst the Indians in New England," 201–2.

90. Increase Mather, *An Earnest Exhortation to the Inhabitants of New England*, 174–75.

91. Johnson, *Wonder-Working Providence*, 132.

92. Williams, *George Fox Digg'd Out of His Burrowes*, 5:309.

93. See Richard P. Gildrie, *The Profane, the Civil, and the Godly: The Reformation of Manners in Orthodox New England, 1679–1749*, 133–56.

94. Cotton Mather, *Frontiers Well-defended: An Essay, to Direct the Frontiers of a Countrey Exposed unto the Incursions of a Barbarous Enemy*, 50; Fitzpatrick, "Figure of Captivity," 7–8.

95. Cotton Mather, *Humiliations Follow'd with Deliverances*, 62–63; this point is made by Fitzpatrick, "Figure of Captivity," 17.

96. Nathaniel Ward [Theodore de la Guard, pseud.], *The Simple Cobbler of Aggawam in America, Willing to Help 'Mend His Native Country, Lamentably Tattered*, 1:227, 1:229. As Richard Hofstadter puts it, Ward's point was that "anyone who was willing to tolerate the active propagation of a religion other than his own was simply not sincere in it," and that "experience would teach Christians that it was far better to live in a united, if somewhat corrupt state than in a state 'whereof some Part is Incorrupt, and all the rest divided' [1:230]" (Richard Hofstadter, *Academic Freedom in the Age of the College*, 79). In this sense *Simple Cobbler*'s hard line on religious tolerance looks forward to the more accommodating pan-Protestantism of later generations.

97. Cotton Mather, *Decennium Luctuosum*, , 206.

98. Increase Mather, *The Order of the Gospel Professed and Practiced by the Churches of Christ in New-England*, 12.

99. Increase Mather, in *Andros Tracts*, ed. William Henry Whitmore, 6:21–22; Gildrie, *Profane, the Civil, and the Godly*, 196.

100. Gildrie, *Profane, the Civil, and the Godly*, 196.

101. Perkins, *Whole Works*, 1:641.

102. Cotton Mather, letter of 31 May 1692, in *A Documentary History of Religion in America to 1877*, ed. Edwin S. Gaustad, 104.

103. Cotton Mather, *A Brand Pluck'd Out of the Burning*, 281–82.

104. *Winthrop Papers, 1498–1649*, 3:149.

105. Mather, general introduction to *Magnalia*, unpaginated.

106. For a vivid and incisive portrait of the religious and racial diversity of the Atlantic colonies, see David W. Wills, *Christianity in the United States: A Historical Survey and Interpretation*, 5–20.

107. Bercovitch, *The American Jeremiad*, 140.

108. Hubbard, *General History of New England* , 34–35.

109. Jenny Franchot, "Unseemly Commemoration: Religion, Fragments, and the Icon," 503.

110. Delbanco, *Puritan Ordeal*, 1.

111. Giles Gunn argues, for example, that scholars of American literature "frequently find themselves in the presence of imaginative materials whose claims to be regarded as in any sense religious are often made in virtually identical terms with their claims to be regarded as somehow American. Obvious examples include such works as *Moby-Dick*, *Leaves of Grass*, 'The American Scholar,' *The Scarlet Letter*, *Walden*, *The Sound and the Fury*, *The Great Gatsby*, *Mont-Saint-Michel*

and Chartres, The Bridge, and *The Deerslayer.* . . . To explore the religious meaning and import of such texts . . . often amounts to the same thing as determining
their status as American" (*The Interpretation of Otherness: Literature, Religion,
and the American Imagination,* 126–27.

CHAPTER TWO
PROTESTANT EXPANSION, INDIAN VIOLENCE, AND CHILDHOOD DEATH:
THE NEW ENGLAND PRIMER

1. Cotton Mather, *Cares About the Nurseries,* 12–13.
2. Cotton Mather, *Magnalia,* bk. 6, 35.
3. Cotton Mather, *A Family Well-Ordered,* 10, 12.
4. Mather, *Family Well-Ordered,* 11.
5. Mather, *Cares About the Nurseries,* 53.
6. Edward Howes to John Winthrop Jr., 20 April 1632, in *Winthrop Papers,*
3:77.
7. Daniel Gookin, *Historical Collections of the Indians in New England,* Massachusetts Historical Society, *Collections,* 1st ser., 1 (1792): 219–21, quoted by
John Canup, *Out of the Wilderness: The Emergence of American Identity in Colonial New England,* 161.
8. Roger Williams, *George Fox Digg'd out of his Burrowes,* 5:240, 5:283.
9. See Sr. Mary Augustina Ray, "The *Protestant Tutor*: A Forerunner of Benjamin Harris' *New England Primer.*"
10. Stationers' Registers (London: Eyre and Rivington, 1683), quoted in Worthington Chauncey Ford, *The Boston Book Market 1679–1700,* 35.
11. "Benjamin Harris, Printer and Bookseller," 49–52.
12. For a checklist of editions before 1830, see Charles Fred. Heartman, *New
England Primer Printed in American Prior to 1830.* The figure of three million is
Paul Leicester Ford's "over conservative claim" (*New England Primer: A History
of Its Origin and Development,* 19). Heartman estimates that between six and
eight million copies of the *Primer* had been circulated by 1830 (xxii).
13. J. Hector St. John Crèvecoeur, *Letters from an American Farmer,* 295. See
James Axtell, "The White Indians of Colonial America."
14. See, e.g., Charles Carpenter, *History of American Schoolbooks,* John A.
Nietz, *Old Textbooks,* William Sloane, *Children's Books in England and America
in the Seventeenth Century.*
15. See, e.g., Daniel A. Cohen, "The Origin and Development of the *New England Primer*"; Elisa New, " 'Both Great and Small': Adult Proportion and Divine
Scale in Edward Taylor's 'Preface' and *The New-England Primer*"; David H. Watters, " 'I Spake as a Child': Authority, Metaphor, and *The New England Primer.*"
16. Lucy Maddox, *Removals: Nineteenth-Century American Literature and
the Politics of Indian Affairs,* 11.
17. Mather, *Magnalia,* bk. 6, 57.
18. I am here indebted to Gauri Viswanathan's formulation of a related argument in her study of the teaching of English literature in India, *Masks of Conquest:
Literary Study and British Rule in India,* 18–20.

19. Quotations from the *Primer* are given without further citation unless they represent unusual additions to standard versions. Almost without exception, editions of the *New England Primer* are unpaginated. See Watters, " 'I Spake as a Child,' " for the contents of a composite, pre-1760 edition. The hymns of Isaac Watts (see below) appear shortly thereafter; "Pleasant Stories" on the rewards of virtue and the consequences of vice appear beginning in the 1780s. See the bibliography for editions consulted for this chapter.

20. New, "Both Great and Small," 121–22.

21. See Richard Slotkin, *Regeneration Through Violence: The Mythology of the American Frontier, 1600–1860*, 52–53, for a suggestive comparison of spiritual conversion as a Puritan initiation rite and the initiation rituals of Indians.

22. John Cotton, *The Powring Out of the Seven Vials*, 156.

23. [Noah Webster], "On Education," 22.

24. John Cotton, *An Exposition upon The Thirteenth Chapter of the Revelation*, 198–99.

25. See, e.g., Jon Butler, *Awash in a Sea of Faith: Christianizing the American People*; Nathan O. Hatch, *The Democratization of American Christianity*; Martin E. Marty, *Righteous Empire: The Protestant Experience in America*; Paul Johnson, *A Shopkeeper's Millennium: Society and Revivals in Rochester, New York, 1815–1837*; Charles Sellers, *The Market Revolution: Jacksonian America, 1815–1846*; Harry S. Stout, "Ethnicity: The Vital Center of Religion in America."

26. Martin E. Marty, *A Nation of Behavers*; Stout, "Ethnicity."

27. Watters, "I Spake as a Child," 195.

28. Richard Brodhead, "Sparing the Rod: Discipline and Fiction in Antebellum America," 87, 90.

29. Elizabeth Barnes, *States of Sympathy: Seduction and Democracy in the American Novel*, 127n1.

30. Wilson Smith, ed., *Theories of Education in Early America, 1655–1819*, 98.

31. See Henry Louis Gates Jr., "Writing 'Race' and the Difference It Makes."

32. John Adams, "A Dissertation on the Canon and Feudal Law" (1765), in *The Political Writings of John Adams*, 12.

33. Davidson, *Revolution and the Word*, 56; see also William J. Gilmore, "Elementary Literacy on the Eve of the Revolution: Trends in Rural New England."

34. Cotton Mather, *Corderius Americanus*, 17–18.

35. For a fuller account of this development see Watters, "I Spake as a Child."

36. On these changes and the editions in which they appear see Ford, *New England Primer*, 27–30.

37. John Foxe, *The Book of Martyrs*, 95.

38. *New England Primer*, 1828 ed., quoted by Sr. Marie Léonore Fell, *The Foundations of Nativism in American Textbooks, 1783–1860*, 9.

39. Here I draw on David Cressy, "National Memory in Early Modern England."

40. On return from "executing the Romish business" with Quebec, the King was greeted with cries of "No Popery! No French Laws! No Protestant Popish King!" *New York Journal*, 25 August 1774, quoted in Charles H. Metzger, S.J., *The Quebec Act: A Primary Cause of the American Revolution*, 43.

41. From a 1755 sermon reprinted in the *Pennsylvania Gazette*, no. 2390, 12 October 1774, submitted by L.S. "for the Amusement of your Readers, leaving them to judge how applicable they may be to that [Quebec] Bill, as well as to the several Acts of Parliament passed in the late and present Reign for enslaving and taxing *America*."

42. John Adams to Abigail Adams, 7 October 1774, in *The Letters of John and Abigail Adams*, 43–44; see also Adams's diary entry for 9 October 1774 in *Works of John Adams*, 3:456.

43. In British primers brought to the colonies, it was common to begin the alphabet with a figure of the cross and to designate the alphabet "Christ's Cross-Row" or the "Cris Cross Row," a convention the *New England Primer* eliminates. Paul Leicester Ford reports on a seventeenth-century text, Morton's *New English Canaan*, in which a minister arrived from England with "a great Bundell of Horne books with him and careful hee was (good man) to blott out all the crosses of them for feare least the people of the land should become Idolaters" (*New England Primer*, 24). The fear of idolatry remained alive among the *Primer*'s adult readers even when religious images became commonplace. Heartman reports a letter written to the publisher of the *New England Primer* on one of the secular images that later replaced the image of Christ: "[I]t is so shocking, that I am obliged to disfigure the picture with my pen, as much as if it were a graven image" (*New England Primer Printed in America*, xxiii–xxiv).

44. I am here indebted to Jenny Franchot's reading of Foxe's *Martyrs* in her *Roads to Rome*, 7–9.

45. Michael Warner, *Letters of the Republic: Publication and the Public Sphere in Eighteenth-Century America*, 25–26.

46. On the ownership of books in eighteenth- and early nineteenth-century America, and their prohibitively high cost, especially for rural and servant populations, see Davidson, *Revolution and the Word*, 15–37.

47. [Noah Webster], *New England Primer, Amended and Improved. By the Author of the Grammatical Institute.*

48. Noah Webster, *Dissertations on the English Language, with Notes, Historical and Critical*, 20, 391, 394.

49. Webster, *Dissertations on the English Language*, 392.

50. Noah Webster, *An American Dictionary of the English Language*, s.v. "CIVILIZATION."

51. Webster, *American Dictionary*, s.v. "SAVAGE."

52. Here again I rely on Viswanathan's argument about British colonial textbooks in India, *Masks of Conquest*, 18–20.

53. Benjamin Franklin to Peter Collinson, 9 May 1753, in *The Papers of Benjamin Franklin*, 4:481–82.

54. Jonathan Mayhew, *A Sermon Preach'd in the Audience of His Excellency*, 31–32.

55. Michael Paul Rogin, *Fathers and Children: Andrew Jackson and the Subjugation of the American Indian*, 85.

56. Most editions of the *Primer* that include the woodblock alphabet have no form for I, but move directly from *Horse* to *Judge*. In this 1800 edition, the alphabet moves from I to K. Beyond marking a shift in lexicographic convention, and

perhaps also a diminution of the role of divine judgment in nineteenth-century American lives, the displacement of Judge by Indian may also record a certain discomfort attendant on white-Indian relations to which Andrew Jackson would give voice thirty years later: "[P]rogress has never for a moment been arrested, and one by one have many powerful tribes disappeared from the earth. To follow to the tomb the last of his race and to tread on the graves of extinct nations excite melancholy reflections" (Andrew Jackson, "Second Annual Message," 2:520–21). Anticipating the ubiquitous African American judges in today's television courtroom dramas, dramas in which these figures' own social or interior lives typically play no role, the Indian here in the place of Judge casts a monitory eye on the historical processes that accord him a token status by denying him history, kinship, and depth.

57. John K. Mahon, *History of the Second Seminole War, 1835–1842*, 218.

58. Samuel Williams, *The Natural and Civil History of Vermont*, 186.

59. Francis Parkman, *The Conspiracy of Pontiac and the Indian Wars After the Conquest of Canada*, 229.

60. Horace Greeley, *An Overland Journey from New York to San Francisco in the Summer of 1859*, 151–52.

61. Butler, *Awash in a Sea of Faith*, 90.

CHAPTER THREE
FROM DISESTABLISHMENT TO "CONSENSUS":
THE NINETEENTH-CENTURY BIBLE WARS AND THE LIMITS OF DISSENT

1. Revolution and disestablishment were not entirely coterminous processes, and were felt by some to be actively at odds. In severing the colonies from Britain, the Revolution had also severed them from their primary source of identity with one another; the proliferation of various Protestant congregations, meanwhile, potentially magnified the specter of disunity against which Anglo-Americans struggled. "Nothing was further from [the] intention" of the new republic's framers, wrote the New England Congregationalist Nathanael Emmons in 1802, "than to introduce a loose, wild, and frantic democracy, which should free the people from all restraint, and set them upon a level" (*A Discourse . . . in Commemoration of American Independence*, 12). On postrevolutionary Protestant anxieties see Winthrop Hudson, *American Protestantism*, 51–62.

2. For a summary of state constitutions on establishment, see Donald E. Boles, *The Bible, Religion, and Public Schools*, 38–43.

3. Ann Douglas, *The Feminization of American Culture*, 5.

4. David Reynolds, *Faith in Fiction: The Emergence of Religious Literature in America*, 2.

5. See, e.g., Jane Tompkins, *Sensational Designs: The Cultural Work of American Fiction*; Shirley Samuels, ed., *The Culture of Sentiment: Race, Gender, and Sentimentality in Nineteenth-Century America*; Elizabeth Barnes, *States of Sympathy: Seduction and Democracy in the American Novel*; Lora Romero, *Home Fronts: Domesticity and Its Critics in the Antebellum United States*; Amy Kaplan,

"Manifest Domesticity"; Cathy N. Davidson and Jessamyn Hatcher, eds., *No More Separate Spheres!*

6. Gauri Viswanathan, *Outside the Fold: Conversion, Modernity, and Belief*, xii. Viswanathan suggests that the "tolerant secular state" became "the foundation for an English national identity in which differences of belief are effaced" (15). By privatizing religion as belief, secular governance renders religion subordinate to the state and its institutions, henceforth identified with the march of reason which belief must either join or for which it must stand aside. Such a move lays bare "the uneven development of colonizing and colonized societies," for it "permit[s] religion to be more 'naturally' identified as a necessary prior stage in the progression toward nationhood" (16). At the same time, the secular state may continue to lay claim to the religious (or "ethnoreligious") identity implicitly aligned with reason and progress. Cf. Ralph Waldo Emerson: "It is very certain that the strong British race which have now overrun so much of this continent, must also overrun that tract [Texas], & Mexico & Oregon also, and it will in the course of ages be of small import by what particular occasions & methods it was done. It is a secular question" (*Journals and Miscellaneous Notebooks of Ralph Waldo Emerson*, 9:74). On the emergence of a pan-Protestant "ethnoreligion" see Harry S. Stout, "Ethnicity: The Vital Center of Religion in America." For an account of how the First Amendment's religion clauses give to the erstwhile secular state the authority to decide what does and does not count as legitimate religion, see Winnifred Fallers Sullivan, *The Impossibility of Religious Freedom*.

7. See Boles, *The Bible, Religion, and Public Schools*, 38–43.

8. 44 U.S. 589 (1845), 12. At issue in the case was the right of New Orleans Catholics to conduct funeral observances in their home churches rather than at the single obituary chapel stipulated for their use by the municipality as a precaution against the spread of cholera.

9. Hudson, *American Protestantism*, 72.

10. Lyman Beecher, "Autobiographical Statement of the Disestablishment of the 'Standing Order' in Connecticut, 1818," 120; emphasis original.

11. Ibid., 122.

12. Lyman Beecher, *The Memory of Our Fathers, a Sermon* , 12.

13. Circular Letter by Rev. William Staughton, minutes of the Philadelphia Baptist Association, held at Philadelphia, October 4th, 5th, and 6th, 1796, in *Minutes of the Philadelphia Baptist Association from 1707 to 1807*, ed. A. D. Gillette, 321, 319.

14. Franklin Hamill Littel, *From State Church to Pluralism: A Protestant Interpretation of Religion in American History*, 32.

15. Although his title, *Religion in America, or, an Account of the Origin, Relation to the State, and Present Condition of the Evangelical Churches of the United States, with Notices of the Unevangelical Denominations,* would class them among the "unevangelical," Baird suggests that Jews, Shakers, and Mormons properly "ought to be called non-Christian rather than non-evangelical, and take rank with Deists and other Infidels" (*Religion in America*, 577). Baird roundly ignored the presence of nonbiblical religions in America, including those of Native Americans. Approximately 20 percent of all slaves brought to America from Africa were Muslims, and many continued to identify religiously with Islam or with

traditional African spiritual practices. Small numbers of Hindus and Buddhists had arrived in America by 1820, and many more Chinese Buddhists came to the West Coast in the gold rush of 1848. See, e.g., Yvonne Yazbeck Haddad, *The Muslims of America*; John Y. Fenton, *Transplanting Religious Traditions: Asian Indians in America*; Albert Raboteau, *Slave Religion: The "Invisible Institution" in the Antebellum South*; Thomas Tweed, *The American Encounter with Buddhism, 1844–1912: Victorian Culture and the Limits of Dissent*.

16. Baird, *Religion in America*, 571, 569, 566, 567.

17. Ibid., 535.

18. Henry Warner Bowden, "Robert Baird: Historical Narrative and the Image of a Protestant America—1855," 154.

19. Baird, *Religion in America*, 534.

20. The literature on religious fragmentation at mid-century is extensive; for general overviews see Sidney E. Mead, *The Lively Experiment: The Shaping of Christianity in America*; Hudson, *American Protestantism*; Timothy L. Smith, *Revivalism and Social Reform in Mid-Nineteenth-Century America*; Robert J. Handy, *A Christian America: Protestant Hopes and Historical Realities*; Moore, *Religious Outsiders*; Nathan O. Hatch, *The Democratization of American Christianity*; Jon Butler, *Awash in a Sea of Faith: Christianizing the American People*. On specific conflicts, see, e.g., Eugene D. Genovese, *"Slavery Ordained of God": The Southern Slaveholders' View of Biblical History and Modern Politics*; Donald M. Scott, "Abolition as a Sacred Vocation"; Albert Raboteau, "The Black Experience and American Evangelicalism: The Meaning of Slavery"; Barbara L. Epstein, *The Politics of Domesticity: Women, Evangelism, and Temperance in Nineteenth-Century America*; Karim Tiro, "Denominated 'SAVAGE': Methodism, Writing, and Identity in the Works of William Apess, a Pequot."

21. Baird, *Religion in America*, 252–53.

22. For a valuable reading of the negotiations of Jehovah's Witnesses, Mormons, and Native Americans with a constitutional order that tacitly privileges particular forms of Protestant Christianity, see Eric Michael Mazur, *The Americanization of Religious Minorities: Confronting the Constitutional Order*.

23. New York's state constitution of 1777, for example, precluded religious establishment as belonging to the "spiritual aggression and intolerance" of "wicked priests" (Boles, *Bible, Religion, and the Public Schools*, 39–40). American Protestants had in fact urged their demands for a separation of church and state along the same lines that the Independent Party in the English Civil War had articulated their separation from the Catholic Church. See Hudson, *American Protestantism*, 14–16. See also Lois W. Banner, "Religious Benevolence as Social Control: A Critique of an Interpretation": "In freeing men from Catholicism [Protestant republicans believed], the Protestant Reformation had liberated them from their attachment to the feudal state and had stimulated them to develop representative governments" (39).

24. Baird, *Religion in America*, 539.

25. Thomas Paine, *Common Sense*, 108, 76. Paine further affirmed that "diversity of religious opinions among us . . . affords a larger field for our Christian kindness" (107).

26. Ezra Stiles, *The United States Elevated to Glory and Honor*, 69.

27. Elhanan Winchester, *An Oration on the Discovery of America . . . October 12, 1792*, 70–71.

28. Noah Webster, *An American Selection of Lessons in Reading and Speaking*, A2.

29. Ibid., 243.

30. Ibid., 329, 331.

31. Noah Webster, *Notes on the Life of Noah Webster*, comp. and ed. Emily Ellsworth Fowler Ford and Emily Ellsworth Ford Skeel (privately printed, 1912), quoted by Harry R. Warfel, *Noah Webster: Schoolmaster to America*, 48.

32. Daniel Dorchester, *Christianity in the United States from the First Settlement down to the Present Time*, 618.

33. See Gerald Shaughnessy, *Has the Immigrant Kept the Faith? A Study of Immigration and Catholic Growth in the United States, 1790–1920*; Jay Dolan, *The Immigrant Church: New York's Irish and German Catholics, 1815–1865*; Randall L. Miller and Thomas Marzik, eds., *Immigrants and Religion in Urban America*; Kerby Miller, *Emigrants and Exiles: Ireland and the Irish Exodus to North America*.

34. Bela Bates Edwards, *The Influence of the United States on Other Nations*, in *Writings*, 2 vols. (New York, 1852), 2:489, quoted by John R. Bodo, *The Protestant Clergy and Public Issues, 1812–1848*, 35.

35. I am here indebted to the argument that Viswanathan makes about religious dissent in Victorian Britain in *Outside the Fold*, 15–16. Lisa Duggan suggestively links religious dissent to gay and lesbian dissent: "a heterosexual presumption has no more place in public life than a presumption of Christianity" ("Queering the State," 9).

36. Protestant-Catholic conflicts similar to those recounted here make up the central act in the three-part drama by which, according to legal scholar Philip Hamburger's 2002 *Separation of Church and State*, the mistaken, even dangerous metaphor of a "wall of separation" has come to dominate American jurisprudence and public discourse on religion. Hamburger points out that Jefferson's first use of the phrase ("wall of separation") in his 1802 letter to the Danbury Baptist Association so failed to capture what Baptists sought in seeking relief from non-Baptist establishment that the Danbury group never even bothered to publish Jefferson's letter in its minutes. What Baptists and other dissenters wanted, in Hamburger's assessment, was a political voice for their own religious views, unconstrained by establishment; neither they nor the establishment clause of the First Amendment ever intended to keep Christian conviction out of American governance, as secularists today insist. As a principle of constitutional interpretation, says Hamburger, separation remained virtually unknown until nineteenth-century Protestants seized on its use to curb the influence of Catholics on civic institutions, including most prominently the public schools. From there Hamburger suggests that anti-Catholic thinking gave rise to a more broad-based attack on Christianity later in the century, whose proponents included not only liberal Protestants who chafed at institutional power but atheists, secular Jews, spiritual seekers, and others who pressed their demand for total separation. Only after this loose coalition failed to amend the constitution to formalize the separation of church and state, says Hamburger, was Jefferson's "wall of separation" metaphor

rescued from obscurity and elevated to the status of original intent. Anti-Catholicism was subsumed but hardly eclipsed in this final act of the drama, the proof of its centrality to separationist jurisprudence being *Everson v. Board of Education* (330 U.S. 1 [1947]), in which the Supreme Court officially adopted the "wall of separation" as the establishment clause's interpretive key. In this, the Court's first case involving (and denying) government aid to parochial schools, Justice (and former Ku Klux Klansman) Hugo Black, who authored the opinion in the case, wrote into law what he had "long before sworn, under the light of flaming crosses, to preserve": " 'the sacred constitutional rights' of 'free public schools' and 'separation of church and state' " (Hamburger, *Separation*, 462). Because it was an ugly anti-Catholicism that raised Jefferson's gloss on the establishment clause to the status of a constitutional principle, Hamburger argues, the very "idea of separation should, at best, be viewed with suspicion" (483)—a point embraced by readers of Hamburger's book in whose view separation unfairly restricts the role of religion in public life. While *Separation of Church and State* is itself no polemic on behalf of a Christian America, those who would remove the principle of separation from American jurisprudence in the interest of strengthening a conservative Christian presence in politics can hardly be blamed for finding support for their position in Hamburger's account. But they are wrong to claim Catholic voices in the nineteenth-century school wars as their historical allies in the project of throwing off separation altogether, as Justices Rehnquist and Thomas have urged (e.g., *Wallace v. Jaffree*, 472 U.S. 38 [1984], Dissenting; *Mitchell v. Helms*, 570 U.S. 793 [2000]); if anything, Catholics in the school conflicts I examine held their opponents to a more Jeffersonian standard for separation than the one their opponents proclaimed. In this respect the central episode of Hamburger's historical drama—the Protestant-Catholic school wars—ought to be read not as a "chilling" case for separation's fatal flaws, as a shuddering reviewer for *First Things* concludes (Stephen F. Smith, "We the Protestants," 43), but instead as confirmation of the far less startling fact that it has been ever unevenly applied.

37. On the Protestant bias of public education, see David Tyack, "The Kingdom of God and the Common School: Protestant Ministers and the Educational Awakening in the West"; Timothy L. Smith, "Protestant Schooling and American Nationality, 1800–1850"; Robert Michaelson, "Common School, Common Religion? A Case Study in Church-State Relations, Cincinnati 1869–70." To demonstrate the march of secularization in American education, John A. Nietz shows that religious subjects account for 85 percent of American textbooks' content before 1775, diminishing to 22 percent by 1825, and then to just 8 percent by 1875 (*Old Textbooks*, 51–57). As portions of textbooks devoted to the subject of religion decreased over this period, however, their broadly Protestant content migrated to lessons in other subjects, including geography, history, morals and conduct, even spelling. See Ruth Miller Elson, *Guardians of Tradition: American Schoolbooks in the Nineteenth Century*, 15–64.

38. *The Northwest Ordinance of 1787*, 95. Emphasis added. See also Edwin Scott Gaustad, "Church, State, and Education in Historical Perspective"; Martha McCarthy, "Religion in Public Schools: Emerging Legal Standards and Unresolved Issues."

39. Gaustad, "Church, State, and Education," 25.

40. Boles, *The Bible, Religion, and the Public Schools*, 25.

41. See Raymond B. Culver, *Horace Mann and Religion in the Massachusetts Public Schools*, 149–62.

42. Mann, "Twelfth Annual Report" (1848), in *The Republic and the School; The Education of Free Men*, 111. On the anti-Catholic front matter of the King James Bible in use in public schools at mid-century see Joan DelFattore, *The Fourth R: Conflicts Over Religion in America's Public Schools*, 21.

43. *Life and Works of Horace Mann*, ed. Mary Mann, 5 vols. (Boston: Walker, Fuller and Company, 1865–68), 4:365, quoted in Culver, *Horace Mann and Religion*, 170.

44. As Colin Greer argues, the "public school was not designed primarily to free the lower-class family from its low self-esteem and advance its members in society. It was an apparatus designed to control most of them, to safeguard society" (*The Great School Legend: A Revisionist Interpretation of American Public Education*, 55). Schooling for black children was segregated in the North and forbidden in the South. Free, compulsory education offered little relief to families, black or white, who needed their children's labor and were doubtful of being able to set them up in independent trades. As impoverished students discovered, the Protestant values of thrift, industry, and internalized authority championed in their textbooks easily converted themselves into ways of perceiving and enforcing social inequality. Poor children, and girls in greater numbers across races and classes, managed more often to elude laws requiring their attendance at school. The literature on the emergence of the public schools in America is immense; those works that usefully set their development within the context of social inequality include Edward H. Reisner, *Nationalism and Education Since 1789: A Social and Political History of Modern Education*; Elson, *Guardians of Tradition*; Bernard Bailyn, *Education in the Forming of American Society*; Greer, *Great School Legend*; Stanley K. Schultz, *The Culture Factory: Boston Public Schools, 1789–1860*; Barbara Finkelstein, "Pedagogy as Intrusion: Teaching Values in Popular Primary Schools in Nineteenth-Century America"; Alexander J. Field, "Educational Expansion in Mid-Nineteenth-Century Massachusetts: Human-Capital Formation or Structural Reinforcement?"; Jane Wiblett Wilkie, "Social Status, Acculturation, and School Attendance in 1850 Boston"; Harvey J. Graff, *The Literacy Myth: Cultural Integration and Social Structure in the Nineteenth Century*; David Nasaw, *Schooled to Order: A Social History of Public Schooling in the United States*; Lee Soltow and Edward Stevens, *The Rise of Literacy and the Common School in the United States: A Socioeconomic Analysis to 1870*; Carl F. Kaestle, *Pillars of the Republic: Common Schools and American Society, 1780–1860*; Richard H. Brodhead, "Sparing the Rod: Discipline and Fiction in Antebellum America"; Dana Nelson Salvino, "The Word in Black and White: Ideologies of Race and Literacy in Antebellum America"; Lynne Vallone, *Disciplines of Virtue: Girl's Culture in the Eighteenth and Nineteenth Century*.

45. Horace Mann, *The Common School Controversy*, 130–31.

46. On these developments, see Ray Billington, *The Protestant Crusade, 1800–1860*; Thomas T. McAvoy, "The Formation of the Catholic Minority in the United States, 1820–1860"; H. M. Gitelman, "No Irish Need Apply"; Michael Feldberg, *The Philadelphia Riots of 1844: A Study of Ethnic Conflict*; Dale T. Knobel,

Paddy and the Republic; Jenny Franchot, *Roads to Rome: The Antebellum Protestant Encounter with Catholicism*; Noel Ignatiev, *How the Irish Became White*.

47. Lyman Beecher, *Plea for the West*, 49, 107.

48. Ibid., 49.

49. Kirwan [Nicholas Murray], *Romanism at Home: Letters to the Hon. Roger B. Taney*, 249–50. Taney, who would notoriously go on to author the Supreme Court's opinion in *Dred Scott v. Sandford* (1857), impressed Murray as a Catholic whose training in rationality had overcome the debilities of his religion: "Brought up to a profession which proverbially sharpens the intellect for just discrimination . . . you are as capable of separating the false from the true, the fiction from the fact, the seeming from the real, as any other American citizen" (18).

50. *Impartial Considerations on the Present State of the Question between Mr Bell and Mr Lancaster* (London, 1802), quoted by Timothy L. Smith, "Protestant Schooling and American Nationality," 685. The writer was commenting on the monitory and reformist Lancaster system of education in England, which sought to educate children from indigent families, and became the model for charity schools in the United States.

51. These examples come from J. A. Cummings, *An Introduction to Ancient and Modern Geography* (Boston: Cummings and Hilliard, 1817), 168; William Channing Woodbridge, *System of Modern Geography* (Hartford, CT: William James Hamersley, 1866), 326; John Frost, *The Class Book of American Literature* (Boston: J.H.A. Frost, 1826), 73, all quoted by Elson, *Guardians of Tradition*, 46–48.

52. Elson, *Guardians of Tradition*, 56. See also Sr. Marie Léonore Fell, *The Foundations of Nativism in American Textbooks, 1783–1860*. Some Protestant leaders lamented that children of immigrant parents, who in their view required the benefits of public schooling the most, were being kept from school because of the sectarian content of textbooks then in use. Governor Seward in New York advocated schools where Catholic immigrants could be instructed by teachers of their own faith, "less from sympathy, than because the welfare of the state demands it, and cannot dispense with it" (Billington, *Protestant Crusade*, 150). Seward's proposal, like the so-called Lowell experiment in Massachusetts, which set moneys aside to educate Catholic children separately from their Protestant peers, was eventually dismantled in the wake of charges that its allocation of resources for the sectarian education of Catholics impoverished the public school fund. On the Irish boycotting of education generally see Field, "Educational Expansion." On the Protestant-Catholic Bible wars in New York, see Billington, *Protestant Crusade*, 142–65; Joseph J. McCadden, "New York's School Crisis of 1840–1842: Its Irish Antecedents"; Diane Ravitch, *The Great School Wars, New York City 1805–1973*; Hamburger, *Separation of Church and State*. On Boston and the Lowell experiment, see Schultz, *Culture Factory*, 252–77; Nasaw, *Schooled to Order*, 66–79.

53. Between 1790 and 1834, Philadelphia offered free schooling to children of its poorest residents only. In 1834, schools were opened to children of all low-income families, not just the indigent, and in 1837 were made available to children of all families regardless of income. Children of the Irish made up the poorest of

the white children in schools, which now educated different classes of children side by side. Protestant parents whose children attended public schools, however, were likely to have been those most at economic risk from the immigrant presence, since wealthier Protestant parents tended to put their children in private schools. Moreover, the Protestant assaults were waged almost entirely against newly arrived Irish Catholics, leaving more established German Catholics and their churches unmolested. See Feldberg, *The Philadelphia Riots of 1844*, especially chaps. 2 and 3. My reading of the Philadelphia conflicts draws also on Mary Ann Meyers, "The Children's Crusade: Philadelphia Catholics and the Public Schools, 1840–1844"; Vincent P. Lannie and Bernard C. Diethorn, "For the Honor and Glory of God: The Philadelphia Bible Riots of 1840"; Billington, *Protestant Crusade*, 220–37; Paul C. Gutjahr, *An American Bible: A History of the Good Book in the United States 1777–1880*, 113–42; Joan DelFattore, *The Fourth R: Conflicts over Religion in America's Public Schools*, 32–51.

54. Circular Letter by Rev. William Staughton, in Gillette, *Minutes of the Philadelphia Baptists*, 319

55. *Philadelphia Catholic-Herald*, 25 November 1841. On this newspaper and its role in the Philadelphia conflicts see Meyers, "Children's Crusade."

56. Isaac Leeser, "Jewish Children Under Gentile Teachers," *The Occident, and American Jewish Advocate* 1.9 (December 1843), 411, 413, quoted by Lannie and Diethorn, "For the Honor and Glory of God," 99n42.

57. *Protestant Banner*, quoted by Meyers, "Children's Crusade," 114–15.

58. *Philadelphia Catholic-Herald*, 21 March 1839.

59. Francis Patrick Kenrick, letter to the Philadelpia Board of Controllers of Public Schools, 14 November 1842, reprinted in the *Philadelphia Christian Observer*, 27 January 1843. The *Christian Observer* remarked: "The Bishop is, no doubt, well aware that our institutions are most intimately connected with the religion taught by the Bible. Christianity forms a most important part of what is called the 'Common Law' of our country. . . . Hence its introduction into our public schools without note or comment, that our youth may imbibe from this pure fountain the great principles of truth, equity, and liberty, on which our institutions are founded. . . . [T]he bishop's letter is nothing less than an attempt to impair confidence in the principles which form the *basis* of our rights and privileges" (*Philadelphia Christian Observer*, 27 January 1843).

60. Rev. Walter Colton, "The Bible in Our Public Schools: A Reply to the Allegations and Complaints contained in the Letter of Bishop Kenrick to the Board of Controllers of [Philadelphia] Public Schools," 17

61. Ibid. Lannie and Diethorn note that Colton's essay was widely distributed in pamphlet form and given to all Philadelphia school teachers ("For the Honor and Glory of God," 63).

62. *Philadelphia Christian Observer*, 7 March 1844.

63. *Philadelphia Catholic-Herald*, 11 April 1844.

64. *Philadelphia Episcopal Recorder*, 9 March 1844.

65. *Philadelphia Catholic-Herald*, 15 February 1844.

66. *Philadelphia Public Ledger*, 8 June 1844, quoted by Feldberg, *Philadelphia Riots*, 95.

67. Quoted by Feldberg, *Philadelphia Riots*, 95.

68. John Hancock Lee, *The Origin and Progress of the American Party in Politics: Embracing a Complete History of the Philadelphia Riots in May and July, 1844*, 246.

69. *Philadelphia Native American*, 7 May 1844, quoted by Lannie and Diethorn, "For the Honor and Glory of God," 73. For other coverage of Schiffler's death and confusions on whether the first shots were fired by Protestants or Catholics, see Lannie and Diethorn, "For the Honor and Glory of God," 100–101n62; Billington, *Protestant Crusade*, 235n15. For popular memorializations of Schiffler, see Gutjahr, *American Bible*, 114–15.

70. Feldberg, *Philadelphia Riots*, 109.

71. *Philadelphia Native American*, 7 May 1844, quoted in Lannie and Diethorn, "For the Honor and Glory of God," 74.

72. *Philadelphia Christian Observer*, 12 July 1844.

73. *Philadelphia Christian Observer*, 19 July 1844.

74. *Minutes of the General Assembly of the Presbyterian Church in the United States of America, 1838–58* (Philadelphia: Presbyterian Board of Publication and Sabbath-School Work, 1894), 173, quoted by Lannie and Diethorn, "For the Honor and Glory of God," 88.

75. Beecher, *Plea for the West*, 37, 142.

76. Mormons and Indians were often conflated in children's textbooks; according to Emma Willard's *Abridged History of the United States or Republic of America* (New York: A. S. Barnes & Co., 1868), for example, Mormonism constituted "the most extraordinary imposture of our age . . . giv[ing] its followers license to commit every crime," but was destined, together with Indians, to be "overwhelmed by the restless wave of civilization" (337–38, quoted by Elson, *Guardians of Tradition*, 59). On Indians in textbooks see Elson, *Guardians of Tradition*, 71–81.

77. George Campbell, *A Sermon . . . at the Ordination of Rev. George H. Atkinson*, 21–22.

78. Cincinnati Board of Education, *Ninth Annual Report* (1838), 2, quoted by Nancy R. Hamant, "Religion in the Cincinnati Schools, 1830–1900," 239–40.

79. *Cincinnati Catholic Telegraph*, 16 May 1834. The British writer Harriet Martineau wrote in 1838 of her recent visit to the United States, including Cincinnati, that "hatred to the Catholics . . . approaches too nearly in its irreligious character to the oppression of the negro. . . . [P]arents . . . put into their children's hands, as religious books, the foul libels against the Catholics which are circulated throughout the country" (*Society in America*, 3:234–35). My reading of these episodes in Cincinnati draws on F. Michael Perko, "The Building Up of Zion: Religion and Education in Nineteenth Century Cincinnati"; Alfred G. Stritch, "Political Nativism in Cincinnati, 1830–1860"; Hamant, "Religion in the Cincinnati Schools"; Michaelson, "Common School, Common Religion."

80. Perko, "Building Up of Zion," 101.

81. "The Bible: A Suitable and Important Class Book for Every School," 235. The editorial warns that "in the nominally Christian countries, where the Bible takes no part in the education of the masses, mental activity ceases, society stag-

nates and sinks into brutal vice. Who, with his eye fixed upon Italy or Spain, or South America, or Mexico, can fail to see a demonstration of these truths?" (238).

82. *Western Christian Advocate*, 15 March 1844; emphasis in original.

83. *Cincinnati Gazette*, 16 November 1844, quoted by Stritch, "Political Nativism in Cincinnati," 244.

84. Stritch, "Political Nativism in Cincinnati," 268–69.

85. Peter R. D'Agostino, *Rome in America: Transnational Catholic Ideology from the Risorgimento to Fascism*, 33.

86. Howard R. Marraro, *American Opinion on the Unification of Italy, 1846–1861* (New York: Columbia University Press, 1932), 70, quoted by D'Agostino, *Rome in America*, 31. My understanding of these events comes from D'Agostino's book, especially 26–37.

87. The Cincinnati *Journal* had greeted the opening of even the first of these schools "with grief and mortification": "[W]e have witnessed the facility with which papists persuade Protestant parents to place their children at the Catholic schools and colleges. It is a well-known fact that these schools are nothing but proselytizing schemes on the part of the Roman hierarchy" (27 July 1831, quoted by Stritch, "Political Nativism in Cincinnati," 259).

88. *Cincinnati Catholic Telegraph*, 26 March 1853, quoted by Perko, "Building Up of Zion," 103.

89. *Western Christian Advocate*, 13 April 1853.

90. Michaelson, "Common School, Common Religion," 203.

91. Perko, "Building Up of Zion," 104.

92. *The Bible in the Public Schools: Arguments before the Superor Court of Cincinnati in the Case of Minor v. Board of Education*, 6–7.

93. Michaelson, "Common School, Common Religion," 207.

94. *Cincinnati Enquirer*, 2 November 1869, quoted in Perko, "Building Up of Zion," 105.

95. *Bible in the Public Schools: Arguments*, 6–15

96. Judicial opinions are reprinted in *Bible in the Public Schools: Arguments*, 350–420. On a "Protestant common denominator" as the "middle ground between sectarianism and secularism," see Tyack, "Kingdom of God and the Common School," 466.

97. *New York Times*, 3 December 1869. For Matthews's complete, far more nuanced argument, see *Bible in the Public Schools: Arguments*, 207–87.

98. The text accompanying these images describes morning exercises at the ideal public school: "a short passage of scripture is read, and with folded hands the little ones repeat the Lord's Prayer." Public schools, the text continues, "constitute our chief safeguard against a relapse into the temporal and spiritual bondage which our fathers sought this country to avoid. . . . The dangers that threaten them in the way of unsecularization, and a diversion of the large portion of the common schools funds for the support of sectarian schools, are only too happily foreshadowed in Mr. Nast's admirable composition on page 140, which requires no comment to enforce its warning admonitions" (*Harper's Weekly*, 26 February 1870, 141–42).

99. *Board of Education of Cincinnati v. Minor,* 23 Ohio State Reports 238 (1872). The opinion appears as the appendix to the 1967 reprint ed. of *Bible in the Public Schools: Arguments,* 422–38.

100. *McGuffey's Newly Revised Eclectic Fourth Reader* (Cincinnati, 1848), 6, quoted by Fell, *Foundations of Nativism in American Textbooks,* 82.

101. Hamant, "Religion in the Cincinnati Schools," 249.

102. *Report of the Proceedings of the State Teachers Association, 1884* (Salem, OR: W. H. Byars, 1884), 39–40, quoted by Tyack, "Kingdom of God and the Common School, 465.

103. See Alvin W. Johnson and Frank H. Yost, *Separation of Church and State in the United States,* 33–40; Boles, *Bible, Religion, and the Public Schools,* 48–57.

104. Emerson wrote in his journal in 1844, "[T]he Catholic religion respects masses of men and ages. . . . The Catholic church is ethnical, and in every way superior. It is in harmony with Nature, which loves the race and ruins the individual. The Protestant has his pew, which of course is only the first step to a church for every individual citizen—a church apiece" (*Journals of Ralph Waldo Emerson,* ed. Edward W. Emerson and Waldo E. Forbes, 10 vols. [Cambridge: Riverside Press, 1909–14], 7:341–43, quoted by Richard D. Birdsell, "Emerson and the Church of Rome," 274).

105. See Greer, *Great School Legend,* 80–104; Elson, *Guardians of Tradition,* 65–185.

106. See Gutjahr, *American Bible,* 63–69.

CHAPTER FOUR
CONVERSION TO DEMOCRACY:
RELIGION AND THE AMERICAN RENAISSANCE

1. The common-school movement in America coincided with the administration by mission boards of programs for the education of "heathen" youth at home and abroad. See Karen Sánchez-Eppler, "Raising Empires Like Children: Race, Nation, and Religious Education"; Amy Kaplan, "Manifest Domesticity." Bible-based common schools in the United States were likewise advanced by the consolidation of foreign mission boards and other benevolent societies under the banner of Protestant unity. "Foreign Missionary Societies, Education Societies, Home Missionary Societies, Bible Societies, Tract Societies, are all of them important, are all of them of one great system; and should indulge no jealousies of each other, so spirit of invidious competition, but cultivate the best mutual understanding, act in the most perfect concord and rejoice each in the success of the other" (Samuel Worcester to Edward Payson, 28 February 1816, American Board of Commissioners for Foreign Missions Papers, Houghton Library, Harvard University, quoted by Clifton J. Phillips, *Protestant America and the Pagan World,* 237).

2. Theodore Parker, *Social Classes in a Republic,* 143. Parker undertook at the end of his life a "History of the Progressive Development of Religion among the Leading Races of Mankind," an attempt, according to his biographer John Weiss, "to establish an historical and philosophical ground for pure theism, by marking

the different epochs of religious development in the races of mankind." In Parker's schema, the religions of savages and the Chinese had the least influence on humankind, the religion of the Puritans the most (Carl T. Jackson, *The Oriental Religions and American Thought*, 75).

3. Thomas Paine, *Common Sense*, 63.

4. Newt Gingrich, quoted in David Samuels, "Tinkers, Dreamers, and Madmen: The New History According to Newt."

5. See Amy Shrager Lang, "The Syntax of Class," 270–71.

6. Walt Whitman, "The Sleepers," in *Leaves of Grass*, ed. Jerome Loving, 331. I am here indebted to Philip Fisher's remark on the relevance of this poem to the acculturative mission of primary education in America ("Democratic Social Space: Whitman, Melville, and the Promise of American Transparency," 71).

7. Herman Melville, *Moby-Dick*, 349.

8. Martin Luther King Jr., "I Have a Dream," excerpt from the speech given 28 August 1963, in *The Words of Martin Luther King, Jr.*, 85–86.

9. Harriet Beecher Stowe, *The Key to Uncle Tom's Cabin*, 40.

10. Harriet Beecher Stowe, *The Interior Life; The Great Atonement; Worldly Conformity; etc.*, 44.

11. Richard H. Brodhead, "Sparing the Rod: Discipline and Fiction in Antebellum America," 70, 71; Horace Bushnell, *Christian Nurture*, 326.

12. Brodhead, "Sparing the Rod," 76.

13. Winthrop Hudson, *American Protestantism*. "Shaping a Protestant America" is the title Hudson gives to the period in his history between the Revolutionary and Civil Wars.

14. Horace Mann, *The Common School Controversy*, 130–31.

15. A classic example of the trope of middle-class adoption comes from Samuel Halliday's *The Lost and Found; or, Life Among the Poor*. Halliday relates the story of Mary Mullen, a nine-year-old girl whom Halliday placed, over her own objections, in New York City's Home for the Friendless, run by Halliday and the American Female Guardian Association. In his zeal to rescue Mullen from her life as a street sweeper, Halliday did not pause to attempt contact with her Irish immigrant family, but did find time to have Mullen pose for a photographer. The resulting picture, a "quite striking" rendering of Mullen "in broom and dress as [Halliday] found her," was widely distributed and became a collectible parlor decoration in middle-class homes. In Halliday's Home for the Friendless, the photograph was eventually displayed alongside its before-and-after companion, a photograph of Mullen on her way to live with a Protestant family in their "pleasant country home." (Hans Bergmann, *God in the Street: New York Writing from the Penny Press to Melville*, 103–4). On the pervasiveness of the theme of middle-class adoption in antebellum sentimental fiction, urban journalism, and the literature of social reform, see Bergmann, *God in the Street*, 93–113; Laura Wexler, "Tender Violence: Literary Eavesdropping, Domestic Fiction, and Educational Reform."

16. Edward Judson, quoted in Hudson, *American Protestantism*, 117.

17. "China and the Sandwich Islands," House Report, 27 Cong. 3 Sess., no. 93, 24 January 1843, 2, quoted in Phillips, *Protestant America*, 243.

18. Jane Tompkins, *Sensational Designs: The Cultural Work of American Fiction, 1790–1860*, 185, 149.

19. Brodhead, "Sparing the Rod," 85, 77.

20. Stuart M. Blumin, *The Emergence of the Middle Class: Social Experience in the American City, 1760–1900*, 2.

21. Michael T. Gilmore, "Hawthorne and the Making of the Middle Class," 216.

22. The new middle-class world stabilizes a productive contradiction at the heart of American Protestantism since the Puritan era—worldly success vs. the inner life—by resolving it into gendered public and private spheres. For women, the importance of affective feeling becomes the calling card of the new middle class, and devotion to home, family, and the welfare of those deemed bereft of normative families and normative homes comes to define the newly "feminized" Protestant Christianity of which they are the bearers. As Thomas L. Haskell explains, an expanding industrial market system brought with it changes in middle-class perceptions of the conventional boundaries of moral responsibility. This enlarged scope of moral agency gave rise to a humanitarian sensibility marked by an interest in children, the poor and infirm, and "primitive" peoples on the part of middle-class whites, who felt newly empowered to "intervene in the course of events and shape the future at will" ("Capitalism and the Origins of the Humanitarian Sensibility, Part I," 361). This is why attention to gender in nineteenth-century texts has for so long eclipsed other social formations except as these figure as objects of white, middle-class, Protestant sympathy, and insofar as such sympathetic identification is taken to characterize middle-class Protestant women's subjectivity.

23. Tompkins, *Sensational Designs*, 149, 144. For a critique of Tompkins as ignoring the sentimental novel's disparagement of religions outside of the evangelical Protestant mainstream, see Terryl L. Givens, *The Viper on the Hearth: Mormons, Myths, and the Construction of Heresy*, 107–8. For an account of the importance of anti-Catholic sentiment to literary constructions of normative Christian and American identity in the nineteenth century, see Susan M. Griffin, *Anti-Catholicism and Nineteenth-Century Fiction*.

24. Mary P. Ryan, *The Cradle of the Middle Class: The Family in Oneida County, New York, 1790–1865*, xiii, 17.

25. According to F. O. Mathiessen, this paradigm's most enduringly influential proponent, "Emerson, Hawthorne, Thoreau, Whitman, and Melville all wrote literature for democracy in a double sense. They felt it was incumbent upon their generation to give fulfillment to the potentialities freed by the revolution, to provide a culture commensurate with America's political opportunity" (*American Renaissance: Art and Expression in the Age of Emerson and Whitman*, xv). To the degree that they took issue with this model, subsequent literary studies typically sought to expand the canon of "literature for democracy" by including works Mathiessen rejected in offering what he called, quoting Ezra Pound, "the history of masterwork, not of failures or mediocrity" (xi). Studies that have instead focused on American literature to illuminate the violence attendant on the expansion of American democracy include Michael Paul Rogin, *Subversive Genealogy: The Politics and Art of Herman Melville*; Anne Norton, *Alternative*

Americas: A Reading of Antebellum Political Culture: Lucy Maddox, *Removals: Nineteenth-Century American Literature and the Politics of Indian Affairs*; William E. Connolly, *The Ethos of Pluralization*, 163–98 ("Tocqueville, Religiosity, and Pluralization").

26. Cathy N. Davidson, *Revolution and the Word: The Rise of the Novel in America*, vii.

27. Nathan O. Hatch, "Elias Smith and the Rise of Religious Journalism," in *Printing and Society in Early America*, ed. William Leonard Joyce (Worcester, MA: American Antiquarian Association, 1983), 183, quoted by Davidson, *Revolution and the Word*, 44–45; see also Hatch, "Millennialism and Popular Religion in the Early Republic."

28. Davidson, *Revolution and the Word*, 44.

29. I am here indebted to Brodhead, who makes a similar point about Nina Baym's claim that "everybody" read novels, "Sparing the Rod," 89.

30. Tompkins, *Sensational Designs*, 185.

31. R. Laurence Moore, "Religion, Secularization, and the Shaping of the Culture Industry in Antebellum America," 228.

32. Dickson D. Bruce Jr., *And They All Sang Hallelujah: Plain-Folk Camp Meeting Religion, 1800–1845* (Knoxville: University of Tennessee Press, 1974), 54, quoted by Moore, "Religion, Secularization," 228. See also Louis Billington, " 'Female Laborers in the Church': Women Preachers in the Northeastern United States, 1790–1840."

33. On African American and Native American contributions to eighteenth- and nineteenth-century evangelicalism see William S. Simmons, "Red Yankees: The Narragansetts in the Second Great Awakening"; Mechal Sobel, *The World They Made Together: Black and White Values in Eighteenth-Century Virginia*; Lynne Wardley, "Relic, Fetish, Femmage: The Aesthetics of Sentiment in the Work of Stowe"; Sylvia R. Frey, "Shaking the Dry Bones: The Dialectic of Conversion"; Karim M. Tiro, "Denominated 'SAVAGE': Methodism, Writing, and Identity in the Works of William Apess, a Pequot."

34. See Catherine L. Albanese, "Exchanging Selves, Exchanging Souls: Contact, Combination, and American Religious History"; Frey, "Shaking the Dry Bones"; Robert L. Hall, "Commentary (on Frey's 'Dialectic of Conversion')"; Tiro, "Denominated 'SAVAGE"; Donald Mathews, *Slavery and Methodism: A Chapter in American Morality, 1780–1845*.

35. According to Nancy A. Hewitt, "By the late 1840s economic stability and ministerial censure convinced most evangelical women to relinquish their radical[ism] . . . and to accept the boundaries of a new religious and cultural norm of womanhood" ("The Perimeters of Women's Power in American Religion," 235).

36. Bushnell, *Christian Nurture*, 13.

37. See, e.g., Mary Kelley, *Private Woman, Public Stage: Literary Domesticity in Nineteenth-Century America*. Moore points to the antebellum production and circulation in the hundreds of thousands of "novels and stories strongly infused with evangelical feeling"—the work of Protestant ministers now assuming the role of writers, and (often female) novelists acting now as preachers—as a means of propagating a broadly Protestant "culture religion" in the guise of secular entertainment ("Religion, Secularization," 227). On the literary and cultural collabora-

tions of middle-class evangelical women and their ministers see Ann Douglas, *The Feminization of American Culture*; Ann-Janine Morey, *Religion and Sexuality in American Literature*.

38. Henry Ward Beecher, *Norwood; or Village Life in New England*, 115.

39. See Reynolds, *Faith in Fiction*, 2–6; Davidson, *Revolution and the Word*, 38–54; Franchot, *Roads to Rome*, 201–2.

40. Edward Everett Hale, *Margaret Percival in America: A Tale* (Boston: Phillips, Samson, and Co., 1850), v, quoted in Reynolds, *Faith in Fiction*, 200.

41. Moore questions the interpretations of David Reynolds, Ann Douglas, and others who suggest that the popularization of religion amounted to secularization, suggesting instead that popularization might well be evidence that "religion was tightening its grip on the American people" ("Religion, Secularization," 216). Perhaps because Moore here accepts the equation of religion with middle-class Protestantism, he fails to see the secular as an arm of the Protestant middle class— that is, to see that what is being secularized is not merely "religion" of whatever variety but a particular strand of post-Calvinist Protestantism whose popularization renders it so pervasive as to become invisible to many observers.

42. Karen Halttunen, *Confidence Men and Painted Women: A Study of Middle-Class Culture in America, 1830–1870*, especially xiv–xvi. The cultural authority of sincerity also maintains the fiction of classlessness, or of the middle class's nondifferentiation from the rest of society. Sincerity ideally renders members of society mutually intelligible to one another, while inscrutability introduces insiders and outsiders, members and observers. See Fisher, "Democratic Social Space," 88–89.

43. Lyof N. Tolstoï, *What is Art?*, 145, 160–61, 144.

44. Catharine E. Beecher and Harriet Beecher Stowe, *The American Woman's Home*, 146–47.

45. Melville, "Hawthorne and His Mosses" (1850) in *Moby-Dick*, 546.

46. Stowe, *The Interior Life*, 16, 19.

47. Tompkins, *Sensational Designs*, 147, 149.

48. For a sampling of critiques of the separate–spheres model in American literary history, see the special issue of *American Literature* ("No More Separate Spheres!" 70.3 [September 1998]) edited by Cathy N. Davidson, as well as Davidson and Jessamyn Hatcher, eds., *No More Separate Spheres!* Davidson makes the point that while both her own *Revolution and the Word* and Tompkins's *Sensational Designs* focus on the writings of both women and men, the fact that they included women's texts at all lodged them in the category of women's literary history. On the marginalization of religious concerns in American literary scholarship, see Jenny Franchot, "Invisible Domain: Religion and American Cultural Studies."

49. In *The American Woman's Home*, for example, Stowe and Catharine Beecher appeal to the Bible to rehabilitate novel-reading as a suitable means of spiritual advancement for the "large portion of the religious world" that might otherwise be moved by Calvinist prohibitions to condemn it. "[T]hat this species of reading [i.e., "fictitious narratives"] is not only necessary but lawful and useful," they countered, "is settled by divine examples, in the parables and allegories of scripture" (*American Woman's Home*, 218).

50. Whitman, "Song of Myself," in *Leaves of Grass*, ed. Loving, 49.

51. Lora Romero, *Home Fronts: Domesticity and its Critics in the Antebellum United States*, 19.

52. As Michael Gilmore points out, the "virile nonconformist" of Emerson's "Self-Reliance" "conformed to the social practices of his time." He was "more entrepreneur than Transcendentalist or sourceless Adam," a product of Jacksonian laissez-faire ideology, a "vocal opponent of customary restrictions on economic development," and a "building block" of the new white Protestant middle class ("Hawthorne and the Making of the Middle Class," 226–27).

53. Melville, *Moby-Dick*, 349.

54. Ibid., 104.

55. Cf. the American Board of Commissioners for Foreign Missions, which in its annual report of 1840 expressed its debt to and affinity with all who extended Christian charity to "the mariner, the imprisoned, the enslaved, and the neglected and outcaste of every condition and character" (American Board of Commissioners for Foreign Missions, *Thirty-First Annual Report*, 195–96, quoted in Phillips, *Protestant America*, 234). Shirley Samuels argues that a commitment to such sympathetic "outreach" is what defines nineteenth-century sentimental culture: "As a set of cultural practices designed to invoke a certain form of emotional response, usually empathy, in the reader, sentimentality produces or reproduces spectacles that cross race, class, and gender boundaries" (*The Culture of Sentiment*, 4–5). In sentimental and evangelical writings, these boundary-crossings are typically authorized by the sentient largesse of Jesus himself, who, Stowe pointed out, "tasted death for every man, the bond as well as the free" (*Key to Uncle Tom's Cabin*, 33). Recent scholarship devoted to dismantling the separate-spheres model in antebellum literary history points to the pervasive strain of sentimental "outreach" in both men's *and* women's writing, controlled in each case by the exigencies of middle-class gender norms. Hence Giles Gunn offers as the fundamental paradigm shaping representative (male) works American literature the encounter with an Other, in response to which the "single, solitary self" ideally finds "deliverance and new life." Here, other selves constitute only one possible version of the Other, which may include, for example, the South, the past, the racial exotic, the urban landscape, the frontier, or nonhuman nature (*The Interpretation of Otherness: Literature, Religion, and the American Imagination*, 191). Such a paradigm places the experimenting, encountering self at the center to which all forms of "otherness" constitute the available reaches—"America isolated yet embodying all, what is it finally except myself?" (Walt Whitman, "By Blue Ontario's Shore," in *Leaves of Grass*, ed. Loving, 275). If, for men, the sentimental encounter satisfies a need for otherness without a compromising loss of self, middle-class women writers tend more typically to find mouthpieces for their own claims for autonomy in those whose otherness, in marking a distance from the writer herself, limns the possibility of a wider world.

56. Stowe, *Key to Uncle Tom's Cabin*, 49; Whitman, preface to *Leaves of Grass*, 1st ed. [1855], in *Leaves of Grass and Selected Prose*, 711; Ralph Waldo Emerson, *Complete Works*, 2:133.

57. Lydia Maria Child, *Hobomok and Other Writings on Indians*, 47–48.

58. Beecher and Stowe, *American Woman's Home*, 337.

59. Melville, *Moby-Dick*, 53; Whitman, "Democratic Vistas," in *Leaves of Grass and Selected Prose*, 467.

60. Timothy Dwight, *A Sermon . . . before the American Board*, 26.

61. Walt Whitman, *The Journalism, Vol. 1: 1834–1846*, 74.

62. American Board of Commissioners of Foreign Missions, *Thirty-seventh Annual Report*, 221, quoted in Phillips, *Protestant America*, 234.

63. Lyman Beecher, *Resources of the Adversary and Means of their Destruction* (Boston, 1827), quoted in Phillips, *Protestant America*, 233–34.

64. Fisher, "Democratic Social Space," 71.

65. At times these forms of removal proceeded simultaneously. Among the federal troops who violently pursued the Nez Perce Indians away from their Oregon homeland in 1877 were some who earlier that year had been withdrawn from the South, marking the end of Reconstruction and a national retreat from federal protections for the rights of African Americans. "The Negro," editorialized *The Nation* in that year, "will disappear from the field of national politics. Henceforth the nation, as nation, will have nothing more to do with him" (*The Nation*, 5 April 1877; Eric Foner, *Reconstruction: America's Unfinished Revolution, 1863–1877*, 582–83).

66. Melville, *Moby-Dick*, 104–5. As Lucy Maddox argues, "the peculiarly unitarian character of American new-nation ideology, and of the rhetoric it produced, meant that tribalism was generally represented as antithetical to the entire project of [democratic] nation building" (Maddox, *Removals*, 10). For an illuminating reading of Tocqueville's *Democracy in America* as neutralizing the violence against Indians that the American nation's "territorialization of [democracy] requires" see William E. Connolly, *The Ethos of Pluralization*, 167–73. For an intriguing argument that Melville makes Jackson's (and Captain Ahab's) "authority over his white equals" depend on his "appropriating the power of people of color" see Rogin, *Subversive Genealogy*, 130.

67. Whitman, "Song of Myself," in *Leaves of Grass*, ed. Loving, 43.

68. Fisher, "Democratic Social Space," 67.

69. Stowe, *The Interior Life*, 5.

70. Melville, *Moby-Dick*, 53.

71. Carolyn L. Karcher, *Shadow Over the Promised Land: Slavery, Race, and Violence in Melville's America*, 64.

72. Melville, *Moby-Dick*, 54.

73. Here I am indebted to the discussion of conversion in Gauri Viswanathan, *Outside the Fold: Conversion, Modernity, and Belief*, especially 83–87.

74. Theodore Dwight, *Open Convents: or, Nunneries and Popish Seminaries Dangerous to the Morals, and Degrading to the Character of a Republican Community*, 123–24. For Dwight, the antidote to Catholic conversion was the opening of convents and seminaries to democratic scrutiny: "Here it is found, in all instances where the insides of these institutions is unfolded to the view of the world, that of all tyrants, the most severe, unfeeling, and unrelenting, is the head of a Convent; of all kinds of human slavery, that of Monks and Nuns is the most abject and degrading" (123–24).

75. Bruce Kinney, *Mormonism: The Islam of America*.

76. Maria Ward, *Female Life among the Mormons* (London, 1855), quoted by Sarah Barringer Gordon, *The Mormon Question*, 44. See also Givens, *Viper on the Hearth*.

77. David Brion Davis, *The Fear of Conspiracy: Images of Un-American Subversion from the Revolution to the Present*, 68. See also Russ Castronovo, "Enslaving Passions: White Male Sexuality and the Evasion of Race."

78. Ernest A. Bell, *Fighting the Traffic in Young Girls, or The War on the White Slave Trade*, 260, 186.

79. Elizabeth Cady Stanton, "Speech to the 1860 Anniversary of the American Anti-Slavery Society," in Stanton and Susan B. Anthony, *The Elizabeth Cady Stanton—Susan B. Anthony Reader: Correspondence, Writing, Speeches*, 80–81.

80. The term "sacred teleology" comes from Sacvan Bercovitch, *The Puritan Origins of the American Self*, 136; see Viswanathan, *Outside the Fold*, 84–86.

81. Fisher, "Democratic Social Space," 71.

82. In an elegant reading of the sentimental novel as a crucial instrument of democratic consensus, Elizabeth Barnes suggests that to yield to the novel's solicitations of sympathy for its characters was to read as an American, since the agreement on the compatibility of inner states of feeling such readings produce was necessary to the consensus-assuming project of democratic self-governance (*States of Sympathy: Seduction and Democracy in the American Novel*).

83. As Harriet Beecher Stowe famously maintained, the abolition of slavery will come about when all "see to it that *they feel right*. An atmosphere of sympathetic influence encircles every human being , and the man or woman who *feels* strongly, healthily and justly, on the great interests of humanity, is a constant benefactor to the human race. See, then, to your sympathies in this matter! Are they in harmony with the sympathies of Christ?" (Stowe, *Uncle Tom's Cabin*, 515). The insistence that even private religious convictions be compatible with democratic institutions also testifies to the success of middle-class Protestantism's disciplinary project of producing subjects ruled by the commands of love and conscience. The graduate of such a program is ruled by head and heart and not by pulpit, pope, principalities, or powers, whose stirrings, in this model, may legitimately accord with those of the disciplined interior but not conflict with them. How could democracy and Catholicism coexist when, as Edward Beecher warned, the "systems are diametrically opposed; one must and will exterminate the other"? (quoted in Davis, *Fear of Conspiracy*, 14–15).

84. Reynolds, *Faith in Fiction*, 15.

85. Royall Tyler, *The Algerine Captive; or, The Life and Adventures of Doctor Updike Underhill . . .* (Walpole, NH: David Carlisle, 1797); Samuel L. Knapp, *Extracts from a Journal of Travel in North America . . . by Ali Bey* (Boston: Thomas Badger, Jr., 1818), both quoted by Reynolds, *Faith in Fiction*, 16–17, 18–19.

86. Emma Curtis Hopkins, "First Lesson in Christian Science" (Chicago, 1888), 16–17, quoted by Stephen Gottschalk, *The Emergence of Christian Science in American Religious Life*, 152. For a warmly sympathetic account of the beginnings of this cosmopolitan American spirituality, one that nods to its "failed inclusions, dubious appropriations, and misguided causes" but elects to leave them largely unexamined in the interest of highlighting a progressive vision and legacy,

see Leigh Eric Schmidt, *Restless Souls: The Making of American Spirituality from Emerson to Oprah* (quotation on p. 287).

87. Jon Butler, *Awash in a Sea of Faith: Christianizing the American People*, 129–30.

88. Albert J. Raboteau suggests that "Conversion, a profound experience of personal acceptance and validation, reoriented the individual slave's view of himself and of the world. . . . Contradicting a system that valued him like a beast for his labor, conversion *experientially* confirmed the slave's value as a human person, indeed attested to his ultimate worth as one of the chosen of God" ("The Black Experience in American Evangelicalism: The Meaning of Slavery," 193); see also Raboteau, *Slave Religion: The "Invisible Institution" in the Antebellum South*.

89. James Axtell, *After Columbus: Essays in the Ethnohistory of Colonial North America*, 54–55. Non-Europeans in nineteenth-century America participated, of course, in an enormous variety of religious practices outside of Christianity. Recent studies of the religious lives of antebellum African Americans have questioned the "black church" bias in scholarship that makes Christian histories and concerns normative for black religious experience. See, e.g., Yvonne Chireau, *Black Magic: Religion and the African American Conjuring Tradition*; Anthony B. Pinn, *Varieties of African-American Religious Experience*. If, as these works show, the massive post-1760 Christianization of slaves that gave rise to the "black church" was never inevitable, neither were individual conversions to Christianity inevitable but strategic, conditional, and transformative, not only for nonwhite converts but for the varieties of faith they adopted.

90. On the emerging of a "black jeremiad," see Raboteau, "Black Experience," 187.

91. Maria Stewart, *Productions of Mrs. Maria W. Stewart*, 19, 18.

92. William Apess, *Eulogy on King Philip*, in *On Our Own Ground: The Complete Writings of William Apess, a Pequot*, 304, 284; Tiro, "Denominated 'SAVAGE,' " 666, 678n52.

93. I am indebted to Lemin Sanneh for this insight.

94. Even those Indians and African Americans who could not read and write English needed to know how to converse inoffensively with whites while maintaining and safeguarding from white comprehension their own modes of communicating information necessary to their survival. The result, as Ann Kibbey observes, was that an "extraordinary knowledge of language use" was required even of those whom white Christian culture continued to deem functionally illiterate ("Language in Slavery: Frederick Douglass's *Narrative*," 180). If those who adopted Christianity or who struggled to learn to read and write were attracted to the forms of respectability these attainments offered as alternatives to conventional images of nonwhite depravities (cf. Tiro, "Denominated 'SAVAGE,' " 662), still the associations in literate Christian culture between illiteracy, primitive spirituality, and subhuman status could be deployed to withhold literacy (or Christian "respectability") from those nonwhite subjects who sought to achieve social recognition as literate Christians. Evelyn Brooks Higginbotham remarks on the strategic mobility required by the "politics of respectability" undertaken by black Baptist women and others who sought spiritual and moral leadership within and beyond their own religious and racial communities. Such a politics, Higginbotham

argues, depended on these women's multiple (not merely double) consciousness, their ability to negotiate complexly interwoven racial, religious, gender, and class identities (*Righteous Discontent: The Woman's Movement in the Black Baptist Church*). Lora Romero reads Maria Stewart's use of middle-class domestic discourse in this light; see her "Black Nationalist Housekeeping" in *Home Fronts*, 52–69. On Native American women's strategic negotiations of domestic discourse, see Wexler, "Tender Violence."

95. Leo Marx, *The Pilot and the Passenger: Essays on Literature, Culture, and Technology in the United States*, x, xi, 8, 16. Davidson's *Revolution and the Word* also reads the rise of the American novel through the lens of Bakhtin, suggesting that its narrative engagement of "surplus humanness," in Bakhtin's term, makes the novel a potentially subversive genre wherever it has been introduced: "subversive of certain class notions of who should and should not be literate; subversive of notions of what is or is not a suitable literary subject matter and form and style, subversive of the term *literature* itself . . . a dangerously inchoate form appropriate for and correlative to a country . . . attempting to formulate itself" (*Revolution and the Word*, 13–14). In a more critical reading of Bakhtin's notion of the novel's form as inherently liberating, Graham Pechey suggests that "there is nothing in the concept of dialogism that prevents us from using it to explain the organization of hegemony itself. . . . Dialogism enables incorporation . . . as well as resistance" ("On the Borders of Bakhtin: Dialogization, Decolonization," 72).

96. Whitman, "Democratic Vistas," in *Leaves of Grass and Selected Prose*, 504; Marx, *Pilot and the Passenger*, 8.

97. Harryette Mullen, "Runaway Tongue: Resistant Orality in *Uncle Tom's Cabin, Our Nig, Incidents in the Life of a Slave Girl*, and *Beloved*," 245.

98. Russ Castronovo, *Fathering the Nation: American Genealogies of Slavery and Freedom*, 80–82. Castronovo cites Carolyn Porter, "Call Me Ishmael, or, How to Make Double-Talk Speak" and Richard H. Brodhead, *Hawthorne, Melville, and the Novel*.

99. On the censoring presence of white readers on and in black narrative, see Raymond Hedin, "Probable Readers, Possible Stories: The Limits of Nineteenth-Century Black Narrative." On the coded language of spirituals, see Raboteau, *Slave Religion*, 249. Jonathan Arac points out that the "vernacular" style, the hero of Marx's (and others') literary historiography, derives its name "from the Latin *verna*, a slave born in the master's house, and it thus carries from its beginnings the problematic of domination and domestication" (*Huckleberry Finn as Idol and Target: The Functions of Criticism in Our Time*, 160.) See also Pechey, "On the Borders of Bakhtin."

100. Whitman, "Democratic Vistas," in *Leaves of Grass and Selected Prose*, 483; Mark Twain, *Adventures of Huckleberry Finn*, 835.

101. Elizabeth Stuart Phelps, *The Silent Partner*. My reading of this work is indebted to Amy Shrager Lang, "The Syntax of Class in *The Silent Partner*." See also Carroll Smith-Rosenberg, "Women and Religious Revivals: Anti-Ritualism, Liminality, and the Emergence of the American Bourgeoisie."

102. Mrs. Mary Matthews to Mrs. Charles Finney, 16 May 1831, Charles Grandison Finney Papers, Oberlin College Library, quoted by Hewitt, "Perimeters of Women's Power," 241.

103. Davidson, *Revolution and the Word*, 70–79, 112–25.

104. Thus Amy Shrager Lang shows how Phelps's middle-class Perley finds her alleged powerlessness as the mill's "silent partner" ostensibly mirrored in the working-class Sip's powerlessness as a factory hand, even as the "fixed gulf of an irreparable lot" divides the two women to the end ("Syntax of Class," 269, 284). In Catharine Maria Sedgewick's *Hope Leslie*, Dana D. Nelson points out, the Pequot Indian Magawisca (given her say before being relegated to the woods that are her "native home") inspires the white heroine's escape from "the contracted boundaries of sectarian faith" by challenging the masculine authority of the Puritan legacy ("Sympathy as Strategy in Sedgwick's *Hope Leslie*," 202). And slave women in the novels of Stowe, Lydia Maria Child, and others, Karen Sánchez-Eppler observes, voice the otherwise "unarticulated and unacknowledged failure of the free woman to own her body in marriage" ("Bodily Bonds: The Intersecting Rhetorics of Feminism and Abolitionism," 97.)

105. Doris Sommer, "Textual Conquests: On Reading Competence and 'Minority' Literature," 147, 150.

106. Harriet Jacobs, *Incidents in the Life of a Slave Girl*, 336.

107. Sommer, "Textual Conquests,"146, 148, 149n18.

108. As Stowe wrote in the *Key*, the "Negro race is confessedly more simple, docile, childlike, and affectionate than other races; and hence the divine graces of love and faith, when in-breathed by the holy spirit, find in their natural temperament a most congenial atmosphere. . . . Considering those distinctive traits of race, it is no matter of surprise to find almost constantly in the narration of their religious histories, accounts of visions, of heavenly voices, of mysterious sympathies and transmission of knowledge from heart to heart without the intervention of the senses, or what Quakers call being 'baptized in the spirit' of those who are distant" (*Key to Uncle Tom's Cabin*, 33, 35).

109. Harriet Beecher Stowe [Christopher Crawford, pseud.], "Repression" (1866) in *Little Foxes*, 384.

110. On black readers' discernment of *Uncle Tom's Cabin*'s simultaneous endorsement of abolition, Christian love, and racist ideology see Marva Banks, "*Uncle Tom's Cabin* and the Antebellum Black Response."

111. Larzer Ziff, *Literary Democracy: The Declaration of Cultural Independence in America*, 298.

112. Giles Gunn, *The Imagination of Otherness*; Fisher, "Democratic Social Space," 80.

113. Mathiessen, *American Renaissance*, ix

114. Ralph Waldo Emerson, *English Traits*, 37.

115. Ibid., 38. "The British Empire is reckoned to contain (in 1848) 222,000,000 souls. . . . So far have British people predominated. Perhaps forty of these millions are of British stock. Add the United States of America, which reckon (in the same year) exclusive of slaves, 20,000,000 people . . . and you have a population of English descent and language, of 60,000,000, and governing a population of 245,000,000 souls" (ibid.).

116. Ibid., 42–43.

117. Ibid., 236.

118. Ibid. Cf. Whitman: "Great is the English brood—what brood has so vast a destiny as the English?/It is the mother of the brood that must rule the earth with the new rule" ("Great Are the Myths," in *Leaves of Grass*, ed. Bradley and Blodgett, 587).

119. Emerson, *English Traits*, 44.

CHAPTER FIVE
FROM ROMANISM TO RACE: *UNCLE TOM'S CABIN*

1. Harriet Beecher Stowe (henceforth HBS), *Uncle Tom's Cabin*, 455. Henceforth cited by page number in the text.

2. The figure of 700,000 converts is for the period 1813–1891 and comes from Sidney E. Ahlstrom, *A Religious History of the American People*, 428. This figure may be high; Gerald Shaughnessy estimates 383,600 Protestant conversions to Catholicism between 1820 and 1900 (*Has the Immigrant Kept the Faith? A Study of Immigration and Catholic Growth in the United States, 1790–1920*, 117, 125, 134, 145, 153, 161, 166, 172). The tables on these pages also include the numbers of Catholic immigrants for each decade. On political themes in antebellum Protestant discourse, see John R. Bodo, *The Protestant Clergy and Public Issues, 1812–1848*; Robert T. Handy, *A Christian America: Protestant Hopes and Historical Realities*; Winthrop Hudson, *American Protestantism*; Martin Marty, *Righteous Empire: The Protestant Experience in America*; Jon Butler, *Awash in a Sea of Faith: Christianizing the American People*.

3. By 1854, anti-Catholic forces were numerically stronger than at any earlier moment in American history (Ray Allen Billington, *The Protestant Crusade, 1800–1860: A Study of the Origins of American Nativism*, 314). Jenny Franchot's *Roads to Rome: The Antebellum Protestant Encounter with Catholicism* offers the most nuanced of recent analyses of the anti-Catholic strain of American abolitionism; my debt to this work is immense and, as I indicate below, will be obvious to its readers. Other valuable reflections on anti-Catholicism and antislavery include William G. Bean, "Puritan Versus Celt, 1850–1860"; Ronald G. Walters, "The Erotic South: Civilization and Sexuality in American Abolitionism"; Douglas C. Riach, "Daniel O'Connell and American Anti-Slavery;" William Gudelunas, "Nativism and the Demise of Schulkyll County Whiggery: Anti-Slavery or Anti-Catholicism"; Michael F. Holt, *The Political Crisis of the 1850s*; Peter Walker, *Moral Choices: Memory, Desire, and Imagination in American Abolitionism*; Stephen E. Maizlish, "The Meaning of Nativism and the Crisis of the Union: The Know-Nothing Movement in the Antebellum North"; Anne Norton, *Alternative Americas: A Reading of Antebellum Political Culture*; Tyler Anbinder, *Nativism and Slavery: The Northern Know-Nothings and the Politics of the 1850s*; and Paul Giles, "Catholic Ideology and American Slave Narratives."

4. Franchot, *Roads to Rome*, xxvi, xix–xx, xxi.

5. Shelley Fisher Fishkin, *Was Huck Black? Mark Twain and African American Voices*, 143.

6. Henry Louis Gates Jr., " 'Authenticity,' or the Lesson of Little Tree," *New York Times Book Review*, 24 November 1991, quoted by Fishkin, *Was Huck Black?*, 142.

7. Fishkin, *Was Huck Black?*, 142. I am indebted for this point to Talal Asad's rich discussion in *Genealogies of Religion: Discipline and Reasons of Power in Christianity and Islam*, 7–13.

8. Mark Twain, *Adventures of Huckleberry Finn*, 626; Fishkin, *Was Huck Black?*, 145. Fishkin argues that Huck's "brilliantly intuitive" mode of "signi-fying" "pays lip service to popular racist stereotypes at those moments when he is undermining them most severely" (66); see her discussion, 60–67. I am grateful to Caroline Gebhard for this insight.

9. Fishkin, *Was Huck Black?*, 144.

10. Eric Lott, *Love and Theft: Blackface Minstrelsy and the American Working Class*, 95.

11. Joseph Louis J. Kirlin, *Catholicity in Philadelphia from the Earliest Mis-sionaries Down to the Present Time*, 54; see also Joseph Butsch, S.J., "Negro Catholics in the United States," 41–42.

12. Elijah Fitch, *A Discourse . . . delivered at Hopkinton . . . March 24th 1776*, 22. On George III as a "Popish king" see Charles H. Metzger, *The Quebec Act*, 43.

13. *Works of the Rev. John Wesley . . . With a Life of the Author by the Rev. John Beecham, D.D.* 11th ed., 14 vols. (London, 1856), 10:183–87, quoted by Sr. Mary Augustina Ray, *American Opinion of Roman Catholicism in the Eighteenth Century*, 79.

14. Franchot, *Roads to Rome*, 54–55.

15. See, e.g., Noel Ignatiev, *How the Irish Became White*; Ku Klux Klan, *Papers Read at the Meeting of Grand Dragons, Knights of the Ku Klux Klan*; Walter Benn Michaels, "The Souls of White Folks."

16. In reference to nuns and convents "black" ostensibly signified the color of the veil worn by those who had taken final vows. One version of the full title of Maria Monk's famed *Awful Disclosures of the Hotel Dieu Nunnery* was *Awful Disclosures of Maria Monk, as Exhibited in a narrative of her sufferings during a residence of five years as a novice, and Two Years as a black nun, in the Hotel Dieu Nunnery at Montreal*; "Black Nunnery" was the title of Monk's third chapter. The frequent appearance of "blackness" in connection with convent life sug-gests that (if not precisely *how*) the symbol of the black veil helped white Protes-tants to assimilate the vexations (and attractions) of racial and religious varieties of spiritual, psychological, and cultural inscrutability.

17. Edward Said, *Orientalism*, 8.

18. On Stowe's orientalized South see Hortense J. Spillers, "Changing the Let-ter: The Yokes, the Jokes of Discourse, or, Mrs. Stowe, Mr. Reed."

19. See Arthur Riss, "Racial Essentialism and Family Values in *Uncle Tom's Cabin*."

20. My reading of the surplus corporeality of "Catholicism" and its extension to the discursive construction of "blackness" is indebted to Franchot, *Roads to Rome*, 324–59; Lott, "White Like Me: Racial Cross-Dressing and the Construc-tion of American Whiteness"; and Norton, *Alternative Americas*, 64–96.

21. Jane Tompkins, *Sensational Designs: The Cultural Work of American Fiction*, 125.

22. See, e.g., Harry Birdoff, *The World's Greatest Hit: Uncle Tom's Cabin*. This reading of the canonical quality of *Uncle Tom's Cabin* is indebted to Elaine Scarry, "Consent and the Body: Injury, Departure, and Desire," 869–70.

23. See David Grimsted, "Uncle Tom from Page to Stage: Limitations of Nineteenth-Century Drama"; Lott, *Love and Theft*, 211–33.

24. J. F. Maclear, "The Evangelical Alliance and Antislavery Crusade," 143.

25. Stowe's invocation of the Inquisition could assume familiarity on the part of her Protestant readers; Billington notes that "nearly every book, pamphlet, or newspaper directed against Catholicism devoted some attention to the Inquisition. . . . The references are too numerous to be cited" (*Protestant Crusade*, 375n66). For antebellum evangelicals, the Inquisition became a favorite site for the historical materializing and resituating of an increasingly remote Calvinist hell, for one result of the softening or "feminization" of American Protestantism in the late eighteenth and nineteenth centuries was that the Calvinist rhetorical genius for describing evil and temptation increasingly focused on Catholic, not Protestant states of sinfulness. In *Uncle Tom's Cabin*, fiery tortures define the hell of the Catholic, and no longer of the Protestant imagination; Legree's Catholic slave Cassy credits the "sisters in the convent" for her feeling of being tormented by devils, her visions of being burned alive (428).

26. Lyman Beecher, *A Plea for the West*, 131.

27. Jonathan Mayhew, *Popish Idolatry, a Discourse Delivered in the Chapel of Harvard-College in Cambridge, New-England, May 8, 1765*, 49.

28. Benjamin Mecom, *To the Publick of Connecticut . . . Another Newspaper*, unpaginated.

29. *Address to the People of Great Britain by the Continental Congress, October 21, 1774*, in *Documents of American Catholic History*, ed. John Tracy Ellis, 138.

30. Address of Frederick Smyth, Chief Justice of New Jersey, to the Grand Jury of Essex County, November 1774, quoted by Metzger, *Quebec Act*, 125n258.

31. *Boston Committee of Correspondence*, Worcester, 18 July 1773, quoted by Ray, *American Opinion*, 271.

32. " 'Popery and Slavery go hand in hand' Said the Father as the American Revolution Began," 15.

33. As John Wolffe suggests, "the effect of Protestantism [in Britain and America] was to channel 'Americanism' into a direction which played down the confrontations of 1775 and 1812 and stressed the common ground possessed by the two nations. American evangelicals saw Britain as a Protestant power blessed by God to an extent only exceeded by themselves, and were particularly anxious that there should be no further wars between the two countries. . . . [Slavery] was to divide Americans from each other far more decisively than it was to separate them from the British" (*The Protestant Crusade in Great Britain, 1829–1860*, 315–16).

34. See Thomas F. Harwood, "British Evangelical Abolitionism and American Churches in the 1830s"; Maclear, "Evangelical Alliance"; Clare Taylor, ed., *British and American Abolitionists: An Episode in Transatlantic Understanding*;

Clare Midgley, *Women Against Slavery: The British Campaigns*; Christine Bolt, *The Women's Movements in the United States and Britain from the 1790s to the 1920s*.

35. Arthur Tappan, in *Slavery in America* 2 (January 1837): 265, quoted by Harwood, "British Evangelical Abolitionism," 306.

36. On Catholic responses to slavery see Daniel R. Goodwin, *Southern Slavery in Its Present Aspects, Containing a Reply to the Late Bishop of Vermont on Slavery*, 146–60; Madeleine Hooke Rice, *American Catholic Opinion in the Slavery Controversy*; Walter Sharrow, "Northern Catholic Intellectuals and the Coming of the Civil War"; Giles, "Catholic Ideology and American Slave Narratives."

37. On this context see Maclear, "Evangelical Alliance."

38. Nassau W. Senior, *American Slavery: A Reprint of an Article on "Uncle Tom's Cabin" of which a portion was inserted into the 206th number of the "Edinburgh Review,"* 4. The writer characterized American slaveholders as an "ultra-Catholic party" and warned of them that "the Clerical, or Jesuitical, or Popish, or Ultra-Montane faction,—whatever name we give to it,—has almost always obtained its selfish objects, because those objects are all that it cares for" (17).

39. N[icholas] Murray, *The Decline of Popery and Its Causes; An Address Delivered in the Broadway Tabernacle*, 346–47.

40. Charles Sumner, *Our Foreign Relations: Showing Past Perils from England and France, Speech of the Honorable Charles Sumner, Cooper Institute, September 10, 1863*, 46.

41. Henry Wilkes, preface to *Lorette, or the History of Louise, Daughter of a Canadian Nun, Exhibiting the Interior of Female Convents*, by George Bourne, ix; George Bourne, *Picture of Slavery in the United States of America*, 151. On the gendered figure of captivity in American anti-Catholic discourses see Tracy Fessenden, "The Convent, the Brothel, and the Protestant Woman's Sphere."

42. Theodore Dwight Weld, *American Slavery as It Is: Testimony of a Thousand Witnesses*, 8.

43. Eugene D. Genovese, *"Slavery Ordained of God": The Southern Slaveholders' View of Biblical History and Modern Politics*, 7. According to Wolffe, transatlantic Protestant Bible and missionary societies of the 1850s presented "Protestantism . . . as a defining characteristic of Americans, and a source of cohesion in a national community in constant danger of being torn apart by the pressure of the slavery issue" (*Protestant Crusade in Great Britain*, 315).

44. George Bourne, *Slavery Illustrated in Its Effects upon Woman And Domestic Society*, 28; Horace Mann, *Slavery: Letters and Speeches*, 477.

45. Bourne, *Slavery Illustrated in Its Effects*, 27; *Speech of Wendell Phillips . . . January 27, 1853*, quoted by Karen Halttunen, "Humanitarian Reform and the Pornography of Pain in Anglo-American Culture," 325; *Liberator*, 29 January 1858, quoted by Walters, "Erotic South," 183. See also Norton, *Alternative Americas*, 69; Billington, *Protestant Crusade*, 53–117; 345–79.

46. Edward Beecher, *Papal Conspiracy Exposed and Protestantism Defended in the Light of Reason, History, and Scripture*, 394.

47. John R. McKivigan, "The Antislavery 'Comeouter' Sects: A Neglected Dimension of the Abolitionist Movement," 143. The metaphor of slavery as the diseased woman of scripture-based anti-Catholic rhetoric is repeated in *The Bible*

on the Present Crisis: The Republic of the U.S. and its Counterfeit Presentment, the Slave Power and the Southern Confederacy, 99, 104, and in Rev. F. H. Hedge, The Sick Woman: A Sermon for Our Time.

48. "American Principles," 410–11. See also Bean, "Puritan Versus Celt."

49. James Russell Lowell, The Antislavery Papers of James Russell Lowell, 2:207–8, 2:111, 2:56. Cf. Edward Beecher on the fervency of the martyred Elijah Lovejoy's abolitionism: "Look at the monstrous abuses practiced by the Romish Church; and at the exposure of them in England, Germany, and Scotland. . . . [I]f Luther had written against popery in such a manner as not to offend the most bigoted and interested of the popish clergy, what would have become of the Reformation?" (Narrative of Riots at Alton, in Connection with the Death of Elijah P. Lovejoy, 14–15).

50. Charles Beecher, The God of the Bible Against Slavery, 7.

51. Though hailed as an abolitionist martyr, Lovejoy saw himself at risk primarily for his anti-Catholicism: "[F]or holding and avowing such [abolitionist] sentiments as these, but especially for honestly endeavoring to open the eyes of my countrymen to the danger which threatens their civil and religious rights, from the workings of a foreign despotic influence, carried forward here by its appropriate instruments, the Jesuits,—for these things, after repeated and long continued threats, I have at length been made the victim of popular violence" (Lovejoy, St. Louis Observer, 10 August 1836, quoted in "Elijah P. Lovejoy as an Anti-Catholic," 180). On the importance of the Lovejoy murder for Beecher's conversion to abolitionism see Joan D. Hedrick, Harriet Beecher Stowe, 109.

52. Catharine Beecher to Sarah Buckingham Beecher, 20 August 1843, quoted in Jeanne Boydston, Mary Kelley, and Anne Margolis, eds., The Limits of Sisterhood: The Beecher Sisters on Women's Rights and Woman's Sphere, 239. On nuns as Beecher's models see Kathryn Kish Sklar, Catharine Beecher: A Study in American Domesticity, 171–72.

53. Beecher, Plea for the West, 37, 131.

54. Lyman Beecher, Autobiography, 2:251. A similar discussion appears in Plea for the West, 61–64. Harriet Martineau mentions Beecher's instigating sermons in connection with the convent riot, Society in America, 3:234. On Beecher's involvement, see also Louisa Goddard Whitney, The Burning of the Convent, 5, 19; Georgianne McVay, "Yankee Fanatics Unmasked: Cartoons on the Burning of a Convent." Other valuable accounts of the convent burning can be found in Billington, Protestant Crusade, 53–117; James J. Kenneally, "The Burning of the Ursuline Convent: A Different View"; Franchot, Roads to Rome, 135–45; Jeanne Hamilton, "The Nunnery as Menace: The Burning of the Charlestown Convent, 1834."

55. On Bishop Purcell's praise of Stowe, see Hedrick, Harriet Beecher Stowe, 70; "Yankee girl" is HBS to Henry Ward Beecher, 29 January 1845, Beecher Family Papers, Sterling Memorial Library, Yale University, quoted by Hedrick, Harriet Beecher Stowe, 168; "Presbyterian nunnery" is from an unsigned note in HBS's hand, William Greene Letters, box 5-753, Cincinnati Historical Society, quoted by Hedrick, Harriet Beecher Stowe, 85; "Committee of Supervision" is HBS, We and Our Neighbors, or, The Records of an Unfashionable Street, 222; "Scarlet Beast of Rome" is HBS, Poganuc People, 55.

56. Norton, *Alternative Americas*, 68.

57. Lovejoy, *St. Louis Observer*, 27 August 1835, quoted by Merton Lynn Dillon, *Elijah P. Lovejoy, Abolitionist Editor*, 41.

58. *United States Catholic Miscellany*, 20 March 1852, quoted by Stephen C. Worsley, "Catholicism in Antebellum North Carolina," 424.

59. The characterization of the nuns as "defenceless" appears in the *Portland (ME) Daily Advertiser*, quoted in Kenneally, "The Burning of the Ursuline Convent," 6; on the plan to parade Mother Mary St. George in effigy see Billington, *Protestant Crusade*, 90.

60. W. C. Anderson, *The Republic and the Duties of Its Citizens* (Dayton, OH, 1847), 10–14, quoted in Bodo, *Protestant Clergy and Public Issues*, 81.

61. The close association between "Catholic" and "heathen" in the antebellum Protestant imagination is made strikingly apparent in "The Game of Pope and Pagan: or, the Siege of the Stronghold of Satan by the Christian Army," a children's board game manufactured by W. and S. B. Ives in Salem, Massachusetts, ca. 1844. The playing board pits an image of "A Hindoo woman on the funeral pyre of her husband," representing "pope and pagan," against a picture of "Missionaries landing on a foreign shore," representing "the siege of the stronghold of Satan by the Christian army." The instructions to the game read in part: "The *white* figures represent the missionaries, as white is the symbol of innocence, temperance, and hope. . . . As heraldic sable denotes grief after a loss, Pope and Pagan are in *black*, both denote gloom of error, and their grief at the daily loss of empire" ("The Game of Pope and Pagan").

62. HBS, *First Geography for Children* 5, 126.

63. Ibid., 42, 200, 198, 42.

64. Ibid., 208,123, 84,128, 74.

65. Ibid., 129, 146, 154, 193.

66. Frederick W. Butler, *The Catechetical Compound of General History Sacred and Profane* (1819), quoted by Sr. Marie Léonore Fell, *The Foundations of Nativism in American Textbooks, 1783–1860*, 85.

67. In relation to the "wicked treacherous and idolatrous population of Mexico," wrote one evangelical, God "is making the United States as he made Assyria of Old, the rod of his anger. . . . But who knows that our turn will not come next?" (*Evangelical Repository* 5 [1847], quoted by Ted C. Hinckley, "American Anti-Catholicism during the Mexican War," 124).

68. HBS, *Key*, 34.

69. Salmon P. Chase in the *Boston Daily Evening Traveller*, 28 August 1849, quoted by Larry Gara, "Slavery and the Slave Power: A Crucial Distinction," 6; HBS, *Key*, 45.

70. Mann, *Slavery: Letters and Speeches*, 474; Murray, *Decline of Popery*, 366–67.

71. *National Era*, 13 May 1847 (citing an editorial in *Blackwoods*), quoted by Thomas F. Harwood, "The Abolitionist Image of Louisiana and Mississippi," 294n34. On antiblack and anti-Catholic rioting in the North during this period see Butsch, "Negro Catholics in the United States."

72. A. Oakey Hall, *The Manhattaner in New Orleans, or Phases of "Crescent City" Life*, 23, 32.

73. A Resident, preface to *New Orleans as It Is*, unpaginated.

74. Resident, *New Orleans as It Is*, 35, 35, 26, 41.

75. See Franchot, *Roads to Rome*, 103, 248; Charles H. Foster, *The Rungless Ladder: Harriet Beecher Stowe and New England Puritanism*, 49–57; Richard Slotkin, *Regeneration Through Violence : The Mythology of the American Frontier, 1600–1860*, 444.

76. The New Orleans Protestant Rev. Joel Parker reported to an audience in his native Hartford, Connecticut that New Orleans Catholic men were "practically atheists; they regard religion as intended for only women and servants" (*Emancipator*, 6 January 1835, quoted by Harwood, "Abolitionist Image," 295).

77. Cf. Lyman Beecher: "[The Catholic Church] is majestic and imposing in its ceremonies, dazzling by its lights and ornaments, vestments and gorgeous drapery, and fascinating by the power of music and the breathing marble and living canvas, and . . . unlimited in its powers of accommodation to the various characters, tastes, and conditions of men. For the profound, it has metaphysics and philosophy—the fine arts for men of taste, and wealth, and fashion—signs and wonders for the superstitious—forbearance for the sceptic—toleration for the liberal, who eulogize and aid her cause—enthusiasm for the ardent—lenity for the voluptuous, and severity for the austere—fanaticism for the excited, and mysticism for moody musing. For the formalist, rites and ceremonies—for the moral, the merit of good works, and for those who are destitute, the merits of the saints at accommodating prices" (*Plea for the West*, 132–34).

78. "Longfellow's poetry has the true seal of the bard in this, that while it is dyed rich as an old cathedral window in tints borrowed in foreign language and literature—tints caught in the fields of Spain, Italy, and Germany—yet, after all, the strong dominant colours are from fields and scenes of home" (HBS, *Uncle Sam's Emancipation*, 155–56).

79. On "partial insanity" as a specifically Catholic trait, cf. Elijah Lovejoy: "No man, in his senses, ever believed fully and fairly the [Roman Catholic] doctrine of transubstantiation. . . . Let us not be misunderstood; there have, doubtless, been many men who *thought* they believed it, but owing to the prejudice of education, their minds, on this point, were dark, and saw things that were not as though they were. So often do we see individuals inflicted with mental imbecility on some particular subject" (Joseph C. and Owen Lovejoy, eds., *Memoir of the Rev. Elijah P. Lovejoy* [New York, 1838], 104, quoted by Dale T. Knobel, *Paddy and the Republic*, 56). On the darkness of mind implied by the Catholic love of "silly gewgaws" see Murray, *Decline of Popery*, 358.

80. On Catholicism's racial (and religious) promiscuities, cf. Lorenzo de Zavola: "As in all Catholic countries, Sunday is a day of diversions in New Orleans. The shops of the Catholics are open; there are dances, music, and feasts. . . . In the Catholic church the negro and the white, the slave and the master, the noble and the poor are gathered before the same altar. Here is a temporary forgetting of all human distinctions. . . . In the Protestant church it is not so. The colored people are excluded or separated into one place by a lattice work or balustrade. The most miserable slave receives from the hand of the Catholic priest all the consolations of religion" (Lorenzo de Zavola, *Viage a Los Estados-Unidos del Norte de America* [1829], in Joseph Paul Ryan, "Travel Literature as Source Mate-

rial for American Catholic History," 317). Franchot remarks on Catholicism as a trope for dangerous mixtures in the antebellum Protestant imagination: "Like the fearsome image of miscegenation that haunted both pro- and anti-slavery white Americans, the threat of spiritual miscegenation as figured in anti-Catholic writing argued that mingling inevitably led to mixture—and in such mixtures all claims to purity were dangerously forsaken" (*Roads to Rome*, 172).

81. HBS, *Uncle Tom's Cabin*, 232, 315. Hungarian rebel Louis Kossuth fled from Austria to Turkey, where he was imprisoned by a Turkish sultan. Kossuth was a rallying point for anti-Catholic voices when he came to the United States in December 1851; his warm reception, according to Billington, was "due in part to the fact that he was a symbol of Protestantism as well as liberty" (Billington, *Protestant Crusade*, 331). Stowe called Kossuth a "great apostle and martyr of *Liberty* and *Christianity*," and defended him from the *Observer*'s slandering of him as a drunkard (Hedrick, *Harriet Beecher Stowe*, 227, 228). Kossuth drew the wrath of abolitionists for refusing to speak out on behalf of the slave, however, and left under a cloud a few months after his arrival (see Ellis, *Documents of American Catholic History*, 341–42). On Austria's Catholic "slaves" see Beecher, *Plea for the West*, 144

82. John R. McKivigan, "The Gospel Will Burst the Bonds of the Slave: The Abolitionists' Bibles for Slaves Campaign," 62.

83. *Miner's Journal*, 1 October 1853, quoted by Gudelunas, "Nativism and the Demise," 230. Franchot discusses charges of Catholic antidomesticity in *Roads to Rome*; see especially 112–34.

84. According to Theodore Dwight, "Roman Priests and Nuns" were "dissevered from society, unlinked from the world . . . even to a change of names, [and] accustomed to a kind of life the opposite of the family state" (*Open Convents*, 165). For Lyman Beecher, the sexual danger marked by "Catholicism" could be read at once as a plot to outpopulate Protestants through seduction and reproduction ("[P]rotestant children, with unceasing assiduity, are gathered into Catholic schools . . . so that every family in process of time becomes six" [*Plea for the West*, 117]) *and* as the impossibility of assimilating a nonreproductive clergy within the American family ("Were they allied to us by family and ties of blood, like the ministry of all other denominations, there would be less to be feared" [*Plea for the West*, 135]). Others suggested that the Church's powers were most dangerous because so protean: the problem of the Catholic immigrant, wrote Samuel F. B. Morse, is the danger of an "anomalous, nondescript, *hermaphrodite*, Jesuit thing, neither foreigner nor native, yet a moiety of each, now one, now the other, both or neither, as circumstances suit" (*Imminent Dangers to the Free Institution of the United States Through Foreign Immigration*, 24).

85. In Stowe's *Little Foxes*, for example, the fire and brimstone of the Calvinist's Hell is relocated to the middle-class household under the mismanagement of a "raw, untrained" Irish Bridget: "There are the gas pipes, the water pipes, the whole paraphernalia of elegant and delicate conveniences . . . the neglect of any of which may flood the house, or poison it with foul air"; "in unskilled, blundering hands" the Protestant household's gas, water, and fire "seem only so many guns in the hands of Satan" (HBS [Christopher Crawford, pseud.], *Little Foxes* , 334–35).

86. *North American Protestant Magazine or Anti-Jesuit* 1 (April 1846), quoted by Billington, *Protestant Crusade*, 354. On voodoo (or *vodou*) and Catholicism in New Orleans see Albert J. Raboteau, *Slave Religion: The "Invisible Institution" in the Antebellum South*, 75–80. According to the Louisiana historian Robert Tallant, "[v]oodoo was at its height by 1850 and Marie Laveau was its essence" (*Voodoo in New Orleans*, 64). Laveau, by various accounts a witch, madam, murderer, doctor, and saint, by her own account a devout Roman Catholic, presided with her daughter (also named Marie Laveau) over the city's voodoo community for the remainder of the century. The profusion of legends surrounding Laveau, however apocryphal, suggests something of the vitality of voodoo's conception of black (and female) spiritual power unfettered by evangelical pieties. At least eight accounts of voodoo in New Orleans appeared in the popular press before the publication of *Uncle Tom's Cabin*; see Blake Touchstone, "Voodoo in New Orleans."

87. See Anbinder, *Nativism and Slavery*, 45.

88. Cf. Maria Monk's "chambers of pollutions above," and "dungeons of torture and death below" (*Awful Disclosures of the Hotel Dieu Nunnery*, 344).

89. Sr. Mary John (Elizabeth Harrison) is referred to as the "Mysterious Lady" in the Boston *Mercantile Journal*, 8 August 1834, quoted by Kenneally, "Burning of the Ursuline Convent," 21n11. "[D]etained in th[e] Convent . . ." is from the *Jesuit*, 16 August 1834, quoted in "Destruction of the Charlestown Convent: Some of the Outrage from Contemporaneous Newspaper Files," 107.

90. "She was the sauciest woman I ever heard talk" is John R. Buzzell, "Destruction of the Charlestown Convent: Statement by the Leader of the Know-Nothing Mob," quoted in Kenneally, "The Burning of the Ursuline Convent," 6. See also the accounts in Hamilton, "Nunnery as Menace," and Whitney, *Burning of the Convent*, 86.

91. Cf. Thomas Ragg, *Popery in Convents*, 9.

92. See John Tracy Ellis, "An English Visitor's Comments on the American Religious Scene"; Paul Laverdure, "Creating an Anti-Catholic Crusader: Charles Chiniquy."

93. Lowell, *Anti-Slavery Papers*, 2:145–48.

94. See Hedrick, *Harriet Beecher Stowe*, 157, 237, 250.

95. On Stowe's trip to England, see Lyman Beecher Stowe, *Saints, Sinners, and Beechers*, 188–89, 191–207; Birdoff, *World's Greatest Hit*; Hedrick, *Harriet Beecher Stowe*, 233–52.

96. HBS, *The Interior Life*, 3–4.

97. *Westminster Review*, January 1853, quoted by Frank J. Klingberg, "Harriet Beecher Stowe and Social Reform in England," 545.

98. Midgley, *Women Against Slavery*, 146.

99. W. L. Garrison, *Liberator*, 9 September 1853, quoted in Grimsted, "Uncle Tom from Page to Stage," 241.

100. Hedrick, *Harriet Beecher Stowe*, 257

101. Holt, *Political Crisis,*161.

102. Flyleaf advertising new books at the end of the text of John M'Clintock, D.D., *The Temporal Power of the Pope*, unnumbered page.

103. On revivals of the *Master Key* see Joan R. Gunderson, "Anthony Gavin's *A Master-Key to Popery:* A Virginia Parson's Best-Seller," 40; on the establishment of Boston's Nunnery Committee see Carleton Beals, *Brass-Knuckle Crusade: The Great Know-Nothing Conspiracy 1820–1860*, 228.

104. Andrew Boyd Cross, *Young Women in Convents or Priests' Prisons*, 24, 22. His defense of Monk's narrative is 14–15.

105. Draft editorial, n.d., Gideon Welles papers, quoted by Michael F. Holt, "The Politics of Impatience: The Origins of Know-Nothingism," 322. Holt notes that the nomination of Frémont came in direct response to Know-Nothing demands for a candidate "fresh from the loins of the people—a mechanic—able and jealous of the hierarchy of Rome" (Thomas J. Marsh to Nathaniel P. Banks, 19 March 1856, quoted in Holt, "Politics of Impatience," 322).

106. Holt, *Political Crisis*, 159–62; Bean, "Puritan Versus Celt," 85; Hedrick, *Harriet Beecher Stowe*, 263.

107. Thomas Whitney, *A Defense of the American Policy* (New York, 1855), 95, quoted by Maizlish, "Know-Nothing Movement," 198.

108. The Missouri cartoon is cited in Beals, *Brass-Knuckle Crusade*, 291; the *Irish-American* notice is cited in Birdoff, *World's Greatest Hit*, 183–84, and in Lott, *Love and Theft*, 229.

109. See Lott, *Love and Theft*, 33, 274n16. On blackness and Irishness, see Lott, *Love and Theft*, 94–96; Knobel, *Paddy and the Republic*, 93, 179; Ignatiev, *How the Irish Became White*, 34–61. Topsy's desire to be "skinned, and come white" (*Uncle Tom's Cabin*, 330) would have been especially recognizable within a minstrel idiom of the Irish as "skinned niggers." Ignatiev notes that if Huck Finn's voice is, as Fishkin has argued, at least partly black, that voice is also, as Twain himself acknowledged, "Irishy" (*How the Irish Became White*, 58).

110. Lowell, *Anti-Slavery Papers*, 1:132, 1:134, 1:206.

111. Sumner, *Our Foreign Relations*, 66

112. H. W. Beecher, *England and America: Speech of Henry Ward Beecher at the Free Tade Hall, Manchester, Oct 9 1863*, 34.

113. See Stowe, *Saints, Sinners, and Beechers*, 207.

114. In Beecher, *England and America*, 7; my emphasis.

115. Diplomatic correspondence, 1864, in Belle Becker Sideman and Lillian Friedman, eds., *Europe Looks at the Civil War*, 254–56.

116. Charles Dilkes, *Greater Britain: A Record of Travel in English-Speaking Countries During 1866 and 1867*, 2 vols (London, 1868), 1:304–5, 318, quoted by Christine Bolt, *The Anti-Slavery Movement and Reconstruction: A Study in Anglo-American Co-operation, 1833–77*, 148. Dilkes's book sold out four editions in England and more in the United States.

117. HBS, preface to *"Tell It All": The Story of a Life's Experience in Mormonism*, by Mrs. T.B.H. Stenhouse, iii.

118. HBS, *House and Home Papers*, 68–69; on the history of this text, see Hedrick, *Harriet Beecher Stowe*, 312–14.

119. Lott, *Love and Theft*, 32.

120. Frederika Bremer, *America of The Fifties: Letters of Frederika Bremer*, 280.

121. HBS, *The Minister's Wooing*, 601.

122. HBS, *Uncle Sam's Emancipation*, 153.

123. Marie Caskey, *Chariot of Fire: Religion and the Beecher Family*, 201, 202. On Mandarin as recalling Sorrento for Stowe see Hedrick, *Harriet Beecher Stowe*, 383; on Stowe's reverence for Mary and her use of Catholic apocrypha see Eileen Razzari Elrod, " 'Exactly Like My Father': Feminist Hermeneutics in Harriet Beecher Stowe's Non-Fiction."

124. HBS, "Introductory Essay" to *The Incarnation; or Pictures of the Virgin and Her Son*, by Charles Beecher (New York: Harper and Brothers, 1849), iv–ix, quoted by Hedrick, *Harriet Beecher Stowe*, 188.

125. I owe this last point to Gillian Brown, who develops it in "Getting in the Kitchen With Dinah: Domestic Politics in *Uncle Tom's Cabin*."

126. My summary of changes in the antebellum family structure draws from Walters, "Erotic South," 191.

127. Catharine E. Beecher and Harriet Beecher Stowe, *The American Woman's Home*, 15. A revised version of Catharine Beecher's 1841 *Treatise on Domestic Economy*, this book includes materials that originally appeared in Stowe's *House and Home Papers* and *Little Foxes*.

128. HBS, *House and Home Papers*, 99.

129. This quotation comes from Job S. Mills, "A Manual of Family Worship" (Dayton, OH, 1900), 34, quoted in Colleen McDannell and Bernhard Lang, *Heaven: A History*, 272. See their discussion, 264–73.

130. Lynne Wardley points to links between Stowe's "sentimental practice" and West African understandings of the afterlife as well as the "fetishism" of African American and Roman Catholic religious worlds: "Stowe's belief that some spirit inhabits all things is not only an exoticized import from the Roman Catholic and African American religions of New Orleans and beyond"; it "is by 1852 one familiar element of the nineteenth-century domestic ideology the tenets of which Stowe's writing reflected and helped to shape" ("Relic, Fetish, Femmage: The Aesthetics of Sentiment in the Work of Stowe," 204–5).

131. Tompkins, *Sensational Designs*, 141, 144. Cf. HBS in *House and Home*: " 'I have often admired,' said I, 'the stateliness and regularity of family worship in the good old families of England,—the servants, guests, and children all assembled,—the reading of the scriptures and the daily prayers by the master or mistress of the family, ending with the united repetition of the lord's prayer by all.' 'No such assemblage is possible in our country,' said Bob, 'our servants are for the most part Roman Catholics, and forbidden to join us in acts of worship.' . . . 'We cannot in this country,' said I, 'give to family prayer that solemn stateliness which it has in a country where religion is a civil institution, and masters and servants, as a matter of course, belong to one church. . . . [O]ur prayers . . . must be more intimate and domestic' " (HBS, *House and Home*, 150–51).

132. See Riss, "Racial Essentialism and Family Values," 532–36. As the work of the (white, middle-class, Protestant) family this move toward essentializing race can usefully be viewed as a function of the cultivation of inwardness and self-government in children that was chief among the tasks of republican motherhood. In *Uncle Tom's Cabin*, the most needful and challenging subject of such a program is Topsy; as Richard Brodhead writes, "Topsy has never known herself as the object of someone's maternal affection; she has never known herself as someone's

child (hence her theory of nonhuman origin: 'I spect I grow'd'); and in the ortho-dox philosophy of domesticity that prevails in *Uncle Tom's Cabin* her lack of the experience of having her life from a loving other is what renders her without facilities for taking social authority up inside herself" ("Sparing the Rod," 86). Eventually Topsy *is* successfully mothered, first by Eva and then Ophelia, and if Topsy's conversion to "be[ing] good" does not have the power to make her "come white" still she can, according to Eva's promise, become a "bright angel" in heaven (*Uncle Tom's Cabin*, 330, 336). Topsy's internalization of Christian mater-nal authority thus primes her to take her place among what Stowe, in *How to Invest Money*, calls the "fair, godlike forms" (among them former black slaves) who greet the subject of this devotional sketch, a generous rich man who discovers on dying that not even "one of his good deeds seemed good enough to lean on; all bore some taint or tinge . . . before the all pure" (HBS, *How to Invest Money*, 46–47, 44). In the blinding light of the All Pure, or what Stowe will elsewhere call "the great Invisible" (HBS, *Men of Our Times, or Great Patriots of the Day*, 386), all taints and tinges are burned away. In this life, meanwhile, blackness (like poverty) will always be with us, and if not race then racism can be purified of taint and tinge. In one sense, the Christian family state replaces the "unchristian prejudice of color" (HBS, *Key*, 31) with the prejudice of class: in England, Stowe observes in *House and Home Papers*, "the higher up the social scale one goes, the more courteous seems to become the intercourse of master and servant; the more perfect and real the power, the more is it veiled in outward expression,—com-mands are phrased as requests, and gentleness of voice and manner covers an authority which no one would think of offending without trembling" (HBS, *House and Home*, 102). This model valorizes the invisible power of middle-class motherhood that training in disciplinary inwardness installs; at the same time, it mirrors the utopic social structure Stowe credits with the power of eradicating prejudice through a trickle-down effect: "The time is coming rapidly when the upper classes in society must learn that their education, wealth, and refinement, are not their own . . . but that they should hold them rather . . . as 'a ministry,' a stewardship, which they hold in trust for the benefit of their poorer brethren. This is the *true* socialism, which comes from the spirit of Christ, and without breaking down existing orders of society, *by love* makes the property and possessions of the higher class the property of the lower" (HBS, *Key* 33).

133. Cf. Ignatiev, *How the Irish Became White*; George Lipsitz, "The Posses-sive Investment in Whiteness: Racialized Social Democracy and the 'White' Prob-lem in American Studies."

134. HBS, *House and Home*, 106, 107.

135. See Mary De Jong, "Dark-Eyed Daughters: Nineteenth-Century Popular Portrayals of Biblical Women."

136. HBS, *Woman in Sacred History: A Series of Sketches Drawn from Scrip-tural, Historical, and Legendary Sources*, 22, 25. Sarah is implicitly likened to the white Protestant mother and wife; see 15.

137. Ibid., 26.

138. Ibid.

139. Ibid.

140. Ibid., 26–27.

141. Ibid., 27, 134.

142. Ibid., 159. See the discussion in DeJong, "Dark-eyed Daughters," 286–93

143. HBS, *Woman in Sacred History*, 27–28.

144. Ibid., 26.

145. HBS, *Men of Our Times*, 385.

146. Cf. Lipsitz, "Possessive Investment in Whiteness," 369; Richard Dyer, "White."

147. A quick sampling of white, Protestant, post-Reconstruction reflection on race: "The races themselves are radically unlike" wrote the Social Gospel theologian George Harris; to belong to a race "is to have certain characteristics which are part of one's constitution, and which one cannot change any easier than the leopard can change his spots, or the Chinaman or negro his coloring" (*Inequality and Progress*, 18). By this logic, according to another American theologian of race, Edgar Gardner Murphy, "the deepest thing about any man—next to his humanity itself—is his race," and thus "no negro can escape, or ought to escape, the Africa of his past" (quoted in Ralph E. Luker, *The Social Gospel in Black and White: American Racial Reform 1885–1912*, 285–86). "We all know it instinctively," said Senator Henry Cabot Lodge, speaking before the 54th U.S. Congress in 1896, "although it is so impalpable that we can scarcely define it, and yet so deeply marked that not even the physiological differences between the [races] are more persistent or more obvious. When we speak of a race, then, we . . . mean the moral and intellectual characteristics which in their association *make the soul of the race*, the product of all its past . . . an unconscious inheritance from all its ancestors, *upon which argument has no effect*" (*Cong. Rec.* 54th Cong., 1 Sess, 2817 ff.; my emphasis). While some commentators on the sexual depravity of non-Anglo-Saxon races made it an object of Progressive reform ("The darkness that rests upon Asia and the midnight that enshrouds Africa, where woman has no rights . . . have their appointed time to pass away in the illumination of which the American Republic is the destined centre" [Joseph Rodes Buchanan, "The Cosmic Sphere of Woman," 679]), others, more typically, figured "primitive" lusts as beyond redemption: "There is something strangely alluring to [black men] in the appearance of a white woman; they are aroused and stimulated by its foreignness to their experience of sexual pleasure, and it moves them to gratify their lust at any cost and in spite of any obstacle" (Philip Alexander Bruce, *The Plantation Negro as Freeman* [New York: Putnam,1889], quoted in Joel Williamson, *The Crucible of Race: Black-White Relations in the American South since Emancipation*, 121). While the vaunted depravities of Catholicism were encoded in the body, those of blackness, of course, were also typically revenged on the body: "If it takes lynching to protect woman's dearest possession from drunken, ravening beasts—then I say lynch a thousand a week if it becomes necessary" (Rebecca Latimer Felton, "Letter to the *Atlanta Constitution*," 411).

148. Cf. Stanley Fish, "How the Right Hijacked the Magic Words," *New York Times*, 3 August 1995.

149. See Henry Louis Gates Jr., "The Trope of the New Negro and the Reconstruction of the Image of the Black."

150. Hedrick, *Harriet Beecher Stowe*, 398.

151. HBS, quoted by Annie Fields, ed., *Life and Letters of Harriet Beecher Stowe*, 204.

152. On seeing the black soprano Elizabeth Greenfield perform in England, Stowe reported, an English lord declared that the "use of these halls for the encouragement of an outcaste race" constituted a "*consecration*," confirming Stowe's view that "there really is no natural prejudice against colour in the human mind" (HBS, *Sunny Memories of Foreign Lands*, 1:284, 1:43; Lott, *Love and Theft*, 235). On the similar consecrations that exemplary Catholics were seen to confer on the Protestant families and nations that accommodated them see HBS, *We and Our Neighbors*, 244–45; Kirwan [Nicholas Murray], *Romanism at Home: Letters to the Hon. Roger B. Taney*, 245.

CHAPTER SIX

MARK TWAIN AND THE AMBIVALENT REFUGE OF UNBELIEF

1. John H. Wallace, "The Case Against Huck Finn," 24, 22.

2. Russell Baker, "The Only Gentleman," *New York Times*, 14 April 1982, excerpted in *Satire or Evasion? Black Perspectives on Huckleberry Finn*, ed. James S. Leonard, Thomas A. Tenney, and Thadious Davis, 243.

3. Christopher Hitchens, "American Notes," *Times Literary Supplement*, 9 March 1985, 258, quoted by Jonathan Arac, *Huckleberry Finn as Idol and Target: The Functions of Criticism in Our Time*, 22

4. George F. Will, "The Politicization of Higher Education," *Newsweek*, 22 April 1991, 72, quoted by Evan Carton, "Speech Acts and Social Action: Mark Twain and the Politics of Literary Performance," 154; George F. Will, "Huck at a Hundred."

5. Arac, *Huckleberry Finn as Idol and Target*, 13, 18. On desegregation and the cold war see Mary Dudziak, "Desegregation as a Cold War Imperative."

6. "The Voice of America," *The New Yorker*, 14 June 1993, quoted by Louis J. Budd, "Mark Twain as an American Icon," 23–24. I follow the increasingly common practice of using "Mark Twain" or "Twain" to refer either to Samuel Clemens or to the literary persona Mark Twain.

7. Leonard, Tenney, and Davis, *Satire or Evasion?*, 274. The observation in these notes that Wallace "opposes *Huckleberry Finn* largely on the ground of improper language" (274) misrepresents his position and suggests concern on the part of the book's editors that Wallace's largely unelaborated objections to Huck's "sacrilegious[ness]" mitigate his antiracist critique. The one other reference to religion in Wallace's essay "The Case Against *Huck Finn*" links his own position to the guidelines offered by the Jewish Community Council in 1981 recommending that "[i]n no event should any student, teacher, or public school staff member feel that his or her own beliefs or practices are being questioned, infringed upon, or compromised by programs taking place in or sponsored by the public school." "I find it incongruent to contend," Wallace writes, "that it is fitting and proper to shelter children from isolation, embarrassment, and ridicule due to their religious beliefs and then deny the same protection to other children because of the color

of their skin. The basic principle is the same." ("The Case Against *Huck Finn*," 20, 19).

8. Mark Twain (hereafter MT), *The Adventures of Huckleberry Finn*, 835. Henceforth cited by page number in the text.

9. Stanley Brodwin, "Mark Twain's Theology: The Gods of a Brevet Presbyterian," 230.

10. *Mark Twain's Notebook*, 198.

11. "Mark Twain Accepts Honorary Degree," *Hartford Courant*, 29 June 1888, excerpted in *Mark Twain Speaking*, 237.

12. Eric Sundquist, "Mark Twain and Homer Plessy," 105.

13. Wallace, "Case Against *Huck Finn*," 20.

14. MT, "Aix, Paradise of Rheumatics," in *The Complete Essays of Mark Twain*, 50.

15. Peaches Henry notes that *Huckleberry Finn*'s "entrenchment in the English curricula of American junior and senior high schools, largely thanks to the praises of Lionel Trilling and T. S. Eliot," coincided with *Brown v. Topeka Board of Education*, "deposit[ing] Huck in the midst of American literature classrooms which were no longer composed of white children only, but dotted with black youngsters as well," where occasionally, as outside Central High School in Little Rock, Arkansas, the word "nigger" was emblazoned on placards protesting integration ("The Struggle for Tolerance: Race and Censorship in *Huckleberry Finn*," 25, 31). On *Huck*'s canonization in the context of federally mandated desegregation see also Arac, *Huckleberry Finn as Idol and Target*, 21.

16. Arthur Schlesinger Jr., "The Opening of the American Mind," *New York Times Book Review*, 23 July 1989, 1, 26, 27, quoted in Arac, *Huckleberry Finn as Idol and Target*, 18

17. Elizabeth P. Peabody, *Reminiscences of Rev. William Ellery Channing, D.D.* (Boston: Roberts Brothers, 1880), 30, 245, quoted by David S. Reynolds, *Faith in Fiction*, 109.

18. Robert G. Ingersoll, "We Build," in *Prose-Poems and Selections from the Writings and Sayings of Robert Ingersoll, 1833–1899*, 44.

19. Ingersoll, "Selections," and "Oration Delivered on Decoration-Day, 1882, before the Grand Army of the Republic," in *Prose-Poems and Selections*, 260, 10.

20. MT to Olivia Langhorne Clemens, 14 November 1879, in *Mark Twain's Letters*, 24:371.

21. Ingersoll, "A Vision of War," and "We Build," in *Prose-Poems and Selections*, 36, 43–44.

22. Will Herberg, *Protestant, Catholic, Jew: An Essay in American Religious Sociology*, 51; see also 94–95.

23. Arac, *Huckleberry Finn as Idol and Target*, 19.

24. Letter of MT to Charles W. Stoddard, 1 June 1885, quoted by John T. Frederick, *The Darkened Sky: Nineteenth-Century American Novelists and Religion*, 152.

25. Jerry Allen, "Tom Sawyer's Town," *National Geographic Magazine*, July 1956, 120–40. http://etext.lib.virginia.edu/railton/tomsawye/nostalgia/56natlgeohp.html.

26. [Bret Harte], unsigned review of Mark Twain's *Innocents Abroad*, 100.

27. "Mark Twain Accepts Honorary Degree," in *Mark Twain Speaking*, 237.

28. Brodwin, "Mark Twain's Theology," 228.

29. Susan Gillman, *Dark Twins: Identity and Imposture in Mark Twain's America*, 9; James D. Wilson, "Religious and Esthetic Vision in Mark Twain's Early Career," 155. Susan Gillman elegantly contests this view; see below.

30. *New York Times*, 14 September 1957, quoted by Henry, "Struggle for Tolerance," 34.

31. Susan Gillman, "Mark Twain's Travels in the Racial Occult: *Following the Equator* and the Dream Tales," 217

32. As Sander Gilman notes, Twain distinguished "whites, negroes, and Jews, suggesting that Jews are a separate race or that they escape race" ("Mark Twain and the Diseases of the Jews," 113), much as Jim momentarily escapes blackness by being disguised in "Arab-face" (MT, *Huckleberry Finn*, 779).

33. To include Christian antislavery voices in the novel, Arac suggests, would be to "diminish the comic miracle of Huck's decision" (*Huckleberry Finn as Idol and Target*, 54).

34. Alan Gribben, " 'When Other Amusements Fail': Mark Twain and the Occult," 173

35. Alfred Kazin, *God and the American Writer*, 189.

36. Dixon Wecter, *Sam Clemens of Hannibal* (Boston: Houghton Mifflin, 1952), 88, quoted by Brodwin, "Mark Twain's Theology," 233.

37. Ralph Ellison, "Change the Joke and Slip the Yoke," 58.

38. MT to Olivia Langdon, in *The Love Letters of Mark Twain*, 44–45, quoted by Jeffrey R. Holland, "Soul Butter and Hogwash: Mark Twain and Frontier Religion," 22–23.

39. MT, "To the Person Sitting in Darkness," 165.

40. MT, partly unpublished sketch of Jane Lampton Clemens, Mark Twain Papers, University of California, Berkeley, quoted by Arthur Gordon Pettit, "Mark Twain, Unreconstructed Southerner, and His View of the Negro, 1835–1860," 20.

41. MT, *Pudd'nhead Wilson*, 955, 927. Henceforth cited by page number in the text.

42. Arthur Pettit notes that Twain preserved in his Nevada scrapbook from the early 1860s a *Boston Post* article (20 May 1859) that portrayed abolitionists as champions of "niggerism" ("Mark Twain's Attitude Toward the Negro in the West, 1861–1867," 55).

43. MT, "Bible Teaching and Religious Practice," in *Complete Essays of Mark Twain*, 570

44. MT, "Greeting to the Twentieth Century," in *Mark Twain and the Three R's: Race, Religion, Revolution—and Related Matters*, 103

45. MT, *Following the Equator*, 21:10, 21:50, 21:9–10, 21:15–16. My reading of *Following the Equator* draws on Gillman, "Mark Twain's Travels in the Racial Occult," and *Dark Twins*, 96–101.

46. MT, "Reflections on Religion," 335, 338.

47. MT, *Christian Science*, 42. Cf. MT, *The Secret History of Eddypus, the World-Empire*, 177.

48. MT, *Mark Twain's Notebook*, 376.

49. Marginal note in Twain's copy of Michelet's *Life of Joan of Arc* (Paris, 1873), 20, Mark Twain Papers, University of California, Berkeley, quoted by Roger B. Salomon, *Twain and the Image of History*, 172.

50. MT, *Personal Recollections of Joan of Arc*, 417.

51. Kazin, *God and the American Writer*, 183

52. Holland, "Soul Butter and Hogwash," 24.

53. MT, *The Adventures of Tom Sawyer*, 38. Henceforth cited by page number in the text.

54. MT, "Reflections on Religion," 342.

55. MT, *Roughing It*, 3:192.

56. MT, *The Innocents Abroad*, 587.

57. Ralph Ellison, "The Negro Writer in America: An Exchange," 216.

58. See, e.g., I. A. Newby, *Jim Crow's Defense: Anti-Negro Thought in America, 1900–1930*, 50–51.

59. *Mark Twain's Autobiography*, 2:193.

60. MT, *Life on the Mississippi*, 364, 259. Henceforth cited by page number in the text.

61. MT, Fragment of a letter to ____, 1891, in *Mark Twain's Letters*, vol. 4 (1886–1900), 109.

62. Bernard DeVoto, ed., *Mark Twain in Eruption*, 49.

63. Victor A. Doyno, *Writing "Huck Finn": Mark Twain's Creative Process*, 204, 209–10; for a critique of Doyno's and similar views see also Jonathan Arac, "Putting the River on New Maps."

64. Salomon, *Twain and the Image of History*, 87

65. MT, *Those Extraordinary Twins*, 310.

66. For a fuller plot summary of *Pudd'nhead Wilson* and its relation to "Those Extraordinary Twins" see Sundquist, "Mark Twain and Homer Plessy," 125n1.

67. See the essays in Susan Gillman and Forrest G. Robinson, eds., *Mark Twain's Pudd'nhead Wilson: Race, Conflict, and Culture*.

68. MT, *Extraordinary Twins*, 426–27.

69. MT, *Extraordinary Twins*, 311.

70. MT, *Innocents Abroad*, 573. I take the term "extraordinary bodies" from Rosemarie Garland Thomson, *Extraordinary Bodies: Figuring Physical Disability in American Culture and Literature*; see also Thomson, *Freakery: Cultural Spectacles of the Extraordinary Body*.

71. MT, *Following the Equator* 21:14, 21:10.

72. MT, Notebook 32a (1), Mark Twain Papers, University of California, Berkeley, quoted in Salomon, *Twain and the Image of History*, 194.

73. MT, *Mark Twain's Letters from Hawaii*, 27; MT, *Mark Twain's Notebook*, 20.

74. Katy Leary (with Mary Lawton), *A Lifetime with Mark Twain* (New York: Harcourt, Brace, and Company, 1925), 213, quoted by Holland, "Soul Butter and Hogwash," 28.

75. MT to Olivia Langhorne Clemens, 29 November1881, in *Love Letters of Mark Twain*, 205.

76. MT, *A Connecticut Yankee in King Arthur's Court*, 65, 67.

77. MT, *Connecticut Yankee*, 216.

78. MT to Miss Darrell, 23 February 1897, typescript in the Mark Twain Papers, University of California, Berkeley; quoted by Susan Gillman, *Dark Twins*, 88.

79. MT, "Reflections on Religion," 333.

80. Stephen Rachman, "Reading Cities: Devotional Seeing in the Nineteenth Century," 667.

81. MT, *Innocents Abroad*, 258, 311.

82. Ibid., 261.

83. Ibid., 472–73.

84. See Pettit, "Mark Twain, Unreconstructed Southerner," 25.

85. Gilman, "Mark Twain and the Diseases of the Jews."

86. MT, "As Regards Patriotism," in *Complete Essays of Mark Twain*, 567.

87. MT quoted in William Gibson, "Mark Twain and Howells: Anti-Imperialists," 446.

88. MT, *Three Thousand Years among the Microbes*, 241

89. MT, *Secret History of Eddypus*, 185.

90. MT, "The Anglo-Saxon Race," in *Mark Twain and the Three R's*, 5.

91. MT, "The Russian Revolution and the USA," in *Mark Twain and the Three R's*, 165.

92. MT, "The Coming American Monarchy II," in *Mark Twain and the Three R's*, 242, 241.

93. MT, *The Chronicle of Young Satan*, in MT, *Mysterious Stranger Manuscripts*, 55.

94. MT, *Mark Twain's Autobiography*, 2:218; Henry Nash Smith, "Mark Twain's Images of Hannibal: from St. Petersburg to Eseldorf," 20; Sholom J. Kahn, *Mark Twain's Mysterious Stranger: A Study of the Manuscript Texts*, 205–6; Gillman, "Mark Twain's Travels in the Racial Occult," 210–13.

95. MT, *No. 44, The Mysterious Stranger*, in MT, *Mysterious Stranger*, 356

96. MT, *Mark Twain's Autobiography*, 2:218.

97. "The Egyptian, the Babylonian, and the Persian rose, filled the planet with sound and splendor, then faded to dream-stuff and passed away; the Greek and the Roman followed, and made a vast noise, and they are gone; other peoples have sprung up and held their torch for a time, but it burned out, and they sit in twilight now, or have vanished. The Jew saw them all, beat them all, and is now what he always was, exhibiting no decadence, no infirmities of age. . . . All things are mortal but the Jew; all other forces pass, but he remains." MT, "Concerning the Jews," in *Complete Essays of Mark Twain*, 249.

98. MT, *Following the Equator*, 21:298–99.

99. MT, "The Savage Club Dinner," in *Mark Twain's Speeches*, 390–91. My reading of Twain's white suit draws on Carton, "Speech Acts and Social Action"; and Gillman, *Dark Twins* 124–25, 184–87.

100. "Mark Twain is Dead at 74," *New York Times*, 22 April 1910.

101. MT, *Following the Equator*, 21:301.

102. Ibid., 21:11

103. Morgan Manuscript of *Pudd'nhead Wilson* in Pierpont Morgan Library, New York, quoted by Gillman, "Racial Occult," 198.

104. MT, "Greeting to the Twentieth Century," in *Mark Twain and the Three R's*, 103.

105. MT, "The Stupendous Procession," in *Mark Twain's Fables of Man*, 418–19.

106. "Interview" in *Mark Twain Speaking*, 530–31; *The World*, 8 December 1906, quoted by Gillman, *Dark Twins*, 186.

107. MT, *Following the Equator*, 21:11–12.

108. Ibid., 21:10–11.

109. A. B. Paine, *Mark Twain: A Biography*, 3:1341–42.

110. Budd, "Mark Twain as an American Icon," 6, 4.

CHAPTER SEVEN
SECULARISM, FEMINISM, IMPERIALISM: CHARLOTTE PERKINS
GILMAN AND THE PROGRESS NARRATIVE OF U.S. FEMINISM

1. Louise Michele Newman, *White Women's Rights: The Racial Origins of Feminism in the United States*, 181.

2. Newman, *White Women's Rights* 19; see 3–21 for a fuller discussion.

3. Catharine Beecher and Harriet Beecher Stowe, *The American Woman's Home*, 337.

4. Harriet Beecher Stowe, *House and Home Papers*, 204.

5. Upton Sinclair, ed., *The Cry for Justice*, 662; William Dean Howells, "The New Poetry," *North American Review* 168 (May 1899): 589–90, quoted by Joanne B. Karpinski, "When the Marriage of True Minds Admits Impediments: Charlotte Perkins Gilman and William Dean Howells," 203. On Gilman in the remarks of Wilson, Debs, and Shaw, see Gary Scharnhorst, "Reconstructing *Here Also*: On the Later Poetry of Charlotte Perkins Gilman," 249.

6. A quick web search in October 2005 turned up more than twelve thousand URLs for college syllabi that include a reading assignment from Gilman's writing.

7. Elizabeth Cady Stanton, "Speech to the 1860 Anniversary of the American Anti-Slavery Society," in *The Elizabeth Cady Stanton—Susan B. Anthony Reader*, 80–81.

8. Ann Braude, *Radical Spirits: Spiritualism and Women's Rights in Nineteenth-Century America*, xxii.

9. Ann J. Lane, "Charlotte Perkins Gilman and the Rights of Women: Her Legacy for the 1990s," 13.

10. Charlotte Perkins Gilman (hereafter CPG), *The Living of Charlotte Perkins Gilman*, 103.

11. CPG, *The Man-Made World, or Our Androcentric Culture*, 28.

12. CPG to George Houghton Gilman, 11 May 1897, Gilman Papers, folder 41, Arthur and Elizabeth Schlesinger Library on the History of Women in America, quoted by Larry Ceplair, in CPG, *Charlotte Perkins Gilman: A Nonfiction Reader*, 88.

13. Lester F. Ward, "Our Better Halves," 274–75. For discussion of the writing of *Women and Economics* see CPG, *Nonfiction Reader*, 88–90.

14. CPG, *Women and Economics: A Study of the Economic Relation between Men and Women as a Factor in Social Evolution*, 36, 43, 9, 109.

15. CPG, *The Home: Its Work and Influence*, 6.

16. CPG, *Women and Economics*, 121.

17. CPG, *Home*, 166.

18. Ibid., 13.

19. Ibid., 5–6

20. Ibid., 5.

21. CPG, "The Ethics of Woman's Work," manuscript of lecture given 1 February 1894, in CPG, *Nonfiction Reader*, 79.

22. CPG, "Thoughts and Figgerings," 28 June 1908, Gilman Papers, folder 16, quoted by Ceplair, in CPG, *Nonfiction Reader*, 93.

23. CPG, "A Summary of Purpose," *The Forerunner* 7 (November 1916), in CPG, *Nonfiction Reader*, 198–202.

24. Carl N. Degler, "Charlotte Perkins Gilman on the Theory and Practice of Feminism," 21.

25. Elaine R. Hedges, " 'Out at Last'? 'The Yellow Wallpaper' after Two Decades of Feminist Criticism," 228. The spare, unnerving "Yellow Wallpaper" has proven to be a later generation's *Women and Economics*: translated into many languages, widely taught in American literature and women's studies classes, and continuously in print since its republication in a book-length edition by the Feminist Press in 1973. Originally published in 1892, "The Yellow Wallpaper" is a firsthand account of advancing psychosis told by a new mother made to undergo the immobilizing "rest cure" prescribed to Gilman by Dr. S. Weir Mitchell in 1886. In the depths of her own postpartum depression, Gilman had diligently applied herself to Mitchell's recommendation of near-total passivity and came "perilously near to losing [her] mind" before managing finally to "cast the noted specialist's advice to the winds and [go] to work again—work, the normal life of every human being, without which one is a pauper and a parasite" (CPG, *Living*, 95–96). Her more conventionally dutiful protagonist in "The Yellow Wallpaper" plunges instead into madness, and ends by "creeping" in circles along the wall of the nursery where she is confined, peeling away layers of the nursery's ancient, discolored wallpaper in order to free the woman she imagines she sees trapped behind the bars of its irregular design. "I wrote it to preach," Gilman remarked of "The Yellow Wallpaper"; "if it is literature that just happened" (quoted in Alexander Black, "The Woman Who Saw It First," 63). Gilman's routine disavowal of literary ambition extended to the Dada-like disclaimer that her poetry collection *In This Our World* was not "a book of poems. I call it a tool box. It was written to drive nails with." (CPG, *Topeka State Journal*, 15 June 1896, quoted by Scharnhorst, "Reconstructing *Here Also*," 249). Among feminist literary critics, who have mostly let such lukewarm self-appraisals stand, Gilman's fiction and poetry deserve esteem less for their literary merit than for their "cultural work," their ability to articulate for an era a set of problems and to propose solutions to those problems. Her fiction is valuable, that is, insofar as the aims of her fiction and nonfiction—"to preach"—are the same. And this way of appreciating Gilman also nicely explains why she would be undervalued according to reigning, implicitly male-gendered standards by which "the mere mention of didacticism" in connec-

tion with fiction "relegates such fiction to [insignificance]" (Sheryl L. Meyering, ed., *Charlotte Perkins Gilman: The Woman and Her Work*, 8). But the embrace of Gilman's writing on these avowedly feminist grounds also allows scholars to read Gilman's fiction expressly in lieu of her nonfiction and so to be spared the starkest and most systematic of her racist pronouncements in favor of what are typically written off as minor lapses of discretion. "Shall we vilify *With Her in Ourland*," ask the editors of *Herland*'s sequel, "because it contains a few (and it really is only a few) ethnocentric lapses?" (Mary Jo Deegan and Michael R. Hill, in CPG, *With Her in Ourland*, 6).

26. Jean E. Kennard, "Convention Coverage or How to Read Your Own Life," 75–94.

27. Meyering, *Charlotte Perkins Gilman*, 9.

28. Braude, *Radical Spirits*, xxii.

29. Karpinski, introduction to *Critical Essays*, 13.

30. Lane, "Charlotte Perkins Gilman and the Rights of Women," 10.

31. Barbara Scott Winkler, "Victorian Daughters: The Lives and Feminism of Charlotte Perkins Gilman and Olive Schreiner," 174.

32. See especially Newman, *White Women's Rights* 132–57; Gail Bederman, *Manliness and Civilization: A Cultural History of Gender and Race in the United States, 1880–1917*, 121–69. See also Susan S. Lanser, "Feminist Criticism, 'The Yellow Wallpaper,' and the Politics of Color in America."

33. CPG, *Home*, 82–84.

34. CPG, "Two Callings," in *Home*, viii.

35. CPG, *Home*, 102.

36. E. B. Tylor, *Primitive Culture*, 1:23–24.

37. CPG, *Women and Economics*, 180.

38. CPG, *Concerning Children*, 4.

39. CPG, "A Suggestion on the Negro Problem," *American Journal of Sociology* 14 (July 1908): 78–85, in CPG, *Nonfiction Reader*, 176–83.

40. Bederman, *Manliness and Civilization*, 135.

41. CPG, *Living*, 37.

42. This list is in CPG, *Nonfiction Reader*, 11–12.

43. Talal Asad, *Genealogies of Religion: Discipline and Reasons of Power in Christianity and Islam*, 18–21, 40–43; Kant quoted on p. 42. For a nuanced account of the emergence of the discourse of "world religions" in conjunction with the universalist aspirations of European modernity see Tomoko Masuzawa, *The Invention of World Religions, or, How European Universalism was Preserved in the Language of Pluralism*.

44. CPG, *Living*, 37–43.

45. CPG, *With Her in Ourland*, 163; CPG, *Man-made World*, 136.

46. CPG, "The Labor Movement: A Prize Essay Read before the Trades and Labor Unions of Alameda County, September 5, 1892," in CPG, *Nonfiction Reader*, 68.

47. CPG, "To My Real Readers," *The Forerunner* 7 (December 1916), 326–28, in CPG, *Nonfiction Reader*, 267.

48. Black, "Woman Who Saw It First," 65–66.

49. Ann J. Lane, *To Herland and Beyond: The Life and Work of Charlotte Perkins Gilman*, 255.

50. CPG, "Human Nature," manuscript of lecture presented to the Pasadena Nationalist Club, 15 June 1890, in CPG, *Nonfiction Reader*, 53.

51. CPG, *Herland*, 1. Cited hereafter by page number in the body of the text.

52. See, e.g., the sparkling feminist encomiums on the back cover of the Pantheon edition: "pure delight" (Susan Brownmiller), "a gentle, witty version of what women can be" (Marge Piercy), "still fresh and very much of today" (Joanna Russ). My reading of *Herland* as a key document in the effort to construct an untarnished intellectual genealogy for U.S. feminism is indebted to Kristin Carter-Sanborn, "Restraining Order: The Imperialist Anti-Violence of Charlotte Perkins Gilman," and to Alys Eve Weinbaum, "Writing Feminist Genealogy: Charlotte Perkins Gilman, Racial Nationalism, and the Reproduction of Maternalist Feminism."

53. Edward Bellamy, *Looking Backward 2000–1887*, 154.

54. Ibid., 106, 98.

55. Ibid., 161.

56. CPG, *With Her in Ourland*, 123.

57. Beecher and Stowe, *American Woman's Home*, 318.

58. On the function of domesticity to construct itself "in intimate opposition to the foreign" see Amy Kaplan, "Manifest Domesticity."

59. CPG, "Is America Too Hospitable?' *The Forum* 70 (October 1923), in CPG, *Nonfiction Reader*, 290; cf. CPG, *With Her in Ourland*, 115–24.

60. Ranu Samantrai, "Continuity or Rupture? An Argument for Secular Britain," 110.

61. CPG, "Is America Too Hospitable?" in CPG, *Nonfiction Reader*, 289, 292–93.

62. Beecher and Stowe, *American Woman's Home*, 146–47.

63. Ellador's rendering of foreign populations as underbred children reflects the ongoing effort to imagine America as home, complete with wayward offspring to be "raised," at a time when its geopolitical boundaries were expanding to include newly enfranchised African American men and new waves of Irish, Eastern European, and East Asian immigrants, together with the inhabitants of Cuba, the Philippines, Hawai'i, the Spanish borderlands, and the recently annexed territories in the mainland United States. More subtly, the image of new and not-yet Americans as children places (American) civil identity at a more advanced stage than (foreign) religious identity, which Gilman, together with Freud, made the equivalent of childhood in world-historical development, "to be outgrown in a civilizing adolescence" (David Lawton, *Blasphemy* [Philadelphia: University of Pennsylvania Press, 1993], 144, quoted in Gauri Viswanathan, *Outside the Fold: Conversion, Modernity, and Belief*, xii; see her discussion, ibid.).

64. Gilman's 1923 essay "The New Generation of Women," for example, commends what she sees as "a new sense of the duty of women to the world as mothers—mothers not merely of their own physical children, but world mothers in the sense in which we speak of city fathers" (CPG, "The New Generation of Women," *Current History* 18 [August 1923]: 731–37, in CPG, *Nonfiction Reader*, 282). Yet even as she casts American women as metaphorical "world mothers" Gilman

sustains—even amplifies—her emphasis on "mere" physical motherhood, the role to which she never warmed and which she lightly surrendered in pursuit of larger freedoms. According to *Women and Economics*, the "rising tide of racial power" belongs to the modern Western wife and mother, who now misuse that power by "pouring . . . [it] into the same old channels that were allowed her primitive ancestors, constantly minister[ing] to the physical needs of her family" rather than to the loftier needs of the race (*Women and Economics*, 120). In "The New Generation of Women," however, Gilman cautioned that the "new status of women [i.e., world-motherhood] is . . . more easily attained by the single woman or the widow than by the wife and mother. Yet wifehood and motherhood are the normal status of women, and whatever is right in woman's new position must not militate against these essentials" (*Nonfiction Reader*, 283).

65. CPG, *His Religion and Hers*, 79, 85–86.

66. CPG, *Man-Made World*, 38.

67. See Janet R. Jakobsen and Ann Pellegrini, "Getting Religion."

68. On the modern construction of religion as belief see, e.g., Malcolm Ruel, "Christians as Believers"; Asad, *Genealogies of Religion*, 27–54; Viswanathan, *Outside the Fold*, xi—xvii; and Winnifred Fallers Sullivan, *The Impossibility of Religious Freedom*.

69. Laura Levitt, "Other Moderns, Other Jews."

70. CPG, *With Her in Ourland*, 166.

71. This point is made by Jakobsen and Pellegrini in "World Secularisms at the Millenium: Introduction"; see also Asad, *Genealogies of Religion*, 8.

72. Braude, *Radical Spirits*, xxii.

73. CPG, *Home*, 175.

74. CPG, *The Charlotte Perkins Gilman Reader*, 178.

Chapter Eight
F. Scott Fitzgerald's Catholic Closet

1. Mitchell Breitwieser, "Jazz Fractures: F. Scott Fitzgerald and Epochal Representation," 361–62.

2. F. Scott Fitzgerald (henceforth FSF), "Absolution," in *The Stories of F. Scott Fitzgerald*, 198. Henceforth cited by page number in the text. On "Absolution" as the original prologue to *Gatsby* see FSF to Max Perkins, 18 June 1924, in *Dear Scott/Dear Max: The Fitzgerald-Perkins Correspondence*, 72.

3. Thomas J. Ferraro, "Butter-and-Egg Men: Response to Breitwieser," 384–85.

4. FSF, *The Great Gatsby*, 60. Henceforth cited by page number in the text.

5. FSF to Max Perkins, ca. 20 June 1922 in *Dear Scott/Dear Max*, 61. See, for example, Joan Allen, *Candles and Carnival Lights: The Catholic Sensibility of F. Scott Fitzgerald*, 103, 114; Paul Giles, *American Catholic Arts and Fictions: Culture, Ideology, Aesthetics*, 180; Giles Gunn, *The Interpretation of Otherness: Literature, Religion, and the American Imagination*, 208; Benita A. Moore, *Escape into a Labyrinth: F. Scott Fitzgerald, Catholic Sensibility, and the American Way*, 331.

6. Consider the *New Republic*'s appraisal of the revived *Vanity Fair* magazine, which debuted in March 1983: "so crude [an imitation of its 1913–36 predecessor] that the twelve pages of ads for Ralph Lauren's clothes stand out as by far the most appealing, likeable, and even interesting thing in the whole 294 pages: even the rather unbelievable picture of the young man (Princeton, Class of '20) who clearly, knowing he is beautiful, does not worry that he may be damned; his left hand caressing his right knee, his deep gaze that of a man who does not need a mirror to look timelessly on himself" (Henry Fairlie, "The Vanity of *Vanity Fair*," 25). Ralph Lauren, né Ralph Lifshitz, rose to prominence after designing the costumes for the 1976 film version of *The Great Gatsby*. See Lisa Keys, "Ralph Lauren's America—and Ours: How the Child of Immigrants Sold WASP Couture, and Culture, to the Masses."

7. Matthew J. Bruccoli, Scottie Fitzgerald Smith, and Joan P. Kerr, eds., *The Romantic Egoists: A Pictorial Autobiography from the Scrapbooks and Albums of F. Scott and Zelda Fitzgerald*, 61.

8. FSF, *This Side of Paradise* (henceforth TSOP) 112. Henceforth cited by page number in the text.

9. Matthew J. Bruccoli, *Some Sort of Epic Grandeur: The Life of F. Scott Fitzgerald*, 79.

10. FSF, "Winter Dreams," in FSF, *Before Gatsby: The First Twenty-Six Stories*, 538. On the relation of this story to *Gatsby*, see 525–27.

11. Marian Ronan, "Tracing the Sign of the Cross: Sexuality and Mourning in U.S. Catholicism," 194.

12. Paul Giles, "Aquinas vs. Weber: Ideological Esthetics in *The Great Gatsby*," 1–3.

13. In 1875 New York City's Cardinal John McCloskey observed: "Even now, the noblest ecclesiastical building ever erected on the City, or in the United States, is slowly going up on Fifth Avenue, and where does the money for it come from? Largely out of the pockets of poor Irish servants, some of whom we have known to give five or eight dollars a month out of their wages to this one special project" (*New York Times*, 7 May 1875, quoted by Delores Liptak, R.S.M., *Immigrants and their Church*, 78. On Thomism and aloofness from wealth see Giles, "Aquinas vs. Weber," 5. My understanding of the Thomist revival in America and the Americanism debate more generally is indebted to Giles, "Aquinas vs. Weber"; Philip Gleason, "The New Americanism in Catholic Historiography"; William M. Halsey, *The Survival of American Innocence: Catholicism in an Era of Disillusionment, 1920-1940*; R. Laurence Moore, *Religious Outsiders and the Making of Americans*, 48-71; and Ronan, "Tracing the Sign."

14. Liptak, *Immigrants and Their Church*, 77.

15. Ronan, "Tracing the Sign," 6–7.

16. This way of framing the debate is Giles's, "Aquinas vs. Weber," 3.

17. In his notebooks Fitzgerald remarked on the "pious nun" of his childhood "who opened the regents' examinations in advance and showed it to her class so that Catholic children might make a good showing to the glory of God." He also recalled "the railroad kings of the pioneer West [who] sent their waitress sweethearts to convents in order to prepare them for their high destinies." FSF, "The Note-books," in *The Crack-up*, 240, 146.

18. My reading of the trajectory of Irish assimilation is indebted to Will Herberg, *Protestant Catholic Jew*, 150–85; Noel Ignatiev, *How the Irish Became White*; Liptak, *Immigrants*, 76–91.

19. Aaron I. Abell, *American Catholicism and Social Action: A Search for Social Justice, 1865–1950* (Garden City: Hanover-Doubleday, 1960), 86, quoted by Giles, *American Catholic Arts and Fictions*, 140.

20. The construction is ungrammatical in Latin.

21. FSF, "Homage to the Victorians," in *F. Scott Fitzgerald on Authorship*, 73.

22. FSF to Edmund Wilson, ca. 7 October 1924, in *The Letters of F. Scott Fitzgerald*, 341; FSF to Carl Van Vechten, June [?] 1924, in *Letters*, 477; FSF, *Dear Scott/Dear Max*, 72; review of TSOP, *America* 23 (29 May 1920): 139. Favorable reviews of Fitzgerald appeared in *Catholic World* 112 (November 1920): 268 and *Catholic World* 112 (December 1920): 290–91, 301; see Moore, *Escape into a Labyrinth*, 242–43.

23. FSF to Shane Leslie, 16 November 1920, in *Letters*, 378.

24. Laura Levitt, "Other Moderns, Other Jews: Rereading Jewish Secularism in America."

25. As Mordecai Kaplan observed in 1917, the American "synagogue is the principle means of keeping alive the Jewish consciousness. . . . [It] is the only institution which can define our aims to a world that would otherwise be at a loss to understand why we persist in retaining our corporate individuality." *Jewish Community Register of New York*, 1917, quoted in Jack Wertheimer, ed., *The American Synagogue: A Sanctuary Transformed*, 31; Levitt, "Other Moderns."

26. Joseph L. Blau, "What's American about American Jewry?" 206. I am indebted to Laura Levitt for the references to both Kaplan and Blau.

27. See, e.g., Allen, *Candles and Carnival Lights*; Jody Bottum, "Gatsby's Epitaph: F. Scott Fitzgerald"; Steven Frye, "Fitzgerald's Catholicism Revisited: The Eucharistic Element in *The Beautiful and Damned*"; Ralph McInerny, "On Being a Catholic Writer."

28. Franchot speaks of the "cultural experience of the loss of religious belief and its recreation as visible memory, or more precisely as souvenir and entertainment," a "seeing that understands itself as a not believing" ("Unseemly Commemoration: Religion, Fragments, and the Icon," 502, 504).

29. By secular Catholic I mean something akin to what Ferraro means by cultural Catholic, one who cultivates and deploys "Catholic ways of knowing and habits of being outside the official precincts and sanction" of the institutional Church in ways that are "deliberately, often tantalizingly, at times insistently, 'religious'—without being or wanting to be catechistic" (*Catholic Lives, Contemporary America*, 8).

30. This distinction from Said's *The World, the Text, and the Critic* is invoked by Jakobsen and Pellegrini, "World Secularisms," 2. In a later interview Said set the "ideal of secular interpretation and secular work" against "submerged feelings of identity" and community that are "geographically and homogenously defined." "The dense fabric of secular life," says Said, can never "be herded under the rubric of national identity" or made to respond to the "phony idea of a paranoid frontier separating 'us' from 'them.' " Secularism understood in this sense offers a way

"of avoiding the pitfalls of nationalism" (*Edward W. Said: A Critical Reader*, 233; Bruce Robbins, "Secularism, Elitism, Progress, and Other Transgressions," 27).

31. I am indebted to Levitt, "Other Moderns," for this account of American pluralism.

32. Giles, "Aquinas vs. Weber," 1. Consider that by the 1930s tens of millions of American Catholics tuned in weekly to the xenophobic and anti-Semitic screeds of radio personality Father Charles Coughlin, who first turned to the airwaves in the wake of a cross burning on his parish lawn. On Irish Catholicism and racism see, e.g., Ignatiev, *How the Irish Became White*; John T. McGreevey, *Parish Boundaries: The Catholic Encounter with Race in the Twentieth-Century Urban North*; William A. Osborne, *The Segregated Covenant: Race Relations and American Catholics*; and the essays in Ronald P. Formisano and Constance Burns, eds., *Boston 1700–1980: The Evolution of Urban Politics*.

33. Ferraro, "Butter-and-Egg Men," 385.

34. FSF, "The Crack-up," in *Crack-up*, 69.

35. Ibid., 70.

36. FSF in *F. Scott Fitzgerald in His Own Time: A Miscellany*, ed. Matthew J. Bruccoli and Jackson R. Bryer, 276.

37. FSF to John O'Hara, 18 July 1933, in FSF, *F. Scott Fitzgerald: A Life in Letters*, 233–34.

38. I am indebted to Benita Moore's discussion of Fitzgerald's Newman years in *Escape into a Labyrinth*, 48–64.

39. FSF, "Who's Who—and Why," in FSF, *Afternoon of An Author: A Selection of Uncollected Stories and Essays*, 84.

40. Jeffrey Meyers, *Scott Fitzgerald, A Biography*, 17; Arthur Mizener, *The Far Side of Paradise: A Biography of F. Scott Fitzgerald*, 42; Andrew Turnbull, *Scott Fitzgerald*, 39.

41. On Fitzgerald's awareness of the novel's gay subtext see FSF to Frances Scott Fitzgerald, 5 October 1940, in FSF, *Letters*, 75.

42. I draw gratefully here on the insights of Eve Kosofsky Sedgwick, particularly her reading of Henry James's *Wings of the Dove* in *Tendencies*, 73–103.

43. Sigourney Fay to FSF, 10 December 1917, in *Correspondence of F. Scott Fitzgerald*, 24; cf. TSOP, 140. According to Shane Leslie, Fitzgerald's letters to Fay were destroyed (Leslie, "Some Memories of F. Scott Fitzgerald," 602).

44. Sigourney Fay to FSF, 19 October 1918, in *Correspondence*, 34.

45. Bruccoli, Smith, and Kerr, *Romantic Egoists*, 16. Although Fitzgerald would also say that he chose Princeton after discovering a campy musical comedy score lying on top of a piano at Newman: "It was a show called His Honor the Sultan, and the title furnished the information that it had been presented by the Triangle Club of Princeton University. That was enough for me. From then on the University question was settled. I was bound for Princeton." ("Who's Who—and Why," *Afternoon of an Author*, 84.)

46. FSF, "Princeton," in *Afternoon of an Author*, 72.

47. The very over-the-top quality of these identifications, of course, makes football a potential locus of queer energies as well. Consider "Basil and Cleopatra," where Basil's star performance in the Princeton-Yale game steels him to release his beloved Minnie Bibble to her possessive escort at the postgame dance,

letting his "heart [go] bobbing off around the ballroom in a pink dress" (FSF, "Basil and Cleopatra," in *Afternoon of an Author*, 68). Or this recollection from "Princeton": "A year ago in the Champs Elysées I passed a slender dark-haired young man with an indolent characteristic walk. Something stopped inside me; I turned and looked after him. It was the romantic Buzz Law whom I had last seen one cold fall twilight in 1915, kicking from behind the goal line with a bloody bandage round his head" (FSF, "Princeton," in *Afternoon of an Author*, 72–73).

48. FSF, "Princeton," in *Afternoon of an Author*, 70–71, 79.

49. My thinking about the overlaps between sexuality and national and religious acculturations is indebted to Magdalena J. Zaborowska, "Americanization of a 'Queer Fellow': Performing Jewishness and Sexuality in Abraham Cahan's *The Rise of David Levinsky*."

50. FSF to Ceci Taylor, 10 June 1917, in *Letters*, 414.

51. FSF, "Sentiment—And the Use of Rouge," in *F. Scott Fitzgerald: The Princeton Years, Selected Writings, 1914–1920*, 127.

52. FSF, "The Note-books," in *Crack-up*, 205.

53. FSF, "The Ordeal," in *F. Scott Fitzgerald: The Princeton Years*, 33–36.

54. Heywood Broun, "Paradise and Princeton," quoted by Alfred Kazin, *F. Scott Fitzgerald: The Man and His Work*, 52.

55. In the "Ledger," his lifelong diary-by-months, Fitzgerald twice remarked on his "Freudian shame" in relation to baring his *feet* to other boys in childhood (Turnbull, *Scott Fitzgerald*, 9, 11). "Clay Feet" was also the title of one of two poems Fitzgerald wrote in 1917 about idealized relationships with other men that cool ("Light fades, noon sickens, and there come times/When I can see but pale and ravaged places/That they have left in exodus . . ."). The other of the two, "On a Certain Man," gives specifics:

> He kissed my hand and let himself, unruddered,
> Drift on the surface of my "youth" and "sin"
> His was the blameless life, and still I shuddered
> Seeing the dark spot where his lips had been.
>
> "How you must hate me, you of joy and brightness
> Who have no sentiment—Ah—I'm a bore—"
> I smile and lie and pray the God, politeness;
> I'll sicken if his curled hair nears once more.
>
> Trembling before the fire, I gasp and rise,
> Yawn some and drawl of sleep, profess to nod,
> And weird parallels image on my eyes
> A devil screaming in the arms of God. (FSF to Ceci Taylor,
>   10 June 1917, in *Letters*, 418–19)

56. Though the two scenes are separated by a hundred-odd pages, the connection between them emerges as Amory's reflections on his "all-American" team of women—now identified with baseball, not football—continue: "Eleanor would pitch, probably southpaw. Rosalind was outfield, wonderful hitter, Clara first base maybe. Wonder what Humbird's body looks like now" (TSOP, 227).

57. FSF, "Handle With Care," in *Crack-up*, 76.

58. FSF to Shane Leslie, late January 1919, in *Letters*, 375.

59. FSF, *The Notebooks of F. Scott Fitzgerald*, 79.

60. FSF to Isabelle Amorous, 26 February 1920, *Correspondence*, 53.

61. Sigmund Freud, "Mourning and Melancholia," *The Standard Edition of the Complete Works of Sigmund Freud*, 14:239–58. My thinking about mourning in connection with Catholicism is indebted to Ronan, "Tracing the Sign"; with Fitzgerald, to Jonathan Schiff, *Ashes to Ashes: Mourning and Social Difference in F. Scott Fitzgerald's Fiction*, which focuses on the deaths of Fitzgerald's two sisters shortly before his birth; with heterosexuality, to Judith Butler, *Gender Trouble: Feminism and the Subversion of Identity* and Sedgwick, *Tendencies*, 73–103.

62. FSF, "Handle with Care," in *Crack-up*. 77.

63. FSF, quoted in Turnbull, *Scott Fitzgerald*, 150.

64. FSF to Anne Ober, 4 March 1938, in FSF, *Life in Letters*, 352.

65. "When Zelda cuttingly referred to his father as an Irish policeman," Nancy Milford reports, "Scott retaliated by slapping Zelda hard across the face" (Nancy Milford, *Zelda: A Biography*, 140). Fitzgerald also wrote Edmund Wilson that he'd wished *Ulysses* were set in America, since "there is something about middle-class Ireland that depresses me inordinately—I mean gives me a sort of hollow, cheerless pain. Half of my ancestors came from just such an Irish strata or a lower one. The book makes me feel appallingly naked" (FSF to Edmund Wilson, 25 June 1922, in FSF, *Letters*, 337).

66. Milford, *Zelda*, 211; FSF, *Correspondence*, 243, 241, 244. In his note-books Fitzgerald wrote (of an unspecified person) that "he had perfected a trick of writing about all his affairs as if his boy friends had been girls, thus achieving feminine types of a certain spurious originality" ("The Note-books," in *Crack-up*, 166.)

67. FSF, "Benediction," in FSF, *F. Scott Fitzgerald: Novels and Stories 1920–22*, 382. Henceforth cited by page number in the text.

68. As Kieth recounts the story for Lois (who has "rather shyly" asked her brother how he "first happen[ed] to do it . . . to come here I mean"): "It was evening and I'd been riding all day [in a Pullman car] and thinking about—about a hundred things, Lois, and then suddenly I had a sense that someone was sitting across from me, felt that he'd been there for some time, and had a vague idea that he was another traveler." As if in response to a telegraphed question put by Kieth to the fellow traveler, the man leans over toward Kieth and says, "I want you to be a priest, that's what I want." Kieth continues: "Well I jumped up and cried, 'Oh my God, not that'—made an idiot of myself before about twenty people, you see there wasn't anyone sitting there at all. A week after that I went to the Jesuit College in Philadelphia, and crawled up the stairs to the rector's office on my hands and knees" (FSF, "Benediction," 388).

69. This is the reading of Edward Gillin in "The Grace of 'Benediction.' "

70. FSF, "My Lost City," in *Crack-up*, 25.

71. See Gillin, "Grace of 'Benediction,' " 35–40.

72. Sedgwick, *Tendencies*, 8.

73. FSF to John Jamieson, 15 April 1934, in *Letters*, 509.

74. Gunn, *Interpretation of Otherness*, 208.

75. Donna J. Haraway, *Simians, Cyborgs, and Women: The Reinvention of Nature*, 188–89. I am indebted to Marian Ronan for this reference.

76. This line of argument begins, as far as I can tell, with Walter Benn Michaels, "The Souls of White Folks."

77. This point is Ronald Berman's, "*The Great Gatsby* and the Twenties," 93–94.

78. Edward Wasiolek, "The Sexual Drama of Nick and Gatsby."

79. See Michaels, "Souls of White Folks," 195.

80. I am indebted here to Judith Butler's discussion of Nella Larsen's *Passing* in *Bodies That Matter: On the Discursive Limits of "Sex,"* 167–86.

81. Michaels, "Souls of White Folks," 203.

82. Mitchell Breitwieser, "*The Great Gatsby*: Grief, Jazz, and the Eye-Witness," 39, 40.

83. John Callahan, *The Illusions of a Nation: Myth and History in the Novels of F. Scott Fitzgerald*, 11.

84. Murray Baumgarten, "Seeing Double: Jews in the Fiction of F. Scott Fitzgerald, Charles Dickens, Anthony Trollope, and George Eliot," 45.

85. Gunn, *Interpretation of Otherness*, 202.

86. Peter Mallios, "Undiscovering the Country: Conrad, Fitzgerald, and Meta-National Form," 381.

87. Elaine K. Ginsberg, ed., *Passing and the Fictions of Identity*, 4, 16

88. Paul Giles, "The Intertextual Politics of Cultural Catholicism: Tiepolo, Madonna, Scorsese," 121.

89. Somewhat differently again, think how readily his episodes of cross-dressing in college have been taken up by his biographers as evidence for Fitzgerald's *hetero*sexuality (e.g., Bruccoli, *Some Sort of Epic Grandeur*, 59; Turnbull, *Scott Fitzgerald*, 61–62)—far be it that, say, arriving at a fraternity dance in lipstick, gown, and heels and captivating the eager men who lined up to dance with him might so much as imply, still less express, a certain heterogeneity of erotic desire; the conventional reading has it that no man not secure in his ramrod-straight "masculinity" would have dared.

90. Sedgwick, *Tendencies*, 225–26; see also 130–42.

91. FSF, *The Last Tycoon: An Unfinished Novel*, 110–11. Henceforth cited by page number in the text.

92. FSF, "The Hotel Child," in FSF, *The Short Stories of F. Scott Fitzgerald: A New Collection*, 600, 604.

93. FSF, "The Trail of the Duke," in *The Apprentice Fiction of F. Scott Fitzgerald, 1909–1917*, 54.

94. FSF, *The Great Gatsby: A Facsimile of the Manuscript*, 54–56. Breitwieser discusses this passage at length in "Jazz Fractures" and in "Grief, Jazz, and the Eyewitness." My transcription corrects for overstrikes and typographical errors.

95. Breitwieser, "Jazz Fractures," 371, 372.

96. FSF, "Ordeal," 35.

97. I am indebted to Breitwieser's discussion of both these passages from *The Last Tycoon*, and to his reading of Fitzgerald's "jazz fractures" more generally, though I depart from his reading at critical points (Breitwieser, "Jazz Fractures").

98. Cf. Andre Siegfried, *America Comes of Age* (New York: Harcourt, Brace, & World, 1927): "A century of experience has proved that Protestants of Nordic origin are readily assimilated, and Calvinists particularly so. There is almost no question of Americanizing an Englishman or a Scotsman, for they are hardly foreigners and feel quite at home for many reasons that go far deeper than the mere similarity of the language. The Dutch, the Germans, the Scandinavians, and the German Swiss all have low melting points. . . . Assimilation only begins to be troublesome with Catholics, even German and Anglo-Saxon Catholics" (22–23), quoted in Charles H Anderson, *White Protestant Americans: From National Origins to Religious Group*, 10.

99. Breitwieser, "Grief, Jazz, and the Eye-witness," 55.

100. FSF, "Pasting it Together," in *Crack-up*, 80.

101. Stephen W. Potts, *The Price of Paradise: The Magazine Career of F. Scott Fitzgerald*, 88–89; the idea was Arnold Gingrich's; see *The Armchair Esquire*, ed. Arnold Gingrich and L. Rust Hills, 93.

102. FSF, "Handle With Care," in *Crack-up*, 78.

103. Matthew J. Bruccoli, "Perkins-Wilson Correspondence," *Fitzgerald-Hemingway Annual 1978*, ed. Matthew J. Bruccoli and Richard Layman (Detroit: Gale Research, 1979), 65, quoted by Scott Donaldson, "The Crisis of Fitzgerald's 'Crack-up,' " 175; Alfred Kazin, "Fitzgerald: An American Confession," *Quarterly Review of Literature* 2 (1945), 342, quoted by Donaldson, "Crisis of Fitzgerald's 'Crack-up,' " 178.

104. FSF, "Handle With Care," *Crack-up*, 76–77.

105. FSF, *Notebooks of F. Scott Fitzgerald*, 300. This was either a story idea or Fitzgerald's gloss on the word "story."

Afterword
American Religion and the Future of Dissent

1. Chapter 2 of Hutchison's *Religious Pluralism in America* is titled "Just Behave Yourselves: Pluralism as Selective Tolerance."

2. Here an exception may prove the rule: Irshad Manji, a Muslim feminist who has been vocal in calling for reform in Islam, reports that she routinely encounters befuddlement and hostility from secularists in Western Europe who find an Islam marked by the values of "tolerance, democracy, justice, equality and freedom"—an Islam that cannot easily be construed as "backwards"—literally unthinkable. Why would an adherent of such values, Manji is frequently asked, need to practice a religion (still less Islam) at all? ("Under the Cover of Islam," *New York Times*, 18 November 2004).

3. See Jane Lampman, "Muslim Scholar Barred from U.S. Preaches Tolerance," *Christian Science Monitor*, 21 September 2004; Don Hill, "Prominent Western Muslim Rejects 'Clash of Civilizations' Idea," Radio Free Europe/Radio Liberty Newsline, 2 December 2004, http://www.rferl.org/featuresarticle/2004/12/daca603e-9f3c-4cd4-a86c-f1025e9c4e07.html; "Tariq Ramadan: American and European Scholars Respond," *American Academy of Religion*, http://www.aar-web.org/about/announce/2004/Ramadan02.asp.

4. Amy Kaplan, "Violent Belongings and the Question of Empire Today," 2.

5. Kaplan, "Violent Belongings," 2, 16n2. Ivo H. Daalder and James Lindsay note that "in the last six months alone, as debate on Iraq peaked, the phrase 'American empire' was mentioned nearly 1,000 times in news stories" ("American Empire, Not 'If' but 'What Kind,' " *New York Times*, 10 May 2003); Kaplan's notes include lengthy lists of recent books and essay on the American empire. As Michael Bérubé observes, "Ten years ago, when scholars in American studies spoke of 'cultures of United States imperialism' [the title of a book edited by Kaplan], they were made . . . to sound as if they were crazed Leninists festooning New York's Upper West Side with wheat-paste posters testifying to the Trilateral Commission's hand in the death of Bruce Lee. Now, however, American studies of the 1990s simply looks like it was ahead of the curve, talking frankly about U.S. imperialism years before anyone else caught on (Bérubé, "The Loyalties of American Studies," 228.

6. Kaplan, "Violent Belongings," 4.

7. Jakobsen and Pellegrini, "World Secularisms at the Millennium: Introduction," 15.

8. Peter van der Veer, "The Foreign Hand: Orientalist Discourse in Sociology and Communalism," 39.

9. Winnifred Fallers Sullivan, *The Impossibility of Religious Freedom*, 154

10. I draw the broad descriptions of these narratives from Kaplan, "Violent Belongings," 4–5, and from Edward W. Said, preface to the 25th anniversary ed. of *Orientalism*, xxi.

11. Kaplan points to the odd circumstance that numbers of civilian and military translators are now charged with "mistranslating" the interrogation of prisoners held at Guantánamo Bay. "Which language was mistranslated?" asks Kaplan. "Pashtun, Farsi, Arabic, English, Russian? Given the notorious lack of language knowledge in the United States, who caught the fine-tuning of these mistranslations? Does this mean that interrogators were not hearing what they expected to hear? Was too much being withheld? Were the translators conducting an altogether different conversation with the prisoners about their experience? Or did the translators translate too much, more than answers to the questions asked?" "If this is an empire threatened by translation," she concludes, "then to speak both Arabic and English, or to practice Islam and be a U.S. citizen, have the potential not of building bridges and cultural exchanges, but instead of exciting the suspicion of treason" ("Violent Belongings," 14). Lest the notion of an empire "threatened by translation" sound far-fetched, consider the fact that in February 2004 the Treasury Department warned that any U.S. scholar who translated or edited written materials from "disfavored nations," including Iran and other nations under U.S. trade embargo, opened themselves to "grave legal consequences." As the literary scholar Nahid Mozaffari told the *New York Times*, "A story, a poem, an article on history, archaeology, linguistics, engineering, physics, mathematics, or any other area of knowledge cannot be translated, and even if submitted in English, cannot be edited in the U.S. . . . This means that the publication of the PEN Anthology of Contemporary Persian Literature that I have been

editing for the last three years would constitute aiding and abetting the enemy" (Adam Liptak, "Treasury Department Is Warning Publishers of the Perils of Criminal Editing of the Enemy," *New York Times*, 28 February 2004); Bérubé, "Loyalties of American Studies," 225.

12. Leo Marx, "Believing in America: An Intellectual Project and a National Ideal," quoted by Bérubé, "Loyalties of American Studies," 231.

13. R. Laurence Moore, *Religious Outsiders and the Making of Americans*, xi.

BIBLIOGRAPHY

Adams, John. *The Political Writings of John Adams*. Edited by George W. Carey. Washington, DC: Regnery, 2000.

———. *Works of John Adams*. Edited by Charles Francis Adams, 10 vols. Boston: Little, Brown, 1850–56.

Adams, John, and Abigail Adams. *The Letters of John and Abigail Adams*. Edited by Frank Shuffleton. New York: Penguin, 2004.

Ahlstrom, Sidney E. *A Religious History of the American People*. New Haven, CT: Yale University Press, 1972.

Albanese, Catherine L. *America: Religion and Religions*. 2nd ed. Belmont, CA: Wadsworth, 1992.

———. "Exchanging Selves, Exchanging Souls: Contact, Combination, and American Religious History." In Tweed, *Retelling U.S. Religious History*, 200–226.

Allen, Jerry. "Tom Sawyer's Town." *National Geographic Magazine*, July 1956, 120–40. http://etext.lib.virginia.edu/railton/tomsawye/nostalgia/56natlgeohp.html.

Allen, Joan. *Candles and Carnival Lights: The Catholic Sensibility of F. Scott Fitzgerald*. New York: New York University Press, 1978.

"American Principles." *Harper's New Monthly Magazine*, February 1857, 410–11.

Anbinder, Tyler. *Nativism and Slavery: The Northern Know-Nothings and the Politics of the 1850s*. New York: Oxford University Press, 1992.

Anderson, Charles H. *White Protestant Americans: From National Origins to Religious Group*. Englewood Cliffs, NJ: Prentice Hall, 1970.

Apess, William. *On Our Own Ground: The Complete Writings of William Apess, a Pequot*. Edited by Barry O'Connell. Amherst: University of Massachusetts Press, 1992.

Arac, Jonathan. *Huckleberry Finn as Idol and Target: The Functions of Criticism in Our Time*. Madison: University of Wisconsin Press, 1997.

———. "Putting the River on New Maps." *American Literary History* 8.1 (1996): 110–29.

Asad, Talal. *Genealogies of Religion: Discipline and Reasons of Power in Christianity and Islam*. Baltimore: Johns Hopkins University Press, 1993.

Axtell, James. *After Columbus: Essays in the Ethnohistory of Colonial North America*. New York: Oxford University Press, 1988.

———. "The White Indians of Colonial America." *William and Mary Quarterly* 32 (1975): 55–88.

Bailyn, Bernard. *Education in the Forming of American Society*. New York: Norton, 1971.

Baird, Robert. *Religion in America, or, an Account of the Origin, Relation to the State, and Present Condition of the Evangelical Churches of the United States, with Notices of the Unevangelical Denominations.* Rev. ed. New York: Harper & Brothers, 1856.

Banks, Marva. "*Uncle Tom's Cabin* and the Antebellum Black Response." In Machor, *Readers in History*, 209–27.

Banner, Lois. "Religious Benevolence as Social Control: A Critique of an Interpretation." *Journal of American History* 60 (June 1973): 23–41.

Barnes, Elizabeth. *States of Sympathy: Seduction and Democracy in the American Novel*. New York: Columbia University Press, 1997.

Baumgarten, Murray. "Seeing Double: Jews in the Fiction of F. Scott Fitzgerald, Charles Dickens, Anthony Trollope, and George Eliot." In Cheyette, *Between "Race" and Culture*, 44–61.

Baxter, Richard. *The Saints Everlasting Rest*. 1650. Reprint, Liverpool: H. Forshaw, 1798.

Beals, Carleton. *Brass-Knuckle Crusade: The Great Know-Nothing Conspiracy 1820–1860*. New York: Hastings House, 1960.

Bean, William G. "Puritan Versus Celt, 1850–1860." *New England Quarterly* 7 (1934): 70–89.

Beauties of the New-England Primer. New York: S. Wood, 1813.

Bederman, Gail. *Manliness and Civilization: A Cultural History of Gender and Race in the United States, 1880–1917*. Chicago: University of Chicago Press, 1995.

Beecher, Catharine E., and Harriet Beecher Stowe. *The American Woman's Home*. Edited by Nicole Tonkovich. Piscataway, NJ: Rutgers University Press, 2002.

Beecher, Charles. *The God of the Bible against Slavery*. New York: New York Anti-Slavery Society, 1855.

Beecher, Edward. *Narrative of Riots at Alton, in Connection with the Death of Elijah P. Lovejoy*. 1838. Reprint, Miami: Mnemosyne Publishing Co., 1969.

———. *Papal Conspiracy Exposed and Protestantism Defended in the Light of Reason, History, and Scripture*. 1855. Reprint, New York: Arno Press, 1977.

Beecher, Henry Ward. *England and America: Speech of Henry Ward Beecher at the Free Trade Hall, Manchester, Oct 9 1863*. Boston: James Redpath, 1863.

———. *Norwood; or Village Life in New England*. New York: Charles Scribner, 1868.

Beecher, Lyman. "Autobiographical Statement of the Disestablishment of the 'Standing Order' in Connecticut, 1818." In Hammack, *Making the Nonprofit Sector in the United States: A Reader*, 118–22.

———. *Autobiography*. Edited by Barbara Cross, 2 vols. Cambridge, MA: Harvard University Press, 1961.

———. *The Memory of Our Fathers, a Sermon*. Boston: T. R. Martin, 1828.

———. *A Plea for the West*. 1835. Reprint, New York: Arno Press, 1977.

Bell, Ernest A. *Fighting the Traffic in Young Girls, or The War on the White Slave Trade*. Chicago, 1910.

Bellamy, Edward. *Looking Backward 2000–1887*. Edited by Daniel H. Borus. Boston: St. Martin's Press, Bedford Books, 1995.

"Benjamin Harris, Printer and Bookseller." *Proceedings of the Massachusetts Historical Society* 57 (1924): 34–68.

Bercovitch, Sacvan. *The American Jeremiad*. Madison: University of Wisconsin Press, 1978.

———. *The Puritan Origins of the American Self*. New Haven, CT: Yale University Press, 1975.

Bercovitch, Sacvan, and Cyrus R. K. Patell, eds., *The Cambridge History of American Literature, vol. 1: 1590–1820*. Cambridge: Cambridge University Press, 1997.

Bergmann, Hans. *God in the Street: New York Writing from the Penny Press to Melville*. Philadelphia: Temple University Press, 1995.

Berman, Ronald. "*The Great Gatsby* and the Twenties." In Prigozy, *Cambridge Companion to F. Scott Fitzgerald*, 79–94.

Bérubé, Michael. "The Loyalties of American Studies." *American Quarterly* 56.2 (2004): 223–33.

Bhabha, Homi K. *The Location of Culture*. London: Routledge, 1994.

"The Bible: A Suitable and Important Class Book for Every School." *Ohio Educational Monthly* 2 (1853): 234–40.

The Bible in the Public Schools: Arguments before the Superior Court of Cincinnati in the Case of Minor v. Board of Education. 1870. Reprint, New York: Da Capo Press, 1967.

The Bible on the Present Crisis: The Republic of the U.S. and its Counterfeit Presentment, the Slave Power and the Southern Confederacy. New York: Sinclair Tousy, 1863.

Billington, Louis. "'Female Laborers in the Church': Women Preachers in the Northeastern United States, 1790–1840." *Journal of American Studies* 19 (December 1985): 369–94.

Billington, Ray Allen. *The Protestant Crusade, 1800–1860: A Study of the Origins of American Nativism*. New York: Macmillan, 1938.

Birdoff, Harry. *The World's Greatest Hit: Uncle Tom's Cabin*. New York: S. F. Vanni, 1947.

Birdsell, Richard D. "Emerson and the Church of Rome." *American Literature* 31 (November 1959): 273–81.

Black, Alexander. "The Woman Who Saw It First." In Karpinski, *Critical Essays on Charlotte Perkins Gilman*, 56–66.

Blau, Joseph L. "What's American about American Jewry?" *Judaism* 7.3 (Summer 1958): 203–18.

Blumin, Stuart M. *The Emergence of the Middle Class: Social Experience in the American City, 1760–1900*. New York: Cambridge University Press, 1989.

Boardman, Henry A., John H. Hopkins, and Nicholas Murray. *Anti-Catholicism in America, 1841–1851: Three Sermons*. New York: Arno Press, 1977.

Bodo, John R. *The Protestant Clergy and Public Issues, 1812–1848*. Princeton, NJ: Princeton University Press, 1954.

Boles, Donald E. *The Bible, Religion, and Public Schools*. Ames: Iowa State University Press, 1965.

Bolt, Christine. *The Anti-slavery Movement and Reconstruction: A Study in Anglo-American Co-operation, 1833–77*. New York: Oxford University Press, 1969.

Bolt, Christine. *The Women's Movements in the United States and Britain from the 1790s to the 1920s.* New York: Harvester Wheatsheaf, 1993.

Boston Synod. *A Confession of Faith.* 1679. In Ziff, *Literature of America: Colonial Period,* 136–42.

Bottum, Jody. "Gatsby's Epitaph: F. Scott Fitzgerald." *Catholic Dossier 5,* no. 4 (July–August 1999): 9–12.

Bourne, George. *Picture of Slavery in the United States of America.* Middletown, CT: E. Hunt, 1834.

———. *Slavery Illustrated in Its Effects upon Woman and Domestic Society.* 1837. Reprint, Freeport, NY: Books for Libraries Press, 1972.

Bowden, Henry Warner. "Robert Baird: Historical Narrative and the Image of a Protestant America–1855." *Journal of Presbyterian History* 47 (June 1969): 149–72.

Boydston, Jeanne, Mary Kelley, and Anne Margolis, eds. *The Limits of Sisterhood: The Beecher Sisters on Women's Rights and Woman's Sphere.* Chapel Hill: University of North Carolina Press, 1988.

Bradford, William. *History of Plymouth Plantation.* Edited by Worthington C. Ford. Boston: Massachusetts Historical Society, 1912. In Miller and Johnson, *Puritans,* 1:91–117.

Bradford, William, and Edward Winslow. *A relation or iournall of the beginning and proceedings of the English Plantation Setled at Plimoth in New England* [commonly known as *Mourt's Relation*]. London: J. Dawson, 1622.

Braude, Ann. "American Religious History *Is* Women's History," in Tweed, *Retelling U.S. Religious History,* 87–107.

———. *Radical Spirits: Spiritualism and Women's Rights in Nineteenth-Century America.* 2nd. ed. Bloomington: Indiana University Press, 2001.

Breckenridge, Carol A., and Peter van der Veer, eds. *Orientalism and the Postcolonial Predicament: Perspectives on South Asia.* Philadelphia: University of Pennsylvania Press, 1993.

Breitwieser, Mitchell. "*The Great Gatsby*: Grief, Jazz, and the Eye-Witness." *Arizona Quarterly* 47.3 (1991): 17–70.

———. "Jazz Fractures: F. Scott Fitzgerald and Epochal Representation." *American Literary History* 12.3 (2000): 359–81.

Bremer, Frederika. *America of the Fifties: Letters of Frederika Bremer.* Edited by Adolph Benson. New York: American-Scandinavian Foundation, 1924.

Brodhead, Richard A. *Hawthorne, Melville, and the Novel.* Chicago: University of Chicago Press, 1976.

———, ed. *New Essays on Moby-Dick.* Cambridge: Cambridge University Press, 1986.

———. "Sparing the Rod: Discipline and Fiction in Antebellum America." *Representations* 21 (Winter 1988): 67–96.

Brodwin, Stanley. "Mark Twain's Theology: The Gods of a Brevet Presbyterian." In Robinson, *Cambridge Companion to Mark Twain,* 220–48.

Brown, Gillian. "Getting in the Kitchen with Dinah: Domestic Politics in *Uncle Tom's Cabin*." *American Quarterly* 36 (1984): 503–23.

Bruccoli, Matthew J. *Some Sort of Epic Grandeur: The Life of F. Scott Fitzgerald.* 2nd rev. ed., Columbia: University of South Carolina Press, 2002.

Bruccoli, Matthew J., and Jackson R. Bryer, eds. *F. Scott Fitzgerald in His Own Time: A Miscellany*. Kent, OH: Kent State University Press, 1971.

Bruccoli, Matthew J., Scottie Fitzgerald Smith, and Joan P. Kerr, eds., *The Romantic Egoists: A Pictorial Autobiography from the Scrapbooks and Albums of F. Scott and Zelda Fitzgerald*. New York: Scribner, 1973. Reprint, Columbia: University of South Carolina Press, 2003.

Bryer, Jackson R., Alan Margolies, and Ruth Prigozy, eds., *F. Scott Fitzgerald: New Perspectives*. Athens: University of Georgia Press, 2000.

Buchanan, Joseph Rodes. "The Cosmic Sphere of Woman." *Arena* 1 (1890): 661–81.

Budd, Louis J. "Mark Twain as an American Icon." In Robinson, *Cambridge Companion to Mark Twain*, 1–26.

Burr, George Lincoln, ed. *Narratives of the Witchcraft Cases, 1648–1706*. New York: Charles Scribner's Sons, 1914.

Bushnell, Horace. *Christian Nurture*. New York: Scribner, Armstrong & Co., 1876.

Butler, Jon. *Awash in a Sea of Faith: Christianizing the American People*. Cambridge, MA: Harvard University Press, 1990.

Butler, Judith. *Bodies That Matter: On the Discursive Limits of "Sex."* New York: Routledge, 1993.

———. *Gender Trouble: Feminism and the Subversion of Identity*. New York: Routledge, 1990.

Butsch, Joseph, S.J. "Negro Catholics in the United States." *Catholic Historical Review*, April 1917, 33–51.

Caldwell, Patricia. *The Puritan Conversion Narrative: The Beginnings of American Expression*. New York: Cambridge University Press, 1983.

Callahan, John. *The Illusions of a Nation: Myth and History in the Novels of F. Scott Fitzgerald*. Urbana: University of Illinois Press, 1972.

Calvin, John. *Institutes of the Christian Religion*. Edited by John T. McNeill. Translated by Ford Lewis Battles. Philadelphia: Westminster Press, 1960.

Campbell, George. *A Sermon . . . at the Ordination of Rev. George H. Atkinson*. Newbury, VT: L. J. McIndoe, 1847.

Canup, John. *Out of the Wilderness: The Emergence of American Identity in Colonial New England*. Middletown, CT: Wesleyan University Press, 1990.

Carpenter, Charles. *History of American Schoolbooks*. Philadelphia: University of Pennsylvania Press, 1963.

Carter-Sanborn, Kristin. "Restraining Order: The Imperialist Anti-Violence of Charlotte Perkins Gilman." *Arizona Quarterly* 56.2 (Summer 2000): 1–36.

Carton, Evan. "Speech Acts and Social Action: Mark Twain and the Politics of Literary Performance." In Robinson, *Cambridge Companion to Mark Twain*, 153–74.

Caskey, Marie. *Chariot of Fire: Religion and the Beecher Family*. New Haven, CT: Yale University Press, 1978.

Cassuto, Leonard. *The Inhuman Race: The Racial Grotesque in American Literature and Culture*. New York: Columbia University Press, 1997.

Castronovo, Russ. "Enslaving Passions: White Male Sexuality and the Evasion of Race." In Fessenden, Radel, and Zaborowska, *Puritan Origins of American Sex*, 145–68.

———. *Fathering the Nation: American Genealogies of Slavery and Freedom.* Berkeley and Los Angeles: University of California Press, 1995.

The Charter of the Colony of Massachusetts Bay in New England, 1628–29. In Shurtleff, *Records of the Government and Company of Massachusetts Bay in New England.*

Chauncey, Charles. *God's Mercy, Shewed to His People, in Giving Them a Faithfull Ministry and Schooles of Learning, for the Continued Supplyes Thereof.* Cambridge, 1655. In Smith, *Theories of Education in Early America*, 1–8.

Chestnutt, Charles W. *The Marrow of Tradition.* Edited by Nancy Bentley and Sandra Gunning. New York: Palgrave, 2002.

Cheyette, Bryan. *Between "Race" and Culture: Representations of "the Jew" in English and American Literature.* Stanford, CA: Stanford University Press, 1996.

Child, Lydia Maria. *Hobomok and Other Writings on Indians.* Edited by Carolyn L. Karcher. New Brunswick, NJ: Rutgers University Press, 1986.

Chireau, Yvonne. *Black Magic: Religion and the African American Conjuring Tradition.* Berkeley and Los Angeles: University of California Press, 2003.

Cogley, Richard W. "John Eliot and the Origins of the American Indians." *American Literature* 21 (1986–87): 210–25.

Cohen, Daniel A. "The Origin and Development of the *New England Primer.*" *Children's Literature* 5 (1976): 52–57.

Colton, Rev. Walter. "The Bible in Our Public Schools: A Reply to the Allegations and Complaints contained in the Letter of Bishop Kenrick to the Board of Controllers of [Philadelphia] Public Schools." *Quarterly Review of the American Protestant Association* 1 (January 1844): 10–22.

Connolly, William E. *The Ethos of Pluralization.* Minneapolis: University of Minnesota Press, 1995.

Cotton, John. *Christ the Fountaine of Life.* London, 1651.

———. "An Enquiry, Whether the Church may not, in the Celebration of the Sacrament, use other Rites." In *Some Treasure Fetched out of Rubbish, or Three Short but Seasonable Treatises.* London, 1660.

———. *An Exposition upon The Thirteenth Chapter of the Revelation.* London: M.S. for Livewel Chapman, 1655.

———. *God's Promise to His Plantations.* London, 1630.

———. *The Powring Out of the Seven Vials.* London: R. S., 1645.

Cressy, David. "National Memory in Early Modern England." In Gillis, *Commemorations*, 61–74.

Crèvecoeur, J. Hector St. John. *Letters from an American Farmer, Describing Certain Provincial Situations.* London: Thomas Davies & Lockyer Davis, 1782.

Cross, Andrew Boyd. *Young Women in Convents or Priests' Prisons.* Baltimore, 1856.

Culver, Raymond B. *Horace Mann and Religion in the Massachusetts Public Schools.* New Haven, CT: Yale University Press, 1929.

Cushman, Robert. "Reason & Considerations Touching the Lawfulnesse of Re-
    mouing out of England into the Parts of America." In Bradford and Winslow,
    Mourt's Relation.

D'Agostino, Peter R. *Rome in America: Transnational Catholic Ideology from
    the Risorgimento to Fascism*. Chapel Hill: University of North Carolina Press,
    2004.

Davidson, Cathy N., ed. "No More Separate Spheres!" Special Issue of *American
    Literature* 70.3 (September 1998).

———, ed. *Reading in America: Literature and Social History*. Baltimore: Johns
    Hopkins University Press, 1989.

———. *Revolution and the Word: The Rise of the Novel in America*. New York:
    Oxford University Press, 1986.

Davidson, Cathy N., and Jessamyn Hatcher, eds. *No More Separate Spheres!* Dur-
    ham, NC: Duke University Press, 2002.

Davis, David Brion. *The Fear of Conspiracy: Images of Un-American Subversion
    from the Revolution to the Present*. Ithaca, NY: Cornell University Press, 1971.

Davis, John, ed., *Religious Organization and Religious Experience*. London: Aca-
    demic Press, 1982.

Degler, Carl N. "Charlotte Perkins Gilman on the Theory and Practice of Femi-
    nism."*American Quarterly* 8.1 (1956): 21–39.

De Jong, Mary. "Dark-Eyed Daughters: Nineteenth-Century Popular Portrayals
    of Biblical Women." *Women's Studies* 19.3–4 (1991): 283–308.

Delbanco, Andrew. *The Puritan Ordeal*. Cambridge, MA: Harvard University
    Press, 1989.

DelFattore, Joan. *The Fourth R: Conflicts Over Religion in America's Public
    Schools*. New Haven, CT: Yale University Press, 2004.

"Destruction of the Charlestown Convent: Some of the Outrage from Contempo-
    raneous Newspaper Files." *U.S. Catholic Historical Society Records and Stud-
    ies* 13 (1919).

DeVoto, Bernard, ed. *Mark Twain in Eruption*. New York: Harper & Brothers,
    1940.

Dillon, Merton Lynn. *Elijah P. Lovejoy, Abolitionist Editor*. Urbana: University
    of Illinois Press, 1961.

Dimock, Wai Chee, and Michael T. Gilmore, eds. *Rethinking Class: Literary Stud-
    ies and Social Formations*. New York: Columbia University Press, 1994.

Dolan, Jay. *The Immigrant Church: New York's Irish and German Catholics,
    1815–1865*. Baltimore: Johns Hopkins University Press, 1975.

Donaldson, Scott. "The Crisis of Fitzgerald's 'Crack-up.'" *Twentieth Century Lit-
    erature* 26 (Summer 1980): 171–88.

Dorchester, Daniel. *Christianity in the United States from the First Settlement
    down to the Present Time*. New York: Hunt & Eaton, 1888.

Douglas, Ann. *The Feminization of American Culture*. New York: Avon, 1977.

Douglas, Mary. *Natural Symbols: Explorations in Cosmology*. New York: Pan-
    theon Books, 1970.

Doyno, Victor A. *Writing "Huckleberry Finn": Mark Twain's Creative Process*.
    Philadelphia: University of Pennsylvania Press, 1991.

Dudziak, Mary. "Desegregation as a Cold War Imperative." *Stanford Law Review* 4 (1988–89): 61–120.

Duggan, Lisa. "Queering the State." *Social Text* 39 (Summer 1994): 1–14.

Dundes, Alan, ed. *Mother Wit from the Laughing Barrel: Readings in the Interpretation of Afro-American Folklore*. Jackson: University Press of Mississippi, 1991.

Dwight, Theodore. *Open Convents: or, Nunneries and Popish Seminaries Dangerous to the Morals, and Degrading to the Character of a Republican Community*. New York: Van Nostrand & Dwight, 1836.

Dwight, Timothy. *A Sermon . . . before the American Board*. Boston: Samuel T. Armstrong, 1813.

Dyer, Richard. "White." *Screen* 29.4 (1988): 44–65.

"Elijah P. Lovejoy as an Anti-Catholic." *Records of the American Catholic Historical Society of Philadelphia* 62 (September 1951): 172–80.

Eliot, John, and Thomas Mayhew. "Tears of Repentance: Or, a Further Narrative of the Progress of the *Gospel* amongst the Indians in New England . . ." Massachusetts Historical Society, *Collections*, 3rd ser., 4 (1834): 197–216.

Ellis, John Tracy, ed. *Documents of American Catholic History*. Milwaukee: Bruce Publishing Co., 1956.

———. "An English Visitor's Comments on the American Religious Scene." *Church History* 36 (March 1967): 42–44.

Ellison, Ralph. "Change the Joke and Slip the Yoke." In Dundes, *Mother Wit from the Laughing Barrel*, 56–65.

———. "The Negro Writer in America: An Exchange." *Partisan Review* 25 (Spring 1958).

Elrod, Eileen Razzari. "'Exactly Like My Father': Feminist Hermeneutics in Harriet Beecher Stowe's Non-Fiction." *Journal of the American Academy of Religion* 53.4 (Winter 1995): 695–720.

Elson, Ruth Miller. *Guardians of Tradition: American Schoolbooks in the Nineteenth Century*. Lincoln: University of Nebraska Press, 1964.

Emerson, Everett, ed., *Letters from New England: The Massachusetts Bay Colony, 1629–1638*. Amherst: University of Massachusetts Press, 1976.

Emerson, Ralph Waldo. *Complete Works*. Edited by Edward Waldo Emerson, 12 vols. Boston: Houghton, Mifflin, 1903–4.

———. *English Traits*. Boston: Houghton, Mifflin & Co., 1881.

———. *Journals and Miscellaneous Notebooks of Ralph Waldo Emerson*. Edited by William H. Gilman et al. 16 vols. Cambridge, MA: Harvard University Press, 1960–82.

———. *Journals of Ralph Waldo Emerson*. Edited by Edward W. Emerson and Waldo E. Forbes. 10 vols. Boston: Houghton Mifflin, 1911.

Emmons, Nathanael. *A Discourse . . . in Commemoration of American Independence*. Wrentham, MA: Nathaniel Heaton, 1802.

Epstein, Barbara L. *The Politics of Domesticity: Women, Evangelism, and Temperance in Nineteenth-Century America*. Middletown, CT: Wesleyan University Press, 1981.

Fairlie, Henry. "The Vanity of *Vanity Fair*." *New Republic*, 21 March 1983, 25–30.

Feldberg, Michael. *The Philadelphia Riots of 1844: A Study of Ethnic Conflict.* Westport, CT: Greenwood Press, 1975.

Feldman, Noah. *Divided By God: America's Church-State Problem—and What We Should Do About It.* New York: Farrar, Straus, & Giroux, 2005.

Fell, Sr. Marie Léonore. *The Foundations of Nativism in American Textbooks, 1783–1860.* 1941. Reprint, New York: Jerome S. Ozer, 1971.

Felton, Rebecca Latimer. "Letter to the *Atlanta Constitution*." In Chesnutt, *Marrow of Tradition*, 409–11.

Fenton, John Y. *Transplanting Religious Traditions: Asian Indians in America.* New York: Praeger, 1988.

Ferguson, Margaret W. "Saint Augustine's Region of Unlikeness: The Crossing of Exile and Language." *Georgia Review* 29 (1975): 842–64.

Ferraro, Thomas J. "Butter-and-Egg Men: Response to Breitwieser." *American Literary History* 12.3 (2000): 382–85.

———, ed. *Catholic Lives, Contemporary America.* Durham, NC: Duke University Press, 1997

Fessenden, Tracy. "The Convent, the Brothel, and the Protestant Woman's Sphere." *Signs: Journal of Women in Culture and Society* 25.2 (Winter 2000): 451–78.

Fessenden, Tracy, Nicholas F. Radel, and Magdalena J. Zaborowska, eds., *The Puritan Origins of American Sex: Religion, Sexuality, and National Identity in American Literature.* New York: Routledge, 2001.

Field, Alexander J. "Educational Expansion in Mid-Nineteenth-Century Massachusetts: Human-Capital Formation or Structural Reinforcement?" *Harvard Educational Review* 46 (1976): 521–52.

Fields, Annie, ed. *Life and Letters of Harriet Beecher Stowe.* Boston: Houghton Mifflin, 1897.

Finkelstein, Barbara. "Pedagogy as Intrusion: Teaching Values in Popular Primary Schools in Nineteenth-Century America." *History of Childhood Quarterly* 2 (Winter 1975): 349–78.

Fisher, Philip. "Democratic Social Space: Whitman, Melville, and the Promise of American Transparency." *Representations* 24 (Fall 1988): 60–101.

Fishkin, Shelley Fisher. *Was Huck Black? Mark Twain and African American Voices.* New York: Oxford University Press, 1993.

Fitch, Elijah. *A Discourse . . . delivered at Hopkinton . . . March 24th 1776.* Boston: John Boyle, 1776.

Fitzgerald, F. Scott. *Afternoon of an Author: A Selection of Uncollected Stories and Essays.* Edited by Arthur Mizener. New York: Charles Scribner's Sons, 1957.

———. *The Apprentice Fiction of F. Scott Fitzgerald, 1909–1917.* Edited by John Kuehl. New Brunswick, NJ: Rutgers University Press, 1965.

———. *Before Gatsby: The First Twenty-Six Stories.* Edited by Matthew J. Bruccoli with the assistance of Judith S. Baughman. Columbia: University of South Carolina Press, 2001.

———. *Correspondence of F. Scott Fitzgerald.* Edited by Matthew J. Bruccoli and Margaret M. Duggan with the assistance of Susan Walker. New York: Random House, 1980.

Fitzgerald, F. Scott. *The Crack-Up*. Edited by Edmund Wilson. 1945. Reprint, New York: New Directions, 1956.

———. *F. Scott Fitzgerald: A Life in Letters*. Edited by Matthew J. Bruccoli with the assistance of Judith S. Baughman. New York: Maxwell Macmillan, 1994.

———. *F. Scott Fitzgerald: Novels and Stories 1920–1922*. New York: Library of America, 2000.

———. *F. Scott Fitzgerald on Authorship*. Edited by Matthew J. Bruccoli with the assistance of Judith S. Baughman. Columbia: University of South Carolina Press, 1996.

———. *F. Scott Fitzgerald: The Princeton Years*. Edited by Chip Deffaa. Fort Bragg, CA: Cyprus House Press, 1996.

———. *The Great Gatsby*. New York: Charles Scribner's Sons, 1925.

———. *The Great Gatsby: A Facsimile of the Manuscript*. Edited by Matthew J. Bruccoli. Washington, DC: Microcard Editions Books, 1973.

———. *The Last Tycoon: An Unfinished Novel*. New York: Charles Scribner's Sons, 1941.

———. *The Letters of F. Scott Fitzgerald*. Edited by Andrew Turnbull. New York: Charles Scribner's Sons, 1963.

———. *The Notebooks of F. Scott Fitzgerald*. Edited by Matthew J. Bruccoli. New York: Harcourt Brace Jovanovich/Bruccoli Clark, 1978.

———. *The Short Stories of F. Scott Fitzgerald: A New Collection*. Edited by Matthew J. Bruccoli. New York: Scribner, 1989.

———. *The Stories of F. Scott Fitzgerald*. Edited by Malcolm Cowley. New York: Charles Scribner's Sons, 1951.

———. *This Side of Paradise*. In *F. Scott Fitzgerald: Novels and Stories 1920–1922*. New York: Library of America, 2000.

Fitzgerald, F. Scott, and Max Perkins. *Dear Scott/Dear Max: The Fitzgerald-Perkins Correspondence*. Edited by John Kuehl and Jackson R. Bryer. New York: Scribner, 1971.

Fitzpatrick, Tara. "The Figure of Captivity: The Cultural Work of the Puritan Captivity Narrative." *American Literary History* 3 (1991): 1–26.

Fleming, William. *Narrative of the Sufferings and Surprizing Deliverances of William and Elizabeth Fleming*. Boston: Green & Russell, 1756.

Fliegelman, Jay. *Prodigals and Pilgrims: The American Revolution against Patriarchal Authority, 1750–1800*. Cambridge: Cambridge University Press, 1982.

Foner, Eric. *Reconstruction: America's Unfinished Revolution, 1863–1877*. New York: Harper & Row, 1988.

Ford, Paul Leicester. *The New England Primer: A History of Its Origin and Development with . . . many Facsimile Illustrations and Reproductions*.1897. Reprint, New York: Teachers College, Columbia University, 1962.

Ford, Worthington Chauncey. *The Boston Book Market, 1679–1700*. 1917. Reprint, New York: Burt Franklin, 1972.

Formisano, Ronald P., and Constance Burns, eds. *Boston, 1700–1980: The Evolution of Urban Politics*. Westport, CT: Greenwood Press, 1984.

Foster, Charles H. *The Rungless Ladder: Harriet Beecher Stowe and New England Puritanism*. Durham, NC: Duke University Press, 1954.

Foxe, John. *The Book of Martyrs: Containing an Account of the Sufferings and Death of the Protestants in the Reign of Queen Mary the First*. London: John Fuller, 1760.

Franchot, Jenny. "Invisible Domain: Religion and American Cultural Studies." *American Literature* 67.4 (December 1995): 833–42.

———. *Roads to Rome: The Antebellum Protestant Encounter with Catholicism*. Berkeley and Los Angeles: University of California Press, 1994.

———. "Unseemly Commemoration: Religion, Fragments, and the Icon." *American Literary History* 9.3 (1997): 502–21.

Franklin, Benjamin. *The Papers of Benjamin Franklin*. Edited by Leonard W. Labaree, Helen C. Boatfield, and James H. Hutson. 33 vols. New Haven, CT: Yale University Press, 1961–.

Frederick, John T. *The Darkened Sky: Nineteenth-Century American Novelists and Religion*. Notre Dame, IN: University of Notre Dame Press, 1969.

Freud, Sigmund. "Mourning and Melancholia." In *The Standard Edition of the Complete Works of Sigmund Freud*, translated and edited by James Strachey, 14:243–58. London: Hogarth, 1978.

Frey, Sylvia R. "Shaking the Dry Bones: The Dialectic of Conversion." In Ownby, *Black and White Cultural Interaction in the Antebellum South*, 21–43.

Frye, Stephen. "Fitzgerald's Catholicism Revisited: The Eucharistic Element in *The Beautiful and Damned*." In Bryer, Margolies, and Prigozy, *F. Scott Fitzgerald: New Perspectives*, 63–77.

"The Game of Pope and Pagan." Peabody and Essex Museum, Salem, Massachusetts, acc. no. 4216.2. Reproduced in Robin Fleming, "Picturesque History and the Medieval in Nineteenth-Century America." *American Historical Review* 100 (October 1995): 1076.

Gara, Larry. "Slavery and the Slave Power: A Crucial Distinction." *Civil War History* 15 (March 1969): 5–18.

Garber, Marjorie, and Rebecca L. Walkowitz, eds. *One Nation Under God? Religion and American Culture*. New York: Routledge, 1999.

Gates, Henry Louis, Jr. "The Trope of the New Negro and the Reconstruction of the Image of the Black." *Representations* 24 (1988): 129–55.

———. "Writing 'Race' and the Difference it Makes." *Critical Inquiry* 12 (Autumn 1985): 1–20.

Gaustad, Edwin Scott. "Church, State, and Education in Historical Perspective." *Journal of Church and States* 24 (Winter 1984): 17–29.

———, ed. *A Documentary History of Religion in America to 1877*. 3rd. ed. Grand Rapids, MI: William B. Eerdmans, 2003.

Geddes, Patrick, and J. Arthur Thomson. *The Evolution of Sex*. London: Scott, 1889.

Genovese, Eugene D. *"Slavery Ordained of God": The Southern Slaveholders' View of Biblical History and Modern Politics*. Gettysburg, PA: Gettysburg College, 1985.

Gibson, William. "Mark Twain and Howells: Anti-Imperialists." *New England Quarterly* 20 (1947).

Gildrie, Richard P. *The Profane, the Civil, and the Godly: The Reformation of Manners in Orthodox New England, 1679–1749.* University Park: Pennsylvania State University Press, 1994.

Giles, Paul. *American Catholic Arts and Fictions: Culture, Ideology, Aesthetics.* New York: Cambridge University Press, 1992.

———. "Aquinas vs. Weber: Ideological Esthetics in *The Great Gatsby.*" *Mosaic* 22.4 (1989): 1–12.

———. "Catholic Ideology and American Slave Narratives." *U.S. Catholic Historian* 15 (Spring 1997): 55–66.

———. "The Intertextual Politics of Cultural Catholicism: Tiepolo, Madonna, Scorsese." In Ferraro, *Catholic Lives, Contemporary America,* 120–40.

Gillette, A.D., ed., *Minutes of the Philadelphia Baptist Association from 1707 to 1807* 1851. Reprint, Springfield, MO: Particular Baptist Press, 2002.

Gillin, Edward. "The Grace of 'Benediction.' " In *New Essays on F. Scott Fitzgerald's Neglected Stories,* edited by Jackson R. Bryer. Columbia: University of Missouri Press, 1996.

Gillis, John, ed. *Commemorations: The Politics of National Identity.* Princeton, NJ: Princeton University Press, 1994.

Gillman, Susan. *Dark Twins: Identity and Imposture in Mark Twain's America.* Chicago: University of Chicago Press, 1989.

———. "Mark Twain's Travels in the Racial Occult: *Following the Equator* and the Dream Tales." In Robinson, *Cambridge Companion to Mark Twain,* 193–219.

Gillman, Susan, and Forrest G. Robinson, eds. *Mark Twain's Pudd'nhead Wilson: Race, Conflict, and Culture.* Durham, NC: Duke University Press, 1990.

Gilman, Charlotte Perkins. *Charlotte Perkins Gilman: A Nonfiction Reader.* Edited by Larry Ceplair. New York: Columbia University Press, 1991.

———. *The Charlotte Perkins Gilman Reader.* Edited by Ann J. Lane. New York: Pantheon, 1980.

———. *Concerning Children.* Boston: Small, 1900. Reprint, Walnut Creek, CA: AltaMira Press, 2003.

———. *Herland.* New York: Pantheon, 1979.

———. *His Religion and Hers: A Study of the Faith of Our Fathers and the Work of Our Mothers.* New York: Century Co., 1923. Reprint, Westport, CT: Hyperion, 1976.

———. *The Home: Its Work and Influence.* New York: McClure, Phillips, 1903. Reprint, New York: Source Book Press, 1970.

———. *The Living of Charlotte Perkins Gilman.* New York: Appleton-Century, 1935.

———. *The Man-Made World, or Our Androcentric Culture.* New York: Charlton Company. 1911. Reprint, New York: Source Book Press, 1970.

———. *With Her in Ourland.* Edited by Mary Jo Deegan and Michael R. Hill. Westport, CT: Greenwood, 1997.

———. *Women and Economics: A Study of the Economic Relation between Men and Women as a Factor in Social Evolution.* Boston: Small, Maynard & Co, 1898. Reprint, New York: Harper & Row, 1966.

Gilman, Sander. "Mark Twain and the Diseases of the Jews." *American Literature* 65.1 (March 1993): 95–115.

Gilmore, Michael T. "Hawthorne and the Making of the Middle Class." In Dimock and Gilmore, *Rethinking Class*, 215–38.

Gilmore, William J. "Elementary Literacy on the Eve of the Revolution: Trends in Rural New England." *Proceedings of the American Antiquarian Society* 92 (1982): 87–178.

Gingrich, Arnold, and L. Rust Hill, eds. *The Armchair Esquire*. New York: Putnam, 1958.

Ginsberg, Elaine K., ed. *Passing and the Fictions of Identity*. Durham, NC: Duke University Press, 1996.

Gitelman, H. M. "No Irish Need Apply." *Labor History* 14 (1973): 56–65.

Givens, Terryl L. *The Viper on the Hearth: Mormons, Myths, and the Construction of Heresy*. New York: Oxford University Press, 1997.

Gleason, Philip. "The New Americanism in Catholic Historiography." *U.S. Catholic Historian* 11 (Summer 1993).

Goodwin, Daniel R. *Southern Slavery in Its Present Aspects, Containing a Reply to the Late Bishop of Vermont on Slavery*. Philadelphia: J. P. Lippincott, 1864.

Gordon, Sarah Barringer. *The Mormon Question*. Chapel Hill: University of North Carolina Press, 2002.

Gottschalk, Stephen. *The Emergence of Christian Science in American Religious Life*. Berkeley and Los Angeles: University of California Press, 1973.

Graff, Harvey J. *The Literacy Myth: Cultural Integration and Social Structure in the Nineteenth Century*. New York: Academic Press, 1979. Reprint, New Brunswick, NJ: Transaction Publishers, 1991.

Greeley, Horace. *An Overland Journey from New York to San Francisco in the Summer of 1859*. New York: C. M. Saxton, Barker & Co., 1860.

Greenblatt, Stephen. *Marvelous Possessions: The Wonder of the New World*. Chicago: University of Chicago Press, 1991.

Greer, Colin. *The Great School Legend: A Revisionist Interpretation of American Public Education*. Rev. ed. New York: Viking Press, 1976.

Gribben, Alan. " 'When Other Amusements Fail': Mark Twain and the Occult." In Kerr, Crowley, and Crow, *Haunted Dusk*, 169–89.

Griffin, Susan M. *Anti-Catholicism and Nineteenth-Century Fiction*. Cambridge: Cambridge University Press, 2004.

Griffith, R. Marie. *Born Again Bodies: Flesh and Spirit in American Christianity*. Berkeley and Los Angeles: University of California Press, 2004.

Grimsted, David. "Uncle Tom from Page to Stage: Limitations of Nineteenth-Century Drama." *Quarterly Journal of Speech* 56 (October 1970): 235–44.

Gudelunas, William. "Nativism and the Demise of Schulkyll County Whiggery: Anti-Slavery or Anti-Catholicism." *Pennsylvania History* 45 (Summer 1978): 225–36.

Gundersen, Joan R. "Anthony Gavin's *A Master-Key to Popery*: A Virginia Parson's Best-Seller." *Virginia Magazine of History and Biography* 82 (January 1974): 39–46.

Gunn, Giles. *The Criticism of Culture and the Culture of Criticism*. New York: Oxford University Press, 1987.

Gunn, Giles. *The Interpretation of Otherness: Literature, Religion, and the American Imagination*. New York: Oxford University Press, 1979.

Gutjahr, Paul C. *An American Bible: A History of the Good Book in the United States, 1777–1880*. Stanford, CA: Stanford University Press, 1999.

Hackett, David G. "Gender and Religion in American Culture, 1870–1930." Typescript, 1994.

———, ed. *Religion and American Culture: A Reader*. New York: Routledge, 1995.

Haddad, Yvonne Yazbeck. *The Muslims of America*. New York: Oxford, 1991.

Hall, A. Oakey. *The Manhattaner in New Orleans, or Phases of "Crescent City" Life*. New York: J. S. Redfield, 1851.

Hall, David D. *Cultures of Print: Essays in the History of the Book*. Amherst: University of Massachusetts Press, 1996.

Hall, Robert L. "Commentary (on Frey's 'Dialectic of Conversion')." In Ownby, *Black and White Cultural Interaction in the Antebellum South*, 44–54.

Halliday, Samuel. *The Lost and Found; or, Life Among the Poor*. New York: Blakeman & Mason, 1859.

Halsey, William M. *The Survival of American Innocence: Catholicism in an Era of Disillusionment, 1920–1940*. Notre Dame, IN: University of Notre Dame Press, 1980.

Halttunen, Karen. *Confidence Men and Painted Women: A Study of Middle-Class Culture in America, 1830–1870*. New Haven, CT: Yale University Press, 1982.

———. "Humanitarian Reform and the Pornography of Pain in Anglo-American Culture." *American Historical Review* 100.2 (April 1995): 303–34.

Hamant, Nancy R. "Religion in the Cincinnati Schools, 1830–1900." *Bulletin of the Historical and Philosophical Society of Ohio* 21 (October 1963): 239–51.

Hambrick-Stowe, Charles E. *The Practice of Piety: Puritan Devotional Disciplines in Seventeenth-Century New England*. Chapel Hill: University of North Carolina Press, 1982.

Hamburger, Philip. *Separation of Church and State*. Cambridge, MA: Harvard University Press, 2002.

Hamilton, Jeanne. "The Nunnery as Menace: The Burning of the Charlestown Convent, 1834." *U.S. Catholic Historian* 14 (Winter 1996): 35–65.

Hammack, David C., ed. *Making the Nonprofit Sector in the United States: A Reader*. Bloomington: Indiana University Press, 1998.

Handy, Robert J. *A Christian America: Protestant Hopes and Historical Realities*. New York: Oxford University Press, 1971.

Haraway, Donna J. *Simians, Cyborgs, and Women: The Reinvention of Nature*. New York: Routledge, 1991.

Harris, George. *Inequality and Progress*. 1897. Reprint, New York: Arno Press, 1972.

[Harte, Bret]. Unsigned review of *Innocents Abroad*, by Mark Twain. *Overland Monthly and Out West Magazine* 4.1 (January 1870): 100.

Harwood, Thomas F. "The Abolitionist Image of Louisiana and Mississippi." *Louisiana History* 7 (Fall 1966): 281–308.

———. "British Evangelical Abolitionism and American Churches in the 1830s." *Journal of Southern History* 28 (August 1962): 287–306.

Haskell, Thomas L. "Capitalism and the Origins of the Humanitarian Sensibility, Part I." *American Historical Review* 90.2 (1985): 339–61.

Hatch, Nathan O. *The Democratization of American Christianity*. New Haven, CT: Yale University Press, 1989.

———. "Millennialism and Popular Religion in the Early Republic." In Sweet, *Evangelical Tradition in America*, 113–30.

Heartman, Charles Fred. *The New England Primer Printed in American Prior to 1830*. Rev. ed. New York: R. R. Bowker Co., 1934.

Hedge, Rev. F. H. *The Sick Woman: A Sermon for Our Time*. Boston: Prentiss & Deland, 1863.

Hedges, Elaine R. " 'Out at Last'? 'The Yellow Wallpaper' after Two Decades of Feminist Criticism." In Karpinski, *Critical Essays on Charlotte Perkins Gilman*, 222–33.

Hedin, Raymond. "Probable Readers, Possible Stories: The Limits of Nineteenth-Century Black Narrative." In Machor, *Readers in History*.

Hedrick, Joan D. *Harriet Beecher Stowe*. New York: Oxford University Press, 1994.

Henry, Peaches. "The Struggle for Tolerance: Race and Censorship in Huckleberry Finn." In Leonard, Tenney, and Davis, *Satire or Evasion?*, 25–48.

Herberg, Will. *Protestant, Catholic, Jew: An Essay in American Religious Sociology*. Garden City, NY: Doubleday, 1955.

Hewitt, Nancy A. "The Perimeters of Women's Power in American Religion." In Sweet, *Evangelical Tradition in America*, 233–56.

Higginbotham, Evelyn Brooks. *Righteous Discontent: The Woman's Movement in the Black Baptist Church*. Cambridge, MA: Harvard University Press, 1993.

Higginson, Francis. *New-Englands Plantation*. London, 1630. In Miller and Johnson, *Puritans*, 1:123–25.

Hinckley, Ted C. "American Anti-Catholicism during the Mexican War." *Pacific Historical Review* 31 (May 1962).

Hofstadter, Richard. *Academic Freedom in the Age of the College*. New Brunswick, NJ: Transaction, 1996.

Holland, Jeffrey R. "Soul Butter and Hogwash: Mark Twain and Frontier Religion." In *"Soul Butter and Hogwash" and Other Essays on the American West*. Edited by Thomas G. Alexander. Provo, UT: Brigham Young University Press, 1978.

Holt, Michael F. *The Political Crisis of the 1850s*. New York: Wiley, 1978.

———. "The Politics of Impatience: The Origins of Know-Nothingism." *Journal of American History* 60 (1973): 309–33.

Hooker, Thomas. *The Application of Redemption by the Effectual Work of the Word, and Spirit of Christ*. London: Peter Cole, 1656.

———. *The Soules Implantation*. London: R. Young, 1640.

Houchins, Sue E., ed. *Spiritual Narratives*. New York: Oxford University Press, 1988.

Hubbard, William. *A General History of New England, From The Discovery to MDCLXXX*. 2nd ed. 1848. Reprint, New York: Arno Press, 1972.

Hubbard, William. *The Present State of New-England, being a Narrative of the Troubles with the Indians in New-England . . . to which is added a Discourse about the War with the Pequods in the year 1637.* London: Tho. Parkhurst, 1677.

Hudson, Winthrop. *American Protestantism.* Chicago: University of Chicago Press, 1961.

———, ed., *Nationalism and Religion in America: Concepts of Identity and Mission.* New York: Harper & Row, 1970.

Hutchison, William R. *Religious Pluralism in America: The Contentious History of a Founding Ideal.* New Haven, CT: Yale University Press, 2003.

Ignatiev, Noel. *How the Irish Became White.* New York: Routledge, 1995.

Ingersoll, Robert G. *Prose-Poems and Selections from the Writings and Sayings of Robert Ingersoll, 1833–1899.* 1910. Reprint, New York: C. P. Farrell, 1925.

Jackson, Andrew. "Second Annual Message." In *A Compilation of Messages and Papers of the Presidents, 1789–1897,* edited by James D. Richardson, 2:520–21. Washington, DC: Government Printing Office, 1897–1917.

Jackson, Carl T. *The Oriental Religions and American Thought: Nineteenth-Century Explorations.* Westport, CT: Greenwood Press, 1981.

Jacobs, Harriet. *Incidents in the Life of a Slave Girl.* In *Classic African American Women's Narratives,* edited by William L. Andrews, 199–360. New York: Oxford University Press, 2003.

Jakobsen, Janet R., and Ann Pellegrini. "Getting Religion." In Garber and Walkowitz, *One Nation Under God?,* 101–14.

———, eds. *World Secularisms at the Millennium.* Durham, NC: Duke University Press, forthcoming.

———. "World Secularisms at the Millennium: Introduction." *Social Text* 18.3 (2000): 1–27.

Jehlen, Myra. "The Literature of Colonization." In Bercovitch and Patell, *Cambridge History of American Literature,* 11–168.

———. "Why Did the Europeans Cross the Ocean? A Seventeenth-Century Riddle." In Kaplan and Pease, *Cultures of United States Imperialism,* 41–58.

Jennings, Francis. *The Invasion of America: Indians, Colonialism, and the Cant of Conquest.* Chapel Hill: University of North Carolina Press, 1975.

Johnson, Alvin W., and Frank H. Yost. *Separation of Church and State in the United States.* 1934. Reprint, Minneapolis: University of Minnesota Press, 1948.

Johnson, Edward. *Wonder-Working Providence of Sions Savior in New England.* 1867. Reprint, Delmar, NY: Scholars' Facsimiles & Reprints, 1974.

Johnson, Paul. *A Shopkeeper's Millennium: Society and Revivals in Rochester, New York, 1815–1837.* New York: Hill & Wang, 1987.

Kaestle, Carl F. *Pillars of the Republic: Common Schools and American Society, 1780–1860.* New York: Hill & Wang, 1983.

Kahn, Sholom J. *Mark Twain's Mysterious Stranger: A Study of the Manuscript Texts.* Columbia: University of Missouri Press, 1978.

Kamensky, Jane. "Talk Like a Man: Speech, Power, and Masculinity in Early New England." In McCall and Yacovone, *Shared Experience,* 19–50.

Kaplan, Amy. "Manifest Domesticity." *American Literature* 70.3 (September 1998): 581–606.

————. "Violent Belongings and the Question of Empire Today—Presidential Address to the American Studies Association, October 17, 2003." *American Quarterly* 56 (March 2004): 1–18

Kaplan, Amy, and Donald E. Pease, eds. *Cultures of United States Imperialism.* Durham, NC: Duke University Press, 1993.

Karcher, Carolyn L. *Shadow over the Promised Land: Slavery, Race, and Violence in Melville's America.* Baton Rouge: Louisiana State University Press, 1980.

Karpinski, Joanne B., ed. *Critical Essays on Charlotte Perkins Gilman.* New York: G. K. Hall & Co., 1992.

————. "When the Marriage of True Minds Admits Impediments: Charlotte Perkins Gilman and William Dean Howells." In Karpinski, *Critical Essays on Charlotte Perkins Gilman.*

Kazin, Alfred. *F. Scott Fitzgerald: The Man and His Work.* 1951. Reprint, New York: Collier Books, 1962.

————. *God and the American Writer.* New York: Knopf, 1997.

Keller, Catherine. "The Lost Fragrance: Protestantism and the Nature of What Matters." *Journal of the American Academy of Religion* 65.2 (Summer 1997): 335–70.

Kelley, Mary. *Private Woman, Public Stage: Literary Domesticity in Nineteenth-Century America.* New York: Oxford University Press, 1984.

Kennard, Jean E. "Convention Coverage or How to Read Your Own Life." In Meyering, *Charlotte Perkins Gilman: The Woman and Her Work.*

Kenneally, James J. "The Burning of the Ursuline Convent: A Different View." *Records of the American Catholic Historical Society of Philadelphia* 90 (March–December 1979): 15–21.

Kerr, Howard, John W. Crowley, and Charles L. Crow, eds. *The Haunted Dusk: American Supernatural Fiction, 1820–1920.* Athens: University of Georgia Press, 1983.

Keys, Lisa. "Ralph Lauren's America—and Ours: How the Child of Immigrants Sold WASP Couture, and Culture, to the Masses." *Forward*, 13 February 2003, http://www.forward.com/issues/2003/03.02.14/fast1.html.

Kibbey, Ann. *The Interpretation of Material Shapes in Puritanism: A Study of Rhetoric, Prejudice, and Violence.* Cambridge: Cambridge University Press, 1986.

————. "Language in Slavery: Frederick Douglass's *Narrative*." *Prospects* 8 (1983): 163–82.

King, John Owen. *The Iron of Melancholy: Structures of Spiritual Conversion in America from the Puritan Conscience to Victorian Neurosis.* Middletown, CT: Wesleyan University Press, 1983.

King, Martin Luther, Jr. *The Words of Martin Luther King, Jr.* Selected by Coretta Scott King. New York: New Market Press, 1987.

Kinney, Bruce. *Mormonism: The Islam of America.* New York: Fleming H. Revell, 1912.

Kirlin, Joseph Louis J. *Catholicity in Philadelphia from the Earliest Missionaries Down to the Present Time.* Philadelphia: J. J. McVey, 1909.

Kirwan [Nicholas Murray]. *Romanism at Home: Letters to the Hon. Roger B. Taney.* New York: Harper & Brothers, 1852.

Klingberg, Frank J. "Harriet Beecher Stowe and Social Reform in England." *American Historical Review* 43 (1938): 542–52.

Knobel, Dale T. *Paddy and the Republic.* Middletown, CT: Wesleyan University Press, 1986.

Ku Klux Klan. *Papers Read at the Meeting of Grand Dragons, Knights of the Ku Klux Klan.* 1923. Reprint, New York: Arno Press, 1977.

Lane, Ann J. "Charlotte Perkins Gilman and the Rights of Women: Her Legacy for the 1990s." In Rudd and Gough, *Charlotte Perkins Gilman: Optimist Reformer,* 3–15.

———. *To Herland and Beyond: The Life and Work of Charlotte Perkins Gilman.* New York: Pantheon, 1990.

Lang, Amy Shrager. "Class and the Strategies of Sympathy." In Samuels, *Culture of Sentiment,* 128–42.

———. "The Syntax of Class in *The Silent Partner.*" In Dimock and Gilmore, *Rethinking Class,* 267–85.

Lannie, Vincent P., and Bernard C. Diethorn. "For the Honor and Glory of God: The Philadelphia Bible Riots of 1840." *History of Education Quarterly* 8 (Spring 1968): 44–108.

Lanser, Susan S. "Feminist Criticism, 'The Yellow Wallpaper,' and the Politics of Color in America." *Feminist Studies* 15.3 (Fall 1989): 415–41.

Laverdure, Paul. "Creating an Anti-Catholic Crusader: Charles Chiniquy." *Journal of Religious History* 15 (June 1988): 94–108.

Lee, John Hancock. *The Origin and Progress of the American Party in Politics: Embracing a Complete History of the Philadelphia Riots in May and July, 1844.* 1855. Reprint, Freeport, NY: Books for Libraries Press, 1970.

Leonard, James S., Thomas A. Tenney, and Thadious Davis, eds. *Satire or Evasion? Black Perspectives on Huckleberry Finn.* Durham, NC: Duke University Press, 1992.

Lepore, Jill. *The Name of War: King Philip's War and the Origins of American Identity.* New York: Knopf, 1998.

Leslie, Shane. "Some Memories of F. Scott Fitzgerald." *Times Literary Supplement,* 31 October 1958.

Levitt, Laura. "Other Moderns, Other Jews." In Jakobsen and Pellegrini, *World Secularisms at the Millennium.*

Lincoln, C. H., ed. *Narratives of the Indian Wars, 1675–1699.* 1913. Reprint, New York: Barnes & Noble, 1952.

Lipsitz, George. "The Possessive Investment in Whiteness: Racialized Social Democracy and the 'White' Problem in American Studies." *American Quarterly* 47 (1995): 369–87.

Liptak, Delores, R.S.M. *Immigrants and Their Church.* New York: Macmillan, 1989.

Littel, Franklin Hamill. *From State Church to Pluralism: A Protestant Interpretation of Religion in American History.* Chicago: Aldine Publishing Company, 1962.

Lott, Eric. *Love and Theft: Blackface Minstrelsy and the American Working Class.* New York: Oxford University Press, 1993.

———. "White Like Me: Racial Cross-Dressing and the Construction of American Whiteness." In Kaplan and Pease, *Cultures of United States Imperialism*, 474–98.

Lowell, James. Russell. *The Antislavery Papers of James Russell Lowell*. Edited by W. B. Parker. 2 vols. 1902. Reprint, New York: Negro Universities Press, 1969.

Luker, Ralph E. *The Social Gospel in Black and White: American Racial Reform 1885–1912*. Chapel Hill: University of North Carolina Press, 1991.

Machor, James L., ed. *Readers in History: Nineteenth-Century American Literature and the Contexts of Response*. Baltimore: Johns Hopkins University Press, 1993.

Maclear, J. F. "The Evangelical Alliance and Antislavery Crusade." *Huntington Library Quarterly* 42 (Spring 1979): 141–64.

Maddox, Lucy. *Removals: Nineteenth-Century American Literature and the Politics of Indian Affairs*. New York: Oxford University Press, 1991.

Mahon, John K. *History of the Second Seminole War, 1835–1842*. Gainesville: University Press of Florida, 1967.

Maizlish, Stephen E. "The Meaning of Nativism and the Crisis of the Union: The Know-Nothing Movement in the Antebellum North." In Maizlish and Kushma, *Essays on American Antebellum Politics*, 166–98.

Maizlish, Stephen E., and John J. Kushma. *Essays on American Antebellum Politics, 1840–1860*. College Station: Texas A & M University Press, 1982.

Mallios, Peter. "Undiscovering the Country: Conrad, Fitzgerald, and Meta-National Form." *Modern Fiction Studies* 47.2 (2002): 356–90.

Mann, Horace. *The Common School Controversy*. Boston, J. N. Bradley, 1844.

———. *The Republic and the School; The Education of Free Men*. Edited by Lawrence A. Cremin. New York: Teachers College Press, 1957.

———. *Slavery: Letters and Speeches*. Boston: B. B. Mussey & Co., 1851.

Martineau, Harriet. *Society in America*. 2nd. ed. 3 vols. London: Saunders and Otley, 1837.

Marty, Martin E. *A Nation of Behavers*. Chicago: University of Chicago Press, 1980.

———. *Righteous Empire: The Protestant Experience in America*. New York: Dial Press, 1970.

Marx, Leo. *The Pilot and the Passenger: Essays on Literature, Culture, and Technology in the United States*. New York: Oxford University Press, 1987.

Mason, John. *A Brief History of the Pequot War, Especially Of the Memorable Taking of their Fort at Mistick in Connecticut*. Boston: S. Kneeland & T. Green, 1736.

Masuzawa, Tomoko. *The Invention of World Religions: Or, How European Universalism Was Preserved in the Language of Pluralism*. Chicago: University of Chicago Press, 2005.

Mather, Cotton. *A Brand Pluck'd Out of the Burning*. In Burr, *Narratives of the Witchcraft Cases*.

———. *Cares About the Nurseries. Two Brief Discourses*. Boston: T. Green for Benjamin Eliot, 1702.

Mather, Cotton. *Corderius Americanus. An Essay Upon the Good Education of Children.* Boston, 1708.

———. *Decennium Luctuosum.* In Lincoln, *Narratives of the Indian Wars.*

———. *A Family Well-Ordered.* Boston: B. Green & J. Allen, 1699.

———. *Frontiers Well-defended: An Essay, to Direct the Frontiers of a Countrey Exposed unto the Incursions of a Barbarous Enemy.* Boston: T. Green, 1707.

———. *Humiliations Follow'd with Deliverances.* Boston: B. Green & F. Allen for Samuel Phillips, 1697.

———. *India Christiana.* Boston: B. Green, 1721.

———. *The Life and Death of the Reverend Mr. John Eliot, who was the First Preacher of the Gospel to the Indians in America.* London: Printed for John Dunton, 1694.

———. *Magnalia Christi Americana: or, the Ecclesiastical History of New-England.* London: Printed for Thomas Parkhurst, 1702.

Mather, Increase. *A Brief History of the War with the Indians in New England* (1676). In Slotkin and Folsom, *So Dreadful a Judgment,* 79–152.

———. *An Earnest Exhortation to the Inhabitants of New England.* Boston: John Foster, 1676. In Slotkin and Folsom, *So Dreadful a Judgment,* 165–206.

———. *The Order of the Gospel Professed and Practiced by the Churches of Christ in New-England.* Boston: B. Green & J. Allen, 1700.

———. *A Relation of the Troubles which have Hapned [sic] in New-England by Reason of the Indians There from the Year 1614 to the Year 1675.* Boston: John Foster, 1677.

Mather, Increase, and Cotton Mather. *The History of King Philip's War.* Edited by Samuel G. Drake. Albany: J. Munsell, 1862.

Mathews, Donald. *Slavery and Methodism: A Chapter in American Morality, 1780–1845.* Princeton, NJ: Princeton University Press, 1965.

Mathiessen, F. O. *American Renaissance: Art and Expression in the Age of Emerson and Whitman.* New York: Oxford University Press, 1941.

Mayhew, Jonathan. *Popish Idolatry, a Discourse delivered in the Chapel of Harvard-College in Cambridge, New-England, May 8, 1765.* Boston: R & S Draper, 1765.

———. *A Sermon Preach'd in the Audience of His Excellency, William Shirley, Esq. . . . May 29, 1754.* Boston: Samuel Kneeland, 1754.

Mazur, Eric Michael. *The Americanization of Religious Minorities: Confronting the Constitutional Order.* Baltimore: Johns Hopkins University Press, 1999.

McAvoy, Thomas T. "The Formation of the Catholic Minority in the United States, 1820–1860." *Review of Politics* 10 (1948): 13–34.

McCadden, Joseph J. "New York's School Crisis of 1840–1842: Its Irish Antecedents." *Thought* 41 (1966): 561–88.

McCall, Laura, and Donald Yacovone, eds. *A Shared Experience: Men, Women, and the History of Gender.* New York: New York University Press, 1998.

McCarthy, Martha. "Religion in Public Schools: Emerging Legal Standards and Unresolved Issues." *Harvard Educational Review* 55 (August 1985): 278–317.

McDannell, Colleen, and Bernhard Lang. *Heaven: A History.* New Haven, CT: Yale University Press, 1988.

McDowell, Deborah E., and Arnold Rampersand, eds. *Slavery and the Literary Imagination.* Baltimore: Johns Hopkins University Press, 1989.

McGreevey, John T. *Parish Boundaries: The Catholic Encounter with Race in the Twentieth-Century Urban North.* Chicago: University of Chicago Press, 1996.

McInerny, Ralph. "On Being a Catholic Writer." *Crisis* 13.11 (December 1995): 32–35.

McKivigan, John R. "The Antislavery 'Comeouter' Sects: A Neglected Dimension of the Abolitionist Movement." *Civil War History* 26 (June 1980): 142–60.

———. "The Gospel Will Burst the Bonds of the Slave: The Abolitionists' Bibles for Slaves Campaign." *Negro History Bulletin* 45 (1982).

M'Clintock, John D. D. *The Temporal Power of the Pope.* New York: Carlton & Phillips, 1855.

McVay, Georgianne. "Yankee Fanatics Unmasked: Cartoons on the Burning of a Convent." *Records of the American Catholic Historical Society of Philadelphia* 83 (September–December 1972).

Mead, Sidney E. *The Lively Experiment: The Shaping of Christianity in America.* New York: Harper & Row, 1963.

Mecom, Benjamin. *To the Publick of Connecticut . . . Another Newspaper.* New Haven, CT: B. Mecom, 1765.

Melville, Herman. *Moby-Dick.* Edited by Harrison Heyford and Hershel Parker. New York: W. W. Norton & Co., 1967.

Merrill, James H. "Some Thoughts on Colonial Historians and American Indians." *William and Mary Quarterly* 46 (1989): 94–119.

Metzger, Charles H., S.J. *The Quebec Act: A Primary Cause of the American Revolution.* New York: United States Catholic Historical Society, 1936.

Meyering, Sheryl L., ed. *Charlotte Perkins Gilman: The Woman and Her Work.* Ann Arbor, MI: UMI Research Press, 1989.

Meyers, Jeffrey. *Scott Fitzgerald: A Biography.* New York: Harper Collins, 1994.

Meyers, Mary Ann. "The Children's Crusade: Philadelphia Catholics and the Public Schools, 1840–1844." *Records of the American Catholic Historical Society of Philadelphia* 75 (June 1964): 103–37.

Michaels, Walter Benn. "The Souls of White Folks." In Scarry, *Literature and the Body,* 185–206.

Michaelson, Robert. "Common School, Common Religion? A Case Study in Church-State Relations, Cincinnati 1869–70." *Church History* 38 (June 1969): 210–17.

Midgley, Clare. *Women against Slavery: The British Campaigns.* London: Routledge, 1992.

Milford, Nancy. *Zelda: A Biography.* New York: Harper & Row, 1970.

Miller, Kerby. *Emigrants and Exiles: Ireland and the Irish Exodus to North America.* New York: Oxford University Press, 1985.

Miller, Perry, and Thomas H. Johnson, eds., *The Puritans.* Rev. ed. 2 vols. New York: Harper Torchbooks, 1963.

Miller, Randall L., and Thomas Marzik, eds. *Immigrants and Religion in Urban America.* Philadelphia: Temple University Press, 1977.

Mitchell, W.J.T. *Iconology: Image, Text, Ideology.* Chicago: University of Chicago Press, 1986.

Mizener, Arthur. *The Far Side of Paradise: A Biography of F. Scott Fitzgerald.* Boston: Houghton Mifflin, 1951.

Monaghan, E. Jennifer. *A Common Heritage: Noah Webster's Blue-Black Speller.* New York: Archon, 1983.

Monk, Maria. *Awful Disclosures of the Hotel Dieu Nunnery.* New York: Howe & Bates, 1836. Reprint, Hamden, CT: Archon Books, 1962.

Moody, Joshua. *Souldiery Spiritualized, or the Christian Souldier Orderly, and Strenuously Engaged in the Spiritual Warre.* Cambridge, 1674. In Miller and Johnson, *Puritans,* 1:367–69.

Moore, Benita A. *Escape into a Labyrinth: F. Scott Fitzgerald, Catholic Sensibility, and the American Way.* New York: Garland, 1988.

Moore, R. Laurence. "Religion, Secularization, and the Shaping of the Culture Industry in Antebellum America." *American Quarterly* 41.2 (1989): 216–42.

———. *Religious Outsiders and the Making of Americans.* New York: Oxford University Press, 1986.

Morey, Ann-Janine. *Religion and Sexuality in American Literature.* Cambridge: Cambridge University Press, 1992.

Morgan, Edmund S., ed. *The Founding of Massachusetts: Historians and the Sources.* Indianapolis: Bobbs-Merrill, 1964.

———. *Visible Saints: The History of a Puritan Idea.* New York: New York University Press, 1963.

Morse, Samuel F. B. *Imminent Dangers to the Free Institution of the United States through Foreign Immigration.* 1835. Reprint, New York: Arno Press, 1969.

Mullen, Harryette. "Runaway Tongue: Resistant Orality in *Uncle Tom's Cabin, Our Nig, Incidents in the Life of a Slave Girl,* and *Beloved.*" In Samuels, *Culture of Sentiment,* 244–64.

Murray, David. *Forked Tongues: Speech, Writing, and Representation in North American Indian Texts.* London: Pinter, 1991.

Murray, N[icholas]. *The Decline of Popery and Its Causes; An Address Delivered in the Broadway Tabernacle.* 1851. In Boardman, Hopkins, and Murray, *Anti-Catholicism in America.*

Nasaw, David. *Schooled to Order: A Social History of Public Schooling in the United States.* New York: Oxford University Press, 1981.

Nelson, Dana D. "Sympathy as Strategy in Sedgwick's Hope Leslie." In Samuels, *Culture of Sentiment,* 191–202.

New, Elisa. " 'Both Great and Small': Adult Proportion and Divine Scale in Edward Taylor's 'Preface' and *The New-England Primer.*" *Early American Literature* 28 (1993): 120–32.

Newby, I. A. *Jim Crow's Defense: Anti-Negro Thought in America, 1900–1930.* Baton Rouge: Louisiana State University Press, 1965.

Newman, Louise Michele. *White Women's Rights: The Racial Origins of Feminism in the United States.* New York: Oxford University Press, 1999.

The New-England Primer, Enlarged, for the More Easy Attaining the True Reading of English. Boston: S. Kneeland & T. Green, 1727.

The New-England Primer, Enlarged, for the More Easy Attaining the True Reading of English. Boston: T. Fleet, 1739.

The New-England Primer, Enlarged, for the More Easy Attaining the True Reading of English. Boston, n.d. Reprint, Germantown, PA, 1754.

The New-England Primer, Enlarged, for the More Easy Attaining the True Reading of English. Boston: T. & J. Fleet, 1770.

The New-England Primer, Enlarged and Improved, or, an Easy and Pleasant Guide to the Art of Reading. Newburyport, MA: John Mycall, 1790.

The New-England Primer, Enlarged and Improved, or, an Easy and Pleasant Guide to the Art of Reading. Boston: Thomas Fleet, 1796.

The New-England Primer, Enlarged, or, an Easy and Pleasant Guide to the Art of Reading. Boston: T. & J. Fleet, 1779.

The New-England Primer, Enlarged, or, an Easy and Pleasant Guide to the Art of Reading. Newport, RI: Oliver Farnsworth, 1800.

The New-England Primer, for the More Easy Attaining the True Reading of English. New York: John Harrisson, 1797.

The New-England Primer, Improved, for the More Easy Attaining the True Reading of English. New York: James Parker, 1750.

The New-England Primer, Improved, for the More Easy Attaining the True Reading of English. Boston: Joseph Bumstead, 1790.

The New-England Primer, Improved, for the More Easy Attaining the True Reading of English. Baltimore: W. Pechin, [1798?].

The New-England Primer, Improved, for the More Easy Attaining the True Reading of English. Hartford, CT: Babcock, 1800.

The New-England Primer, Improved, for the More Easy Attaining the True Reading of English. Hartford, CT: Hudson & Goodwin, 1800.

The New-England Primer, Improved, for the More Easy Attaining the True Reading of English. New York: T. Jansen & Co., 1800.

The New-England Primer; Much Improved, Containing a Variety of Easy Lessons for Attaining the True Reading of English. Philadelphia: T. Dobson, 1799.

The New-England Primer, or, an Easy and Pleasant Guide to the Art of Reading. Baltimore: Cushing & Jewett, 1818.

Nietz, John A. *Old Textbooks . . . from Colonial Days to 1900*. Pittsburgh: University of Pittsburgh Press, 1961.

Noll, Mark A, Nathan O. Hatch, and George M. Marsden. *The Search for a Christian America*. Westchester, IL: Crossway 1983.

The Northwest Ordinance of 1787. From *Journals of the Continental Congress, 1774–1789*, edited by Worthington C. Ford. In Sargent, *Political Thought in the U.S.*, 91–96.

Norton, Anne. *Alternative Americas: A Reading of Antebellum Political Culture*. Chicago: University of Chicago Press, 1986.

Orsi, Robert A. *Between Heaven and Earth: The Religious Worlds People Make and the Scholars Who Study Them*. Princeton, NJ: Princeton University Press, 2004.

———. "On Not Talking to the Press." *Religious Studies News*, AAR ed., 19.3 (May 2004): 19.

Osborne, William A. *The Segregated Covenant: Race Relations and American Catholics*. New York: Herder & Herder, 1967.

Ownby, Ted, ed. *Black and White Cultural Interaction in the Antebellum South.* Jackson: University Press of Mississippi, 1993.

Packer, Barbara. "Emerson and the Overgod." Paper presented at the 1994 meeting of the American Historical Association, San Francisco.

Paine, Albert Bigelow. *Mark Twain, A Biography.* New York: Harper & Brothers, 1912.

Paine, Thomas. *Common Sense.* New York: Penguin, 1986.

Parker, Theodore. *Social Classes in a Republic.* Centenary ed. Boston: American Unitarian Association, n.d.

Parkman, Francis. *The Conspiracy of Pontiac and the Indian Wars after the Conquest of Canada.* 1851. Reprint, Lincoln: University of Nebraska Press, 1994.

Pearce, Roy Harvey. *Savagism and Civilization: A Study of the Indian and the American Mind.* Baltimore: Johns Hopkins University Press, 1967. Reprint, Berkeley and Los Angeles: University of California Press, 1988.

Pechey, Graham. "On the Borders of Bakhtin: Dialogization, Decolonization." *Oxford Literary Review* 9.1–2 (1987): 59–84.

Perkins, William. *The Whole Works of that Famous and Worthy Minister of Christ.* 3 vols. London: John Legatt, 1631.

Perko, F. Michael. "The Building Up of Zion: Religion and Education in Nineteenth Century Cincinnati." *Cincinnati Historical Society Bulletin* 38 (Summer 1980): 96–114.

Perry, Lewis, and Michael Fellman, eds. *Antislavery Reconsidered: New Perspectives on the Abolitionists.* Baton Rouge: Louisiana State University Press, 1979.

Pettit, Arthur Gordon. "Mark Twain, Unreconstructed Southerner, and His View of the Negro, 1835–1860." *Rocky Mountain Social Science Journal* 7 (April 1970): 17–28.

———. "Mark Twain's Attitude Toward the Negro in the West, 1861–1867." *Western Historical Quarterly* 1 (January 1970): 51–62.

Phelps, Elizabeth Stuart. *The Silent Partner.* Boston: J. R. Osgood, 1871.

Phillips, Clifton J. *Protestant America and the Pagan World: The First Half Century of the American Board of Commissioners for Foreign Missions, 1810–1860.* Cambridge, MA: East Asian Research Center, Harvard University, 1969.

Pinn, Anthony B. *Varieties of African-American Religious Experience.* Minneapolis: Fortress Press, 1998.

Pope, Robert. *The Half-way Covenant: Church Membership in Puritan New England.* Princeton, NJ: Princeton University Press, 1969.

" 'Popery and Slavery go Hand in Hand' Said the Father as the American Revolution Began." *American Catholic Historical Researches* 21.1 (January 1904): 15–18.

Porter, Carolyn. "Call Me Ishmael, or, How to Make Double-Talk Speak." In Brodhead, *New Essays on Moby-Dick.*

Potts, Stephen W. *The Price of Paradise: The Magazine Career of F. Scott Fitzgerald.* San Bernardino, CA: Borgo Press, 1993.

Prigozy, Ruth, ed. *The Cambridge Companion to F. Scott Fitzgerald.* Cambridge: Cambridge University Press, 2002.

Raboteau, Albert J. "The Black Experience and American Evangelicalism: The Meaning of Slavery." In Sweet, *Evangelical Tradition in America,* 181–98.

———. *Slave Religion: The "Invisible Institution" in the Antebellum South*. New York: Oxford University Press, 1978.

Rachman, Stephen. "Reading Cities: Devotional Seeing in the Nineteenth Century." *American Literary History* 9.4 (1997): 653–75.

Ragg, Thomas. *Popery in Convents*. London, 1837.

Rapson, Richard L. "The Religious Feelings of the American People, 1845–1935: A British View." *Church History* 35 (1966): 311–27.

Ravitch, Diane. *The Great School Wars: New York City, 1805–1973*. New York: Basic Books, 1974.

Ray, Sr. Mary Augustina. *American Opinion of Roman Catholicism in the Eighteenth Century*. 1936. Reprint, New York: Octagon Press, 1974.

———. "*The Protestant Tutor*: A Forerunner of the *New England Primer*." *U.S. Catholic Historical Society Records and Studies* 30 (1939): 65–139.

Reisner, Edward H. *Nationalism and Education since 1789: A Social and Political History of Modern Education*. New York: Macmillan, 1922.

A Resident, *New Orleans as It Is*. Utica, NY: De Witt Clinton, 1849.

Reynolds, David S. *Faith in Fiction: The Emergence of Religious Literature in America*. Cambridge, MA: Harvard University Press, 1981.

Riach, Douglas C. "Daniel O'Connell and American Anti-Slavery." *Irish Historical Studies* 20 (March 1976): 3–25.

Rice, Madeleine Hooke. *American Catholic Opinion in the Slavery Controversy*. 1944. Reprint, Gloucester, MA: P. Smith, 1964.

Riss, Arthur. "Racial Essentialism and Family Values in *Uncle Tom's Cabin*." *American Quarterly* 46 (December 1994): 513–44.

Robbins, Bruce. "Secularism, Elitism, Progress, and Other Transgressions: On Edward Said's 'Voyage In.' " *Social Text* 40 (Fall 1994): 25–37.

Robinson, Forrest G., ed. *The Cambridge Companion to Mark Twain*. Cambridge: Cambridge University Press, 1995.

Rogin, Michael Paul. *Fathers and Children: Andrew Jackson and the Subjugation of the American Indian*. 1975. Reprint, New York: Vintage, 1976.

———. *Subversive Genealogy: The Politics and Art of Herman Melville*. New York: Knopf, 1983.

Romero, Lora. *Home Fronts: Domesticity and Its Critics in the Antebellum United States*. Durham, NC: Duke University Press, 1997.

Ronan, Marian. "Tracing the Sign of the Cross: Sexuality and Mourning in U.S. Catholicism." PhD dissertation, Temple University, 2002.

Ross, Andrew. *No Respect: Intellectuals and Popular Culture*. New York: Routledge, 1989.

Rowlandson, Mary. "A Narrative of the Captivity and Restauration of Mrs. Mary Rowlandson." In Lincoln, *Narratives of the Indian Wars*.

Rudd, Jill, and Val Gough, eds. *Charlotte Perkins Gilman: Optimist Reformer*. Iowa City: University of Iowa Press, 1999.

Ruel, Malcolm. "Christians as Believers." In Davis, *Religious Organization and Religious Experience*, 9–31.

Ryan, Joseph Paul. "Travel Literature as Source Material for American Catholic History." *Illinois Catholic Historical Review*, April 1928, 301–63.

Ryan, Mary P. *The Cradle of the Middle Class: The Family in Oneida County, New York, 1790–1865.* Cambridge: Cambridge University Press, 1981.

Said, Edward W. *Culture and Imperialism.* New York: Knopf, 1993.

———. *Edward Said: A Critical Reader.* Edited by Michael Sprinker. London: Blackwell, 1992.

———. *Orientalism.* New York: Vintage, 1979.

———. Preface to the 25th anniversary ed. of *Orientalism.* New York: Random House, 2003.

———. *The World, the Text, and the Critic.* Cambridge, MA: Harvard University Press, 1983.

Salomon, Roger B. *Twain and the Image of History.* 1957. Reprint, New Haven, CT: Yale University Press, 1961.

Salvino, Dana Nelson. "The Word in Black and White: Ideologies of Race and Literacy in Antebellum America." In Davidson, *Reading in America,* 140–56.

Samantrai, Ranu. "Continuity or Rupture? An Argument for Secular Britain." *Social Text* 18.3 (Fall 2000): 105–21.

Samuels, David. "Tinkers, Dreamers, and Madmen: The New History According to Newt." *Lingua Franca* 5 (January–February 1995): 32–39.

Samuels, Shirley, ed. *The Culture of Sentiment: Race, Gender, and Sentimentality in Nineteenth-Century America.* New York: Oxford University Press, 1992.

Sánchez-Eppler, Karen. "Bodily Bonds: The Intersecting Rhetorics of Feminism and Abolitionism." In Samuels, *Culture of Sentiment,* 92–114.

———. "Raising Empires Like Children: Race, Nation, and Religious Education." *American Literary History* 8.3 (Fall 1996): 399–425.

Sargent, Lyman Tower, ed. *Political Thought in the U.S.: A Documentary History.* New York: New York University Press, 1997.

Scarry, Elaine. "Consent and the Body: Injury, Departure, and Desire." *New Literary History* 21 (Fall 1990): 867–96.

———, ed., *Literature and the Body: Essays on Populations and Persons.* Baltimore: Johns Hopkins University Press, 1988.

Scharnhorst, Gary. "Reconstructing *Here Also*: On the Later Poetry of Charlotte Perkins Gilman." In Karpinski, *Critical Essays on Charlotte Perkins Gilman,* 249–68.

Schiff, Jonathan. *Ashes to Ashes: Mourning and Social Difference in F. Scott Fitzgerald's Fiction.* Selinsgrove, PA: Susquehanna University Press, 2001.

Schmidt, Leigh Eric. *Restless Souls: The Making of American Spirituality from Emerson to Oprah.* San Francisco: HarperSanFrancisco, 2005.

Schultz, Stanley K. *The Culture Factory: Boston Public Schools, 1789–1860.* New York: Oxford University Press, 1973.

Scott, Donald M. "Abolition as a Sacred Vocation." In Perry and Fellman, *Antislavery Reconsidered.*

Sedgwick, Eve Kosofsky. *Tendencies.* Durham, NC: Duke University Press, 1993.

Seed, Patricia. *Ceremonies of Possession in Europe's Conquest of the New World, 1492–1640.* Cambridge: Cambridge University Press, 1995.

Sellers, Charles. *The Market Revolution: Jacksonian America, 1815–1846.* New York: Oxford University Press, 1991.

Senior, Nassau W. *American Slavery: A Reprint of an Article on "Uncle Tom's Cabin" of which a portion was inserted into the 206th number of the "Edinburgh Review."* London: Longman & Co., 1856.

Sharrow, Walter. "Northern Catholic Intellectuals and the Coming of the Civil War." *New York Historical Society Quarterly* 58 (January 1974): 35–56.

Shaughnessy, Gerald. *Has the Immigrant Kept the Faith? A Study of Immigration and Catholic Growth in the United States, 1790–1920.* 1925. Reprint, New York: Arno Press, 1969.

Shepard, Thomas. "The Clear Sunshine of the Gospel breaking Forth Among the Indians in New-England" (1648). In Massachusetts Historical Society, *Collections*, 3rd ser., 4 (1834): 39–67.

Shurtleff, Nathaniel B., ed. *Records of the Governor and Company of the Massachusetts Bay in New England.* 5 vols. Boston: W. White, 1853–54.

Sideman, Belle Becker, and Lillian Friedman, eds. *Europe Looks at the Civil War.* New York: Orion Press, 1960.

Simmons, William S. "Cultural Bias in the New England Puritans' Perception of Indians." *William and Mary Quarterly* 38 (1981): 56–72.

———. "Red Yankees: The Narragansetts in the Second Great Awakening." *American Ethnologist* 10.2 (May 1983): 253–71.

Sinclair, Upton, ed. *The Cry for Justice.* Philadelphia: Winston, 1915.

Sklar, Kathryn Kish. *Catharine Beecher: A Study in American Domesticity.* New Haven, CT: Yale University Press, 1973.

Sloane, William. *Children's Books in England and America in the Seventeenth Century.* New York: Columbia University Press, 1955.

Slotkin, Richard. *Regeneration through Violence: The Mythology of the American Frontier, 1600–1860.* Middletown, CT: Wesleyan University Press, 1973.

Slotkin, Richard, and James K. Folsom, eds. *So Dreadful a Judgment: Puritan Responses to King Philip's War, 1676–77.* Middletown, CT: Wesleyan University Press, 1978.

Smart, Peter. *A Sermon Preached in the Cathedrall Church of Durham, Iuly 7, 1628.* London: Bernard Alsop & Thomas Fawcet, 1640.

Smith, Henry Nash. "Mark Twain's Images of Hannibal: From St. Petersburg to Eseldorf." *Texas Studies in English* 37 (1958): 3–23.

Smith, Stephen F. "We the Protestants." *First Things* 128 (December 2002): 43–47.

Smith, Timothy L. "Protestant Schooling and American Nationality, 1800–1850." *Journal of American History* 53 (March 1967): 679–95.

———. *Revivalism and Social Reform in Mid-Nineteenth-Century America.* New York: Abingdon Press, 1967.

Smith, Wilson, ed. *Theories of Education in Early America, 1655–1819.* Indianapolis: Bobbs-Merrill, 1973.

Smith-Rosenberg, Carroll. "Women and Religious Revivals: Anti-Ritualism, Liminality, and the Emergence of the American Bourgeoisie." In Sweet, *Evangelical Tradition in America*, 199–232.

Sobel, Mechal. *The World They Made Together: Black and White Values in Eighteenth-Century Virginia.* Princeton, NJ: Princeton University Press, 1987.

Soltow, Lee, and Edward Stevens. *The Rise of Literacy and the Common School in the United States: A Socioeconomic Analysis to 1870*. Chicago: University of Chicago Press, 1981.

Sommer, Doris. "Textual Conquests: On Reading Competence and 'Minority' Literature." *Modern Language Quarterly* 54 (1993): 141–53.

Spillers, Hortense J. "Changing the Letter: The Yokes, the Jokes of Discourse, or, Mrs. Stowe, Mr. Reed." In McDowell and Rampersand, *Slavery and the Literary Imagination*, 25–61.

Stanton, Elizabeth Cady, and Susan B. Anthony. *The Elizabeth Cady Stanton— Susan B. Anthony Reader: Correspondence, Writing, Speeches*. Edited by Ellen Carol DuBois. Rev. ed. Boston: Northeastern University Press, 1992.

Stenhouse, Mrs. T.B.H. *"Tell It All": The Story of a Life's Experience in Mormonism*. Hartford, CT: A. D. Worthington, 1874.

Stewart, Maria. *Productions of Mrs. Maria W. Stewart*. Boston: Friends of Virtue, 1833. In Houchins, *Spiritual Narratives*.

Stiles, Ezra. *The United States Elevated to Glory and Honor, a sermon . . . at the anniversary election*. New Haven, CT, 1783. In Hudson, *Nationalism and Religion in America*, 63–70.

Stout, Harry S. "Ethnicity: The Vital Center of Religion in America." *Ethnicity* 2 (June 1975): 204–24.

Stowe, Harriet Beecher [Christopher Crawford, pseud.]. *Little Foxes*. In *Stories, Sketches, and Studies*. Vol. 14, *The Riverside Edition of the Writings of Harriet Beecher Stowe*. Boston: Houghton Mifflin. Reprint, New York: AMS Press, 1967.

———. *First Geography for Children*. Boston: Phillips, Sampson, & Co., 1855. Originally published as *Primary Geography for Children, on an Improved Plan with Eleven Maps and Numerous Engravings*, by Harriet Beecher. Cincinnati: Corey & Farbank, 1833.

———. *House and Home Papers*. 1864. Reprint, Boston: Ticknor & Fields, 1865.

———. *How to Invest Money*. London, 1852.

———. *The Interior Life; The Great Atonement; Worldly Conformity; etc*. In *The Christian Diadem: A Monthly Series Of Doctrinal and Devotional Essays* 1 (1853).

———. *The Key to Uncle Tom's Cabin*. 1854. Reprint, New York: Arno Press, 1968.

———. *Men of Our Times, or Great Patriots of the Day*. Hartford, CT: Hartford Publishing Co., 1868.

———. *The Minister's Wooing*. In *Three Novels: Uncle Tom's Cabin, The Minister's Wooing, and Oldtown Folks*. New York: Library of America, 1982.

———. *Poganuc People*. 1878. Reprint, Boston: Houghton Mifflin, 1896.

———. Preface to *"Tell It All": The Story of a Life's Experience in Mormonism*, by Mrs. T.B.H. Stenhouse. Hartford, CT: A. D. Worthington, 1874.

———. *Sunny Memories of Foreign Lands*. 2 vols. Boston: Phillips, Sampson, & Company, 1854.

———. *Uncle Sam's Emancipation: Earthly Care A Heavenly Discipline; and Other Tales and Sketches*. 1853. Reprint, Freeport, NY: Books for Libraries Press, 1970.

————. *Uncle Tom's Cabin.* 1852. In *Three Novels: Uncle Tom's Cabin, The Minister's Wooing, and Oldtown Folks.* New York: Library of America, 1982.

————. *We and Our Neighbors, or, The Records of an Unfashionable Street.* New York: J. B. Ford & Co., 1875.

————. *Woman in Sacred History: A Series of Sketches Drawn from Scriptural, Historical, and Legendary Sources.* New York: J. B. Ford & Co., 1874.

Stowe, Lyman Beecher. *Saints, Sinners, and Beechers.* London: Ivor Nicholson & Watson, 1935.

Stritch, Alfred G. "Political Nativism in Cincinnati, 1830–1860." *Records of the American Catholic Historical Society of Philadelphia* 48 (September 1937): 227–78.

Sullivan, Winnifred Fallers. "Diss-ing Religion: Is Religion Trivialized in American Public Discourse?" *Journal of Religion* 75.1 (January 1995): 69–79

————. *The Impossibility of Religious Freedom.* Princeton, NJ: Princeton University Press, 2005.

Sumner, Charles. *Our Foreign Relations: Showing Past Perils from England and France, Speech of the Honorable Charles Sumner, Cooper Institute, September 10, 1863.* Boston: Wright & Potter, 1863.

Sundquist, Eric. "Mark Twain and Homer Plessy." *Representations* 24 (Fall 1988): 102–28.

Sweet, Leonard I., ed. *The Evangelical Tradition in America.* Macon, GA: Mercer University Press, 1984.

Tallant, Robert. *Voodoo in New Orleans.* 1946. Reprint, Gretna, LA: Pelican, 1990.

Taylor, Clare, ed. *British and American Abolitionists: An Episode in Transatlantic Understanding.* Edinburgh: Edinburgh University Press, 1974.

Thomas, G. E. "Puritans, Indians, and the Concept of Race." *New England Quarterly,* March 1975, 3–27.

Tillich, Paul. *Theology of Culture.* Edited by Robert C. Kimball. London: Oxford University Press, 1964.

Tiro, Karim M. "Denominated 'SAVAGE': Methodism, Writing, and Identity in the Works of William Apess, a Pequot." *American Quarterly* 48.4 (December 1996): 653–79.

Tolstoï, Lyof N. *What is Art?* Translated by Aylmer Maude. New York: Thomas Y. Crowell & Co., 1899.

Tompkins, Jane. *Sensational Designs: The Cultural Work of American Fiction.* New York: Oxford University Press, 1985.

Thomson, Rosemarie Garland. *Extraordinary Bodies: Figuring Physical Disability in American Culture and Literature.* New York: Columbia University Press, 1997.

————, ed. *Freakery: Cultural Spectacles of the Extraordinary Body.* New York: New York University Press, 1996.

Touchstone, Blake. "Voodoo in New Orleans." *Louisiana History* 13 (1972): 371–86.

Turnbull, Andrew. *Scott Fitzgerald.* New York: Scribner, 1962.

Twain, Mark. *Adventures of Huckleberry Finn.* In *Mississippi Writings.* New York: Library of America, 1982.

Twain, Mark. *The Adventures of Tom Sawyer.* In *Mississippi Writings.* New York: Library of America, 1982.

———. *Christian Science.* Amherst, NY: Prometheus Books, 1993.

———. *The Complete Essays of Mark Twain.* Edited by Charles Neider. New York: Da Capo, 2000.

———. *A Connecticut Yankee in King Arthur's Court.* Berkeley and Los Angeles: University of California Press, 1983.

———. *Europe and Elsewhere.* New York: Harper & Brothers, 1923.

———. *Following the Equator.* In *The Definitive Edition of the Writings of Mark Twain,* vols. 20 and 21. New York: Gabriel Wells, 1923.

———. *The Innocents Abroad.* New York: Oxford University Press, 1996.

———. *Life on the Mississippi.* In *Mississippi Writings.* New York: Library of America, 1982.

———. *Literary Essays.* In *Writings of Mark Twain,* vol. 22.

———. *The Love Letters of Mark Twain.* Edited by Dixon Wecter. New York, Harper, 1949.

———. *Mark Twain and the Three R's: Race, Religion, Revolution—and Related Matters.* Edited by Maxwell Geismar. Indianapolis: Bobbs-Merrill Company, 1973.

———. *Mark Twain Speaking.* Edited by Paul Fatout. Iowa City: University of Iowa Press, 1976.

———. *Mark Twain's Autobiography.* 2 vols. Edited by Albert Bigelow Paine. New York: Harper, 1924.

———. *Mark Twain's Fables of Man.* Edited by John S. Tuckey. Berkeley and Los Angeles: University of California Press, 1972.

———. *Mark Twain's Letters.* Edited by Albert Bigelow Paine. In *Definitive Edition of the Writings of Mark Twain,* vol. 24. New York: Gabriel Wells, 1923.

———. *Mark Twain's Letters.* Vol. 4 (1886–1900). Arranged by Albert Bigelow Paine. Fairfield, IA: First World Library, 2004.

———. *Mark Twain's Letters from Hawaii.* Edited by A. Grove Day. 1966. Reprint, Honolulu: University of Hawai'i Press, 1975.

———. *Mark Twain's Notebook.* Edited by A. B. Paine. New York: Harper & Brothers, 1935.

———. *Mark Twain's Speeches.* With an introduction by William Dean Howells. Reprint, New York: Oxford University Press, 1996.

———. *Mysterious Stranger Manuscripts.* Edited by William M. Gibson. Berkeley and Los Angeles: University of California Press, 1969.

———. *Personal Recollections of Joan of Arc.* 1896. Reprint, New York: Oxford University Press, 1996.

———. *Pudd'nhead Wilson.* In *Mississippi Writings.* New York: Library of America, 1982.

———. "Reflections on Religion." Edited by Charles Neider. *Hudson Review* 16 (1963): 335–38.

———. *Roughing It.* In *Definitive Edition of the Writings of Mark Twain,* vol. 3. New York: Gabriel Wells, 1923.

———. *The Secret History of Eddypus, the World-Empire.* In Twain, *Tales of Wonder,* 176–225.

———. *Tales of Wonder*. Edited by David Ketterer. Lincoln: University of Nebraska Press, 2003.

———. *Those Extraordinary Twins*. In *The Tragedy of Pudd'nhead Wilson, and the Comedy, Those Extraordinary Twins*. New York: Oxford University Press, 1996.

———. *Three Thousand Years among the Microbes*. In Twain, *Tales of Wonder*, 233–326.

———. "To the Person Sitting in Darkness." *North American Review* 172.2 (February 1901): 161–76.

———. *The Writings of Mark Twain*. 25 vols. New York: Harper & Brothers, 1911.

Tweed, Thomas A. *The American Encounter with Buddhism, 1844–1912: Victorian Culture and the Limits of Dissent*. Bloomington: Indiana University Press, 1992.

———, ed. *Retelling U.S. Religious History*. Berkeley and Los Angeles: University of California Press, 1997.

Tyack, David. "The Kingdom of God and the Common School: Protestant Ministers and the Educational Awakening in the West." *Harvard Educational Review* 36 (Fall 1966): 447–69.

Tylor, E. B. *Primitive Culture*. 2 vols. London: John Murray, 1871.

Vallone, Lynne. *Disciplines of Virtue: Girl's Culture in the Eighteenth and Nineteenth Century*. New Haven, CT: Yale University Press, 1995.

Van der Veer, Peter. "The Foreign Hand: Orientalist Discourse in Sociology and Communalism." In Breckenridge and Van der Veer, *Orientalism and the Postcolonial Predicament*.

Viswanathan, Gauri. *Masks of Conquest: Literary Study and British Rule in India*. New York: Columbia University Press, 1989.

———. *Outside the Fold: Conversion, Modernity, and Belief*. Princeton, NJ: Princeton University Press, 1998.

Walker, Peter. *Moral Choices: Memory, Desire, and Imagination in American Abolitionism*. Baton Rouge: Louisiana State University Press, 1978.

Wallace, John H. "The Case against *Huck Finn*." In Leonard, Tenney, and Davis, *Satire or Evasion?*, 16–24.

Walters, Ronald G. "The Erotic South: Civilization and Sexuality in American Abolitionism." *American Quarterly* 25 (May 1973): 177–201.

Ward, Lester F. "Our Better Halves." *Forum* 6 (November 1888).

Ward, Nathaniel [Theodore de la Guard, pseud.]. *The Simple Cobbler of Aggawam in America, Willing to Help 'Mend His Native Country, Lamentably Tattered*. London, 1647. In Miller and Johnson, *Puritans*, 1:226–36.

Wardley, Lynne. "Relic, Fetish, Femmage: The Aesthetics of Sentiment in the Work of Stowe." In Samuels, *Culture of Sentiment*, 203–20.

Warfel, Harry R. *Noah Webster: Schoolmaster to America*. New York: Macmillan, 1936.

Warner, Michael. *Letters of the Republic: Publication and the Public Sphere in Eighteenth-Century America*. Cambridge, MA: Harvard University Press, 1990.

Wasiolek, Edward. "The Sexual Drama of Nick and Gatsby." *International Fiction Review* 19.1 (1992): 14–22.

Watters, David H. " 'I Spake as a Child': Authority, Metaphor, and *The New England Primer.*" *Early American Literature* 20.3 (1985–86): 193–213.

Weber, Max. *The Protestant Ethic and the Spirit of Capitalism.* Trans. Talcott Parsons. New York: Scribner's, 1930.

Webster, Noah. *An American Dictionary of the English Language.* 2 vols. 1828. Reprint, New York: Johnson Reprint Co., 1970.

———. *An American Selection of Lessons in Reading and Speaking.* 3rd. ed. Philadelphia: Young & M'Culloch, 1787.

———. *Dissertations on the English Language, with Notes, Historical and Critical.* Boston: Isaiah Thomas, 1789.

[Webster, Noah]. *The New-England Primer, Amended and Improved, by the Author of the Grammatical Institute.* New York: J. Patterson, 1789.

———. "On Education." *American Magazine* 1 (December 1787): 22–26.

Weinbaum, Alys Eve. "Writing Feminist Genealogy: Charlotte Perkins Gilman, Racial Nationalism, and the Reproduction of Maternalist Feminism." *Feminist Studies* 27.2 (Summer 2001): 271–302.

Weld, Theodore Dwight. *American Slavery as It Is: Testimony of a Thousand Witnesses.* 1839. Reprint, New York: Arno Press, 1968.

Wertheimer, Jack, ed. *The American Synagogue: A Sanctuary Transformed.* Cambridge: Cambridge University Press, 1987.

Wexler, Laura. "Tender Violence: Literary Eavesdropping, Domestic Fiction, and Educational Reform." In Samuels, *Culture of Sentiment,* 9–38.

White, John. *The Planter's Plea.* London, 1630.

Whitman, Walt. *The Journalism, Vol. 1: 1834–1846.* Edited by Herbert Bergman, Douglas A. Noverr, and Edward J. Recchia. New York: Peter Lang, 1998.

———. *Leaves of Grass.* Edited by Scully Bradley and Harold W. Blodgett. New York: W. W. Norton, 1973.

———. *Leaves of Grass.* Edited by Jerome Loving. New York: Oxford University Press, 1998.

———. *Leaves of Grass and Selected Prose.* New York: Modern Library Edition, 1950.

Whitmore, William Henry, ed. *Andros Tracts: Being a Collection of pamphlets and official papers issued during the period between the overthrow of the Andros government and the establishment of the second charter of Massachusetts.* Boston: Prince Society, 1868–74.

Whitney, Louisa Goddard. *The Burning of the Convent.* 1877. Reprint, New York: Arno Press, 1969.

Wilkes, Henry. Preface to *Lorette or the History of Louise, Daughter of a Canadian Nun, Exhibiting the Interior of Female Convents,* by George Bourne. Edinburgh: Waugh & Innes, 1836.

Wilkie, Jane Wiblett. "Social Status, Acculturation, and School Attendance in 1850 Boston." *Journal of Social History* 11 (Winter 1977): 179–92.

Will, George. "Huck at a Hundred." *Newsweek,* 18 February 1985, 92. In Leonard, Tenney, and Davis, *Satire or Evasion?,* 268.

Willard, Emma. *Abridged History of the United States or Republic of America.* New York: A. S. Barnes & Co., 1868.

Williams, Roger. *The Bloudy Tenent of Persecution*, ed. Samuel L. Caldwell (Providence, RI: Publications of the Narragansett Club, 1867). In Miller and Johnson, *Puritans*, 1:216–23.

———. *George Fox Digg'd out of his Burrowes.* Vol. 5, *The Complete Writings of Roger Williams.* Edited by Reuben Aldridge Guild. New York: Russell & Russell, 1963.

———. *A Key into the Language of America.* London: Gregory Dexter, 1643.

Williams, Samuel. *The Natural and Civil History of Vermont.* Walpole, NH: Isaiah Thomas, 1794.

Williamson, Joel. *The Crucible of Race: Black-White Relations in the American South since Emancipation.* New York: Oxford University Press, 1984.

Wills, David W. "The Central Themes of American Religious History: Pluralism, Puritanism, and the Encounter of Black and White." *Religion and Intellectual Life* 5 (Fall 1987): 30–41.

———. *Christianity in the United States: A Historical Survey and Interpretation.* Notre Dame, IN: University of Notre Dame Press, 2005.

Wilson, James D. "Religious and Esthetic Vision in Mark Twain's Early Career." *Canadian Review of American Studies* 17.2 (Summer 1986): 155–72.

Winchester, Elhanan. *An Oration on the Discovery of America . . . October 12, 1792* (London, 1792). In Hudson, *Nationalism and Religion in America*, 70–72.

Winkler, Barbara Scott. "Victorian Daughters: The Lives and Feminism of Charlotte Perkins Gilman and Olive Schreiner." In Karpinski, *Critical Essays on Charlotte Perkins Gilman*, 173–83.

Winthrop, John. "Reasons to be Considered, and Objections with Answers" [1629?]. In Morgan, *Founding of Massachusetts.*

———. *A Short History of the Rise, Reign, and Ruine of the Antinomians.* Edited by Thomas Weld. London, 1644.

———. *Winthrop Papers.* Edited by Allyn B. Forbes and Malcolm Freiberg, 5 vols. Boston: Massachusetts Historical Society, 1929–92.

———. *Winthrop's Journal: "History of New England," 1630–1649.* Edited by James Kendall Hosmer. New York: Scribner's, 1908.

Wolffe, John. *The Protestant Crusade in Great Britain, 1829–1860.* Oxford: Clarendon Press, 1991.

Worsley, Stephen C. "Catholicism in Antebellum North Carolina." *North Carolina Historical Review* 60 (October 1983): 399–430.

Zaborowska, Magdalena J. "Americanization of a 'Queer Fellow': Performing Jewishness and Sexuality in Abraham Cahan's *The Rise of David Levinsky*, with a Footnote on the (Monica) Lewinsky'd Nation." In Fessenden, Radel, and Zaborowska, *Puritan Origins of American Sex*, 213–34.

Ziff, Larzer. *Literary Democracy: The Declaration of Cultural Independence in America.* New York: Viking Press, 1981.

———, ed. *The Literature of America: Colonial Period.* New York: McGraw Hill, 1970.